BRITISH SHIPBUILDING, 1500–2010

# BRITISH
# SHIP
# BUILDING
# 1500–2010

*a history by*
## ANTHONY SLAVEN

CRUCIBLE

ISBN 978-1-905472-16-1

*British Shipbuilding: a history, 1500–2010*

First edition

Published in 2013 by Crucible Books
an imprint of Carnegie Publishing Ltd
Chatsworth Road,
Lancaster LA1 4SL
www.carnegiepublishing.com

*British Library Cataloguing-in-Publication data*
A catalogue record for this book is available from the British Library

ISBN 978-1-905472-16-1

Designed, typeset and originated by Carnegie Publishing
Printed and bound by in the UK by Short Run Press Ltd, Exeter

# Contents

# Tables

# Preface

The research upon which this book is founded stretches over a period of nearly forty years, and has involved the support and contribution of many individuals. Beginning in the 1970s. I was aided greatly by two research colleagues, Jean Verth and David Clark. Jean worked with me over many months researching the records of the Shipbuilding Conference, held at that time in the Brass Foundry at Woolwich Arsenal. She worked particularly on the records and minutes of National Shipbuilders Security Ltd, and, being expert in shorthand, made copious notes from the minutes, which have since disappeared. The notes fortunately remain. With David Clark this work was extended to research on records in the Bank of England, and the Public Record Office at Kew. His work with me also extended into the business records of the Scottish shipbuilding companies, which were at that time being rescued and accumulated in the University of Glasgow, mainly by Michael Moss, John Hume, Richard Dell and me. Research on the shipbuilders themselves was undertaken in the 1980s, and biographies of the leading men were compiled by a team involving the late Sydney Checkland, Sheila Hamilton, Nicholas Morgan, Charles Munn and Brenda White. At the same time collaborative research was undertaken with colleagues at the University of Goteborg, Jan Kuuse, Thommy Svensson and Bo Strath, and with Fred Walker at the National Maritime Museum, Greenwich. This collaboration produced specialist conferences and publications from Glasgow, Goteborg, London and Helsinki. Later in the 1980s Ian Buxton at Newcastle linked with Fred Walker and me to research the nationalised British Shipbuilders. On my part in this involved extensive interviews with the leading men in the industry, and the civil servants, unionists and politicians. Philip Taylor was my colleague in this, travelling widely throughout Britain over a period of two years to record the response of the men to a raft of questions, and to listen to their own recollections and opinions. These interviews were subsequently organised and edited by Hugh Murphy when working as my research fellow in the Centre for Business History in Glasgow University, and have been drawn on in the account of British Shipbuilders in this book.

My thanks is also due to the staff of many libraries and archives, notably those of the Bank of England, the Public Record Office, Kew, the then Brass Foundry staff at

Woolwich, The National Maritime Museum, the University of Glasgow Library and Archive Services, The Mitchell Library, Glasgow ,and my friends and colleagues in the Institution of Engineers and Shipbuilders in  Scotland. Particular thanks are due to my colleagues in the Ballast Trust, the late Dr Bill Lind, Delaine Colquhoun, Duncan Winning and especially to Kiara King as archivist there.

Preparing the many versions of the manuscript inevitably involved the skills of many ladies struggling with my handwriting, especially Christine Leslie and Linda Craig. The final version transferred to disc for my publisher was the work of Megan Lee Butler. Finally, at Carnegie Publishing, Alistair Hodge and Laura Tristram have been endlessly patient and supportive. My thanks and appreciation is due to all of them. The book owes much to them all, but responsibility for all that appears here is solely mine.

# CHAPTER ONE

# Wood and sail, 1500–1815

## Foundations, 1500–1700

As an island nation with thousands of miles of coastline, estuaries and riverbanks, Britain had no shortage of locations suited to the building of boats and ships. This was particularly true before the nineteenth century, when vessels were of small size, mainly of much less than 100 tons. Competent carpenters with limited tools such as axes, adzes, saws, hammers, drills and chisels, could lay down a keel and build a small hull almost anywhere. From the earliest times the need was for ships for fishing, for the transport of commodities, and for defence. For hundreds of years these small wooden ships were capable of plying the narrow seas to Ireland, to the Baltic and the Low Countries, and across the Channel to France, and southward to Portugal and the Mediterranean. As long as these features set the scope and scale of merchant shipping, the demand for tonnage was low and irregular, and the activity required to build it had little continuity. However, from the beginning of the sixteenth century, new circumstances came into play which began to foster a recognisable shipbuilding craft to meet the growing demand for ships for trade, war and state power.

Until the sixteenth century and for most of the seventeenth, most trade between Europe and the Orient followed the great overland routes from Asia to the Middle East and the Mediterranean. As long as this was the case England and Scotland remained small nations on the periphery of the great Eurasian land-based empires. This remoteness was shared by the emerging north-west European states. New opportunities, however, began to appear, beginning with the great voyages of discovery between 1492 and 1522. There then followed the opening of long-distance deep-sea routes to the Americas, to India, to the Spice Islands, to Africa and China.[1] Competition for influence in, and control of, the new trades and territories fostered conditions in which by the end of the eighteenth century England was to emerge as the leading maritime power in the world. In this long transition and transformation the growth of shipping and shipbuilding were to be major engines of Britain's new economic and political power. Yet, tracing the foundation and emergence of shipbuilding as a significant industry for Britain is not easy; indeed, we have no reliable or systematic data for ship tonnage constructed or registered until the last quarter of the eighteenth century. Before then we have, at best, occasional windows that allow some light to be thrown on developments in shipbuilding through the growth of the royal navies, and by way of some early estimates of the growth of the merchant fleet.

Following the voyages of discovery, the new maritime and colonial power of Portugal and Spain exercised the commercial envy and strategic concern of the Tudors. This in turn led to a determination to improve coastal defences and to develop a strong royal navy.[2] There was also official encouragement to expand a merchant fleet which could be adapted to supply ships and men in support of the Navy in times of conflict. Henry VIII in 1541, and Elizabeth I in 1563, introduced Acts to confine and control the carriage of goods to English ships, and in 1559 Elizabeth had also attempted to prohibit the export of English ships.[3] Four years later Elizabeth also attempted to exclude foreign-owned ships from engaging in English coastal trade. Important as these protective measures were in encouraging English shipping, it was the Tudor emphasis on building ships of war that was more influential in establishing an identifiable shipbuilding industry.

When Henry VIII came to the throne in 1509 he inherited a navy of five ships. He then set about establishing a permanent naval force, building more than 40 warships and creating dockyards at Deptford and Woolwich on the Thames. At his death in 1547 his navy consisted of 58 ships with a combined total of between 11,000 to 12,000 tons. It is likely that most of these were built at Deptford and Greenwich,[4] making the Thames the centre of the emerging shipbuilding industry. Even so, a settled and available workforce was slow to develop. Consequently when Henry commissioned the *Grace à Dieu* in 1518, a vessel of 1,400 tons, he had to press men from every main port from Exeter in the west to York in the north, to provide labour.[5] Similarly in Scotland when James IV in 1507 commissioned the *Michael* of 1,000 tons, he had to build a new dock at Newhaven and import shipwrights from France.[6] During his reign James added 38 ships to the Scottish Navy, and had dockyards at Leith, Newhaven, Dunbar and Dumbarton. While these ships demonstrated that shipwrights could build very large vessels from an early date, they were ships of war, and merchant ships were generally small, a great ship being one of 100 tons or more.*

War and statecraft were also linked to the promotion of trade and, in the second half of the sixteenth century, the English crown granted monopoly trading rights to what became great chartered trading companies. The Muscovy Company of 1555 was set up to promote trade with Russia through Archangel, the principal medieval Russian port located on the White Sea. It was followed in 1581 by the Levant Company to develop trade to the Mediterranean. Next, and perhaps the greatest of the new monopolies, was the East India Company which was established in 1599. It was the

---

* A brief description of measures of ships' tonnages is given in Appendix 1, pages 268–9.

subsequent demands of these organisations for larger deep-water ships which, by creating sufficient regular demand, became the catalyst to encourage a new growth in merchant shipbuilding, and the flourishing of the English merchant marine. Ralph Davis estimated the English fleet at not more than 50,000 tons in the 1560s. By 1583 this had grown to a fleet comprising 1,300 to 1,400 ships and totalling some 67,000 tons. Since only 173 of these ships were said to be over 100 tons, the fleet was clearly made up predominantly of very small vessels, the average being around 50 tons.[7]

The establishment of the Royal Dockyards, and the growth of the chartered trading companies, added to the traditional demands for tonnage for the transportation of coal, salt, timber, grain and other commodities, as well as for the fishing fleet. Taken together, these provided a larger flow of work which encouraged coteries of skilled workmen to grow and to find more regular employment. The skilled shipwrights employed in the Royal Dockyards were also able to work in private yards, and indeed to branch out and establish their own concerns. By Elizabeth's reign some well-known private yards were thriving on the Thames, notably those of Matthew Baker, William Pell, Edward Steveny, William Stephen, Richard Chapman, John Addy and William Bright.[8] By the end of Elizabeth's reign in 1603, her policies and statecraft had not only overcome the Spanish Armada in 1588, but had rescued a declining navy to have a fleet of 42 warships of 17,000 tons with over 8,000 seamen.[9] By that time too the merchant fleet was well established, its largest ships built and repaired on the Thames.

While naval construction had been a spur to the growth of shipbuilding under the Tudors, the Stuarts were less consistent builders, although both James VI and I and Charles I built some large ships. James built 10 new ships and rebuilt another 11, each being over 500 tons. His son Charles also commissioned 10 large warships, the largest, the *Sovereign* of 1,522 tons.[10] By the 1630s many new private yards had opened on the Thames, including the Blackwall yard, which in scale was said to be similar to the Royal Dockyards.[11] Although naval work and merchant work for the chartered companies were focused on the Thames, Medway and East Anglia, shipbuilding in the western ports responded to the large demands for fishing vessels. In 1634, for example, the west-coast ports were said to have supplied 26,720 tons of shipping and 10,680 men for the Newfoundland fisheries.[12] In addition, the herring industry was reputed to employ up to 300 small busses at this time.[13]* Whaling and coal also made growing demands for new tonnage and, by the mid-seventeenth century, both Hull and Newcastle were important shipbuilding centres. J. F. Clarke has estimated that by 1660 colliers were carrying around 500,000 tons from the great North East coalfield to London, making the Tyne, along with the Thames, the two main centres of shipbuilding in the second half of the seventeenth century.[14]

---

* A 'herring buss' was a type of fishing vessel first developed by the Dutch in the fifteenth century. If has a broad beam and rounded stem and stern, giving a broad deck suitable for processing the catch on board.

By the time of the restoration of the monarchy in 1660 the demands of these industries had driven a large expansion of the English merchant fleet, from a total of 115,000 tons in 1629 to some 200,000 tons by 1660.[15] An earlier estimate by Harper gives a lower tonnage of 160,000 in the 1660s.[16] Significant as this is, it was dwarfed by the Dutch fleet which Unger estimated at 450,000–550,000 tons at the same time.[17] Unger argues that the lightly built Dutch ships had a short lifespan of 10 years, with the fishing smacks lasting double that. Domestically built English ships were heavier and more robust, and probably had a lifespan of 20–25 years. If that was the case then the fleet of 200,000 tons as estimated by Davis in the 1660s would have required 8,000 to 10,000 tons of new ships each year simply to sustain the fleet at that level. Not all of this new tonnage, however, would have come from domestic construction, since perhaps one quarter to one third of tonnage was built outside England at that time.[18]

Nevertheless, even allowing for this, domestic shipbuilding had become a substantial industry by the second half of the seventeenth century, particularly as trade with the Americas expanded. While initial settlement of the colonies was slow, it accelerated after 1630, and between 1630 and 1643 some 100,000 settlers had crossed the Atlantic from England.[19] As colonial trade became more important, in 1651 the Commonwealth under Cromwell enacted the Navigation Act to prevent Dutch ships trading to the colonies. The Act was replaced by new legislation in 1660, the new Act a more wide-ranging measure that enumerated colonial products which could only be shipped directly and exclusively to England, Ireland, or to another English colony. The intention was to exclude European powers, and especially the Dutch, from participation in the burgeoning trade with the American colonies. The commercial and political tension between the English and the Dutch resulted in three Anglo-Dutch wars in the second half of the century. The first, of 1652–54, followed from the trade exclusions resulting from the 1651 Navigation Act. The second war, of 1665–67, followed upon the capture of New Amsterdam (New York) in 1664 by the English, while the third war of 1672–74 was part of a wider European conflict of 1672–78 during which the Dutch former American settlements were ceded to England, all of these losses weakening Dutch competition.

In spite of these conflicts the value of English trade grew from an annual average of £6.7 million between 1665 and 1669 to £8.3 million between 1699 and 1701.[20] As a consequence the merchant fleet had expanded to 323,000 tons in 1702, according to Ralph Davis, while Harper again gives a lower figure of 267,000 tons.[21] In either case both estimates indicate that between the Restoration and 1702 the merchant fleet had expanded its tonnage in the order of 60 per cent, by which time it was beginning to be a more serious rival to the Dutch fleet. Moreover, the power of the Royal Navy (so named from 1660) had also increased, from the 50 ships of around 23,000 tons in 1663 to 272 ships of 159,000 tons by the time of William III's death in 1702.[22] Significantly for the future, a considerable tonnage of naval ships was being contracted out to private builders, mainly on the Thames and Medway.

## Expansion, war and trade: 1700–1776

During the eighteenth century trade and war once more strongly influenced the demand for new tonnage. Trade grew moderately in the first half of the century by about 0.8 per cent per year to £12.7 million by 1750,[23] this raising its contribution to national income from 8 to 12 per cent. The growth rate then accelerated sharply between 1750 and 1775, doubling to 1.7 per cent annually, and the export ratio to national income rose from 12 per cent to nearly 15 per cent.[24] The expansion of exports was driven by textiles, mainly wool before the 1780s, together with iron products for the colonies. In imports the demand was for consumer products, mainly sugar, tea, coffee and tobacco, and increasingly for raw materials for use by the expanding manufacturing sector of the British economy. By the middle of the eighteenth century domestic pig iron producers could supply only about half of home demand, the balance being made up of imports of bar iron from Russia and the Baltic. Increasingly imports featured hemp, flax, silk, wool, cotton, iron, timber, tallow and grain. This involved a gradual switch away from imports sourced from north-west Europe and the Mediterranean to a heavier dependence on supplies emanating from North America, and the West and East Indies. In this growing trade the value of imports considerably exceeded that of exports, but this was largely offset by the burgeoning re-export trade. Under the Navigation Acts, the re-export of colonial products was kept firmly in the hands of British merchants, and carried in British and colonial ships. In addition, as foreign trade grew, coastwise trade also expanded, especially in the coal trade. Shipments of coal from the Tyne and Wear to London nearly trebled in volume, from 650,000 tons in 1700 to 1.8 million tons by the 1780s.[25] By then J. F. Clarke notes that colliers made about eight voyages each year and, in 1777, this involved 547 vessels making 4,370 round trips.[26] The Tyne was by then the major builder of colliers, although Ipswich was also an important centre of production. There is also evidence of active coal shipments from the river Forth, and smaller exports from Ayrshire ports to Ireland.

The increasing significance of trade clearly had important consequences for the demand for new tonnage, and for the growth of the merchant fleet. At the beginning of the century the estimates by Harper and Davis measured the fleet between 267,000 and 323,000 tons.[27] By mid-century Brown estimates that it had grown to 421,000 tons,[28] a net gain of 100,000 tons over Davis, and more than 150,000 tons increase from the Harper estimate. This is a modest expansion over a period of 50 years and mirrors the relatively slow growth in trade over the same period. Shipbuilding, shipping and trade, were undoubtedly affected by the disruption of the three prolonged conflicts involving Britain, France and Spain between 1707 and 1763.

The slow expansion of the fleet in the first five decades of the century does not suggest the existence of a large demand for new tonnage. Assuming a twenty-year lifespan for the average merchant ship, then a fleet of some 300,000 tons in 1700 would have generated an annual replacement demand of around 15,000 tons, while the larger fleet of 1750 would have absorbed annual replacement orders for around 21,000 tons. There would have been some new tonnage additions to increase the fleet by up to 150,000 tons to 1750. Not all of these orders, however, were available to domestic builders, for between one third and one half of the tonnage in the fleet was supplied from the colonies, from Europe, and by wartime prizes. Between 1700 and 1750, British shipbuilders did not enjoy a large or particularly buoyant market. However, for some builders, an increasingly important factor was the spill-over of wartime naval demand into private yards.

Between 1700 and 1775 Britain was at war for 35 years with France and Spain. The competition and struggle for supremacy expanded the Royal Navy from 272 ships of 159,000 tons in 1702 to 340 ships of 321,000 tons by 1760.[29] While at the beginning of the century the six Royal Dockyards built and repaired virtually all the tonnage required by the Navy, the exigencies of the War of the Spanish Succession (1702–13) saw an extension of contracts into private yards. At the end of the seventeenth century only three or four yards on the Thames were recognised by the Navy Board as fit to build to Navy specification. However, by the end of the war, the Navy Board had 12 yards on the Thames on its list as able to build warships.[30] This was to set the pattern for the rest of the century. In the War of Jenkins' Ear and Austrian Succession (1739–48), merchant yards built and launched 140 warships of 77,591 tons for the Navy Board. The Thames was predominant, building 73 ships of 35,000 tons, but Liverpool and Hull each contributed 12 ships, Ipswich and Harwich 9 ships apiece, and the Solent and Isle of Wight built 26 ships of 17,000 tons.[31] With most of the work going to yards on the Thames and Medway, Banbury identifies 17 yards there as being active in naval construction during the war.[32] Then, after only eight years of peace, Britain was again embroiled in conflict with France and Spain in the Seven Years War of 1756–63. During this conflict Roger Knight identifies orders for 161 warships going to the private yards. The Thames again took over half the tonnage, delivering 39 ships of 25,984 tons, and for the first time some private yards built ships of the line. Thames yards built five seventy-fours, another two came from yards in Essex and Suffolk, and one from the Isle of Wight. A lesser sixty-four gun ship was also constructed at Hull.[33]

In total, in the two wars of 1739–48 and 1756–63, merchant yards built 214 warships of 127,219 tons, which in merchant equivalent tons and value terms was possibly twice that. While this was a major boost to the merchant market before the 1760s, the work was not widely spread. Yards from Hull to the Solent did attract orders, with Liverpool a small outlier, but most work was concentrated in the Thames yards, and to a lesser extent on the Medway. These yards attracted half of all the naval tonnage built in merchant yards in these years. Since the Thames also held the monopoly of building and repairing East Indiamen, the character of shipbuilding there diverged sharply from other districts. Even by the 1770s the average British merchant ship was only a vessel of 100 tons. In contrast to this, East Indiamen were in the range of 800–1,200 tons, and the standard third-rate warship was 1,500 tons. By the 1770s the Thames concentrated mainly on larger, high-value vessels. Conversely, on the east coast from East Anglia to Whitby, construction was more diverse, ranging from coasters and colliers to whalers and general cargo ships. Elsewhere, in the south-west and north-west ports, there was a range of building from fishing smacks to coastal vessels, and larger ships for the West Indies and slave trades. In Scotland and Ireland construction was generally of smaller craft for fishing and coastwise trade, although on the Clyde, larger ships for the West Indies trades were appearing more regularly.

In spite of the disruption of the Seven Years War, the acceleration in the growth of trade after 1750 added 711,000 tons of ships to the merchant fleet, taking it to 1,132,517 tons by 1776.[34] A fleet of that scale would, on a 20-year replacement cycle, have required an annual new build in the order of 57,000 tons, simply to maintain it. To cope with that, and to add an average of another 30,000 tons each year to reach the 1776 fleet tonnage, the shipping market must have been absorbing 80–90,000 tons of new ships each year. However, not all of that fell to the order books of domestic shipbuilders. From 1776, Lloyds Register provides information on the place of build of ships. Joseph Goldenberg's analysis of the 1776 Register shows that, of the fleet of 1,132,517 tons, fewer than half was British built, comprising some 561,563 tons, or 49.6 per cent of the total. The importance of colonial supplies is demonstrated, with 361,435 tons, 31.9 per cent, originating in British America. Moreover 18.5 per cent of the fleet was foreign-built, with Norway, Germany and the Low Countries delivering half of that.[35]

The Lloyds data also confirm the North East coast as the main merchant shipbuilding district in Britain. The yards on the Tyne, Wear and Tees, together with Whitby, Scarborough and Hull, had built 40 per cent of all English tonnage on the Register, or 35 per cent of British tonnage when Scottish built vessels are included. Whitby, Newcastle and Scarborough were the leading ports of origin in the district. In contrast, because of its focus on naval construction, the Thames built just over 19 per cent of the English merchant tonnage on the Register, followed by the North West with 14 per cent. East Anglia contributed nearly 10 per cent, and the South West ports nearly 9 per cent of the total. A further 5 per cent originated in South East ports, while less than 3 per cent originated in Wales. According to the Register, Scotland contributed only 29,165 tons, 5.2 per cent of the British built tonnage.

The 1776 Register is certainly not a complete record, but whatever its imperfections, it reveals a flourishing and geographically widespread industry which must have constructed at least half of the 711,000 tons added to the fleet between 1750 and 1776. The industry had developed substantially since 1700 but clearly suffered from the keen competition of the colonial builders, particularly those of New England and the Chesapeake. In 1776, however, with the Declaration of Independence by the thirteen British American colonies, the industry entered into new and more protected market conditions.

## War and the shipbuilding districts, 1776–1815

The 1776 Declaration of Independence placed the colonial shipbuilders outside the Navigation Acts, and excluded them as suppliers of tonnage to British ship-owners. Competition from the colonies was immediately removed. When this was followed by the Revolutionary and Napoleonic conflicts, the effect was seemingly to deliver a growing and captive market to British shipbuilders. Indeed in the 40 years from 1775 to 1815 there were 35 years of conflict involving Britain in four wars; the American War of Independence, 1775–82; the French Revolutionary Wars of 1793–1802, and the Napoleonic Wars of 1803–15, this overlapping with the American conflict of 1812–14. Such constant and prolonged hostilities inevitably had repercussions for shipping and shipbuilding. Nevertheless, despite the years of warfare, the British merchant marine more than doubled in scale from 1,132,517 tons in 1776 to 2,478,000 tons in 1815.[36] In addition the tonnage of ships clearing from British ports engaging in foreign trade also more than doubled, from 1,904,000 tons to 4,764,000 tons in the same period.[37]

It is clear from these data that shipping and trade were buoyant and growing rapidly. The fleet added 1,284,000 tons, and tonnage clearing in foreign trade expanded by 2,860,000 tons. Yet the activity in British merchant shipbuilding did not mirror these trends. The recorded output of new tonnage built and first registered in Britain in 1787, the first year after the Registration Act of 1786, was 91,700 tons, and for the next 27 years to 1815, this level of output was only exceeded in five years, 1800–03 inclusive, and in 1815.[38] For the remainder of the 22 years the production of merchant tonnage languished, rarely exceeding 60–80 per cent of the 1787 output. As a consequence, a considerable part of the growth of tonnage in the merchant fleet must have come from other sources, for the war years were clearly a more difficult environment for the shipbuilder than for the ship owner. Indeed, a large part of the increased tonnage came from captured prizes. Prize tonnage on the Register already stood at 369,563 tons in 1801, and peaked at 563,346 tons in 1811, this represented by an addition of 4,023 vessels to the fleet.[39] From 1801 to 1815 prizes represented over 20 per cent of the tonnage in the merchant marine. Allowing for this the domestic additions to the fleet were a modest 644,000 tons between 1776 and 1811, a growth of 51 per cent over four decades. During this time the heavy share of colonial-built tonnage receded from around 32 per cent in 1776 to 20 per cent of the total 1801. The shortfall had, however, been filled by prize tonnage rather than domestic production. Purely British-built tonnage had edged up to 55 per cent of the fleet.

British builders clearly faced difficult conditions in these forty years, this reflected in the sharp fluctuations in output, and the frequently modest level of production of new merchant tonnage. Nevertheless, in spite of the volatility of demand and production, the industry did grow and change significantly. These developments can be traced more clearly than in earlier years because of the improvement in systematically recording the tonnage built and registered. National series are available from 1787, though there are breaks in 1803 and for 1812−13 for British and Empire data, and from 1806−13 inclusive, for British constructed tonnage alone. In addition these series are supplemented by the Goldberg analysis of the 1776 Lloyds Register, and by a more comprehensive analysis of merchant and naval output on a port by port basis, as compiled by J.F. Clarke for the period between 1776 and 1813.[40] These data are summarised on a regional basis in Tables 1.1 and 1.2.

*Table 1.1*   Regional shares of British-built merchant tonnage, 1776−1813

| Tonnage built | 1776 520,128[1] | | 1801−02 182,143[2] | | 1786−1813 1,806,610[3] | |
|---|---|---|---|---|---|---|
| By region | '000 tons | % | '000 tons | % | '000 tons | % |
| North East[a] | 197.2 | 37.9 | 72.6 | 39.8 | 742.2 | 41.0 |
| Thames[b] | 94.9 | 18.3 | 13.5 | 7.4 | 234.7 | 12.9 |
| South East[c] | 24.9 | 4.8 | 6.2 | 3.4 | 100.5 | 6.1 |
| South West[d] | 43.3 | 8.3 | 18.6 | 10.2 | 255.7 | 14.1 |
| East Anglia[e] | 48.1 | 9.2 | 14.7 | 8.1 | 145.3 | 8.0 |
| North West[f] | 68.7 | 13.2 | 24.2 | 13.3 | 264.1 | 14.6 |
| Wales | 13.7 | 2.6 | 8.4 | 4.6 | 54.1 | 3.0 |
| Scotland | 29.2 | 5.6 | 23.9 | 13.1 | — | — |

[1] Compiled from J. Goldberg, 'An Analysis of Shipbuilding Sites in Lloyd's Register of 1776', *The Mariners Mirror*, 59 (1973), no. 4.

[2] J.F. Clarke, 'Shipbuilding in Britain about 1800', unpublished paper, pp. 1−40; 2,000 ship sample of Lloyd's Register, 1801−02.

[3] J.F. Clarke, *Shipbuilding in Britain about 1800*. Total output compiled by port, 1786−1813 (excludes Scotland).

*Definition of regions*:

[a] North East: Berwick to Hull              [b] Thames: Thames and Medway

[c] South East: Dover to Isle of Wight       [d] South West: Poole to Gloucester

[e] East Anglia: Boston to Colchester        [f] North West: Chester to Whitehaven

*Table 1.2*  Regional shipbuilding, 1786–1813 ('000 tons, builder's measure)

| Region | Merchant Tons ('000) | % | Naval Tons ('000) | % | Total Tons ('000) | % |
|---|---|---|---|---|---|---|
| North East | 742.2 | 41.0 | 14.5 | 4.6 | 756.7 | 35.7 |
| Thames | 234.7 | 12.9 | 180.6 | 57.2 | 415.4 | 19.6 |
| South East | 100.5 | 6.1 | 63.4 | 20.0 | 176.9 | 8.3 |
| South West | 255.7 | 14.1 | 28.8 | 9.2 | 284.5 | 13.4 |
| East Anglia | 145.3 | 8.0 | 22.6 | 7.0 | 167.9 | 7.9 |
| North West | 264.1 | 14.6 | 2.6 | 0.8 | 266.7 | 12.6 |
| Wales | 54.1 | 3.0 | — | — | 54.1 | 2.3 |
| England and Wales | 1,806.60 | | 315.60 | | 2,122.20 | |

*Source*: Compiled from J.F. Clarke, 'Shipbuilding in Britain about 1800'; tonnage launched in each port (unpublished paper).

The overall pattern confirms the dominance of the North East district, which supplied 41 per cent of all new tonnage built between 1786 and 1813. Newcastle alone supplied more than 27 per cent of the regional output, with Hull and Sunderland each contributing another 22 per cent, while Whitby delivered 17.6 per cent of the district output. The strengthening of shipbuilding in both the North East ports and in the South West region, as rivals to the Thames, is also clear. Both out-build the Thames in merchant tonnage in these years. In the North West district Whitehaven contributed one third of that district's tonnage, closely followed by Liverpool with 30 per cent. In the South West of England the main centres were Bristol, Dartmouth, Exeter and Plymouth, while in the South East district, Dover, Southampton, Cowes and Lyne were the main producers. The major centres in East Anglia were Ipswich and Yarmouth. From these port-based data Clarke identifies more than 70 ports in England and Wales, and more than 30 ports in Scotland, regularly building ships at this time. Over the period 1786–1813 his data cover 26 years (that of 1803 is missing). From this he records a total merchant output from England and Wales of 14,859 ships, with an aggregate total of 1,806,610 tons. This gives an average annual output of 69,500 tons, with the average ship measuring 121.6 tons. Within this analysis Clarke reviews output from Scotland between 1786 and 1805, the average being in the range of 10–11,000 tons per year, about 13 per cent of the British output.[41] This is consistent with his analysis of some 2,000 ships in the Lloyds Register of 1800–01. Scottish tonnage in that sample was 23,939 tons, 13 per cent of the British total.[42]

The regional analysis and the port data also confirm a relatively small contribution to merchant tonnage from the yards on the Thames and the south coast. It is here that, most notably, the impact of war and demands for naval tonnage have most influence on the fortunes of the industry. Compilations from Clarke's port data for the period 1786–1813 record a naval output of 315,581 tons in the private yards.[43] Over half of this, 57.2 per cent, came from yards on the Thames and Medway, and a further 20 per cent was built in the yards from Dover to the Solent. While Clarke suggests that the work content of this naval tonnage was up to double the equivalent merchant output, simply adding this builders' measure tonnage to the other merchant output on the Thames lifts the river's share in total output to nearly 20 per cent, keeping it in second place behind the North East coast among the shipbuilding districts. Adding this naval tonnage to the merchant tonnage lifts the total output of the industry to 2,122,000 tons in the 26 years from 1786 to 1813, and annual average of some 82,000 tons (see Table 1.2). If the estimated Scottish production of 10–11,000 tons is added, Clarke's port data indicate that the industry was working with an output of 90,000–95,000 tons per year. If allowance is made for the view that, in work content, naval tonnage is equivalent to double the merchant work, the adjusted output of the merchant industry increases to circa 105,000–110,000 tons annually throughout the war years.

Naval construction in the private yards was clearly an important component of the industry, and Roger Knight has produced more detailed data to assess its significance. His analysis of the years from 1755 to 1815 concludes that the private yards delivered 432,000 tons of warships, two thirds of the total built in the period.[44] This indicates an even greater addition to the workload of the merchant yards. In the critical war years of 1803–15, the private yards built 242,619 tons of warships, over 70 per cent of all naval production in these years. This comprised no fewer than 433 ships.[45] In addition to orders placed on the Thames and Medway, this boom of construction delivered orders to another 51 yards, these stretching as far north as Leith and Berwick on the east coast, and to Liverpool and Chester in the west.[46] Yards on the Thames produced one third of the tonnage, amounting to 84 ships with an average size of 952 tons. The Medway delivered another 14 per cent, where the average ship was smaller at 671 tons. Eleven yards on the Thames and five on the Medway delivered this tonnage, one third of the ships and 47 per cent of the tonnage constructed.

The second greatest concentration of warship building in the private yards was on the Solent and Isle of Wight. Yards there built 87 ships and nearly 17 per cent of the tonnage. Outside of the Thames, the largest ships were produced at Hull, 11 ships of 9,971 tons, averaging 906 tons. In this pressure of wartime demand even the Tyne, Wear and Tees delivered 25 warships of 10,126 tons, an average of 405 tons per vessel. To put all this in context, the Royal Dockyards built 82 ships of 94,960 tons, an average size of 1,158 tons. These were the largest ships of the line.[47] When this naval shipbuilding is examined, it is evident that the relatively small purely merchant output emanating from the Thames, Medway, and yards in Kent, Sussex and Hampshire, is greatly offset by the huge effort in supplying ships of war. The industry on the Thames, Medway and on the South East coast was essentially diverted from peacetime to wartime production, thus allowing the Dockyards to concentrate on building the largest ships of the line, and on the enormous burden of repairs and rebuilding arising out of the prolonged conflict and blockade.

Early in the renewed warfare, in 1804, the Admiralty commissioned a survey of merchant shipyards to assess the availability of skill, capital and labour that might be called on to aid the war effort.[48] Clarke cautions that the returns were not complete, having no information on the North West ports, or for Aberdeen. With these exceptions the survey enumerated 520 yards in existence. Allowing for the omissions, Clarke suggests the actual number of yards working in 1804 must have been in excess of 550. Considering that Knight identified 67 yards obtaining naval orders between 1803 and 1815, perhaps only some 10–12 per cent of all yards were drawn on to build ships of war. The orders clearly went to the larger yards, and in spite of the length and severity of the conflict, most shipyards were unaffected directly by naval demand. The survey demonstrated that the average employment in the shipyards was only 17 men, and that about 13 per cent of the yards employed fewer than ten men. Indeed one third of the entire workforce was in yards employing 20 or fewer men. However, at the other end of the scale, the survey identified 41 yards all employing more than 50 workers. These yards accounted for 38 per cent of the entire workforce of shipwrights, caulkers and apprentices. The four largest yards all employed more than 150 men. These were Bulmer, in South Shields, with 181 men, Perry and Wells Blackwall yard in London, with 173 men, F. Hurry at Howden Dock, with 155 employees, and Scott's at Greenock with 151 men. Another six yards employed between 100 and 150 men. Of these 41 yards, 17 were in the North East, of which six were located in South Shields. Another 11 of the yards were on the Thames and Medway, and four were in Scotland, three in Greenock and one in Leith. The North West district had three of the largest yards, two of them in Liverpool and one at Chester. Four of these largest yards were in the South West, two of them in Bristol, while the two remaining were in the Channel Islands.[49]

The total workforce enumerated in the survey was 9,160 men and apprentices. When allowance is made for the lack of returns for Whitehaven, Aberdeen and Stockton, which together contributed ten per cent of the 1804 tonnage, the total workforce in the merchant yards must have been in the order of 10,000 men. At the same time the Royal Dockyards employed 3,248 shipwrights.[50] By 1814 the Dockyard labour force had grown to 5,369 shipwrights and 10,227 others, a total of 15,596 employees. While the output and employment in the merchant yards fluctuated widely in these years, the 1804 output of 84,000 tons was close to the 1814 production of 80,000 tons. It is then reasonable to assume that the workforce would have been similar to the 10,000 at work at the earlier date. Consequently the total workforce in shipbuilding, naval and merchant, at the end of the Napoleonic Wars must have been in excess of 25,000 men.

In the course of the eighteenth century the shipbuilding industry had grown substantially in scale and had developed clear regional locations and patterns of production. The Thames and South East coast were the major suppliers of larger ships, East Indiamen and naval craft. In contrast the industry in the South West and North West increasingly built for the West Indian and slave trades, as well as for the more local coasting and fishing trades. Shipbuilding in the west of Scotland shared some of these features though still built more for local than for deep-water markets. Yards in the East of Scotland catered for the fisheries and ships for trade to the Baltic in fish, grain and timber, and to the Low Countries. Colliers, and coal and salt shipments from the river Forth, were also a feature. But this was a pale reflection of the scale and dominance of the industry strung along the North East coast from Berwick to Hull. Here were the main builders of general cargo ships, colliers, fishing smacks, and whalers. Colliers, fishing busses and general cargo ships also characterised the yards in East Anglia, but this district was slowly losing dynamism as the North East yards increased their hold on the industry at large.

Impressive as these developments were, shipbuilding was not transformed by the forces that were beginning to reshape the economy. At the beginning of the eighteenth century Britain was an agrarian, rural and craft based economy, but by the beginning of the nineteenth century, trade, towns and factory-based manufactures had assumed a new importance. In contrast to earlier centuries, population grew and was sustained by other shifts in economy and society. Between 1701 and 1811 the population of Great Britain and Ireland doubled from 9.4 to 18.1 million,[51] and although the population living and working on the land continued to grow, the share of agriculture in national income slipped from around 45 per cent in 1701 to about one third at the end of the century. In contrast, the combined share of industry, trade, and building edged upward from one quarter to one third of national product.[52] While these were not huge changes they were signals that the traditional craft of shipbuilding had increasingly to relate to an economy beginning to transform itself by manufactures, trade and urban living. Significant in this transition was the employment of inanimate power, first the exploitation of water power to drive the new spinning mills, and more gradually the addition of forms of steam power to drain mines, lift coal, and drive machinery. Steam power was still in its infancy for even in 1800 there were only 1,200–1,300 steam engines in operation in Britain, 500 of them being of the improved Watt design. At that time steam only supplied about 10 per cent of the horsepower consumed by mines and factories.[53] Nevertheless the signs were there of the potential of steam to transform production, especially in the environment emerging with the linking of rural and urban markets through the network of 2,000 miles of canals, and more than 2,000 miles of navigable rivers made available by 1800.[54]

In the developing economy the leading manufactures were textiles, first woollens and then especially cotton, together with the expansion of the iron and coal-mining industries. The scale of these new enterprises dwarfed that of the shipbuilding industry. While the largest cotton mills employed in excess of 1,500 in 1815,[55] the largest merchant shipyards employed only one tenth of that number, although the

Royal Dockyards were still among the largest capital enterprises and employers in the country. Moreover, while the value of cotton goods produced in the early years of the nineteenth century was in excess of £10 million annually,[56] the value of merchant ships built was in the range of £2.0–£2.5 million,[57] though this compared more favourably with £2.8 million for the pit head value of coal, and £3.0 million for the value of silk output in 1800.[58] At these values shipbuilding contributed perhaps 1.0–1.5 per cent of national income, though with naval construction in the private yards considered, shipbuilding may have contributed up to 2.0 per cent of the national product at the beginning of the nineteenth century.

In general, while some sectors of the economy were moving rapidly to adopt large plants, steam power and metal machinery, the shipyards were largely untouched by these advances. Labour, even in the Dockyards, remained firmly on a craft basis of masters, journeymen and apprentices, all relying on the acquisition and transmission of knowledge and skills by demonstration, by hands-on practice, and by rule of thumb. While there were some moves to provide written principles of ship construction and naval architecture, these made slow headway. Perhaps the best known treatise was that by Frederich Heinreich Chapman, chief constructor and Admiral Superintendent of the Swedish Naval Dockyard in Karskrona. This was published in 1775 and was still the main text being drawn on in the Dockyards in the 1840s.[59] Chapman also demonstrated how to calculate the stability of a vessel by establishing its metacentre.[60] Some theoretical advances also came from outside the industry. Isaac Newton in England and Christian Huygens in Holland demonstrated that doubling the speed of a hull in the water quadrupled the resistance, implying that hull design should increase in length in relation to breadth for improved efficiency.[61] Interest in improving hull design certainly grew as captured French vessels frequently displayed finer lines, and enjoyed greater speed. Stimulated by this, the Society of Arts offered a prize of £100 for an improved hull design, but had little success. In similar vein the Admiralty set up a School of Naval Architecture at Portsmouth in 1810, but it had little support or influence.[62] More practical measures, such as introducing copper sheathing to protect hulls, and the substitution of iron and copper bolts and nails to replace wooden pins, and iron knees and brackets to connect beams and side timbers, all met with more success, especially in naval craft. Gabriel Snodgrass, Surveyor for the East India Company, promoted the use of iron knees and brackets, while Robert Seppings, who became Surveyor of the Navy, particularly advocated the use of diagonal bracing of the hull, a feature which allowed wooden hulls to be extended from a maximum of 200 to 300 feet.[63] Technical advances and their adoption were small and slow in the Navy, and were mainly ignored in the merchant yards, where the design of ships had changed little between the time of the Tudors and the Napoleonic Wars, although what had been called a great ship in the sixteenth century, one of 100 tons, had by 1800 become an average in the merchant fleet, though many were still much smaller than that.

Davis, however, argues that this appearance of slow change and stagnant practice may be misleading. He suggests that in the eighteenth century English builders responded to growing trade by gradually adopting ship designs similar to the box-like hulls of the Dutch fluitschips, these providing greater cargo capacity. Moreover progressive changes in rigging saw a significant reduction in crew numbers, with a consequent improvement in efficiency.[64] It is not clear, however, how widespread such changes were. The fact that vessels of less than 100 tons still comprised the largest part of the merchant fleet suggests that the industry as a whole still clung to traditional practice, and was slow to adopt changes. It was encouraged in this by equally conservative ship owners who preferred the familiar to the novel.

Irrespective of this, shipbuilding had grown to be an industry of considerable scale by the end of the eighteenth century. But large as it was in number of yards, in output and employment, it was not yet a national industry in terms of its market. It remained an industry of strong regional identities, with production predominantly for local markets. However, the acceleration in the development of the industrial economy, and renewed American competition in shipping after 1815, began to erode localism and conservatism, as did experimentation with steam power. These were among the influences that were to transform shipbuilding from local to national significance, and to launch it into international leadership in the course of the nineteenth century.

# Two industries:
# from 1815 to the 1880s

The partnerships of wood and sail, and steam and iron, dominate the development of shipbuilding between 1815 and 1885. Each pair of resources supported the development of two quite distinct industries which grew side by side, interacting and interlocking to transform the nature and scale of shipbuilding. This is not so much a case of a declining sector being replaced by a new and growing activity, but rather of a great craft at the apogee of achievement quite dramatically replaced by a superior product. This displacement of an historic craft by a modern engineering assembly trade involved great changes in the scale and location of the industry, revolutionary innovations in construction and forms of propulsion, and a transformation of the nature of the firms and their markets.

## Growth and fluctuations

As an industry shipbuilding relies upon investment in high-value capital products; its activity is carried upward or downward by sharp swings in demand from ship owners. Orders ebb and flow with the course of trade, fluctuations in freight rates, and the relative price of new and second-hand tonnage. In these relationships a ship owner could plunge for a new ship, buy a second-hand vessel, or simply defer replacement over a lengthy period of time. Caught between the unpredictability of demand and the need to be able to respond quickly to the prospect of attracting an order, shipbuilders typically tended to develop over-capacity. Indeed, capacity available in relation to current demand is central to understanding the fluctuations that have always characterised the industry.

Between 1815 and 1883 the annual output of ships grew more than sevenfold, to 768,000 tons. This vast increase took Britain to first place among shipbuilding nations, and this expansion was achieved through great turbulence, rather than with smooth and regular growth. During these seventy years the industry experienced seven great cycles of expansion and contraction, each roughly of nine to ten years duration (see Table 2.1). The industry peaks and troughs are broadly in line with those of the general trade cycle, as would be expected since it delivered the ships to carry world cargoes, though often with a lag of one or two years at the turning points. The fluctuations in output could also be influenced by the time taken to absorb the tonnage produced. When the huge building effort of the Napoleonic Wars and the subsequent sale of prize tonnage, saturated the shipping market, the consequence was that, during the next 22 years, the 1815 tonnage was only exceeded in three years, 1825–26 and 1837. Similarly the surge of tonnage produced to meet the demands of expanding eastern trade, and the effects of the first Chinese (Opium) War, meant that the 211,300 tons produced in 1840 was not passed until 1855. It was then another nine years before that output of 323,200 tons was surpassed in 1864, these lags again reflecting the capacity problem of absorbing large increases of tonnage into the shipping market. Consequently, although the industry was expanding, its overall experience to the 1850s was of three short booms separated by two long periods of slack trade, as the market slowly absorbed the capacity produced at the peaks of production.

*Table 2.1*  Ships built and first registered in the UK, 1815–1883 (net tons)

|  | 1815 | 1850 | 1870 | 1883 |
|---|---|---|---|---|
| *All ships* |  |  |  |  |
| Total tonnage | 102,900 | 133,700 | 342,700 | 768,600 |
| Number of ships | 913 | 689 | 974 | 1,174 |
| Average ship tonnage | 113 | 194 | 352 | 655 |
| *Sail ships* |  |  |  |  |
| Tonnage | 102,100 | 119,100 | 117,000 | 146,800 |
| Number of ships | 904 | 621 | 541 | 368 |
| Average ship tonnage | 113 | 192 | 216 | 399 |
| *% sail* | *99.2* | *89.0* | *34.1* | *19.1* |
| *Steam ships* |  |  |  |  |
| Tons | 800 | 14,600 | 225,700 | 621,800 |
| Number of ships | 9 | 68 | 423 | 806 |
| Average ship tonnage | 89 | 215 | 533 | 771 |
| *% steam* | *0.8* | *11.0* | *65.9* | *80.9* |

*Source*: Compiled from B R Mitchell and P Deane, *Abstract of British Historical Statistics*, Cambridge, 1962, ch. VIII. Transport, Table 2, pp. 220–2.

During the first half of the nineteenth century the industry was completely dominated by wood and sail construction. In 1815, apart from nine steamboats, all tonnage was in wood and sail. Even by 1850 sail tonnage represented 89 per cent of all output, and wood provided 90 per cent of all hull tonnage. The wood and sail industry was then approaching its maximum scale, reaching that position in 1855 with an output of 211,000 tons, two thirds of the production of the entire industry. It is only from then that the two industries begin to display some variation in the peaks and troughs of their activity. In the 1849–57 cycle, sail tonnage bottomed out in 1854, with steam later in 1857. This variation became more pronounced in the 1867–79 cycle, during which sail and steam tonnages moved in opposite directions. They were then almost completely alternative preferences for ship owners, steam tonnage in demand in the upswing, with demand for cheaper sail tonnage recovering sharply after the peak of 1874.

Throughout these decades the fluctuations in output were severe, and before 1850 made for a slow growing industry. The merchant fleet was static in tonnage at between 2.3 and 2.5 million tons from 1815 to 1839, slowly absorbing the post-war surplus capacity. In the 1840s it began to grow, adding a million tons to 1850, and then doubling in scale to 7.2 million tons by 1883.[1] From 1850 the trend in shipbuilding output is relentlessly upward, and was strong enough to cope with the fluctuations in the succeeding cycles. The upward trend from 1850 absorbed these fluctuations almost without trace in a long expansion that did not show any significant break until 1882. This is not to suggest that shipbuilders did not suffer greatly in downturns, with many failures among firms, but recovery came more quickly, with each trough less deep than the previous one, and each new peak surpassing the previous level of output.

The great surge in the scale of shipbuilding, and the doubling in size of the merchant marine, were supported by a threefold growth in Britain's foreign trade,[2] this driving up net credits earned by British shipping from £13 million to over £52 million by the 1870s.[3] The expansion of trade after the repeal of the Navigation Acts in 1849 was clearly linked to the huge increase in the carrying capacity of the merchant fleet. It was also stimulated by the sharp reduction in turn-round times in ports as a consequence of the growing impact of the screw-driven iron steamship from the 1850s.[4] While sail tonnage still represented three quarters of the fleet in the 1850s, contemporaries already argued that in carrying capacity one steam ton was equivalent to three to four sail tons.[5] The inference is that the steamer fleet was already equal in carrying capacity to the much larger sail fleet in the 1850s.[5] Thereafter, the relentless growth of the iron steamship meant that by 1870, the output of wood and sail tonnage contributed only 30 per cent of the output of the industry. A decade later this had dwindled to 19 per cent, the steamship contributing the rest. At the same time iron hulls had grown from one quarter of the industry output in 1850, to around 90 per cent of output in 1880. The combination of steam and iron had by then completely supplanted the traditional craft of wood and sail, and had also transformed the regional location of the main shipyards.

## Regional changes

While it is evident that there were great changes among the leading shipbuilding districts after 1815, the absence of systematic information on regional output and employment obscures the nature, scale, and timing of the shifts. National output data are reliable from 1814, and census employment enumerations improve in coverage from 1831, though when compared with occasional detailed regional compilations, the census appears to understate the scale of the workforce. Nevertheless the broad outline of regional growth and decline can be discerned.

During the eighteenth century the main concentrations of shipbuilding had emerged on the Thames and South East coast, and on the north-eastern rivers from the Tyne to the Humber, and this was still the case by 1820. However, with the disappearance of naval demand, the balance of leadership began to move in favour of the North East coast. In 1820 the yards between the Tyne and the Wash delivered 30 per cent of national production, outpacing the yards from the Thames and south coast. This was now clearly the second ranking district, with less than a quarter of national output (see Table 2.2). Third place in regional production was in the Bristol Channel and South West yards, followed in fourth place by the Mersey and North West district. Four fifths of UK production came from the industry in England and Wales, with Scotland contributing 16 per cent. Within Scotland the east-coast industry, from the Moray Firth to the river Forth, dominated with over half the Scottish output. The Clyde produced around one third of Scottish tonnage, and less than 6 per cent of national output, giving little indication of its later achievement. It was then still a very small scale producer in wood and sail, far behind the rivers of the north of England and the Thames. The industry in Ireland was smaller still, delivering only 1,684 tons, with the yards around Belfast and others in the south-west being the main areas of production.

*Table 2.2*  UK shipbuilding: regional output, 1820 and 1871 (net tons)

| Region | 1820 | | 1871 | |
|---|---|---|---|---|
| | *Tons* | *% UK* | *Tons* | *% UK* |
| *England* | | | | |
|     Thames and South East | 12,574 | 18.9 | 13,038 | 3.3 |
|     South coast | 2,480 | 3.7 | 3,903 | 1.0 |
|     Thames, South and South East (total) | 15,054 | 22.6 | 16,941 | 4.3 |
| South West/Bristol Channel | 10,019 | 15.0 | 9,663 | 2.5 |
| Mersey and North West | 8,222 | 12.3 | 28,837 | 7.4 |
| East Anglia | 2,371 | 3.6 | 2,491 | 0.6 |
|     Tyne | 2,222 | 3.3 | 55,398 | 14.2 |

| | | | | |
|---|---|---|---|---|
| Wear | 7,560 | 11.3 | 73,196 | 18.7 |
| Tees | 3,533 | 5.3 | 37,034 | 9.5 |
| Humber | 4,055 | 6.1 | 28,410 | 7.3 |
| North East coast (total) | 17,370 | 26.0 | 194,038 | 49.6 |
| *Wales* | 618 | 0.9 | 833 | 0.2 |
| Total, England and Wales | 54,014 | 81.0 | 252,803 | 64.6 |
| *Scotland* | | | | |
| Clyde | 3,961 | 5.9 | 115,136 | 29.0 |
| Forth | 2,360 | 3.5 | 1,557 | 0.4 |
| Tay | 1,794 | 2.7 | 6,090 | 1.6 |
| Aberdeen and north-east Scotland | 2,092 | 3.1 | 7,314 | 1.9 |
| West coast and the islands | 797 | 1.2 | 44 | – |
| Total, Scotland | 11,004 | 16.5 | 130,141 | 33.3 |
| *Ireland* | | | | |
| Belfast | 634 | 1.0 | 7,842 | 2.0 |
| Dublin | 240 | 0.4 | 412 | 0.1 |
| South-west Ireland | 810 | 1.1 | – | |
| Total, Ireland | 1,684 | 2.5 | 8,254 | 2.1 |
| Total UK | 66,702 | 100.0 | 391,198 | 100.0 |

Sources: 1820: Compiled from British Sessional Papers, HC 1826–27, Vol XVIII; 1871: British Sessional Papers, HC 1872, Vol LIII

The occupational returns of the 1831 census provide some check on this pattern.

The 1831 employment pattern does not mirror the 1820 output distribution. The Thames and South East district take first place in employment, with 26 per cent of the workforce, displacing the North East coast to second place with just over 20 per cent of employment. Similarly the South West and North West districts reverse their output rankings, the North West in third place with 17 per cent of male employment compared to 13 per cent in the South West. Scotland's share in this is only 12 per cent, some 60 per cent of this employed in the east-coast yards, and another quarter of the workforce on the Clyde. In 1831 the centre of gravity of the industry in employment still lies in the shipbuilding towns from the Thames to the Bristol Channel where nearly half the total adult male workforce was located. The anomaly of the North East leading in output, but the Thames concentrating more of the workforce, may reflect the need to employ more labour to undertake the work on the larger and higher value merchant and naval tonnage which was the typical output of the Thames and South

East districts. In the combination of employment and tonnage produced, the Thames and the North East coast were still finely balanced in the competition for overall leadership in the industry.

From the 1830s the historic dominance of the industry located from the Thames to the Bristol Channel began to be overtaken, not as yet by any absolute decline of employment there, but by the more rapid growth of the industry along the North East rivers, and on the Clyde (see Table 2.3). By 1851 the North East district had become the leading area in terms of both employment and output, while the most rapid growth had taken place on the Clyde whose employment in 1851 had trebled over 1831. These trends accelerated between 1851 and 1871, the total workforce growing by four fifths. The slowest growth of less than one quarter was in the Thames and southern districts, while the North East captured one quarter of the entire workforce. The fastest expansion among the English districts was a doubling of employment in the Mersey and North West, but even this paled in relation to the fourfold expansion in Scotland, this driven by the Clyde where employment grew more than six times to 12,829 adult males, this being marginally ahead of the combined employment on the Tyne, Wear and Tees. By 1871 these four northern rivers held more than 44 per cent of the workforce, the share of the southern districts having been cut in half to 18 per cent. Between 1831 and 1871, the centre of gravity of British shipbuilding had shifted inexorably from the south of England to the north-east of England and to Scotland.

While the North East and Scotland had overtaken the Thames and south coast in both employment and output, the Thames industry had stagnated in output, rather than having contracted. Thames yards produced 13,038 tons of shipping in 1871 compared with 12,574 tons in 1820. This district still employed 10 per cent of the workforce, but delivered less than three per cent of tonnage produced. In strong contrast, with only one quarter of employment, the North East rivers produced 165,628 tons, 42 per cent of the total. Similarly, the Clyde delivered 30 per cent of output, with only 20 per cent of the workforce. These anomalies seem to point to unlikely productivity differences, but are more likely to highlight under-recording of employment in the census with its listing only of adult men over twenty years of age. Consequently, by 1871, the regional tonnage data appear as a more reliable guide to the relative positions of the shipbuilding districts. On tonnages the leading district, with over 42 per cent of tonnage, is clearly the North East coast. Within the district the Wear leads with 19 per cent ahead of the Tyne on 14 per cent, and the Tees in third place (see Table 2.2). The Clyde is easily in second place with 30 per cent of output, followed by the Mersey and Humber with similar shares of over 7 per cent of output, with smaller contributions of 4 per cent from the east of Scotland and 2 per cent from Ireland.

*Table 2.3*   Adult male employment in British shipbuilding, 1831–1871

| | 1831 | | 1851 | | 1871 | |
|---|---|---|---|---|---|---|
| Total employed, Great Britain | 16,942 | | 31,062 | | 56,476 | |
| *By district* | *No.* | *%* | *No.* | *%* | *No.* | *%* |
| Thames | 2,514 | 14.8 | 5,069 | 16.3 | 6,135 | 10.9 |
| South East | 1,939 | 11.4 | 1,839 | 5.9 | 2,169 | 3.8 |
| South coast | 1,241 | 7.3 | 1,583 | 5.1 | 2,208 | 3.9 |
| Thames, South and South East (total) | 5,694 | 33.6 | 8,491 | 27.3 | 10,512 | 18.6 |
| North East coast | 3,016 | 17.8 | 7,809 | 25.1 | 12,134 | 21.5 |
| Humber | 475 | 2.8 | 1,349 | 4.3 | 2,480 | 4.4 |
| North East district (total) | 3,491 | 20.6 | 9,158 | 29.5 | 14,614 | 25.9 |
| Bristol and South West | 2,233 | 13.2 | 3,047 | 9.8 | 4,170 | 7.4 |
| Mersey and North West | 2,834 | 16.7 | 3,887 | 12.5 | 7,786 | 13.8 |
| Wales and other | 635 | 3.7 | 2,096 | 6.7 | 2,955 | 5.2 |
| England and Wales (total) | 14,887 | 87.8 | 26,679 | 85.9 | 40,037 | 70.9 |
| Clyde | 559 | 3.3 | 1,960 | 6.3 | 12,829 | 22.7 |
| Forth | 313 | 1.8 | 452 | 1.5 | 951 | 1.7 |
| Tay | 239 | 1.4 | 599 | 1.9 | 1,399 | 2.5 |
| Aberdeen and north-east Scotland | 451 | 2.7 | 599 | 1.9 | 1,260 | 2.2 |
| Other | 493 | 2.9 | 705 | 2.3 | | |
| Scotland (total) | 2,055 | 12.1 | 4,395 | 14.1 | 16,439 | 29.1 |

*Source*: Compiled from Censuses of England and Wales, and Scotland.
*Note*: On a pro rata basis derived from Irish output, employment in Irish shipbuilding in
the 1820s must have been small, around 300–400 adult males, with half based in Belfast. By
1871 employment in Ireland was probably between 2,500 and 3,000, with over 90 per cent
concentrated in Belfast.

The new regional pattern is clear with the North East as the giant among the
districts. However, when individual rivers are considered, the Clyde emerges as the
largest producer with an output of 115,136 tons, far ahead of the Wear in second place
with 73,196 tons, and Tyne and Tees with still smaller outputs. In 1871 the Clyde is
by some distance the largest producer of tonnage of any river in Britain, and also
ahead of any other shipbuilding river in the world at that time. This lead was only of
very recent origin. As late as 1861, in employment, the Thames still had 8,284 men
as against 6,758 on the Wear, and 5,912 on the Clyde. It was the acceleration of iron
steamship building in the 1860s, linked to the disruption of the American Civil War

and the ensuing failure of Thames firms in the financial crisis of 1867, that finally and abruptly diminished the Thames, and propelled the Clyde and Wear to overtake the Thames significantly in output and employment. This reversal in the fortunes of the Thames is also to some extent linked to the growing advantage of the northern and Scottish rivers located on their own coal and iron fields, as the industry switched to iron steamship production. However, changes in the nature of the shipping market, and differentials in costs of production and prices are also significant in the weakening position of the Thames, and the growth in strength of the Clyde and North East. These elements are interlocked with the course of invention, innovation and technical change in the two industries before the 1870s.

## The traditional industry

In the first half of the nineteenth century construction in wood and sail dominated shipbuilding, not only in Britain, but worldwide. In Britain in the 1850s wooden hulls still represented 70 per cent of all tonnage being built, and sail power provided over three quarters of propulsion. Sail tonnage indeed held its position longer than wooden hulls, since iron hulls greatly prolonged the life of the sailing ship. The apogee of iron sail tonnage was not reached until as late as 1875, when its output peaked at nearly 200,000 tons.

Throughout these years the progress of Britain's traditional shipbuilding in wood and sail was overshadowed by the skill and rivalry of American builders. Between 1815 and 1850 the British and American industries were similar in scale, although the measures, in net and gross tons respectively, are not directly comparable. In Britain the annual average production from 1816–20 was 82,000 net tons, and in America, 86,000 gross tons. There appeared to be no great difference in scale until the 1840s when American tonnage began to grow very rapidly. In the five-year period 1851–55 Britain launched on average 159,000 net tons of sailing ships compared with 346,000 gross tons each year in America. In the next five years the respective annual tonnages were 211,000 in Britain and 300,000 tons from American yards. However, the disruption of the Civil War gifted world leadership to Britain in the following decades. There had been considerable rivalry between the two nations until the Civil War and, before then, many of the changes and improvements introduced in Britain had been stimulated by American example.

The nature of the traditional industry made it difficult for builders to benefit from economies of scale, dominated as it was by hundreds of very small yards with fewer than 20 employees. In such an environment entry was easy and exit frequent in the cycles of expansion and contraction that typified the industry. Growth in output came not so much from large increases from established yards, but more from the quick appearance of new small-scale enterprises attracted by an escalation in local demand. In these conditions familiar and long-established methods of construction prevailed, concentrating on ships of familiar design and scale. Builders and ship owners were encouraged in this inertia by the constraints imposed by the antiquated Tonnage Laws consolidated in 1773 and 1775. These enshrined 'Builders Old Measure' in the legislation, a measure of tonnage based on maximum length and beam of a ship, but excluding depth from the calculation. Since this was the measure of tonnage for port and cargo taxes, the depth of a vessel could be increased without affecting the measure of tonnage for taxation. The outcome was to build deep and narrow hulled ships with large cargo capacity, but which were slow and unhandy sailors. British builders and owners stuck to these features in spite of the visible evidence of the superior speed and manoeuvrability of competing American vessels. This had been amply demonstrated in the Napoleonic Wars when the American blockade runners had even out-sailed Royal Navy frigates, and had captured much of the Mediterranean fruit trade.[7]

The influence of the Tonnage Laws was not universal in the industry, having little effect on the designs emerging from the Royal Dockyards, especially in developments in naval small craft and fast packets, or in the work in yards building East Indiamen. These were the best areas of British design, and it was from these that significant improvements began to emerge. Under the influence of Sir Robert Seppings, Surveyor of the Navy from 1813 to 1832, modifications in the designs of both the bow and stern were introduced in order to improve speed. He also advocated the introduction of diagonal bracing to strengthen the wooden hulls, a measure which allowed the tonnage of ships of the line to be doubled from 2,000 to 4,000 tons.[8] In the case of East Indiamen, which plied monopoly long-distance routes, cost and economy in design were not dictated by the Tonnage Laws, and these large ships of 1,200–1,500 tons were fine sailing vessels. In these cases it is clear that English shipyards could build well-designed, fast and efficient ships. However, these demonstrations were not taken up in the majority of the yards; nor did they have much influence on the typical wood and sail vessels of the time. This lack of interest was reinforced by the Navigation Laws which extended protection to both coastal and deep-sea trade, and hence sheltered both builders and owners from competition.

It is no coincidence that it was the winding down of trade monopolies to India from 1814, and to China from 1834, which stimulated the first major improvement in hull design and efficiency among larger vessels. There was also a revision of the Tonnage Laws in 1835 which introduced depth into the tonnage calculation. This was initially in response to the growing number of steamships with much space given over to machinery, and a need for a better way to represent a ship's tonnage, but it was soon to have beneficial effects in the design of sailing ships too. This new law allowed for more flexibility in the relationship of the dimensions of length, breadth and depth of hulls. As a consequence hull design was better able to respond to the challenge of increasing competition on the routes thrown open to India and China. These long routes were served mainly by three-masted full-rigged ships, and the pressure to produce improved versions was met first by the innovation of what became known as the Blackwall frigates. These were first designed and built by Wigram and Green at their Blackwall yard on the Thames. The first two were launched in 1837, introducing finer hull lines and sharper bows.[9] They were the first steps in Britain that would lead eventually to the development of the clipper ship. This first step reflected American developments in which their builders were in the 1830s increasing the size of ships by steadily extending the length of the hull in relation to breadth and depth. This resulted in ships with ever sharper bows and finer sterns, linked to flat decks and huge sail plans.[10]

In Britain the Blackwall frigates were the first real departure from traditional ship design. Over 120 were built between 1837 and 1875, a few in Indian yards, and around half from yards on the North East coast, as the efficiency of the design was appreciated. Following rapidly on Wigram and Green's innovation, Alexander Hall in Aberdeen built a schooner in 1839, the *Scottish Maid*, the first to have the concave or forward curving Aberdeen Bow, which significantly improved speed and sailing performance. Hall's sons, James and William tested various hull forms in a small water tank, and found that their curved bow design was the most effective shape to benefit from the 1835 revision of the Tonnage Laws. While this revision measured the overall depth and breadth of a ship, the length was measured only at half mid-ship depth. Consequently any length of the hull above that line created cargo space free of tax. Not surprisingly the Aberdeen Bow became a design feature that was quickly and widely adopted.[11] Experimentation with hull form in the wake of the revision of the Tonnage Laws must have been fairly common. Scott's of Greenock were certainly known to have experimented with and tested different hull forms in the early 1840s in their graving dock. They were also testing models to scale in the waters of their local Loch Thom in the hills above Greenock.[12]

The spur of competition certainly began to erode generations-old custom and practice in design and construction. Moreover, the climate of change was accelerated by the repeal of the Navigation Laws in 1849 which opened Britain's deep-sea trade to competing fleets, this soon followed in 1854 with the removal of protection from the coastal trade. This coincided with the introduction of the Merchant Shipping Act of 1854, which swept away the last vestiges of centuries-old legislation designed to protect and encourage British shipping.[13] At the same time the Tonnage Law of 1835 was completely overhauled with the introduction of the Moorsom System. This revised the means of calculating the tonnage of ships, allowing for the deduction of space occupied by machinery and other non-revenue producing space in the hull.[14]

This pivotal period from 1849–54 encompassed three other influences and events which sharpened competition and widened markets. The discovery of gold in California in 1849 sparked off a hectic gold rush from 1849 to 1854 during which about 150,000 prospectors were shipped to the west coast of America from all parts of the globe. This was followed by another gold discovery in Australia at Ballarat in New South Wales, and at Warrandyte in Victoria in 1851. In 1852 some 370,000 migrants were shipped to Australia. The effect of these demands on shipping was to trigger a great boom in shipbuilding in both Britain and America. In Britain tonnage launched jumped from 118,000 to 203,000 tons by 1853. The effect in America was even greater, where output doubled to 583,000 tons between 1849 and 1855.[15] In both cases it was the output of sailing vessels that benefited most, three quarters of the British tonnage being in sail, and 80 per cent of American tonnage likewise. The third occurrence stimulating demand was the Crimean War of 1853–56, with huge demands for the carriage of men and material between 1854 and 1856.

While the British market was opened to competition from American builders and ship owners from 1849, British builders and ship owners were excluded from access to the Californian emigrant market by American protective measures. That, however, did not prevent them from picking up on the improvements in design innovated in America. In response to the gold rush, to the rising tide of emigrant traffic, and to escalating shipments of raw cotton to Britain, American builders adopted yet longer and narrower hulls with sharper bows and sterns. The result was to increase the average size of passenger and cargo ships to around 1,500 gross tons. On the passenger routes from Europe and Britain to America, the traffic was largely dominated by the fast American sailing packets, such as the Black Ball, Black Cross and Red Star Lines.[16] Against such competition on the Atlantic, British builders and owners responded with the steamship, but on the long-distance hauls to the Far East and the Antipodes, both British and American builders moved on from the schooner to evolve the true clipper ship.

In Britain, the empirical improvements introduced in the Blackwall frigates and Aberdeen schooners were refined in John Scott Russell's conception of the wave line hull form, which revolutionised design in naval architecture.[17] In America, where wood was still inexpensive and plentiful, the builders pushed ship size up to 2,000 tons, but in Britain costs of timber constrained size and limited the extent of following the American path in wood sail construction. In part compensation, John Jordan of Liverpool developed the compromise of composite construction, a method of combining iron frames together with wooden planking sheathed in copper to save on costs, and to try to overcome the problem of the fouling of iron hulls with marine growths.[18] Building on these developments, and drawing on American experience, British builders then developed their own versions of the true clipper ship. These were generally smaller than their American counterparts, usually in the range of 700–1,200 tons. Like their American rivals, there were the greyhounds of the seas, with sleek hulls for high-value cargoes such as tea and silk. Significant builders included Alexander Hall and Walter Hood in Aberdeen, Robert Steele at Greenock, William Pile at Sunderland, Maudslay Sons and Field at Greenwich, and many others. Among the other builders was Scott's of Greenock whose clipper, *Lord of the Isles*, in 1853, is widely thought to have at least equalled the fine design and speed of the great American clippers. By the 1850s, British builders of sailing ships had left old constraints behind, and had demonstrated a new and growing capacity to build some of the best sailing ships in the world. In the 1860s many of these were in excess of 2,000 tons, and the average tonnage of a sailing ship had trebled from 1815 to 300 tons. It is an irony of history that this late flourishing of great sailing ships flowing from British yards was curtailed abruptly with the opening of the Suez Canal in 1869. American competition had been removed by the disruption of the Civil War, but by drastically reducing the distance to be sailed to the Far East, the Suez Canal opened the way for the steamship to penetrate the remaining stronghold routes of the sailing ship. The shipwrights building in wood and sail had barely achieved ascendency over the Americans when their success was to be overwhelmed and surpassed by the newer industry in metal and steam.

## The new industry: innovation in steam and iron

By the last quarter of the eighteenth century, while steam power was in common use in mines, and was making inroads in cotton mills, it had barely begun to be considered for driving ships. Early experimentation was hindered by the size and weight of the Newcomen atmospheric engine in which the expanding power of steam alternated with atmospheric pressure to move the piston up and down in the cylinder. The waste of energy in alternately heating the cylinder, then cooling it by spraying it with cold water to create a vacuum, made it impractical for installation in small wooden hulls. This possibility had to await the insight of James Watt who overcame this inefficiency by condensing the steam in an outside vessel or cylinder. The separate condenser conserved heat and allowed the expanding power of steam to be applied on both sides of the piston. Watt's improved engine also disposed of the array of rods and beams of Newcomen's engine, and when linked to a crank converted vertical to rotary motion capable of driving machinery. Watt patented his separate condenser in 1769, and opened the way for experimenting with marine versions of the steam engine.

The French experimented first, though unsuccessfully, in 1776. Then in 1783 an engineer, Jouffray D'Aubons, had a successful demonstration of a small paddle steamer, the *Pyroscaphe*, on the river Saône. However, any chance of an early French lead vanished with the turmoil of the Revolution, and pioneering work fell to Britain and America. In America in 1787, John Fitch is credited with a successful trial of a small steam boat on the Delaware, but engine problems and patent and financial difficulties did not allow him to build on this initial success. Contemporaneously in 1787, a successful steamboat trial was conducted on Dalswinton Loch in Dumfriesshire by Patrick Miller, James Taylor and William Symington. Miller was a successful private banker and shareholder in the Carron Ironworks, and had invested heavily in improving the carronade. He had also experimented in propelling a small leisure craft by hand cranked paddle. The step to replacing human by steam power was encouraged after examining a model of a proposed land steam-carriage built by his near neighbour, William Symington, engineer at the nearby Wanlochhead Lead Mines. James Taylor was tutor to Miller's children, and had himself been experimenting with stabilising boats by developing double hulls. It was in such a small double hulled pleasure craft (25 ft × 8 ft) that Miller and Symington fitted Symington's small engine, a modified Newcomen engine with separate condenser, which probably contravened Watt's patent. This successfully propelled the boat at five miles per hour, utilising two central-line paddle wheels.[19]

Encouraged by this demonstration Miller commissioned Symington to build a more powerful engine to be installed in a larger 60 foot double-hulled paddle steamer. This had a partially successful trial on the Forth and Clyde Canal in 1801, which attracted the attention of Lord Dundas, Governor of the Canal. At his instigation Symington built a second boat named *Charlotte Dundas*, after the governor's daughter. This was 56 ft × 18 ft, powered by Symington's own design of a double-acting single-cylinder engine connected directly to a crank to turn the paddle wheels. After a short initial trial on the canal at Glasgow in January 1803, the first full voyage took place on 28 March 1803, when the *Charlotte Dundas* steamed from Grangemouth to Glasgow towing two laden barges, a voyage of 18.5 miles against a strong headwind, in just under nine hours. In achieving this, Symington became the first in Europe to demonstrate a successful commercial steamboat, but the opportunity to develop it further was lost when the canal proprietors abandoned the trials, fearing that the wake of the paddleboat might damage the banks of the canal.

In America Fitch's early trials were not followed up until 1807 by Robert Fulton. Fulton had worked in England as an engineer on the canals in the 1780s, and had tried, unsuccessfully, to sell Napoleon a design for a submarine in 1801. Returning to America he experimented with steam power, and in 1806 built a boat in which he installed Boulton and Watt engine and boilers. His boat, *Clermont*, sailed impressively up river on the Hudson from New York to Albany in August 1807, a distance of 150 miles in 32 hours. He followed this by establishing the first regular passenger river steamer service in the world.[20] In accomplishing this Fulton had built on the examples of Fitch, Miller and Symington. None of them was a shipbuilder, but mainly engineers who had successfully assembled hulls, engines, boilers, and paddles, supplied by specialist firms. In Britain this was soon to be emulated by Henry Bell.

Henry Bell was an engineer and hotelier in Helensburgh on the Clyde, and had been apprenticed in the famous London firm of John Rennie. Bell had witnessed the voyage of the *Charlotte Dundas* in 1803, and had been in correspondence with Fulton on his experiments. Bell's strategy copied that pioneered by Symington, Fitch and Fulton, by commissioning the components for his steamboat from established manufacturers. The hull was built by John Wood at Port Glasgow, the engine made by John Robertson in Glasgow, and the boiler came from David Napier's Camlachie Foundry, also in Glasgow. The result was Henry Bell's *Comet* of 1812, a small wooden craft of 43 feet 6 inches in length, powered by a four horsepower single-cylinder double-acting side-lever engine. The *Comet* achieved a speed of five miles per hour in good conditions, and had a square rigged sail set up on the smokestack to help in poorer conditions.[21] In August 1812 the *Comet* steamed from Glasgow to Greenock, a journey of 19 miles, in 3½ hours. This success led Bell to inaugurate a regular steamboat service on the Clyde, plying between Glasgow, Greenock and Helensburgh. His successful innovation, and simple assembly technique, was followed quickly on other major rivers, and by 1820 only the river Wear had not built its own version of the new steamboats. Between 1812 and 1820 Clyde builders launched no fewer than 42 steamboats totalling 3,200 tons. The hulls were supplied by eleven different shipbuilders, including two from Dundee, while the machinery came from ten suppliers, including two sets from Boulton & Watt's Soho factory in Birmingham.[22]

The Clyde was the first mover in steamboat building in Britain, but was soon overtaken by the Thames, drawing on its wealth of established engineers and shipbuilders. Some insight into these early developments can be gained from the analysis of a 20 per cent sample of all ships on Lloyds Register from 1810–49.[23] Although there was a rush of steamboat construction before 1820, only nine steamboats appear in the 20 per cent sample for the decade to 1819. Two thirds of these came from the Clyde, and 15 per cent from the Thames. In the much larger sample of 58 steamboats of 11,800 tons identified in the succeeding decade of 1820–29, the Thames leads with 37 per cent, the Mersey and North West ports, 23 per cent, and the Clyde in third place on 21 per cent of steam tonnage. The Thames's dominance extended to nearly half the steam tonnage in the sample for 1830–39, but in the years 1840–49, the Thames and Clyde were nearly equal with 31 per cent and 29 per cent of tonnage respectively. Over these four decades the sample captured a registration of 181 steamboats of 83,024 tons. Of these the Thames delivered over one third, and the Clyde more than one quarter, of both ships and tonnage. The Mersey and North West district was in third place with 15 per cent of the boats and 10 per cent of the tonnage.

This sample picture of the early decades of steamboat building can be amplified and deepened by drawing on the lists of steam tonnage built and first registered in the UK as recorded in the Parliamentary Papers.[24] G. R. Porter compiled these for the period 1814–1849, his lists identifying no fewer than 1,544 steamboats of 202,500 tons. These allocate 1,004 ships, 65 per cent, and 124,442 tons, 61.4 per cent of tonnage, to England. Scotland, contributed 412 ships, 27 per cent, and 84,800 tons, 42 per cent of tonnage. Ireland delivered only 18 ships of 5,000 tons. This allocation is broadly in line with the 20 per cent sample survey which allocated two thirds of tonnage to England, and one third to Scotland in years to 1849. Yet another snapshot is provided in Lloyds Register in 1840, in a table of 'Ships Navigated by Steam'. This identifies 124 ships, three with no tonnage recorded. The remaining 121 steamboats totalled 24,813 tons, an average of 205 tons per ship. London was the place of build of 32 per cent of the tonnage, followed by the Clyde with 19 per cent, and Liverpool with 15 per cent. This evidence, however incomplete, consistently points to the Thames, Clyde and Mersey as the main pioneers in the early decades of steamboat building in Britain.

The initial lead of the Clyde was rapidly overhauled by the much larger industry on the Thames, but by 1850 the Thames and Clyde are vying for leadership in this new industry. On these rivers the pioneer builders quickly ran into problems arising from the unreliability and inefficiency of the engines and boilers. They also soon found it necessary to experiment to find the best way of propelling the new steamships.

The period before 1850 was one of continuous trial-and-error experimentation to improve engines, boilers and paddles, culminating in the introduction of the screw propeller. The main advances in the early engines and boilers were made by the firms of Maudslay Sons and Field, and Penn, on the Thames, by Boulton and Watt in Birmingham, and by David Napier and his cousin Robert, on the Clyde. The first side-lever engines worked with very low pressures and weak boilers and had a prodigious appetite for fuel, consuming as much as 10 lbs of coal per horse power hour. With their connecting rods, spur wheels and cogs, they also occupied a lot of hull space, leaving little room for paying cargo and passengers. One approach to minimising space was pioneered by David Napier, who introduced his Steeple Engine in 1831. This dispensed with spurred cogs, and its height left more useful space in the hull. It became a popular engine for fast paddle steamers. A different and better solution to the problem of space came from John Penn, who first introduced his oscillating engine in 1825. This was initially adopted more slowly, but its low and compact form gained popularity, and it was fitted regularly in paddle steamers up to the 1880s. It overcame the problem of connecting rods by linking the piston directly to the crank shaft.

The success of these refinements depended on related advances in the strength and efficiency of their boilers. The first type installed were Watt land boilers, although these soon gave way to marine versions of the 'box boilers', these quickly supplemented by marine versions of the locomotive fire-tube boilers.[25] These developments gradually raised steam pressures from under 4 lbs per square inch, to between 20 and 30 lbs per square inch. At these levels the engines and boilers were sufficiently economical to enable steamboats to work successfully on river, estuary and short sea crossings. Longer deep-sea crossings required still greater economy, and this was to be achieved by a combination of improved direct-acting engines with higher pressure fire-tube boilers.

In the 1830s the tide of European migration to America began to swell, and initially most of this was captured by the fast American sailing packets. This was an expanding market, and the opportunities of challenging the American dominance with the steamship were quickly explored. Two companies were formed in 1836 with the objective of introducing a trans-Atlantic steamer service. These were The Great Western Steamship Company, and the British and American Steam Navigation Company. The first was formed by the engineer, Isambard Kingdom Brunel, and his Bristol business partners, to establish a route from Bristol to New York. The rival was sponsored by an expatriate American, Junius Smith, to sail between London and New York.

Brunel designed his ship, the *Great Western*, as a wooden-hulled paddle steamer of 1,350 tons. It was built in Bristol by Patterson and Mercer, the engines by Maudslay Sons and Field in London. Smith had his ship, the *British Queen*, designed by Macgregor Laird at 1,850 tons. The hull was commissioned to Curling and Young on the Thames, and the engines initially to Girdwood on the Clyde. Girdwood liquidated and the engine contract then went to Robert Napier, but the delay gifted the lead to Brunel. Smith was, however, still determined to be the first across the Atlantic, and responded by chartering the much smaller SS *Sirius* of 700 tons, which had been designed to sail the London to Cork route. The *Sirius* left Cork on 4 April 1838, while the *Great Western* did not leave Avonmouth until four days later. *Sirius* arrived in New York on 22 April having taken 18 days, only hours ahead of the larger and faster *Great Western* which docked on the 23rd, having made the crossing in 15 days.[26] These were the first west-bound passages made entirely under steam. The remarkable crossing times of 18 and 15 days respectively, cut the west-bound voyage time in half compared with the fastest American sailing packets which in the 1830s were averaging 34 days on the westward voyage against the wind.[27]

Contemporaneous with this demonstration of the speed and power of the large ocean-going paddle steamer, the potential and practicality of the screw propeller were being established. Archimedes had demonstrated the principle of the screw to raise water, and early designs of propellers were in effect elongated rotating screws. Various patents were taken out by Woodcroft in 1826, and separately in 1836 by Thomas Petit Smith and Captain John Ericson. Ericson's version was more generally taken up in America, while Smith's was preferred in Britain. After registering his patent Smith joined with the London engineer John Rennie to establish their Steam Propeller Company. In 1838 they installed a screw propeller in the steamer *Archimedes*, which proved the reliability of the screw in a 2,500-mile round-Britain voyage.[28] This success attracted the attention of the Admiralty, whose trials in 1844 involving a tug-of-war between HMS *Rattler*, fitted with screws, and HMS *Prometheus*, fitted with paddles, demonstrated convincingly the superiority of the propeller. Further trials were carried out, notably between HMS *Rattler* and HMS *Alecto*, with *Rattler* again proving the advantage of the screw over the paddle. Brunel was so persuaded by these demonstrations that, at a late date, he decided to install screw propellers instead of the planned paddles in his second large steamer, the *Great Britain*. This was under construction for the Great Western Steamship Company, after the success of the *Great Western* on the Atlantic crossing. Brunel also decided to take the bold step of building the hull in iron, even though Lloyds did not recognise iron in construction until 1844. Launched in 1843, the *Great Britain* made its maiden voyage from Liverpool to New York in July 1845, crossing in 14 days and 21 hours, becoming the first iron steamship to make the Atlantic crossing.[29] In the *Great Britain* gearing had to be employed to deliver the necessary high revolution speed to the propellers, but by 1850 the best engines allowed direct connection to the screws.[30]

By 1850 the steamship industry was on the cusp of a leap forward in the power and efficiency of its machinery, and on the brink of a revolution in construction through the adoption of iron. The timeline to the take-up of iron was long and hesitant, the pioneers having to confront the apparent common-sense prejudice that iron could not float. This was first done in 1787 when the Shropshire iron master, John Wilkinson, built and launched his barge, the *Trial*, on the Severn. The *Trial* was 70 feet long and was made of cast-iron plates.[31] In spite of this early success there was no rapid adoption of the innovation, although several iron barges were said to be working on the Midland Canal by 1813. More than 30 years were to pass before the next significant step of building an iron passenger barge was taken, with the *Vulcan* in 1819. Keen to reduce operational costs on the Forth & Clyde Canal, the Executive Council of the canal drew up plans for an iron barge. The contract was given to Thomas Wilson, a boat builder with a small yard at Faskine on the Monkland Canal at Glasgow. The *Vulcan* was 61 ft × 14 ft, and was built with a two-ply riveted keel, the iron plates being laid in vertical strakes butted flush with an angle iron behind each butt. This set out principles of construction in the new industry.[32] Three years later another pioneer vessel was launched on the Tyne by Hawks of Gateshead.[33]

The use of both iron and steam in shipbuilding was being pioneered at the same time in the opening decades of the nineteenth century, but they had not initially been brought together in a single ship. This innovation followed quickly in 1821. Not surprisingly this step was taken by an iron master, Aaron Manby, at his Horsley Ironworks in Staffordshire, rather than in a wood shipyard. Named the *Aaron Manby*, the ship was built to the design of the client, Captain Charles Napier, dismantled and taken in sections and reassembled and engined at Rotherhithe on the Thames. The ship was a flat-bottomed barge of 116 tons, and at 120 feet was twice the length of the *Vulcan*. It was the first sea-going iron steamship, crossing from London to Le Havre on 10 June 1822, before sailing on up the Seine to Paris. It was, for some years, used for pleasure trips on the Seine as part of Napier's fleet.

Following this innovation, pioneering ships combining iron and steam appeared more frequently. Aaron Manby built other iron steamships, notably in 1825 the *Marquis of Wellesley*, this re-erected at Liverpool.[34] Two years later, on the Clyde, David Napier adopted this technique in building the *Aglaia*, then re-erecting it for service on Loch Eck. By 1829, John Laird and John Vernon were building iron steamers on the Mersey,[35] followed in 1830 by William Fairbairn building three iron stern-wheelers at his works in Manchester. Then, in 1831, Laird at Birkenhead, and Neilson at Glasgow, where both building iron steamers, and, in 1832, Maudslay Sons and Field, on the Thames, joined the pioneers with an iron steamer for the East India Company.[36] The attraction of the superior strength of iron over wood in construction was so compelling that in 1834 Tod and MacGregor on the Clyde took the step of laying down a new yard exclusively for iron steamship construction. Similarly convinced of the merits of iron, William Fairbairn branched out from his works in Manchester to open a yard at

Millwall, on the Thames, in 1837.[37] The Tyne then joined the early builders in iron and steam with T. D. Marshall in 1839, and Coutts and Company in 1840.[38]

From then on, progress was even more rapid, John Grantham claiming as early as 1842 that iron was no more expensive than wood for vessels of 300 feet, and was steadily cheaper beyond that length.[39] As the building of iron steamers accelerated, Lloyds granted its first A1 classification to an iron steamer in 1844, though separate rules for iron construction did not follow until 1855. By then it was clear that an iron steamship was stronger and lighter, and had a larger carrying capacity, than a wooden steamship of similar dimensions, these advantages over-riding the problems of iron causing compass deviation, and of marine growth fouling on iron hulls.

In these early years of iron steamship building, most of the pioneers were engineers and iron masters with little or no experience in the older industry of building in wood and sail. However, since official statistics only begin recording tonnages in wood and iron from 1850, the critical pioneering decades from 1820 to 1850 do not easily yield a clear picture of the progress of, and leadership in, early iron steamship building. The 20 per cent sample of all ships on Lloyds Register before 1850, compiled by John Raper, provides some insight, but is insufficient to draw firm conclusions. It does at least confirm that, between 1820 and 1829, iron was still a novelty in construction, only one iron ship being sampled in the 1820s, and nine in the 1830s. It is in the decade 1840–49 that the pace quickens, the sample yielding 78 iron ships of 26,154 tons. Prior to 1849 the sample shows 37 per cent of iron tonnage coming from the Clyde, 24 per cent from the Mersey, and 21 per cent from the Thames. In contrast to this, the Lloyds Register of 1845 lists 37 iron ships of 9,500 tons, of which 35 per cent was constructed on the Thames, 20 per cent in Scotland, and 16 per cent on the Mersey. Leadership evidently varied from year to year among the three main rivers, which were clearly the Clyde, Thames and Mersey.

It is difficult to judge what confidence to place in these early data, since other evidence appears to indicate that it was the Thames which was the magnet for iron and steam building in these early years, attracting Fairbairn from Manchester in 1835, David Napier from Glasgow in 1836, he then followed later by John Scott Russell. The outcome was that, in the early 1840s, eight major yards on the Thames were building iron-hulled ships, mainly steamboats but some also in sail.[40] While specific output information is lacking, this level of activity in Britain's main shipping market suggests that the Thames was in the van in the pioneering years of the 1830s and early 1840s. From then, however, the Thames appears to have been overtaken by the Clyde, where 20 yards were building iron steamships by 1852.[41] Lacking local coal and iron ores, the Thames relied more on supplies of high-quality scrap iron for beating into plates. This was to become one of a number of cost disadvantages which steadily made it more difficult for Thames shipbuilders to compete with producers enjoying elastic supplies of rolled iron plates on the Clyde, and progressively on the Mersey, and on the Tyne, Wear and Tees.

Some more detailed district output compilations give a sharper focus on the leading producers of the new iron steamers from the late 1840s. John Strang's paper to the British Association in 1852 lists the number and power of iron steamboats built at all Clyde ports between 1846 and 1852, a total of 233 ships of 129,273 tons.[42] This compares with 26,063 tons of iron steamships built on the Mersey over the longer period of 1840–49.[43] More directly comparable for the years 1847–53, the yard lists of the Thames iron shipyards record a total of 80,756 tons of ships, although it is not clear what proportion might be of steam or sail.[44] While there undoubtedly are omissions and anomalies in these compilations, the iron steamship tonnage produced on the Clyde is already much larger than that built on the Thames, with the Mersey a long way behind. The builders on the Clyde appear to have committed to iron and steam more completely than elsewhere, stealing a lead that was difficult for builders on the other rivers to overtake.

Strang's compilations for the Clyde are certainly more comprehensive than those available for the Thames and Mersey, but it is probable that these rivers produced larger tonnages than recorded here. It is certain that the returns of vessels built and first registered in the UK do not capture the total output of the industry. Strang's subsequent compilation of Clyde tonnages, for 1853–58, illustrates this anomaly.[45] He reports that the Clyde yards launched 576 iron steamships of 366,596 tons in these years, while the data for the UK as a whole report 906 ships of 339,260 tons in the same period. It is certain that the Clyde could not have produced more iron steamship tonnage than that of the UK as a whole, so we must be cautious in giving credence to these data. Strang later compared Clyde to national output between 1856 and 1860, and again from 1861 to 1865. In these periods he claimed that the Clyde built 76 per cent and 62 per cent respectively of iron steamship tonnage in the UK. While these comparisons cannot be accepted fully at face value, the evidence is strong enough to support the conclusion that the Clyde, with the Thames and Mersey, were the prime movers in both iron and steam construction before 1850, and that from the mid-century, the Clyde pulled ahead of them, and that builders on the North East rivers only then began to follow on.

The relative position of the main shipbuilding rivers is very clear by 1871. In that year the Clyde launched more iron steam tonnage than any other river: 103,254 tons, or 31.5 per cent of the UK total. The Wear, Tyne and Tees followed in that order, collectively building 46 per cent of total output, making the North East by far the largest shipbuilding district. In contrast, the Thames, historically the main shipbuilding river, now produced less than 3 per cent of iron steam tonnage, even though it was still home to some very important yards, such as Samuda Brothers, and the Thames Ironworks and Shipbuilding Company. It was also still important enough to attract two new specialist builders in the 1860s, namely Thorneycroft and Yarrow.

The switch of production to Scotland and the northern rivers was certainly linked to the growth of iron and coal industries there, but was ultimately driven more by a continuing series of path-breaking innovations in the efficiency and economy of marine engines and boilers, improvements that were quickly taken up in these expanding districts. In the 1840s the linking of direct oscillating engines to fire-tube boilers had cut coal consumption by half to around 4–5 lbs per horsepower-hour in the first successful Atlantic crossings. Engineers knew that the answer to yet further economies lay in achieving still higher boiler pressures, and more efficient consumption of coal and use of steam. The innovation which began to deliver this came through improving the oscillating engine with the introduction of a marine version of the compound expansion engine. In compound engines the power of steam was first released through expansion in a high-pressure cylinder, and then further expanded in a low-pressure cylinder, hence considerably increasing the use of the energy. Compound land engines had been in regular use since the English engineer, Arthur Wolff, had patented a version in 1805. Marine versions seem to have been experimented with in America as early as 1834, and on the Rhône in 1847. However, it was on the Clyde in January 1853 that the engineering partnership of Charles Randolph and John Elder introduced their successful compound engine. They combined it with steam jacketing to cut down heat loss from the cylinders, and installed it in the SS *Brandon* in 1854. They claimed in correspondence with prospective customers that 'our patent double cylinder expansion engines, expanding steam to six volumes … [give] a saving of about 40 per cent in the fuel required for the ordinary engine'.[46]

This was a seminal development, but its ultimate success still required improvement in the strength of boilers to enable them to deliver pressures regularly in excess of 40 lbs per square inch. It was not until 1862 that this was assured when another Glasgow engineer, James Howden, introduced his 'Scotch Boiler'.[47] This initiated a move away from the normal rectangular box boiler to a cylindrical form capable of sustaining higher pressures. The Holt Line quickly adopted the combination of compound expansion engines with Howden's Scotch boilers, fitting them in their SS *Cleator* in 1863, and in the SS *Agamemnon* in 1865. With the saving in fuel this made possible, the *Agamemnon* sailed non-stop for 8,500 miles from Liverpool to Mauritius.[48] This had not been possible previously, and dramatically demonstrated the breakthrough achieved with the compound engines and Scotch boilers. With this combination the full 40 per cent saving in fuel promised by Randolph and Elder in 1853 could be reliably achieved. The adoption of these innovations was so rapid that by 1871 the improved compound engines were said to have supplied one-third of the horsepower employed in the British merchant fleet, this increasing to three-quarters of the horsepower by 1876.[49]

This was a timely conjunction and innovation, for the price of coal doubled in the early 1870s, and the saving of 40 per cent in coal consumption offset this cost problem for ship owners. The improved engines and boilers worked at pressures of 60 lbs or more per square inch, and consumed only 2.1 lbs of coal per horsepower-hour. In addition the power-to-weight ratio of the engines and boilers had been reduced from around one ton of coal, 5,280 lbs, per horsepower in the first steamships, to around 480 lbs in the 1870s, giving dramatic savings in space for cargo and passengers.[50] These developments happened to coincide with the opening of the Suez Canal in 1869, which brought the longest routes to the Far East and Antipodes within the range of the new generation of more efficient steamers. The combination of steam and iron had transformed the nature and scale of shipbuilding after 1850, and had also begun to re-shape the nature of the shipbuilding firms, which were to dominate the new industry.

## The firms

From the Admiralty Survey of 1804 we know that there were then more than 500 yards in existence, with an average employment of 17 men, and that only 41 of these yards had 50 or more men in the workforce. In the wooden shipbuilding industry the shipyards were characteristically small, with a high rate of entry and failure. On the river Wear, for example, from 1810 to 1860, between one-half and two-thirds of all yards setting up in the industry had failed within two years.[51] Similarly on the Thames, between 1815 and the 1870s, more than 30 significant firms were in operation at one time or another, and there were also a penumbra of up to 20 smaller establishments coming in and out of the industry.[52] On the Clyde there were over 30 early steamboat builders in operation before 1845, but only eight survived beyond 1850.[53] This pattern of a high turnover of firms was also true of the Mersey and North West. In that district 34 yards were in operation at some time between 1815 and 1840, but only six were left by the 1870s.[54]

At the beginning of the nineteenth century, the typical small shipyard worked with simple slipways, rough wooden scaffolding, sheer legs for lifting, or perhaps a derrick in the larger yards. Working equipment would have included a saw pit, large saws, a steam box, borers and bolt cutters. Hand tools – including small saws, adzes, axes and planes – would normally have been supplied by the workmen, the journeymen shipwrights and carpenters. Even substantial builders called themselves shipwrights, or master shipwrights, stressing their craft skill, rather than their function as a shipbuilder. In the very largest yards, such as the Blackwall yard on the Thames, Martin's yard in Dublin, or Scott's at Greenock, capital requirements could amount to several thousand pounds. Robert Martin's Dublin yard is said to have cost £5,000 in 1812.[55] However, in the generality of small yards, capital requirements were low. When Alexander Stephen bought up his deceased brother's yard in Arbroath in 1829, it cost him £505 for all the materials, including a ship on the slipway. The yard then employed 27 men, typical of the majority of the yards of the period.[56] It was a feature common to all these yards that the value of the ship on the slipway was typically larger than the capital employed in the yard.

That the industry could function with small fixed capitals was due to a number of characteristic features. Yards were not usually owned, but rather leased or rented, often from port, harbour and river authorities, or from local landowners. The timbers required in construction were frequently purchased through commercial bills drawn on local banks, or sometimes supplied directly by the ship owner. This last was common practice on the Tyne and Wear, where ships were also often built speculatively without an owner of the outset. This was particularly common among the fringe of very small builders attracted into the industry in boom conditions. The day-to-day need for working capital for the purchase of materials frequently relied on commercial credits, while the funds for paying wages and other outlays often came from instalment payments made by the customer at agreed stages during construction. Three or four stage instalments were common, although the regularity could falter in slack trade conditions. In that circumstance builders might have to rely more heavily on discounting bills of exchange, rather than having immediate access to cash payments. Builders could also become ship owners when a ship built on speculation did not find a purchaser. On occasion they might also have had to accept an older vessel in part payment for the new ship, hoping to re-sell the trade-in when the market improved.

This pattern of activity, with its large population of small firms, remained typical of shipbuilding in the first half of the nineteenth century, and the nature of the firm only began to change from the 1840s as the advance of steam, and the adoption of iron, began to affect the industry. The way forward for a shipbuilder turning to steamboat building, was shown as early as 1821 by David Napier on the Clyde. Already established as an engineer and iron founder at his Camlachie Foundry, he made his first marine engine in 1816, and for a number of years continued to supply engines for ships built for him by local shipbuilders. Then, in 1821, he moved his business to Lancefield, where he set up a shipyard adjacent to his engineering shop. This did not constitute full integration of activities, but he was the first entrepreneur to have both shipbuilding and engine-making in his own hands. This step was to be developed more fully on the Thames, initially promoted mainly by engineers. When Fairbairn moved from Manchester in 1835, he established at Millwall, a shipyard, an engineering shop, and iron and brass foundries on the one site. Not only did he build ships there, but also made a variety of general engineering products such as beams and iron bridges. His Manchester and Millwall establishments together employed more than 1,000 men.[57] In similar fashion, the Samuda brothers were established engineers and iron founders located, from 1832, at Southwark, making marine engines. By 1842 they added a shipyard at Blackwall to begin iron shipbuilding. This transition was also made by John Rennie's sons, George and John, who added locomotive building to their general engineering business in 1837, then entered marine engine building, before setting up a shipyard at Norman Road in Greenwich. While it was mainly engineers and iron founders who added iron shipbuilding to their engineering businesses, a few established builders in wood also moved in that direction. In 1843 the historic Blackwall yard was divided to allow George Green to continue to build in wood, while permitting Money and Henry Loftus Wigram to begin building in iron.

From these pioneering linkages, it was a relatively short step to fuller integration on a single site for slipways, engine and boiler shops, and in some cases also iron works and rolling mills. On the Thames, C.J. Mare took these steps between 1847 and 1853, dissolving his earlier partnership with Ditchburn. By 1853 he controlled three yards connected by ferry, his works having cost £225,000 at a time when an iron shipyard typically had a capital of £25,000.[58] This move to single site integration of iron-working, engine-building, boiler-making and shipbuilding, went further on the Thames than on other rivers, but by the 1870s all the main districts had similar developments. On the Clyde firms such as Elder, Napier, and Tod & MacGregor had adopted this form of organisation, as had Laird on the Mersey, and Mitchell, Palmer, and Doxford in the North East. On the Clyde and North East rivers, the new iron shipyards generally specialised in shipbuilding, in contrast to the combination with general engineering common on the Thames, where many of the companies continued to produce a variety of engineering products. This more diversified pattern of operation was in the end a less competitive foundation, and Thames firms were gradually outpaced by the companies on the Clyde, Tyne, Wear and Tees. These integrated establishments were the largest in the industry, but even in the 1870s they were the exception. The more common pattern was for a shipyard to buy in its engines and boilers from specialist producers, and to develop customary links with suppliers. In the North East the main suppliers of marine engines were the firms of Hawthorne, Stephenson, and Clarke.[59] On the Clyde, Caird, Kincaid, Napier and Elder were the main engine builders, while on the Thames the main suppliers were Maudslay, Penn and Rennie. Such arrangements generated a complex pattern of inter-related engineering firms in all the main shipbuilding districts, and helped to spread the risk, and limit capital outlay, in this new and growing industry.

Capital outlay was not immediately an insuperable barrier to entry to the new iron shipbuilding industry. Prospective entrants in the 1850s could expect to outlay around £25,000,[60] and it could be accomplished with much less than that. When Alexander Stephen moved from Dundee to open a yard on the Clyde at Kelvinhaugh in April 1850, he and the landowner, Robert Black, each laid out some £9,000 on site and slipway improvements, and the annual rental was set at £1,224.[61] At the same time the Denny family at Dumbarton had £50,000 invested in their Leven shipyard, and a further £87,000 involved in shipping interests.[62] These were modest outlays in relation to the £225,000 expended by C.J. Mare at his Blackwall premises, but he was bankrupt in 1856, at which point the valuation of buildings and plant was set at £175,000.[63] When the company was reformed in 1857 as the Thames Ironworks and Shipbuilding Company, the new capitalisation had been reduced to £100,000.[64]

Before the revision and extension of company law in 1862 to embrace limited liability fully, shipbuilding firms were either partnerships, or sole proprietorships, with family dynasties emerging in each of the districts. Then in the frantic conditions in the shipping market during the American Civil War, escalating demand induced a brief burst of company formation. Eleven companies were floated between 1863 and 1865, with a nominal capital of £5.5 million.[65] Three of the largest were on the Thames: the Thames Ironworks, the Millwall Ironworks, and the London Engineering and Shipbuilding Company. The largest, however, was on the Tyne, where Charles Palmer floated his Palmers Shipbuilding and Iron Company in July 1865. This had a nominal capital of £2 million in 40,000 shares of £50 each. This linked iron mines, blast furnaces, engine and boiler shops, and a shipyard in Jarrow, and was more like the largest enterprises on the Thames, than the other companies in the North East, or indeed elsewhere in shipbuilding.[66]

The range of capital provision in the emerging iron shipbuilding companies was considerable, but in the 1870s the investment in the largest iron yards was typically in the order of £200,000–£300,000. On the Clyde the new Fairfield yard, engine works and fitting-out basin cost £260,000 when opened in 1870.[67] In 1872 Tod & MacGregor's yard changed hands for £200,000, while the outlay in setting up J. & G. Thomson's new yard at Clydebank had risen to £190,000.[68] When Robert Napier's yard was sold in 1878 it fetched £270,000.[69] Similar outlays were made at Belfast where the partner capital in Harland & Wolff was £87,500 in 1873, but by 1880 partner and loan capital had risen to £263,225.[70]

By the 1870s the large number of small wooden shipyards, typical of the industry at the beginning of the century, had disappeared from the Clyde, the Tyne and Tees. Some remained on the Wear, and were still the mainstay in boatbuilding on the south coast, and in the South West ports. Elsewhere, the new large iron shipyards now dominated the industry. The inspector of Factories Return of 1871 listed 90 such establishments employing 23,306 men in England, and 25,011 men in Scotland, a total of 48,317. On the North East coast there were 28 iron shipyards with 12,416 men, an average employment of 443 per yard. The Thames was credited with 18 iron yards employing 9,110 men, some 506 per establishment. The Clyde had 27 such works with 24,003 employees. The largest iron yards were clearly on the Clyde, the average workforce of 889 men being nearly twice that in the other main districts.[71] Since only 17 of these 90 yards had taken public company status, the firms in all the shipbuilding districts still remained family and partnership in form. While continuity of ownership over long years could be discerned – Laing and Pile in the North East, Scott, Denny and Stephen on the Clyde, and Rennie, Penn and Maudslay on the Thames – most of the leading companies in the 1870s were young firms, formed mainly in the 1840s and 1850s. In the new iron shipyards, all the companies were adopting an organisation based on functional departments, engine shop, boiler shop, drawing office, shipyard, and so on, each relying increasingly on specialised departmental management. In the growth of the new industry, these organisational changes were at least as important as the technical innovations in re-shaping shipbuilding in these years, and reinforced the tendency of the iron yards to be in the hands of mainly new men and new firms.

## Prices and profits

Although the tonnage of ships launched annually increased more than sixfold between 1815 and 1880, the price per ton of vessels increased more modestly. In the wood and sail industry, tonnages built increased from 87,000 tons in 1815, to 117,000 tons in 1850, but the evidence suggests that there was little general increase in price. On tonnage rates quoted in Builders Old Measure, the Stephen diaries show little or no general increase between 1824 and 1851. There were considerable fluctuations form a peak rate of £12.2 in 1825 to a low of £7.3 in 1829, but the average was between £9 and £11 per ton.[72] These prices were drawn variously from the Stephen yards at Aberdeen, Arbroath and Dundee, and are similar to those in yards on the North East coast, as evidenced to the Commissions of 1833 and 1848. On the Thames, however, tonnage rates were as much as one-third above these, reflecting the higher rated vessels normally built there.[73]

After 1850 price information is clearer. Maywald has estimated prices per gross register tons for steamers, and his hull prices may be taken to represent the cost of sail tonnage. He takes wood as the main construction material to 1862, and iron thereafter.[74] These can be compared with contract prices drawn from the business papers of Denny at Dumbarton, and Stephen at Kelvinhaugh and Linthouse, on the Clyde.[75] On the evidence of these series there were considerable price fluctuations, year to year, but no significant general increase in either sail or steam tonnage rates. The fluctuations in price emerge more clearly in the yard contract prices than in the Maywald estimates, especially in the Crimean War and Civil War years, when the Denny prices show particularly sharp increases. The contract prices also support the common claim that wood-sail tonnage was more costly than iron-sail tonnage in the 1850s. Moreover, composite hulls seem to have been up to £2 per ton more expensive than iron hulls, while there was little difference in price for composite steamers, and iron steamers in the Stephen contracts (Table 2.4).

Until the early 1870s there appears not to have been any general increase in tonnage prices, and it is the fluctuation in prices within the cycles that was more significant for the builder. Price fluctuations, which could increase or decrease tonnage rates by one-quarter, or one-third, and on occasion by half, within a few years, were the visible indicators of the uncertain and unstable market conditions in which the shipbuilders had to work. When these prices, as estimated by Maywald, are applied to output tonnages, the value of ships built increased from about £2.0 million per year in the decade after the Napoleonic Wars, to around £15.0 million in the post Civil War decade, and to £16.0 million in the 1870s.[76] When the Clyde contract prices are used, these estimate annual output value in the 1850s at £4.4 million as against £4.7 million by Maywald, and £12.4 million between 1870–75, compared to Maywald's estimate of £12.6 million.

On these estimates, the value of ships produced increased about sixfold between the 1820s and the 1870s, and did so in an environment characterised by sharp changes

*Table 2.4*  Average price of constructing steam and sail vessels
per gross register ton (£)

| Year | Maywald steamers | Denny iron steamers | Stephen iron steamers | Maywald sail | Stephen Wood sail | Stephen Iron sail | Stephen Composite sail |
|---|---|---|---|---|---|---|---|
| 1850 | 25.0 | 25.0 | | 16.0 | | | |
| 1855 | 25.1 | 33.2 | 25.0 | 18.0 | 20.4 | 17.5[3] | |
| 1860 | 26.1 | 21.6 | 27.2 | 18.7 | 19.0[1] | 16.0 | |
| 1865 | 28.6 | 29.7 | 27.0[5] | 22.1 | 27.0[2] | 18.7 | 17.0 |
| 1870 | 23.9 | 27.7 | 28.7 | 19.2 | | 14.6 | 17.7 |
| 1875 | 31.1 | 28.5 | 29.2 | 23.4 | | 16.5 | 23.5[4] |

[1] 1861   [2] 1864   [3] 1856   [4] 1873   [5] 1864

For a more detailed table see A. Slaven, 'The Shipbuilding Industry' in Roy Church (ed.), *The Dynamics of Victorian Business* (London, 1980), p. 118.

*Sources*: K. Maywald: 'The Construction Costs and the Value of the British Merchant Fleet, 1850–1938', *Scottish Journal of Political Economy*, vol. 3, 1956. NB: Maywald's estimates are for steamers, but his hull prices may be taken as equivalent to sail vessels. In his calculations wood is taken as the main construction material to 1862, iron thereafter.

Denny prices: University of Glasgow Business Record Centre, Denny Papers, UGD3/5/1–3, Contracts; and also, D S Lyon, The Denny List, vol. 1, 1975.

Stephen prices: University of Glasgow, UGD4/8/1–7 and UGD4/18/7.

in tonnage prices. Such fluctuations clearly made shipbuilding a risky business in which profit was far from certain, and failure an ever-present hazard. These instabilities are clearly reflected in the Denny accounts on the Clyde. In the downturn of 1843–45, Denny experienced losses of up to 7 per cent on the contracts, but this was compensated by profits of 10–11 per cent in the succeeding recovery. In the hectic market conditions during the Crimean War, profits on Denny contracts ranged between 12 and 27 per cent, and then collapsed to losses of up to 6 per cent between 1859 and 1861. In the Civil War boom years of 1863–64, profits were restored to around 10 per cent, while the Stephen contracts made profits of 20 per cent in the same period. Ten years later, Denny contracts averaged 6–7 per cent profit. In 1864, in the Stephen yard, gross profit as a return on capital employed of £76,000 was 36 per cent, and averaged 10 per cent on a capital of £150,000 a decade later.

When choosing how to price a contract shipbuilders would quote on a cost-plus basis whenever they could. This would normally be a mark-up in the range of 7–10 per cent, although in depressed conditions, contracts could be taken at, or even below cost, in order to keep the yard in operation. It was taking orders for six wooden gunboats on this basis that tipped C.J. Mare into insolvency in 1855.[77] Contracts taken at cost were expected to break even, while a small profit was implied in a contract with only a small mark-up. These expectations, however, could be overtaken by unexpectedly sharp rises in factor costs, unforeseen delays in construction, and changes in specification along the way. Among factor costs, changes in wage rates were less of a problem than other supply costs. In Britain, nominal wages were in general stationary, or falling slowly, between 1815 and 1850, before rising consistently to the peak of the mid-Victorian boom in 1873. On the Clyde, shipwrights' time rates were stationary, at 21 shillings per week, from the 1820s to 1850, rose sharply to 31 shillings in 1852, then averaged 24 shillings in 1862. In 1860 shipwrights building in wood averaged between 24 and 26 shillings per week on the Clyde, compared to 30 shillings on the Mersey and North East coast, and as high as 42 shillings on the Thames. Variations in rates among the districts were substantial before 1850, and remained so in the traditional craft grades of work. But in the new occupations in the iron shipyards, near uniformity of rates was evident. For riveters and platers the range was 30–32 shillings in most districts, with London between 33 and 38 shillings per week. This is consistent with the evidence presented by Samuda to the Royal Commission on Trade Unions in 1867–68.[78] He maintained that Thames rates were about 15 per cent above those in the other districts and, when other factors were included, this meant the wage-cost element represented about 30 per cent of the cost of the ship. This was not dissimilar to the position on other rivers, and suggests that wage differentials were unlikely to be a critical element in the decline of shipbuilding on the Thames.

When the wage-rate indices compiled by Bowley and Wood are considered, between 1850–60 wage rates increased by 12 per cent on the Clyde, Tyne, and Wear, and at Belfast, while being static on the Mersey and the Thames. Then between 1860 and 1864 Clyde rates advanced rapidly by 31 per cent, compared to 28 per cent on the Tyne, 24 per cent on the Wear, and 23 per cent in Belfast. Conversely, rates were again advancing more slowly on the Mersey and Thames, at increases of 16 and 7 per cent respectively. Labour rate differentials were consequently quite small in the expanding iron shipbuilding sector, and were certainly less than 10 per cent among the major rivers. The rates were, however, more flexible upward than downward, this provoking many strikes and lock-outs in the main districts. But ultimately the rates were forced down, enabling the shipbuilders to keep the wage-cost component roughly steady at between 25–30 per cent of the cost of the ship throughout these years.[79] This price control helped make the new iron steamship an attractive and competitive product in both the national and international shipping markets.

# The market

The shipbuilding market changed dramatically in scale and nature between 1815 and 1880. Under the Navigation Acts the British merchant marine was a monopoly market for British shipbuilders, and remained so after their repeal, through British leadership in technological innovation, and in competitive pricing. The merchant fleet expanded from 2.5 million tons in 1815 to 6.6 million tons in 1880, and within that the market for steam tonnage grew from nothing to 2.7 million tons. In addition the sail fleet grew from 2.5 million tons in 1815 to 4.6 million tons in 1870, before beginning to be a contracting sector of demand. The addition of steam tonnage to the fleet more than doubled between 1860 and 1870, and doubled again to 1880. By then the British merchant marine represented one-third of all world tonnage, and nearly half of world steam tonnage. At this scale the British fleet was larger in tonnage than all the fleets of the European nations combined, and was four times larger than the fleet of Norway, and of the seaborne tonnage of the USA, and six times larger than that of Germany. Not only did this provide a huge market for British builders, but the annual sale of over 5 per cent of used tonnage to foreign owners created a steady replacement demand for new tonnage. As a consequence the British fleet was by 1880 composed of the largest and most modern vessels in the world, easily enabling Britain to become the world's largest carrier.[80]

This huge growth in the scale of the merchant fleet, in which the steamship became the leading sector, also changed the nature of the market of British shipbuilders. Before 1850, the major customers for British builders were local ship owners, with only small sales of tonnage going outside the local market. This was true even of the industry on the Thames, which though having a national reputation for large, high-quality ships, still gained its orders mainly from the demand of London-based ship owners and companies. Competition was mainly with neighbouring firms, rather than from other districts, although the demand for colliers and Indiamen in part transcended the rule of locality.

The introduction and uptake of steam, and then of iron, profoundly changed the economics of competition in the industry. When the industry was dominated by a population of hundreds of very small producers, none had sufficient scale to influence price effectively, nor to control the supply and price of materials. However, as the industries of coal and iron began to grow, close proximity and preferential access to the collieries, iron works and foundries began to be an advantage. When linked to the innovations in construction and propulsion, pioneering firms gained advantages in costs, and stimulated differential regional growth, and product differentiation. The Clyde specialised early in fast packets, and passenger and cargo liners, while the Tyne, Wear and Tees expanded as a result of their tramp cargo and bulk carrier specialisms. Competition began to be inter-regional as the new iron and steam industry concentrated on the Clyde, in the North East, on the Mersey, and at Belfast.

This market and regional product differentiation was also accelerated by the creation of new market sectors. These included the Atlantic passenger liners, the subsidised mail routes, and ships for the mass migration of Europeans to North America, and to Australia and New Zealand. The first major beneficiary of a mail contract on the north Atlantic was Samuel Cunard. In partnership with George Burns from Glasgow, and David McIvor from Liverpool, he formed the British and North American Royal Mail Steam Packet Company, later to be Cunard. He had the first four ships built on the Clyde by Robert Napier, who had brokered the deal. This began a long relationship between Cunard and Napier, and other builders on the Clyde. Similarly, in 1839, James McQueen gained a contract to carry mails to the West Indies, and to North and South America, and founded the Royal Mail Line. The same dynamic promoted the formation of the Peninsular Steamship Company, to carry mails initially from Falmouth to Gibraltar, this growing into the Peninsular and Oriental Steamship Company, to extend the mail service overland to Suez, and then on to Calcutta. The power and efficiency of the new iron steamship also impacted on the traditional tramp market, and began to create long-distance cargo liner services. The first such was developed by Alfred Holt, whose Blue Funnel Line, established in 1865, became the world's first regular long-distance cargo-liner service to China and the Far East.

These passenger and cargo liner services began to grow rapidly from the 1850s, and builder–owner links became a prominent feature in these new market areas, developing preferential repeat order arrangements. The other new market development was the increasing importance of building ships on foreign account. This was mainly a demand from foreign owners for British expertise in iron steamships. In the second half of the 1850s, export tonnage was 12 per cent of UK output, this increasing to 16 per cent between 1870 and 1875. The share of steam tonnage in exports rose from 78 per cent to 96 per cent in the same period, opening up a lucrative market, in which builders on the North East coast were prominent.

Naval orders had also been an important market up to the Napoleonic Wars, especially for the larger yards on the Thames. After 1815 the naval market withered, and this left the larger Thames yard to languish, or to adapt to new demands. There were almost no new naval orders for private yards until the 1830s, and even then there was only a trickle of contracts over the next twenty years. From 1832 to 1850, naval orders to private yards amounted to a mere 34,000 tons. About 40 per cent of this was built on the Thames, mostly by Fletcher and Fearne, and Ditchburn and Mare.[81] In the 1850s the naval market expanded to 104,000 tons, the Thames capturing four-fifths of this, with the yards of Mare, Green, Pitcher, and Wigram, the main builders. This preference for giving orders to Thames yards persisted in the 1860s, with over half of the contracts being awarded. The main builders were the Thames Ironworks, Westwood and Baillie, Wigram, Samuda, and Scott Russell. In contrast barely 16 per cent of tonnage was built on the Clyde, 10 per cent on the Mersey, and the balance of nearly 20 per cent in the North East. Outside London, the builders were Napier and Elder on the Clyde, Laird at Birkenhead, and Palmer, and Mitchell on the Tyne. This market developed even more rapidly after the French built the *La Gloire*, the first ironclad warship, in 1859. This was quickly followed in 1860 by HMS *Warrior*, Britain's first iron-hulled warship, constructed by the Thames Ironworks. This market expanded even more rapidly after the Civil War, naval orders to private yards amounting to 235,500 tons between 1869 and 1878. Only 19 per cent of these then went to the Thames, against 23 per cent to the Clyde, and a small 5 per cent to the Mersey. Just over half the contracts went to the Tyne, orders going predominantly to Palmers' yard at Jarrow, and to Armstrong Mitchell at their Walker yard. Large as this naval order book was, it only represented 7 per cent of Armstrong Mitchell's output from 1866 to 1881.[82]

By 1880 the growth in scale of output, the development of market differentiation, and product specialisation, had all contributed to the demise of the small wooden shipyards, and to the concentration of the new industry on the North East rivers, the Clyde, Mersey and Belfast. The age of iron and steam had transformed shipbuilding from a craft in wood and sail into a complex assembly industry. Momentous as these developments were, they were soon to be eclipsed in the age of steel and armaments, which was to dominate the industry from 1880 to the First World War.

# CHAPTER THREE

# Leading the world: the 1880s to the First World War

The long rivalry in shipping and shipbuilding between Britain and America was ended effectively by the disruption of the Civil War. From that opportunity British shipbuilding gained world leadership in construction, and for the next hundred years no country was to surpass Britain's output of merchant tonnage. The market ascendancy gained by British shipbuilders was truly remarkable, and was unrivalled by any other British industry at the end of the nineteenth century. In the two decades before the First World War British shipyards constructed over 60 per cent of world tonnage (*see* Table 3.1), and the output of ships in the rest of the world was less than two-thirds of that of Britain. The nearest rival was Germany, whose launchings of 465,000 gross tons in 1913 was less than a quarter that of Britain, while that of the US was only 18 per cent. This dominance also stretched into world markets where about 30 per cent of all world tonnage built for non-British registration also came from British yards.

This leadership grew out of the interplay of many factors in the last third of the nineteenth century, but four developments stand out as highly influential. In the first instance it is clear that Britain's pivotal position in shipping, trade and finance in the emerging world economy offered favourable opportunities to British shipbuilders which they were quick to exploit. Within this context British leadership in marine technology, and in ship design and construction, effectively crowded out foreign competition from the domestic market. In this near-monopoly market the opportunities for investment and growth encouraged both an increasing regional concentration and growth in scale in the industry, whose multiplier effect created powerful locally supportive infrastructures of sub-contractors. In addition, the size of the British merchant fleet, at over 40 per cent of the world fleet in 1913, contributed scale economies to British builders that were not readily accessible to rivals. In effect, the scale and nature of the British economy, together with its role in the emerging world economy, created conditions which for a time endowed British shipbuilders with a competitive advantage that could not easily be replicated or challenged seriously by other nations before the First World War.

*Table 3.1*  World and UK merchant tonnage launched, 1894–1913
(quinquennial averages in '000 gross tons)

| | World | UK | UK % of world | World tonnage for non UK registration | UK share |
|---|---|---|---|---|---|
| 1894–98 | 1,463 | 1,091 | 74.6 | 628 | 40.9 |
| 1899–1903 | 2,338 | 1,400 | 59.9 | 1,261 | 25.6 |
| 1904-08 | 2,406 | 1,439 | 59.8 | 1,394 | 30.6 |
| 1909–13 | 2,489 | 1,522 | 61.1 | 1,329 | 27.2 |
| Average 1894–1913 | 2,174 | 1,363 | 62.7 | 1,153 | 29.7 |

*Sources*:  Tonnage launched compiled from Committee on Industry and Trade: Survey of the Metal Industries, Appendix I, p. 462. HMSO, 1928.

Tonnage for Non-UK Registration and UK Shares compiled from S. Pollard and P.L. Robertson, *The British Shipbuilding Industry, 1870–1914*, Appendix B.

*Note*: Net tons converted to gross tons by 1.6.

See also *Survey of the Metal Industries*, p.462.

## Technical change

As pioneers and prime movers in applying metal and steam technology to ships, British shipbuilders and marine engineers created for themselves an unassailable leadership in that technological paradigm. In the closing decades of the nineteenth century refining and improving these technologies provided powerful and commercially attractive solutions to the ever-present challenge of developing and sustaining the best combination of efficiency, economy and reliability in the metal steamship. From 1880 Britain led the world in making the transitions from iron to steel for hulls, in exploiting the margin of efficiency to be gained in extending the principle of compound expansion to triple- and quadruple-expansion engines, and in opening up new horizons of power and speed in applying the principles of the turbine to steam propulsion. These developments depended in turn upon exploiting fully the potential of the Scotch and the water-tube boilers, and linking these to advances in the design, construction and variety of ship types.

Howden's innovation of his Scotch boiler in 1862 had introduced steel plates to improve strength, and forced draught to increase temperatures, which when combined in a cylindrical tank raised pressures to 80 lbs psi. In the following year Babcock and Wilcox had introduced a more sophisticated water-tube boiler in which the combustion gases surrounded a complex honeycomb of pipes, delivering pressures in excess of 100 lbs psi. While the Scotch boiler made gains in the merchant fleet the water-tube boiler proved unreliable, and languished. Indeed, the full potential of both the Scotch boiler and the water-tube version was only to be realised after 1880. In 1882, A.C. Kirk at Fairfield on the Clyde, linked the Scotch boiler to his innovation of a triple-expansion engine in the SS *Aberdeen*. This proved to be a great success, delivering a further saving of 17 per cent in fuel over the standard combination of Scotch boiler and compound engines. This new combination was to become the workhorse of the merchant fleet for the next fifty years.[1]

It was also now that the potential of the water-tube boiler was finally to be realised, but in a naval vessel, rather than in a merchant ship. In 1884, a version by Thorneycroft was the first satisfactory installation in a torpedo boat. In spite of this success, the Admiralty turned to installing a French design, the Belleville boiler, rather than those being developed by Yarrow, Thorneycroft and Babcock and Wilcox, and this area of British design struggled for another 20 years before gaining ascendency in naval orders.

The coming together of the triple-expansion engine, the Scotch boiler, and water-tube boilers coincided with the push to replace iron with steel in construction and with the patenting of Charles Parsons' turbine in 1884. Some steel vessels had been constructed on the Thames during the American Civil War, and the French were experimenting with mild steel for warships from 1873. But, as with iron, it was Clydeside builders who most eagerly adopted steel plates, whose superiority in strength and elasticity was well known.[2] It was also clear that thinner plates could be used and a saving of up to 16 per cent in weight could be achieved over iron construction. The constraint for ship owners was the higher initial cost, for in 1880 steel plates were still up to 50 per cent more expensive than iron. However, as the Siemens Martin process for open hearth steel, and the Gilchrist Thomas process utilising basic ores came on stream, prices dropped rapidly and by 1890 were virtually equal with iron.[3] Within these ten years iron was all but abandoned and steel construction represented about 90 per cent of all tonnage launched in 1890.

The final step in exploiting the potential of marine stream engines came with Charles Parsons' turbine. In 1884 he patented his direct-acting turbine in which the expanding power of steam impacted on vanes arranged in a circular form. This was capable of very high revolutions, and was first applied to generate electricity on land and in ships. A decade elapsed before he established his own company, the Parsons Marine Steam Turbine Co., in an effort to develop and exploit the innovation, and it was not until 1897 that the dramatic demonstration of the power, speed and manoeuvrability of the launch *Turbinia* captured attention at the Naval Review at Spithead. By that time Parsons' radial-flow turbine was one of four types on offer, the others emanating from Curtis in the USA, and the de Laval and Rateau from France.

Parsons' breakthrough came in cooperation with William Denny and Brothers of Dumbarton who together with a Clydeside ship owner, Captain John Williamson, formed the Turbine Steamer Syndicate in 1901. The result was Denny's *Kind Edward* launched in 1901 as the world's first turbine-driven merchant vessel. As with the compound engine, and the Scotch and water-tube boilers, nearly twenty years of persistence had to be financed and endured before the technical advance flourished as a commercial innovation. Thereafter progress was swift, and by 1913 Parsons claimed that of the 28 million horsepower estimated in use in world merchant and naval vessels, 12 million horsepower was being delivered by direct-action turbines.[4] Even so, it was the triple-expansion engine, and Walter Brock's refinement of quadruple expansion that dominated the merchant marine.

With these inter-linked developments British marine engineers and shipbuilders established a technical leadership which in scale of operation could not be rivalled by competitors. The divergent path to motor vessels was not yet a challenge, Rudolph Diesel patenting his engine only in 1892. Again it was 20 years before it was translated into operational form when the East Asiatic Co. of Copenhagen commissioned two identical vessels, the *Selandia* launched at Burmeister and Wains Copenhagen yard in 1911, and the *Jutlandia* in 1912 launched by Barclay Curle & Co. on the river Clyde. The British licence, initially with a special company, the Atlas Mercantile Co. Ltd, passed to Harland & Wolff in 1912, who as early movers were investing in building the new engines at both their Glasgow and Belfast establishments. At the same time Doxford in Sunderland was laying the foundation for British diesel engine development.

While the changes in construction and propulsion were the most dramatic in re-shaping the industry in these years, ship design also responded to the challenge of improving efficiency and economy. The expansion of world trade and the development of different trades encouraged the design of specialised carriers. The first tank steamer for carrying oil was constructed in 1887 and the problem of the huge stresses and strains imposed on the vessel then became an important area of investigation.[5] These vessels were initially transversely framed, and a significant advance in strength came after 1910 with the introduction of the Isherwood system of longitudinal framing which was also widely adopted for general cargo vessels.[6] General cargo ships had also been improved with the development of both the well-deck cargo vessel, and the turret-decker tramp. Designers were also increasingly drawn to the problems of stability and resistance. The former was tackled successfully from 1880 with the introduction of the integrator to simplify stability calculations, and resistance trials were given prominence when Denny of Dumbarton established the first test tank in commercial use in 1883, building upon the experimental work inaugurated by Froude in 1872 in the Admiralty tank at Torquay. These were at the cutting edge of experimentation, and other British shipbuilders benefited by empirical imitation more than by similar technical investment. Nevertheless, the cumulative outcome of the many refinements was to develop a distinctive competitive advantage for British shipbuilders in reciprocating steam engines, steel hulls, and in large-scale and volume merchant ship production before the First World War.

# Structure and scale

The third development contributing to the competitive strength of British shipbuilding before the First World War was the changes in location, organisation and scale which produced a powerful regional concentration in the industry. The decline of shipbuilding on the Thames and on the south coast, well under way by the middle of the century,[7] was completed, and two districts comprising four rivers had come to dominate the industry (Table 3.2). By the beginning of the twentieth century half of all UK merchant shipbuilding output was concentrated on the North East coast between the Tyne and the Humber. Within this district the three northern rivers of Tyne, Wear and Tees delivered over 42 per cent of the total, and they were at the centre of the most extensive shipbuilding district in Britain, and together formed the heart of the UK industry. The second great concentration of the industry was on the Clyde which regularly delivered around 30 per cent of new merchant tonnage each year. No other single shipbuilding river in the world exceeded the concentration of activity on the Clyde. In 1913, 38 of the 104 yards in operation in Britain clustered on the banks of the Clyde, while 40 yards were located on the Tyne, Wear, Tees and Humber.

This high degree of concentration was mirrored in the pattern of output. With an average of 102 firms operating between 1911 to 1912, over one-quarter of production came from only six firms, and half of all output was delivered by 14 companies (Table 3.3). Only two of the yards regularly built in excess of 100,000 tons each year, Swan Hunter & Wigham Richardson, and Harland & Wolff, and another nine yards built between 50,000 and 100,000 gross tons annually. The average scale of output of all the yards was only 19,000 grt each year.

However, although there was a large number of yards in the industry, the production in each main district was dominated by a few larger yards. On the Tyne, with 13 companies, over 60 per cent of production came from only three yards. On the river Wear, again with 13 companies, over half the output came from Doxford, Thompson, and Shorts. Similarly on the Clyde with its 38 companies, over half of all output came from only seven of these. Consequently, even within these regional concentrations, a few dominant yards overshadowed the work of a larger number of smaller companies on each river.

Part of the attraction of these areas to shipbuilders was the advantage of the proximity to coal, iron, steel and their products. Modern shipbuilding is a complex engineering assembly industry in which at least 60 per cent of the value of the ship represents materials purchased by the shipyard, and a supporting infrastructure of supplier and component industries was a necessary adjunct if a shipyard was not to undertake the manufacture of every item from steel to finishing paint. Consequently, in these shipbuilding districts there emerged a vast array of companies which were linked functionally, and sometimes formally. In both the North East and on the Clyde, the major shipbuilders had ready access to iron and steel mills, foundries, forges, pipe,

*Table 3.2* Merchant and naval tonnage launched in '000 gross tons
Average of 1911–1912

| District | '000 grt | % UK |
|---|---|---|
| Tyne | 383.7 | 19.3 |
| Wear | 308 | 15.5 |
| Tees | 146.5 | 7.4 |
| Hartlepool | 130.9 | 6.6 |
| Humber | 42.2 | 2.1 |
| North East coast (total) | 1,011.4 | 50.8 |
| Barrow to Workington | 53.6 | 2.7 |
| Mersey | 52.1 | 2.6 |
| North West coast (total) | 105.7 | 5.3 |
| Thames and East Anglia | 8.9 | 0.4 |
| South coast | 7.4 | 0.3 |
| Bristol Channel | 1.8 | 0.1 |
| South England (total) | 18.1 | 0.8 |
| England and Wales, total | 1,135.4 | 57.0 |
| River Clyde | 626.1 | 31.5 |
| River Forth | 27.1 | 1.4 |
| River Tay | 15.9 | 0.8 |
| Aberdeen and nort-east Scotland | 9.6 | 0.5 |
| Scotland (total) | 678.8 | 34.1 |
| Belfast | 173.8 | 8.7 |
| Dublin | 1.8 | 0.1 |
| Ireland (total) | 175.6 | 8.8 |
| Total UK tonnage launched, 1911–12 | 1,898.8 | 99.9 |

*Source*: Compiled from Fairplay, 1912.

*Table 3.3*  Rank order of UK shipyards, 1911/12

| | Yard | District | '000 grt | % UK | % cumulative |
|---|---|---|---|---|---|
| 1 | Swan Hunter & Wigham Richardson | Tyne | 119.4 | 6.0 | |
| 2 | Harland & Wolff | Belfast | 97.9 | 4.9 | |
| 3 | Wm Doxford & Sons | Wear | 88.5 | 4.4 | |
| 4 | Wm Gray & Co. | Hartlepool | 77.2 | 3.9 | |
| 5 | Workman Clark | Belfast | 75.9 | 3.8 | |
| 6 | Russell & Co. | Clyde | 71.7 | 3.6 | 26.6 |
| 7 | Sir W.G. Armstrong Whitworth | Tyne | 57.8 | 2.9 | |
| 8 | Northumberland Shipbuilding Co. | Tyne | 55.4 | 2.8 | |
| 9 | Irvine's Shipbuilding Co. | Hartlepool | 53.7 | 2.7 | |
| 10 | Cammell Laird | Birkenhead | 52.1 | 2.6 | |
| 11 | Vickers Ltd | Barrow | 51.4 | 2.6 | 40.2 |
| 12 | Palmers Shipbuilding & Iron Co. | Tyne | 49.1 | 2.5 | |
| 13 | Scotts Shipbuilding & Engineering Co. | Clyde | 44.9 | 2.3 | |
| 14 | John Brown & Co. | Clyde | 44.2 | 2.2 | |
| 15 | C. Connell & Co. | Clyde | 42.0 | 2.1 | |
| 16 | Barclay Curle & Co. | Clyde | 41.8 | 2.1 | 51.4 |
| 17 | J.L. Thompson & Sons | Wear | 39.7 | 2.0 | |
| 18 | R. & W. Hawthorn Leslie | Tyne | 38.5 | 1.9 | |
| 19 | Fairfield Shipbuilding & Engineering Co. | Clyde | 38.4 | 1.9 | |
| 20 | Ropner & Sons | Tees | 36.5 | 1.8 | |
| | Top 20 yards | | 1,175.6 | | 59.1 |
| | All 102 yards in UK | | 1,989.8 | | 100.0 |

*Sources*: Compiled from Fairplay, 1911 and 1912, and A.W. Kirkaldy, *British Shipping* (London: Kegan Paul, 1919), Appendix VI, pp. 584–7.

tube, wire, chain and galvanising works. The local trade directories reveal long lists of suppliers of copper and brass products, lead products, nails, rivets, nuts, bolts, plates, sheets, bars, sections, keel blocks, and every conceivable product required by a vast range of ships from small coasters to deep-sea tramps, and from yachts to liners and warships.

The close-knit industrial structure developed and nurtured by these dependencies of supply and demand created an industrial complex or, as Alfred Marshall described it, an 'industrial atmosphere'. These inter-relationships delivered economies of management, scale and capital utility, and benefits in productivity, that could not be matched by builders in isolated localities, or in economies where shipbuilding represented a much smaller component of industrial activity. Lorenz has demonstrated the profound advantage this industrial district environment delivered to British shipbuilding in terms of labour productivity. The high load factors of British yards linked to abundant skilled labour achieved an output per head of 15.2 tons per year in 1909, well ahead of the 6.3 tons achieved in Germany, and the 4.7 tons recorded in France.[8] Moreover, the advantage of agglomeration and concentration in two very large shipbuilding districts also influenced the scale, specialisation, and degree of integration of the shipbuilding companies. The influence of small numbers of relatively large companies in total output has been noted, and this reflected significant changes in the organisation and investment in shipbuilding companies in the closing years of the nineteenth century, and in the decade before the First World War.

In the 1870s and 1880s it is clear that ownership and control in British shipbuilding firms was a local affair, each district having its own network of owner-capitalist and family-based firms. The new iron shipyards with larger demands for capital showed some tendency to take the new public company form,[9] although only 17 of the 90 iron yards enumerated by the Factory Inspectors had done so. The largest of these yards had cost £200,000–£300,000, and the smallest around £30,000. Estimating on the basis of fragmentary evidence of sale-prices of yards suggests the capital invested in British shipbuilding in the 1870s was probably not less than £7 million, and could have been as large as £10 million. Pollard and Robertson suggest a capitalisation of £19 million by 1886, this rising sharply to £73 million by 1911.[10] The acceleration from the 1880s was partly in response to the increasing scale of world shipping and the increasing capital required to keep pace with the technologies called on to produce larger, more powerful engines, boilers and hulls. But even more influential was a move to forward integration by steel and armament producers anxious to secure an outlet for their products.

The earliest move in this direction was in 1882 when the ordnance firm of Sir W.G. Armstrong took over the shipbuilders C. Mitchell & Co., and established a naval yard at Elswick on the Tyne. The Manchester engineering company of Sir Joseph Whitworth and Co. was added in 1897, as was Robert Stephenson & Co. in 1899. In 1888 the Barrow yard was acquired by the Naval Construction and Armaments Co.

Ltd, part of the Cavendish family interest in steel, shipping and shipbuilding. This set-up was subsequently acquired in 1897 by Vickers Sons & Maxin Ltd for £425,000.[11] Two years later the Sheffield armaments firm of John Brown & Co. purchased the Clydebank Shipbuilding and Engineering Co. for £923,255.[12] This first penetration of Scottish interests by English capital stimulated Beardmore, the Scottish forge masters and armour plate manufacturers, to acquire the Govan yard of Robert Napier & Sons and to plan to lay out a new yard at Dalmuir adjacent to John Brown's Clydebank establishment. The strain on Beardmore resources precipitated a significant injection of English capital by Vickers in 1902. The English firm acquired a half share in Beardmore, exchanging 389,500 Vickers £1 shares for 750,000 £1 Beardmore stock. By 1906 this combine was establishing an ordnance work in Glasgow and when the Dalmuir yard was complete in 1907, the outlay had been £923,036.[13] The pace of armament manufacturers' interest continued in 1903 when Charles Cammell & Co. of Sheffield acquired the Birkenhead shipbuilders of Laird & Co. and commenced the erection of Ordnance Works at Coventry.[14] In 1905 Cammell Laird acquired half the ordinary shares in the Fairfield Shipbuilding and Engineering Co. on the Clyde, which in turn took a quarter interest in the Coventry Ordnance Works of £187,500. At the same time John Brown & Co. acquired a half-interest in the Coventry works so that by 1905, Cammell Laird, John Brown, and Fairfield were inter-connected in an armaments network to create a combine at least as large as the Vickers Sons & Maxim empire, though not so closely integrated. As a consequence of these moves the five great armament firms – Vickers Sons & Maxim, John Brown & Co., Sir W.G. Armstrong Whitworth & Co., Cammell Laird & Co., and Beardmore – were deeply enmeshed in shipbuilding by the turn of the century, and to an extent were linked to each other. Cammell's and Browns were linked to the Coventry Ordnance Works, while Vickers had penetrated Beardmore in which Armstrong Whitworth also purchased an interest in 1911.

These armaments networks were not the only ones being developed in shipbuilding before the First World War. In 1903, three Tyneside firms – C.S. Swan and Hunter, Wigham Richardson & Co., and the Tyne Pontoon and Drydock Co. – came together to form the firm of Swan Hunter & Wigham Richardson, with a controlling interest in the Wallsend Slipway and Engineering Co. This was certainly the largest of the purely shipbuilding and engineering combines outside the armaments groups. In contrast, Palmers at Jarrow opted for internal expansion and the creation of a vertically integrated operation from coal, iron and steel, through to its shipyards and engineering works. It also developed another link with shipping when Lord Furness acquired a large shareholding. Furness was indeed a major influence in linking ship-owning and shipbuilding, acquiring the Hartlepool yard of Henry Withy in 1883 and subsequently adding Irvines Dry Dock Co. at Hartlepool, and the Northumberland Shipbuilding Co. at Howden. Later, in 1901, the Wilson line, part of Furness's links with Lord Pirrie of Harland & Wolff, acquired Earles Shipbuilding Co. at Hull. Furness was also involved in 1900 bringing together William Allan & Co. of Sunderland, Westgarth & Co. of Middlesbrough, and Thos Richardson & Sons of Hartlepool to form Richardsons, Westgarth & Co. with a capital of £1,050,000 to create one of the largest shipbuilding and marine engineering enterprises in Britain.

The penetration of shipbuilding by shipping interests and vice-versa was not uncommon in these years. Peter Denny at Dumbarton had major interests in the Irawaddy Flotilla Co., the Platense Flotilla Co., the British and Burmese Steam Navigation Co. and several others. Scotts of Greenock were large shareholders in the China Navigation Co., and were intimately linked with the Liverpool shipping firms of Holts and Swires. Sir John Ellerman as a major shareholder sat on the boards of both Barclay Curle & Co. in Glasgow and Swan Hunter Wigham Richardson in Newcastle, and it was he who negotiated the purchasing of Barclay Curle by Swan Hunter & Wigham Richardson in 1912. William Tod Lithgow was reported to hold shares in as many as eighty-one shipping lines, partly as a single ship operator, but also as a means of cementing networks with prospective purchasers.

Perhaps the most extensive penetration of shipbuilding by ship-owning was erected through the association of William Pirrie of Harland & Wolff, and Owen Phillips, later Lord Kylsant, of the Royal Mail Group. This developed in three stages, the first in 1902 when as part of the negotiation to form the International Mercantile Marine Co., Pirrie secured for Harland & Wolff the undertaking that the new tonnage orders for the combined shipping line, together with heavy repairs required in Britain, would go to the Belfast yard.[15] This built on the 51 per cent share Pirrie already held in the Hamburg-Amerika Line as a source of orders. Five years later Pirrie negotiated a link with John Brown & Co., the armament firm taking the largest single stake in Harland & Wolff by which they gained ship orders, and Pirrie secured a supply of steel shafting, forgings, and especially turbines without the need to establish independent facilities.[16] Quickly thereafter in 1907 Pirrie & Phillips acquired the deceased Sir Alfred Jones's shipping interests in Elder Dempster, the African Steam Ship Co., the British and African Steam Navigation Co., and the Imperial Direct West India Mail Service.[17] The interlocked shipping and shipbuilding interests acquired gave Harland & Wolff and John Brown access to a very wide market for orders.

The other major functional connection, or network, that developed in these years was that between the shipbuilders and the marine engineers. The importance of engines and boilers to the final cost of vessels – anything from one-quarter to forty per cent for merchant vessels[18] – actively encouraged major builders to provide their own engineering facilities. By the first decade of the twentieth century Todd claims that of 74 marine engineering establishments in operation, 50 were vertically linked with the shipbuilders.[19] Another source of evidence, the annual returns of HP delivered and published in Fairplay, indicated 67 firms making returns in 1911 and 1912. Of these 41, or 61 per cent, were directly linked with shipbuilding companies. The main districts, however, displayed rather different patterns. The formal linkage of marine engineering and shipbuilding was very strong on the Clyde, with over 75 per cent of HP delivered emanating from the integrated shipbuilding and engineering firms. In contrast, on the Tyne less than 30 per cent of engine power was constructed in integrated establishments, over 70 per cent flowing from concerns separated from the main shipyards. Even when allowance is made for the engine output of Richardson Westgarth, the Central Marine Engine Works, and the Wallsend Slipway and Engineering Co., all effectively controlled by shipbuilding companies, but operating as separate establishments, the independent firms on the North East coast still delivered half the engine power in the district. These differences in part reflect different demand patterns of specialism in building. Nevertheless, networks of formal and informal dependence characterised the relationships of the shipbuilders and marine engineers.

The outcome of these mergers and associations was to concentrate capital, as well as production, in fewer and larger firms by the eve of the First World War (Table 3.4). Of the 104 firms in operation, 18 were public limited companies. The top five were all armament companies, and the only purely shipbuilding and engineering firm roughly on the same scale was Swan Hunter & Wigham Richardson (Table 3.5). At £1.5 million the capitalisation of SHWR is arguably a better indication of the shipbuilding assets of the five armaments combines than the authorised or paid-up capital of these entire enterprises, since in these combines the shipyards operated as the shipbuilding division of more complex operations. The preference for public company, private company and proprietorship, clearly varied among the shipbuilding districts. Public companies had only made a significant impact on ownership patterns on the upper Clyde around Glasgow, and on the Tyne. Proprietorships conversely were still the most popular type of firm on the Tyne and still significant on the Clyde and Wear. The private limited company had, however, been adopted with vigour in all the main districts, and was by far the most common form on the Wear and Tees, and lower Clyde. But with few exceptions, whatever the legal form, it is clear that these firms were effectively family-based operations. Family dynasties, either singly, or jointly, were in long continued control of the enterprises. The nature of the firms, and the men who ran them, also created significant strengths for British shipbuilding before the First World War.

## The men and the firms

The foundations of competitive strength emanating from the structure, scale and regional clustering of the industry were further enhanced by particular characteristics of the men, employers and workers alike, as well as the nature of the firms as organisations. Most of the great shipbuilding firms in the North East and on the Clyde were established in the middle decades of the nineteenth century, and the men who set them up, and their sons and nephews, continued to control them for very long periods. An analysis of the leaders of the Scottish shipbuilding firms demonstrates that business

*Table 3.4*  District company structure, 1910

| District | No. of public companies | No. of private companies | No. of proprietors | Total |
|---|---|---|---|---|
| Glasgow | 8 | 9 | 5 | 22 |
| Greenock and Port Glasgow | 0 | 12 | 4 | 16 |
| River Clyde (total) | 8 | 21 | 9 | 38 |
| Aberdeen and north-east Scotland | 0 | 2 | 1 | 3 |
| River Tay | 0 | 2 | 0 | 2 |
| River Forth | 0 | 2 | 3 | 5 |
| Scotland (total) (capitalisation £8.6 m) | 8 | 27 | 13 | 48 |
| Tyne | 4 | 4 | 5 | 13 |
| Wear | 1 | 8 | 4 | 3 |
| Tees | 0 | 4 | 2 | 6 |
| Hartlepool | 1 | 1 | 0 | 2 |
| Humber | 1 | 2 | 3 | 6 |
| North East coast (total) (£8.2 m) | 7 | 19 | 14 | 40 |
| Mersey | 1 | 0 | 0 | 1 |
| Barrow in Furness | 1 | 0 | 1 | 2 |
| Thames to East Anglia | 0 | 2 | 4 | 6 |
| South Coast | 1 | 1 | 1 | 3 |
| Bristol Channel | 0 | 1 | 0 | 1 |
| England except North East (£8.0 m) | 3 | 4 | 6 | 13 |
| England total (£ 16.2 m) | 10 | 23 | 20 | 53 |
| Belfast | 0 | 2 | 0 | 2 |
| Dublin | 0 | 1 | 0 | 1 |
| Ireland, total | 0 | 3 | 0 | 3 |
| UK total (£ 24.8 m) | 18 | 53 | 33 | 104 |

*Source*:  Compiled from Stock Exchange Yearbook, 1910.

*Table 3.5*   Capitalisation of public limited companies in UK shipbuilding, 1910

| | Company | Location | Authorised £m | Paid-up £m |
|---|---|---|---|---|
| 1 | Vickers Ltd | Barrow | 5.20 | 5.20 |
| 2 | Armstrong Whitworth | Tyne | 4.21 | 4.21 |
| 3 | John Brown & Co. | Clyde | 4.00 | 3.71 |
| 4 | Beardmore & Co. | Clyde | 2.50 | 2.00 |
| 5 | Cammell Laird | Mersey | 2.50 | 2.37 |
| 6 | Swan Hunter & Wigham Richardson | Tyne | 1.50 | 1.17 |
| 7 | Palmers Shipbuilding Co. | Tyne | 0.883 | 0.698 |
| 8 | D. & W. Henderson | Clyde | 0.600 | 0.525 |
| 9 | R.W. Hawthorn Leslie | Tyne | 0.557 | 0.462 |
| 10 | Fairfield Shipbuilding & Engineering Co. | Clyde | 0.500 | 0.500 |
| 11 | Wm Doxford & Sons | Wear | 0.500 | 0.450 |
| 12 | London & Glasgow | Clyde | 0.450 | 0.211 |
| 13 | Wm Gray & Co. | Hartlepool | 0.350 | 0.350 |
| 14 | J.I. Thorneycroft & Co. | S Hampton | 0.350 | 0.346 |
| 15 | Wm Simons & Co. | Clyde | 0.250 | 0.250 |
| 16 | Bow McLachlan & Co. | Clyde | 0.160 | 0.160 |
| 17 | Earles Shipbuilding & Engineering | Hull | 0.150 | 0.150 |
| 18 | Flemming & Ferguson | Clyde | 0.150 | 0.150 |
| | Total | | £24.8 m | £22.92 |

*Source*: Compiled from the Stock Exchange Year Book, 1910.

leadership owed a great deal to early and successful establishment of families in the business,[20] and that few men outside the controlling families reached top positions in management. Moreover, the leading role of founding families was generally retained in the transition to public company form, and was certainly reinforced in adopting private company status. In Scotland, for example, the Dennys, Stephens and Lithgows all retained family control when private company status was adopted, as did the families of the Gilchrists, Fergusons and MacLeans, when Barclay Curle took public company form. In the North East the Doxford family continued in control of their company, as did the Gray family when their company took public form. To these men the business was more than a place of work; it was in effect a way of life, carrying with it strong and enduring loyalties and commitments.

As a group the shipbuilders were more men of practical experience than of theoretical inclination or training. While a few were technically well-qualified engineers or naval architects, the majority had little formal education beyond the classroom, and gained their expertise through formal and informal apprenticeship, combined with shop-floor training. The common apprenticeships were as engineers, shipwrights, ships' draughtsmen and naval architects.[21] In this approach to training, the famous firms were themselves the training ground much sought after by families seeking to place their sons as premium apprentices. On the Clyde the works of Napier, Denny and Elder & Co. (later Fairfield) were particularly noted as training establishments, while in the North East, training in Hawthorns, St Peters Engineering works, and in Wigham Richardsons' establishment was similarly valued.

The owners and managers of the firms were consequently deeply rooted in the practical expertise of shipbuilding and marine engineering, and in that respect shared common ground with their workmen. As metal and steam technology captured shipbuilding, the craftsmen-based production and skills of the wood and sail era was translated into new forms in which the main tasks of metal fabrication, engineering, and fitting-out became increasingly structured in formal craft unions, until by the end of the century at least seventeen unions could be found representing members in a typical shipyard.[22] Masters and men shared a common training and a common command of the craft technologies upon which their product depended. The work process itself grew out of this apprentice and shop-floor experience-based system, and in large measure, management and labour jointly evolved a hierarchical system of management and control. This defined clear decision rules for each process or stage of production, which in turn was largely in the hands of a specific craft group in the shipyard, engine works, or boiler shop. Centralised and authoritarian control at the top of the firm was combined with a decentralised allocation of work on the slipway or shop floor, at which point the appropriate craftsmen effectively coordinated and controlled the day-to-day work. Moreover, through the craft apprentice system, and the closed-shop practices becoming common from the 1890s, these craftsmen also controlled entry to, and the training of, the workforce.

In this complex way masters and men essentially learned from each other, making the firm an effective teaching and learning forum which was capable of maintaining, adapting and improving products and product technologies in a routine and sustainable way. The technical history of shipbuilding and marine engineering is one of continuous refinement and improvement of engines and boilers by empirical experimentation and adaptation, each yard finding its own way of adapting the fundamental innovations which were well publicised and discussed in the professional and technical journals of the Institutions of Shipbuilders and Engineers, Naval Architects, and in mercantile journals such as *Fairplay*.

The firms which succeeded before the First World War linked the skills and experience of the entrepreneurs, managers and workmen in this way, and in so doing developed organisations which were adaptive, and whose abilities technically were well attuned to responding to changes in the technologies which they themselves had largely developed. Concentrated in two major districts, as these firms were, constant local rivalry was endemic, and this encouraged efforts constantly to improve and refine products and processes in order to maintain reputation, attract orders, and improve market share. The cheek-by-jowl location of these firms, run by men from similar backgrounds, men well known to each other from close association in professional bodies, and who shared responsibilities in their local communities, ensured that advances made in one establishment were soon emulated in others, this contributing powerfully to the competitive strength of the district, and of the industry as a whole.

## Markets

The nature of the market and of demand for ships in the later decades of the nineteenth century proved to be another source of strength for the industry. The market was both highly volatile and rapidly growing, as mean freight rates oscillated wildly. If the level of freights in 1900 is taken as 100, it declined by 40 per cent between 1889 and 1896. It then recovered by 25 per cent to 1900, only to collapse again by 40 per cent to 1908, before rising rapidly by 50 per cent to 1912. These fluctuations were broadly reflected in output volumes, but because the carrying capacity and efficiency of ships improved so rapidly, a fall in freight rates did not necessarily mirror a decline in profitability for the ship owner, nor lead to an automatic reduction in orders.[23] Volatility in freights was consequently offset in part by the speed, scale and efficiency in the new vessels.

Consequently, in spite of apparently unfavourable trends in mean freight rates, world shipping continued to expand rapidly. The total world fleet grew from around 29 million gross tons of shipping in 1890 to 47 million tons by 1913, a gain of 63 per cent. Steam tonnage alone, however, exploded from 16 million tons to 42 million, a gain of 2.6 times in 24 years. As the major world producer of steam tonnage, Britain captured the largest share of this. Between 1890 and 1913 British yards poured out over 24 million gross tons of new steamships; about 19 million tons were taken by British ship owners, the remainder going to overseas buyers. The large British merchant marine, which grew from 11 million grt to nearly 19 million grt by 1913, was entirely the reserve of British builders. Between 1909 and 1913, for example, only 24,679 gross tons of shipping were built abroad for British owners. By 1913 British ship owners controlled 40 per cent of the world fleet and 42.6 per cent of all world steam tonnage, delivering to British shipbuilders a market of unrivalled size and scope. The British fleet had increased by some 4.5 per cent per year between 1890 and 1913, and another 2.5 per cent of total fleet tonnage was replaced each year.[24] This annual addition of around 7 per cent of fleet tonnage meant a secure average demand for British shipyards in the order of 1.3 million gross tons. When overseas tonnage is added, British shipbuilders could expect 300,000–400,000 tons of orders from foreign buyers each year (Table 3.1) providing an average expected workload with orders of 1.6–1.7 million tons.

A merchant market on this scale was simply not available to builders in other countries. The flow of orders, year on year, was quite remarkable. If we take each ship launched as one order, then over the 24 years from 1890 to 1913, British yards launched 19,229 merchant vessels, 80 per cent for home ship owners, 20 per cent for foreign buyers. This represented an average order book of 801 vessels per year, the average size climbing from 1,300 grt in the early 1890s to about 1,700 grt by 1913. A workload of this volume encouraged both regional and firm specialisation, developments which again reinforced the competitive strength and advantage of Britain's shipbuilding industry.

With about half of Britain's output, the North East was the main builder of cargo tramps. The river Wear was specially noted for this type, with Shorts, Pickersgills, Laings, Grays and Thomsons, all leaders in the sector. Most also produced cargo liners, but the tramps predominated. This was the river that developed the Turret-Decker, a vessel designed to maximise carrying capacity in relation to measurement upon which port dues would be levied. Doxfords played a significant part in developing this type. On the neighbouring river Tees, a similar pattern of specialisation emerged, but with the balance of production including whalers, while Smiths Dock Co. also produced trawlers and whalers. The Tyne, in contrast, was more diversified. Cargo liners were as prominent as cargo tramps in construction, while Palmers and Armstrongs were among the pioneers of tanker construction in the 1890s. Armstrongs, like most of the largest yards in Britain, could produce a full range of vessels if required, and also had a naval capability. Similarly, Swan Hunter & Wigham Richardson could build across the range of ships, and was noted for its liner construction.

In the other main district, on the river Clyde, the pattern was more varied, and while yards such as Connells and Duncans, and Russells (later Linthgow) produced tramps, the emphasis was on cargo liners, passenger cargo, and passenger liner construction. The Clyde also had a wider range of specialist builders, from dredgers, produced by a number of small yards such as Simons, Lobnitz, Ferguson, and Fleming and Ferguson, to cross-channel and estuarine craft from Denny, and the highest class of passenger liners from John Brown, Beardmore, Scott's of Greenock, and Fairfield. This last group were also naval contractors. Vickers at Barrow and Cammell Laird at Bickenhead shared these characteristics. Across the Irish Channel, Harland & Wolff could produce any type of vessel, but was particularly noted for cargo liners and passenger liners, as was their neighbour Workman Clark.

The final element in the market that gave strength to British shipbuilding before 1914 was the rapid growth of naval construction in the private shipyards. This market developed erratically in the 1860s and 1870s, mainly in response to the willingness or otherwise of the Admiralty Board to provide plans for warships designed by the Royal Corps of Naval Constructors, and to be supplied to private yards for orders for foreign navies.[25] The real stimulus, however, came with the Navy Defence Act of 1889 which provided for a very large, five-year building programme costing £21.5 million, a large part of which was beyond the capacity of the Royal Dockyards and therefore had to be put out to tender in private yards.[26] Concerns arising from the acknowledged obsolescence of the Navy, and fears of expanding French and Russian tonnage, produced a consensus in the House of Commons which became known as the 'Two Power Standard', by which it was held that the Royal Navy should be kept on a scale at least equal to the naval strength of any two other countries. This initially meant France and Russia, although the equation was later compromised by the rapid growth of German naval power. But from 1889 to the First World War, the 'Two Power Standard' and the succession of naval building programmes, had profound consequences for the growth of British shipbuilding (Table 3.6).

The naval programmes between 1889 and 1913 delivered 2.8 million displacement tons of warships for service with the Royal Navy. Over half of this, 1.6 million tons or 56.4 per cent, was concentrated in private shipyards, the balance flowing from the Royal Dockyards at Chatham, Sheerness, Portsmouth, Devonport and Pembroke. In addition to this, the private yards attracted orders from overseas governments for 480,000 tons of warships, giving a naval market for the private yards in the order of 2.1 million tons. Admiralty orders represented 77 per cent of this, and foreign orders 23 per cent. The work allocated by the Admiralty Board between 1889 and 1913 favoured the Clyde over the other rivers. The Clyde yards, mainly Clydebank, Dalmuir, Fairfield, Scotts and Denny, supplied almost 45 per cent of tonnage against 21 per cent from the North East coast, mainly Armstrongs, with another 24 per cent more from the Barrow yard, and the Cammell Laird yard. Many of the smaller yards gained about 10 per cent of the Admiralty orders (Table 3.6).

*Table 3.6*   UK warship construction, 1889–1913
('000 displacement tons by five-year period)

|  | 1889–93 | 1894–98 | 1899 – 03 | 1904–08 | 1909–13 | Total (m. tons) |
|---|---|---|---|---|---|---|
| Private UK yards | 188.7 | 230.2 | 399.2 | 248.8 | 534.1 | 1.6 |
| Private foreign A/C | 22.9 | 136.4 | 88.3 | 82.6 | 150.3 | 0.48 |
| Total from private yards | 211.6 | 366.6 | 487.5 | 331.4 | 684.4 | 2.08 |
| Royal Dockyards | 210.2 | 266.0 | 216.7 | 245.8 | 298.3 | 1.24 |
| Naval construction in UK | 398.9 | 496.2 | 615.9 | 494.6 | 832.4 | 2.83 |
| Total naval (inc. foreign) | 421.8 | 632.6 | 704.2 | 577.2 | 982.7 | 3.32 |
| *Share of UK Naval* | % | % | % | % | % | % |
| Clyde | 26.3 | 52.3 | 47.7 | 39.6 | 47.1 | 44.4 |
| North East coast | 38.2 | 8.2 | 14.4 | 32.4 | 20.3 | 21.1 |
| Barrow and Mersey | 17.1 | 31.0 | 28.8 | 16.3 | 24.0 | 24.2 |
| Other | 18.4 | 8.5 | 9.1 | 11.7 | 8.5 | 10.3 |

Sources: Compiled from S. Pollard and P.L. Robertson, *The British Shipbuilding Industry, 1870–1914*, p. 217, and *Survey of the Metal Industries*, Balfour Cttee Report, HMSO, 1928, Appx II: Warships Launched.

The export of warships also developed strongly at this time, expanding the warship order book by 23 per cent between 1889 and 1913. Of the 480,000 tons supplied to foreign governments the Clyde contributed only 28,250 tons.[27] In strong contrast, on the Tyne Armstrong had by 1912 supplied 322,000 tons of warships to foreign buyers, mainly to Japan, Brazil, Chile and China.[28] Vickers Sons & Maxim at Barrow, and Cammell Laird at Birkenhead, supplied most of the rest, with significant smaller tonnage, especially of the new torpedo boat destroyers, coming from specialist builders such as Thorneycroft and Yarrow.

The total naval market was highly important in the development of British shipbuilding in the 25 years before the First World War. Merchant tonnage launched was 32.8 million gross tons, while warship tonnage for home and overseas contributed 2.1 million displacement tons, equivalent to around 5.2 million tons gross in work content and value terms. At this level the naval order book represented 15.9 per cent of the merchant orders between 1889 and 1913. If the output of the naval dockyards is added, the total warship tonnage launched in Britain in those years was in excess of 3.3 million tons displacement, roughly equivalent to 8.3 million tons gross. In the total scale of ship production in the UK in those years that was roughly equivalent to 25 per cent of all merchant construction. Considering that naval construction was concentrated in relatively few yards, the significance of that market takes on even greater weight, especially in Birkenhead, Barrow, Newcastle and Glasgow. On the Clyde, for example, the significance of warship work is readily seen in relation to the profitability of two of the greatest naval yards, Fairfield and Clydebank. Between 1899 and 1906, naval work contributed between 75 and 80 per cent of net profits in these yards.[29] Moreover, in the lean years from 1907 to 1911, when profitability was difficult to obtain on merchant work, warship work still contributed much more strongly to overheads and profits than did merchant work. Peebles demonstrates that at Clydebank and Fairfield between 1905 and 1910 naval work contributed to overheads and profit at about twice the rate of merchant work. This increased to more than three times between 1910 and 1915 for Clydebank, and remained at twice the rate at Fairfield.[30] The contribution to profits was clearly much higher for naval than for merchant work, and the significance of the naval market was much greater than tonnage alone suggests. Of all market segments developing before the First World War, the warship sector was potentially the most profitable but also the most volatile and unpredictable. It nevertheless was a major foundation of the scale, strength and capability of British shipbuilding by the first decade of the twentieth century.

On the eve of the First World War, British shipbuilding was the colossus of the world industry, its market ascendancy and leadership in output unrivalled by any other nation, although competition was beginning to grow strongly, especially from Germany. The competitive advantage of the industry grew out of Britain's pivotal position as world trader,[31] carrier and financier, the opportunities this provided being exploited in technical leadership and innovation in marine steam and metal technology. When this technical base developed into regional concentrations of production and support industries dominated by adaptive firms and men, their exploitation and monopoly of the huge British merchant fleet combined with these strengths to propel Britain into world leadership in shipbuilding in the three decades before the First World War. While individually and collectively these characteristics gave great strength to the industry, none was a static condition, nor without elements of weakness. The ascendancy held by the industry in 1913 appeared robust, but it was soon to come under pressure as the relative strengths of these roots of competitive advantage began to change.

# CHAPTER FOUR

# War and depression: 1914–1939

## The First World War

The First World War introduced a major distortion into the shipbuilding and shipping markets with both immediate and longer term consequences for the development of both industries. On 3 August 1914 the government published a royal proclamation by which the Admiralty was authorised to requisition any British ships.[1] At the same time all shipyards received notices placing them under Admiralty control for the duration of the hostilities.[2] Work on merchant vessels on the slipways was subject to suspension, and priority was given to the introduction of an emergency naval construction programme. During 1915 and 1916 almost no new merchant orders were taken, and the flow of launches diminished sharply to barely one-third of the 1914 level as war construction priorities only slowly allowed merchant tonnage in progress to be cleared from the berths (Table 4.1). During these two years the control of shipping tightened to the extent that British ship owners were prohibited from selling ships to foreign owners, ending the customary large second-hand market. In addition British ships over 500 gross tons were prohibited from carrying cargo outside the British Empire, save by special licence, thus withdrawing British vessels from many markets and trades.

From the outbreak of the war the Admiralty Transport Arbitration Board had prepared and issued recommended rates of hire for requisition of vessels in a 'Blue Book', the rate subsequently known as 'Blue Book Rates'.[3] While these were initially above open-market rates, the withdrawal of large sections of British tonnage from tramp and subsequently liner cargo trades drove up market rates as demand for tonnage accelerated for both neutral and belligerent fleets. Even in 1916 about half of Britain's tramp tonnage, and most of its liner tonnage, remained outside Admiralty control, and with sharply rising freights, shipping profits grew to a level that caused much public disquiet and brought in the Excess Profits Duty in September 1915.[4] This was initially set at 50 per cent of extra profit calculated on the average profit earned in 1912–13, but was raised abruptly to 60 per cent in April 1916, and 80 per cent in January 1917. By then the New Ministries and Secretaries Act of December 1916 had

*Table 4.1*   UK tonnage launched, 1914–1919

| Year | Merchant ships ('000 gross tons) | Warships ('000 displacement tons) | |
|------|------|------|------|
| | | Royal Dockyards | Private yards[1] |
| 1914 | 1,683 | | |
| 1915 | 651 | | |
| 1916 | 608 | 653 | 634 |
| 1917 | 1,163 | 427 | 409 |
| 1918 | 1,348 | 517 | 514 |
| 1919 | 1,620 | 242 | 242 |
| Total, 1914–19 | 7,043 | 1,839 | 1,799 |

[1] 251,000 displacement tons cancelled leaving wartime output of 1.58 million displacement tons, equivalent to nearly 4.0 million gross tons in work and value content.

*Source*: Compiled from Lloyds Register, Annual summary of merchant ships launched.

created a Minister of Shipping, titled the Shipping Controller, with responsibility for the operation and control of merchant shipping and shipbuilding. Consequently, by early 1917 virtually all British merchant tonnage was either under requisition, or directly controlled by the government.

The appointment of the shipping controllers, and the advent of Lloyd George as prime minister in December 1916, heralded a significant change in policy in relation to new ship construction. By 1917 losses of merchant tonnage amounted to nearly 4 million gross tons, while replacement tonnage had been sharply curtailed by the emergency naval construction programme (Table 4.1). Growing fears of a failure in food and raw material supplies encouraged a renewed emphasis on merchant tonnage, and output recovered significantly in 1917 and 1918. Government fears were at such a level that it insisted that all new merchant tonnage commissioned should conform to approved standard types, and should also be owned by the State, and operated on its behalf by selected ship owners acting as government shipping managers.[5]

While the intervention of the new Minister of Shipping increased production, it also separated control of merchant and naval construction. This quickly caused problems of coordination, and in May 1917 the government transferred responsibility for merchant shipbuilding back to the Admiralty. While the Minister, or Shipping Controller, retained responsibility for shipping operations, construction was now centralised under the direction of a new 'Navy Controller', initially Sir Eric Geddes, succeeded in July 1917 by Sir Alan Anderson. The pressure on merchant tonnage was then so intense that Geddes and Anderson conceived a policy of state support for extending shipbuilding facilities. One aspect of this was capital grants to modernise and extend existing capacity, especially in major naval yards; the other was a proposal to establish up to three entirely new state-owned shipyards on the river Severn. This policy was implemented, but no tonnage had been launched from the Severn yards before the Armistice.[6]

The immediate consequence of these policies of control, direction and intervention on shipping and shipbuilding was to place shipbuilding under intense pressure with a huge workload of construction and repair. The wartime emergency programme placed orders of 1.79 million displacement tons with the private shipyards, of which 251,655 tons were cancelled in 1919.[7] This comprised 480 warships and 414 sloops and smaller vessels, and was a workload of 1.46 million displacement tons in addition to merchant construction and repair work. The warship work was roughly equivalent to 3.65 million gross tons which, when added to merchant output of 5.48 million tons, gave the shipyards an output in excess of 9 million gross tons during the war, an average annual workload in the order of 1.8 million tons.

A sustained output at this level would have meant that tonnage under construction on the slipways would always have been well in excess of 2 million gross tons, and that throughout the war, shipyards were effectively stretched to full capacity. An immediate consequence was investment in new berths, and in some cases in new yards. The outcome was that by 1920, British shipbuilding had extended its number of operational berths from 580 in 1914 to 806, a gain of 40 per cent.[8] While many of these were additions to existing yards, some 28 new shipbuilding companies were established.[9] In addition to government yards on the Severn at Chepstow and Monmouth, significant new ventures included the Furness Shipbuilding Company with a greenfield site at Haverton Hill, Cleveland, in 1917, the Burntisland Shipbuilding Company established on the river Forth in 1918 by Amos and Wilfred Ayre, and the Lloyd Royal Belge (UK) company and the Blythswood Shipbuilding Company, both on the river Clyde, in 1916 and 1919 respectively.

The new investments also brought new shipbuilding groupings to prominence, groups based mainly on merchant shipbuilding which now joined the armaments groups as dominant forces in the industry. On the river Clyde considerable regrouping was accomplished around the Harland & Wolff and Lithgow interests. Harland & Wolff had bought out the London and Glasgow Engineering and Shipbuilding Company in 1912, but added Caird & Co. of Greenock in 1916, undertook the management of the Ardrossan Dockyard and Archibald MacMillan in 1918, and acquired control of D. & W. Henderson and A. & J. Inglis in 1919. From their base in Port Glasgow Lithgows acquired Robert Duncan & Co. in 1915, the marine engineering company of David Rowan Co. in 1917, and the yards of Dunlop Bremmer & Co., and William Hamilton & Co. in 1919. In the same year the Northumberland Shipbuilding Company converted to public company form, increased its capital to £2.4 million and acquired a controlling interest in the Fairfield Shipbuilding and Engineering Company and the Blythswood

Shipbuilding Co. on the Clyde, Workman Clarke Co. at Belfast, Doxford and Son at Sunderland, and the Monmouth Shipbuilding Co. on the Severn at Chepstow. This burst of wartime and immediate post-war investment increased the public companies in shipbuilding from the 18 registered in 1911 to 23 in 1920. Authorised capital advanced from £24.8 million to £81.9 million while capital issued and paid up moved from £22.9 to £62.2 million. While this appears a large increase, the wholesale price index for iron and steel products jumped from 100 in 1913 to 358 in 1920, suggesting that in real terms the capitalisation of the major public companies in shipbuilding had not improved. Consequently, while shipbuilding emerged from the war with enlarged capacity, it is doubtful whether any significant investment in depth had been accomplished in line with the increase in scale.

## Capacity, costs and competition

While the war had distorted the production pattern and scale of shipbuilding in Britain, there were similar effects on shipbuilding and shipping internationally, each with profound consequences for British shipbuilding in the longer term. While before the war Britain had regularly constructed 60 per cent of all new world tonnage, during the war that contribution slipped to one-third. At the same time construction capacity and production increased sharply in other countries, laying the foundation of increased competitive power. Where before 1914 no other country had produced as much as one-quarter of Britain's tonnage, by 1919 the USA launched over 4 million gross tons, more than double that of Britain. While this was a wartime emergency response, and soon to diminish, the productive power of other nations was more permanently extended. Japan and Sweden had made striking progress: Japanese production in particular edged into third place in the world behind America and Britain. World output had more than doubled from 3.3 million tons in 1913 to 7.1 million in 1919, and productive capacity had grown from about 4 million tons to 7.5 million. If the USA is excluded, capacity in the rest of the world had increased to about 4 million tons, nearly doubling from the pre-war figure. The incidence of extended capacity varied from about 40 per cent in Britain, as measured by the increase in number of berths, to more than twice in Denmark, 59 per cent and 55 per cent respectively in Norway and Sweden, 37 per cent in Holland, 30 per cent in France, and a small 15 per cent in Germany.[10]

These adjustments in capacity are understandable in the context of tonnage losses and the demand for new shipping during the war. British merchant tonnage lost during the war as a result of enemy action was 8.36 million gross tons, and over 9.0 million tons when normal marine accident is added.[11] Total losses of merchant tonnage worldwide were in excess of 13 million gross tons,[12] a wastage rate of 30 per cent of the tonnage afloat in 1913. That volume of tonnage could have been replaced by the world shipbuilders with their pre-war capacity fully occupied, but the diversion of nearly half of Britain's energies to naval construction, and Germany similarly preoccupied, left scope for the acceleration of shipbuilding capacity in other countries.

The distortion of war also accelerated changes in the composition of the world flag fleet. At the end of the war the British merchant fleet was about 3.5 million tons smaller than in June 1914. Even the rapid acquisition from the Navy Controller of 156 completed standard ships and another 115 still under construction, together with the purchase of much second-hand tonnage from Norway, Sweden, Greece, Spain and America, and most of the German tonnage confiscated under the terms of the Treaty of Versailles, left the British Fleet at 18.1 million tons in 1920, still 800,000 tons below its 1914 level.[13] By then the world fleet had grown from 43.08 million tons in 1913 to 47.9 million tons in 1919 and 53.9 million tons in 1920. Britain's share had declined from 42.4 per cent of world tonnage afloat in 1913, to 33.5 per cent in 1920. Apart from the United States whose ocean-going fleet had grown by 10 million tons, the other significant gains in tonnage were Japan with an increase of 1.49 million tons and France with 1.2 million. Most other European flag fleets also added tonnage and gained market share at Britain's expense.

The war not only set in motion swift changes in the composition of the shipping market for British shipbuilders, but injected new technology in the shape of the motorship, and of oil burning to raise steam. Only 2.6 per cent of the world fleet used oil to raise steam in 1914, but this had increased to over 20 per cent by 1922. Moreover, while the launch of the *Jutlandia* and *Selandia* in 1912 had inaugurated the ocean-going motorship, 938,160 gross tons of motorships were in service by 1920, some. 1.7 per cent of world tonnage. These were new departures, and, especially in the case of the motorship, the pressures of war had ensured that Britain had made slower progress than other countries. In 1920 Britain owned 137,000 tons of the world's 938,000 tons of motorships.[14] The competition in the new product and new technology had clearly accelerated under wartime conditions, and did so in an environment of rapidly escalating costs and prices. Fairplay's standard 7,500 tons deadweight single-deck steamer rose in price from £42,500 in June 1914 to £258,750 in March 1920, a sixfold advance, effectively twice the increase on the wholesale price index in the same period, and a doubling in the real cost of tonnage in the course of the war.

British shipbuilding therefore emerged from the war changed in significant ways from its condition in 1913. Its overall capacity had enlarged by about 40 per cent while its captive domestic market, in the shape of the British merchant marine, had stood still in aggregate tonnage and had lost world share, declining from 42 to 33 per cent of the world fleet. Its building priorities had been distorted from civil to wartime work, with naval construction having represented up to 40 per cent of workload, and much more in value, compared with 17 per cent before the war. The export market, which had represented 25–30 per cent of the annual output of the industry, had been temporarily eliminated, and competitive shipbuilding companies and flag fleets had increased in strength. The post-war market for replacement and new tonnage held promise, but the outlook for naval construction was uncertain. Moreover, real costs had doubled, and replacement tonnage at the 1920 peak cost at least four times, and as much as six times, the pre-war price. Optimism and uncertainty confronted the shipbuilders in equal measure in 1920, but that at least was nothing new in an industry long used to violent fluctuations of demand, price and production.

## Structural changes

The ascendancy of British shipbuilding before 1914 had been embedded in the international economic arrangements which had placed Britain at the heart of a Euro-centric world economy, an economy of limited industrialisation but one with a complex specialisation of production based in part on comparative advantage linking producers of manufactures and primary products. World trade was based on an exchange of these two groups of products in a system of multi-lateral trade and settlement among relatively open economies. The exchange of these products had been lubricated and made possible by the mechanism of the gold standard, a system operated and financed by Britain, by virtue of the strength of Sterling, and by Britain's role as the major world financier.

This system had been under pressure before 1914 through the rise of economic power in the USA and Germany, which brought with it increasing protectionism and restriction of open markets. These were minor weaknesses and before 1914 the system functioned effectively. However, the war accelerated changes that had been in train before 1914, noticeably through the spread of industrialisation and the worldwide increase in primary production. Quite predictably, too, it dismantled the multi-lateral exchange and settlement system by rupturing trade, breaking international investment flows, and forcing countries off the gold standard to protect their reserves. By the end of the war the UK had been greatly damaged, and the role of national lender had shifted to the USA. Wartime destabilisation of currencies merged with post-war reparations and indebtedness to hinder reorganisation and recovery.

These immediate problems had the effect of obscuring the underlying structural changes that the war had accelerated, changes which had fundamentally altered the old trade relationships that had underlain the pre-war system. The spread of industry had enhanced the potential for export competition for manufacturers, and the rise of economic nationalism, which protected agriculture in Europe and manufacturers in primary producing nations, weakened the old basis of exchange and dependency. The attempt to reinstate the pre-1914 multi-lateral settlement system as a framework for trade growth, partly achieved with the new gold exchange standard in 1926, dominated British and European political economy in the 1920s, and diverted attention from the underlying changes in economic power, which meant that most European countries were confronted with a need to reallocate resources away from staple export industries whose products were no longer in high demand in the changed economic environment of the 1920s. This need was not quickly recognised, and the failure to respond promptly in part explains the weak performance of world trade, and the especially weak condition of British exports between the wars. The evidence that the international economic environment had shifted adversely for Britain is set out sharply in Britain's foreign trade performance in relation to trends in world trade (Table 4.2).

The volume growth of world trade was barely 8 per cent between 1920 and 1928, and in aggregate then grew by only one per cent to the peak of the recovery boom in 1937. Britain's manufactured exports languished well behind even this modest level of trade activity. In strong contrast to the decade before the war when world trade was growing in excess of 4 per cent, the inter-war years were typified by sluggish trade; the market environment for British shipping, and hence for British shipbuilding, had weakened decisively.

*Table 4.2*  Index of world and UK exports (1913 = 100)

| Year | World exports | UK manufactured exports |
|------|---------------|-------------------------|
| 1913 | 100 | 100 |
| 1928 | 113 | 81 |
| 1937 | 114 | 82 |

Source: D.S. Landes, *The Unbound Prometheus* (Cambridge: CUP, 1969, pp. 365–6.

## Market trends and market shares

The market conditions for shipbuilding and shipping between the wars were broadly set by the injections of new tonnage into operation during the war, and in the hectic post-war replenishment boom which broke in the middle of 1920. In spite of the tonnage destroyed in war, the world fleet had added nearly 5 million tons by 1919, and absorbed more than another 14 million tons by 1923, taking it to 62.3 million tons. The optimism engendered by the post-war boom had placed 7.18 million tons of ships under construction on world slipways by 1920, coinciding with the upward rush of world freights to their peak of 599 in March 1920, (1913 = 100) before declining sharply to 234 at the end of the year. By 1923 freights had slipped further, to 109, barely above the 1913 level, indicating that shipping supply was fast out-running cargoes to be carried. By 1927 freights had dropped below the 1913 level, and with the exception of 1937, generally remained below that baseline until the outbreak of war in 1939.[15] The orgy of shipbuilding between 1919 and 1923 had driven world tonnage sharply beyond the immediate needs of a weakly expanding world trade, and ushered in a prolonged period of weak demand, excess capacity, and severe competition for new tonnage.

The pattern of response to this was not the same among the major world shipbuilders, the difference broadly reflecting the additions of tonnage to domestic flag fleets and the incidence of support and protection afforded by national governments. Over one-third of all tonnage built in the world between the wars had already been launched by 1924 (Table 4.3) and over 60 per cent by 1929. In fact Britain had launched two-thirds of her inter-war output by 1929, with a consequently weak production record in the very difficult decade of the 1930s. Conversely Belgium, Denmark, Norway, Sweden and Japan all beat world trends to build increasing shares of tonnage in these years. Britain's loss of market share accelerated sharply in the 1930s after a vigorous comeback in the 1920s, the outcome being a serious contraction, from contributing half the world tonnage between 1925 and 1929, to only one-third of output in the five years before the Second World War. The loss of position was made more serious by the fact that while world output was actually at the same level, 11.6 million tons in each of these periods, British shipbuilders were unable to hold on to their earlier share.

*Table 4.3*   Merchant tonnage launched, 1920–1939
('000 gross tons)

|  | World | UK | % UK | % abroad |
|---|---|---|---|---|
| 1920–24 | 16,567 | 6,710 | 40.5 | 59.5 |
| 1925–29 | 11,645 | 5,920 | 50.8 | 49.2 |
| 1930–34 | 6,690 | 2,760 | 41.2 | 58.7 |
| 1935–39 | 11,685 | 3,935 | 33.7 | 66.3 |
| Total, 1920–39 | 46,595 | 19,325 | 41.5 | 58.4 |

*Source*: Lloyds Register of Shipping. *Annual Summary of Merchant Ships Launched.*

Britain's declining market share and much reduced level of output, in association with the considerable extension of capacity which had taken place, meant that the industry worked at very low load factors, which increased the burden of fixed charges on the value of ships under construction. In the 1920s this was thought to add £500,000 annually to the industry's costs.[16] The pressure on costs was made even more severe by the sharp decline in ship prices from the 1920 peak. The Fairplay standard cargo ship had then cost £258,700, but by 1926 had slumped to £52,500, squeezing the margin available to the shipbuilder. Competition grew so fierce that one prominent shipbuilder lamented that 'each of the larger firms in turn, when short of work, make a plunge, taking an important contract with practically no charges, and the result of this is that the new market price on which owners appear to base estimates of what new construction will cost, is fictitiously low'.[17]

But even with prices so low, and competition so keen, the industry was losing ground to European competitors. The Furness Withy case in 1926, when that shipping line placed an order for five vessels with a German yard, revealed that the British tender, at £213,000, even without charges included, was 28 per cent above the German figure of £153,000.[18] By the end of the 1930s the differential was reported to be about 20–25 per cent comparing British prices with those of Swedish yards for the largest cargo vessels, and about 17.5 per cent above that for general cargo and tanker ships.[19]

While these price differentials were a serious and persistent problem, they do not of themselves explain Britain's loss of world market share; that was closely linked to depending heavily for orders on the British fleet. The price problem does, however, loom large in the ability of British builders to develop their export market. Before the war the sale of tonnage to overseas buyers represented between 25 and 30 per cent of the output of British yards, a market in the order of 400,000 tons per year. In the 1920s Britain's share of world ship exports slipped to 16 per cent, but by the end of the 1930s was down to just over 7 per cent of a rising market. This weakening, and then near-collapse of export sales, goes some way to explain the reduction in British construction, especially in the 1930s, but the lack of work for the shipbuilders was more directly linked to the contraction of demand for naval tonnage, and to demand from British ship owners.

The flow of naval orders to the private yards ceased with the Armistice, and cancellations quickly followed, the last 18,000 displacement tons in the pipeline being launched in 1920. In the following year the Washington Treaty for the Limitation of Naval Armament eliminated any prospect of orders for new capital ships. Where Britain had seemed to be on the verge of embarking on a construction programme to replace its ageing warships and maintain Royal Navy supremacy over other powers, the Treaty froze that position by imposing restrictions on Japan in the number of both its battleships and cruisers, and set Britain at a parity with the USA, this removing the need for extra tonnage.[20] The naval market which had provided up to 20 per cent of the industry workload before the war was wiped out overnight, presenting the great naval yards with immense problems of utilising capacity in the merchant sector alone. The naval orders that did materialise amounted to about 7 per cent of a much reduced workload for the industry. Before the war the private yards had launched 534,000 displacement tons of warships in only five years from 1909 to 1913. In the twenty years between the wars, only 580,000 tons were launched, nearly half of that concentrated in the rushed re-armament programme from 1935 to 1938. The collapse of this market, so important and so profitable to British shipbuilders before 1914, exacerbated the problems of surplus capacity and gravely weakened the competitive power of the major producers by creating for them a huge burden of overhead charges that had to be earned from a much smaller order book. On the Clyde the problem crippled the great Dalmuir yard and led swiftly to its closure, and seriously weakened Clydebank, Fairfield and Scotts. Vickers at Barrow, Camell Laird at Birkenhead, and

Armstrong Whitworth at Newcastle were similarly affected, plunging all of their yards more deeply into seeking orders in the merchant sector.

Serious as weak export performance and vanishing naval orders were, the root cause of Britain's contracting output and declining market share was the faltering flow of orders from domestic shipping lines. Before the war British yards could regularly expect the British merchant marine to deliver new orders in excess of one million tons each year, amounting to at least two-thirds of the industry order book. Between the wars this dependence on domestic demand increased to over 70 per cent, but the volume of construction was considerably reduced. The tonnage built for British ship owners in the 1920s, 9.5 million grt, was 12 per cent below the average for the decade before the war, while the poor performance of 4.6 million tons in the 1930s was only 42 per cent of the pre-war level of construction for the domestic flag fleet.

This severe contraction was a direct reflection of the altered circumstances of the British merchant marine. While other flag fleets continued to expand, British tonnage increased only modestly to 20.3 million tons in 1930, before declining steadily to 17.9 million tons in 1939, nearly half a million tons less than in 1913, this representing only 26 per cent of world tonnage compared to over 42 per cent before the war. Sturmey has linked this eclipse to changes in the structure of world trade, both in routes and in commodities, and also to shifts in the competitive strength of British shipping arising from operating costs and the types of vessels being deployed. The impact of protection, causing trade diversion from British ships to indigenous flag fleets, also operated through the growing incidence of tariffs, subsidies and quotas.[21] Had these factors not operated, or if the British merchant marine had been more competitive and maintained its pre-war level of growth, Sturmey suggests that the British flag fleet should have been five million tons larger in 1939 than it was. This represents a huge lost market for British shipbuilders, and would have increased total order books by a quarter, if these lost orders had been placed.

This performance was in striking contrast to merchant fleets and shipbuilding elsewhere. Between 1920 and 1939 non-UK flag fleets added over 19 million tons of new shipping, and foreign shipyards launched 27 million tons of a new vessels. Outside Britain, both shipping and shipbuilding remained industries of modest growth and represented opportunities for gaining new orders. The Norwegians in particular captured a larger share of the world carrying trade, especially in oil, through a notable advance in efficiency and speed in their vessels.[22] If Britain's ship owners had responded in a similar fashion it is arguable that they could have held on to a larger share of world trade, and then have maintained a higher level of orders to British shipbuilders. Equally, it is clear that the British order book could have been improved if British shipbuilders had gained greater access to the orders being placed by foreign owners. That neither British shipping nor British shipbuilders penetrated growing overseas market opportunities to any great extent underlines the significance of the decline in orders from the British flag fleet as a major factor in the contraction of Britain's share of world output in these years.

The deteriorating position of British shipbuilding was also related to structural changes in the market induced by the innovation of the motorship and the development of the tanker. The rise of the motorship transformed world shipping and world shipbuilding in the 1920s and 1930s. In 1920 the 938,000 tons of motorships in service was less than 2 per cent of tonnage afloat, but by 1939 nearly 17 million tons of motorships were in service, approximately one quarter of the world fleet tonnage. This achievement rested on a rapid growth of motorship construction in all the main shipbuilding countries, a trend in which Britain lagged behind major rivals, notably Sweden, Japan and Germany. While the sheer scale of British shipbuilding meant that its production of 5.4 million tons of motorships was well ahead of the motorship tonnage achieved by any other builder, and accounted for 32 per cent of all world motorship construction, this represented under 28 per cent of all merchant work in British yards, while foreign shipbuilders on average built 42 per cent of their tonnage in the new motorship. In some cases such as Sweden and the Netherlands, steamship construction was virtually abandoned, while in Germany in the 1930s three-quarters of output was motorship tonnage. With the exception of Germany, none of these countries had a significant shipbuilding industry before the war, and none had any substantial commitment to the technology of the marine steam engine. The operating economy of the motorship over equivalent steamship tonnage, clearly demonstrated in the 1920s, heavily influenced the purchasing preferences of ship owners in European countries, and this was dramatically reflected in the changing construction pattern of their indigenous shipbuilding industries.

The other major development in the shipping market in the 1920s and 1930s was the growing popularity of the tanker. In 1914 the world tanker fleet was only 1.48 million tons, a mere 3 per cent of the world merchant fleet. This doubled to 2.93 million tons, 5.4 per cent of the fleet by 1920, and then added another 5 million tons in the 1920s. The rate of addition diminished to 4 million tons in the 1930s, as the boom in 1920s construction was slowly absorbed, but by 1939 tankers represented 17 per cent of the world fleet, 11.6 million tons, and had been a buoyant market sector for two decades. As with the motorship, British yards produced the largest tonnage of tankers, launching over 3 million tons, or 37 per cent of the world total, which represented 18.6 per cent of the British order book. This compared with tankers comprising nearly one-quarter of the production in other shipbuilding countries, again signifying the relatively slower uptake of this type of tonnage in Britain. As a consequence Britain's share of the world tanker fleet declined from one-third to one-quarter, as nations such as Germany, Norway and Sweden took up the tanker more quickly. This outcome is difficult to comprehend, since Britain's ship owners had lost millions of tons of cargo with the decline in the coal trade, and the bulk carriage of oil must have been an obvious substitute. This was certainly the attraction for Norway, Sweden and Germany, who vigorously attacked the growing international oil market.[23]

All the main market trends of the 1920s and 1930s point to a deterioration in the market position of British shipbuilding. In terms of sheer scale and volume of output

Britain remained the premier world shipbuilder, but that market dominance was being eroded significantly, especially in the growing market areas of the motorship and the tanker, where foreign builders succeeded in capturing ever larger shares. The decline in Britain's position appears to be directly linked to the dependence on the British merchant navy for the bulk of the orders for British shipyards, a market area which stagnated between the wars. The continued reliance on this stagnant market was not an outcome of neglect, but was more a consequence of the product lines developed by the shipbuilders, and the links which they had developed with the ship owners.

## Products and production

Between 1920 and 1939 the statistics collected by the Shipbuilding Conference record production from no fewer than 164 companies, some only operating briefly and launching perhaps only one small craft. The total output of the industry in these twenty years was 6,874 ships of 19.9 million tons, ranging over twelve main categories of vessel (Table 4.4). As before the war, cargo tonnage dominated the industry with one-third of the ships and half the tonnage, but tankers had displaced colliers in the market place, and ranked third in line behind passenger vessels. These three types – cargo, passenger and tanker – comprised 90 per cent of the work of the industry in tonnage, but only half the number of ships built. Nearly half of all the passenger ships were built on the Clyde, while the North East coast launched about half the cargo tonnage and over half of all the tankers.

*Table 4.4*   UK vessel types and gross tonnage launched, 1920–1939

| Vessel type | Number | '000 tons | % of total | Average tons per vessel |
|---|---|---|---|---|
| Passenger | 598 | 4671 | 23.4 | 7,811 |
| Cargo | 2,349 | 10,093 | 50.6 | 4,296 |
| Tanker | 543 | 3,353 | 16.8 | 6,175 |
| Collier | 234 | 467 | 2.3 | 1,996 |
| Other | 3,696 | 1,382 | 6.9 | 374 |
| All vessels | 6,874 | 19,962 | 100.0 | 2,903 |

*Sources*: The Shipbuilding Conference: National Maritime Museum. Compiled from vol. II, *Merchant Shipbuilding in Great Britain and Ireland, 1920–38*, and vol. III, *1939–45*.

But even though so many companies were in operation, the output was concentrated in a relatively small number of larger firms (Table 4.5). Three giant groups, Harland & Wolff, Swan Hunter and Lithgows, each built more than one million tons, and together held over 22 per cent of UK production. The top three firms before the war had only concentrated 15 per cent of output in their hands. Another ten firms built over half a million tons and with the first group contributed over half the total tonnage. Four-fifths of all construction came from only 31 firms, leaving more than 130 smaller firms to share 20 per cent of the market.

*Table 4.5*  Rank order of UK shipbuilders
in '000 gross tons, launched, 1920–1939

|  | Builder | District | '000 tons | % UK | % exported |
|---|---|---|---|---|---|
| 1 | Harland & Wolff | Belfast/Clyde | 1,983 | 10.0 | 8.6 |
| 2 | Swan Hunter | Tyne | 1,448 | 7.3 | 43.9 |
| 3 | Lithgow | Clyde | 1,017 | 5.1 | 24.2 |
| 4 | William Gray | Hartlepool/Sunderland | 810 | 4.1 | 24.7 |
| 5 | Armstrong Whitworth | Tyne | 693 | 3.5 | 48.9 |
| 6 | Cammell Laird | Birkenhead | 657 | 3.3 | 19.1 |
| 7 | Furness Shipbuilding Co. | Tees | 629 | 3.2 | 46.9 |
| 8 | Barclay Curle | Clyde | 591 | 3.0 | 37.9 |
| 9 | Workman Clark | Belfast | 551 | 2.8 | 20.3 |
| 10 | Palmers Shipbuilding Co. | Tyne | 530 | 2.7 | 21.7 |
| 11 | Vickers Armstrong | Barrow | 523 | 2.6 | 13.5 |
| 12 | John Brown & Co. | Clyde | 522 | 2.6 | 28.7 |
| 13 | Wm Doxford & Sons | Sunderland | 507 | 2.5 | 38.1 |

Source:  Compiled from Shipbuilding Conference: Merchant Shipbuilding Statistics, vol. I, *1920–38*, and vol. III, *1939–45*. National Maritime Museum.

The regional concentration of the industry was also relatively stable between the wars, although the Clyde increased its share of total output from 31 per cent before the war to 35 per cent, while the North East slipped back modestly from 42 to 40 per cent. Belfast remained the third great area of concentration with nearly 10 per cent of the total output. Each of these districts, and the other smaller centres of shipbuilding, had their own distinctive mix of products. The Aberdeen area, for example, built very little tonnage in the three main groups, but coasters, trawlers and colliers were its specialisms. The Humber specialised similarly in smaller craft, with trawlers the main market segment, while on the Thames and in East Anglia coasters and small coastal craft took up half the output.

These product mixes also influenced the profile of marine engineering in the shipbuilding districts. The traditional reciprocating steam engine remained the favoured power plant for tramps, coasters, trawlers and small craft, and was the main installation on the Humber, in the Hartlepool yards, and on the Wear and Tees. In contrast, where liner and passenger cargo construction was the main product, the steam turbine was the favoured engine, and was the most popular unit installed on the Clyde, the Tyne and at Barrow, as well as on the Mersey and at Belfast. The new diesel engine had made its appearance in all these districts, most vigorously in Belfast and on the Clyde, but still had made little impact on building styles in the tramp and small vessel areas. These combinations of ship types and engines created specific and distinctive packages of products in the main shipbuilding areas, and set out the market segments preferred by the builders. The district specialisms were also directly linked to the customer base developed by the builders, and help to explain the dependence on the British merchant fleet for most of the order book. These patterns of dependence also underlie the declining market share and stagnation of output experienced by the industry between the wars.

## Building patterns and networks

The permutation of 33 major shipyards with the three main ship types, passenger, cargo and tanker, produced a complex structure of product markets which in general terms grouped themselves into five main market segments: full-line builders; passenger specialist; passenger cargo groups; cargo specialists; and cargo-tanker builders. Only three companies could properly be described as full-range builders, their order book normally being fairly evenly spread over the three main groups. Of these the largest and most significant was Swan Hunter & Wigham Richardson. Their scale was such that the company could and did regularly build outside these sectors, and it was also a major naval yard. No other company rivalled the spread and diversity of production of Swan Hunter & Wigham Richardson, although the sheer scale of output by Harland & Wolff gives it some claim to full-range status, even though its order book was more specialised. Two smaller companies, Caledon on the Tay, and Hawthorn Leslie on the Tyne, also built evenly across the main market sectors.

The other end of the market from these very varied builders was the pure cargo specialists, where eight companies built more than three-quarters of their tonnage; some such as Connells, Grays, Readhead, Shorts, and Henderson, built virtually no other type (Table 4.6). Related to this market area, but more diversified with a twin specialism, were nine firms combining cargo and tanker construction. Four of these, Armstrong Withworth, Palmers, Blythswood and Laings, led with tanker construction, the others with cargo-building. The two remaining market areas were the passenger and passenger/cargo sectors. Five firms built more than 60 per cent of their tonnage in the passenger class, and three, Vickers Armstrong, John Brown, and Fairfield, concentrated more than three-quarters of their construction in liners. It was no accident that these were also among the most important naval yards. The passenger/cargo groups comprised six main yards, of which Harland & Wolff was the greatest.

*Table 4.6*  Main builders by specialisation, 1920–1939

---

1. *Full line builders* (even spread in main categories)

   Swan Hunter & Wigham Richardson, Hawthorn Leslie, Caledon Shipbuilders

2. *Passenger liner specialists* ( >60% of tonnage)

   Vickers Armstrong, John Brown, Fairfield, Beardmore, Scotts

3. *Passenger cargo* ( >80% tonnage)

   Harland & Wolff, Cammell Laird, Barclay Curle, Workman Clark, Stephens, Dennys

4. *Cargo specialists* ( >75% tonnage)

   Connells Co., Wm Gray & Co., Short Bros, D. & W. Henderson, Northumberland Shipbuilding, Redhead & Sons, Doxford & Sons, J. Thompson & Sons, Burntisland Shipbuilding

5. *Cargo/tanker* ( >50% tonnage)

   Lithgow, Furness Shipbuilding, Hamilton & Co., Duncan & Co., Greenock Dockyard

   *Tanker/cargo* ( >60% tonnage)

   Armstrong Whitworth, Palmers Shipbuilding, Blythswood Shipbuilding, J. Laing & Sons

---

Source: compiled from Shipbuilding Conference. Merchant Shipbuilding Statistics, Vol. 1, 1920–38. National Maritime Museum.

These building patterns clearly influenced the scope for competition among the major shipbuilders. Each market area had its noted specialists, and most firms developed two specialisms, allowing them regularly to tender in more than one segment. A very few companies were geared up to compete and build in all the main market sectors, and in addition the great liner yards, with their large berths and specialised design departments, were capable of tendering for, and constructing, any type of tonnage. However, they were at a distinct disadvantage in competing for pure cargo tonnage, since this type of work did not fully employ their skills, plant, and fitting-out facilities. Equally, even the largest cargo specialist such as Gray, Connell, or Doxford, would generally be excluded from liner and naval work, since their yards lacked the specialised design staff, berths, and fitting-out capabilities. Moreover, in an industry dominated by custom and reputation, little credibility would have been attached to tenders from cargo builders in the liner and naval markets. The ability of companies to compete outside their selected specialisms clearly depended on the mixtures of segments cultivated, and also partly on the scale of the enterprise. Most smaller yards had little ability to move outside their chosen areas, and even the largest yards could only do so at a disadvantage.

# Builder–client networks

The scope for competition was also constrained by the development of networks of dependency that grew up between builders and ship owners, irrespective of whether those were British or foreign. The 164 companies listed by the Shipbuilding Conference as building ships in Britain between the wars delivered their vessels to more than 2,200 shipping companies,[24] yet only 69 of these shipping concerns were large-scale purchasers with more than 50,000 tons acquired between 1920 and 1939. These 69 companies took 11.2 million tons of new ships, 56 per cent of the entire output of the industry between the wars. The orders for the balance of 8.7 million tons were distributed among more than 2,150 shipping companies, whose average order in twenty years was under 4,000 gross tons. Many of these companies ordered only one ship during the whole period.

Among the major shipping lines placing orders with British builders, only 14 were not British-registered, and of these three were Dominion lines. Of the eleven foreign lines in the main group of customers, three were Norwegian, two French, two Dutch, and one each from Spain, Italy, Greece, and the USA. These eleven companies ordered over 803,000 tons of ships, about 20 per cent of all export tonnage from Britain between the wars. Since over half the total tonnage built between the wars was delivered to only 69 companies, it is clear that most of the main British shipbuilders obtained their orders from a relatively small group of shipping lines who placed work with them regularly.

The order books of the 13 largest shipbuilding companies, representing over half the output of the industry between the wars, reveals that although more than 2,200 shipping lines were in the market, the major shipbuilders filled their orders from their links with only 497 ship owners.[25] The client base varied from as few as 20 for John Brown of Clydebank, to as many as 130 for Swan Hunter & Wigham Richardson. But even when a builder had a large number of clients on his books, up to half the total tonnage built was ordered from a very small number of customers in each case, many of whom had exclusive links with a particular shipbuilder (Table 4.7). Four of the top yards had a large number of clients exclusive to themselves, building between one-quarter and one-third of their ships for these owners; these were Armstrong Whitworth, Doxford, Furness Shipbuilding Company, and Swan Hunter & Wigham Richardson. At the other extreme, three builders, John Brown, Vickers Armstrong and Workman Clark, had little dependence on exclusive owner arrangements. All were specialist liner builders, a market segment with only a small number of potential customers. Since both the customer base and producer pool were small, neither side could afford exclusive arrangements. No liner company could guarantee such a regular flow of orders as to employ a large yard fully, and no shipyard could set aside exclusive berth space for a specific owner for prolonged periods, although preferential arrangements were common.[26] Between these two groups the others occupied a middle ground, with up to 17 per cent of output being constructed for exclusive owners who formed about one-quarter of their clientele.

*Table 4.7*  Number of shipping lines on order books of main UK shipbuilders, 1920–1939

| | | *Number of clients* | *Number exclusive to builders* | *Number of clients to provide % of tonnage* | | |
|---|---|---|---|---|---|---|
| | | | | 10% | 25% | 50% |
| 1 | Harland & Wolff | 68 | 16 | 1 | 2 | 6 |
| 2 | Swan Hunter | 130 | 63 | — | 4 | 13 |
| 3 | Lithgow | 66 | 15 | — | 4 | 13 |
| 4 | Wm Gray & Co. | 48 | 15 | 1 | 2 | 5 |
| 5 | Armstrong Whitworth | 73 | 26 | 2 | 5 | 16 |
| 6 | Cammell Laird | 45 | 4 | 1 | 2 | 6 |
| 7 | Furness Shipbuilding Co. | 57 | 29 | 1 | 3 | 12 |
| 8 | Barclay Curle | 44 | 13 | 1 | 2 | 5 |
| 9 | Workman Clark | 29 | 3 | 1 | 2 | 5 |
| 10 | Palmers Shipbuilding Co.[1] | 31 | 9 | 1 | 1 | 5 |
| 11 | Vickers Armstrong | 21 | 2 | 1 | 1 | 3 |
| 12 | John Brown & Co. | 20 | 0 | 1 | 1 | 2 |
| 13 | Doxford & Sons | 52 | 23 | 1 | 4 | 13 |
| | Total builder–client contacts | 684[2] | 218 | 12 | 33 | 105 |

[1]  Palmers closed 1931.

[2]  Since many shipping lines ordered from more than one shipbuilder, these 684 client contracts emerged from the 497 shipping lines which provided half the total tonnage of these 13 companies.

*Source*: as Tables 4.3–4.6.

The common feature is that these larger yards, and the smaller companies, established their production, their mix of vessels, and their sales outlets, on the basis of a small range of regular customers. Many of these were long-standing and carefully cultivated relationships in which the satisfied customer delivered many repeat orders over the years. For instance, the Swires and the Holts regularly placed their business with Scotts of Greenock. Canadian Pacific had long-standing links with John Browns and Armstrong Whitworth, while Cunard routinely built with Swan Hunter, Armstrong Whitworth, Cammell Laird, and John Brown. Peninsular and Oriental favoured Armstrong Whitworth, Vickers and Barclay Curle, and Union Castle linked with Harland & Wolff and Armstrong Whitworth.

In some cases these arrangements were based on more formal ownership linkages, the Royal Mail Group being part of the Kyslant and Pirrie empires, delivering orders to Harland & Wolff yards at Belfast and on the Clyde. Similarly the Furness Withy group held interests in the Northumberland Shipbuilding Company, itself the controlling interest in a combine of shipyards including Doxford, Workman Clark, Fairfield and Blythswood, while Lord Inchape held a controlling interest in Stephens of Linthouse. The connection also worked the other way, with many shipbuilders having interests in shipping lines. The Dennys held controlling interest in the Irrawady Flotilla Co., Swan Hunter & Wigham Richardson owned the Hopemount Shipping Co., while Lithgow was connected with the Denholm Line and the Dornoch Shipping Company.

Similar routine linkages penetrated the export market. British shipbuilders sold ships to more than 50 different countries between the wars, in addition to those in the Empire and Dominions. Some 4.1 million tons, or 20.6 per cent of total output, was sold to foreign nationals, but three-quarters of this was delivered to only eight markets: in order of significance, Norway, France, the Netherlands, Italy, the United States, Greece, Sweden and Spain. Indeed only three of these markets took over half the export sales, Norway (29 per cent) France (15 per cent) and the Netherlands (11 per cent). Consequently, although there was a large network of potential purchasers, the main foreign market network was concentrated on only three main outlets.

Such a concentration of demand encouraged a large number of British shipyards to enter the export sector, and no fewer than 101 companies, two-thirds of the total in operation, entered the market on at least one occasion between the wars. At the lower end of penetration 17 of the companies sold less than 10 per cent of their production overseas. Another 38 builders exported between 11 and 29 per cent of their tonnage, and 21 companies sold from 30 to 49 per cent of output to foreign nationals. A much smaller number of companies exported more than half their output, 19 exporting 50–79 per cent of tonnage, while a very small group, six builders, exported in excess of 80 per cent of their output. The major shipbuilders straddled the lower half of the pattern, only Beardmore exporting more than half its output in the 1920s. A few, such as Hawthorn Leslie, and Harland & Wolff, had little or no exposure in exports, and two, John Brown and Vickers Armstrong, while they had extensive Dominion customers, had virtually no foreign shipping lines on their books. As liner and naval builders these companies found little interest in their products outside Britain and the Dominions, as most countries supplied their own naval and liner tonnage.

Most of the other major builders (Table 4.5) sold over 20 per cent of their tonnage overseas, and Armstrong Whitworth, Swan Hunter & Wigham Richardson, Furness Shipbuilders, and Smiths Dock all exported more than 40 per cent of output. Norway figured prominently in all their order books, Swan Hunter & Wigham Richardson having Hoegh Leif & Co. as a regular customer, while Armstrong Whitworth had a favoured connection with Westfal Larsen & Co. Smiths Dock and Furness Shipbuilders also had a firm Norwegian connection with Johan Rusmussen & Co.

Exports were indeed sufficiently important to the main builders for most of them to have a small group of foreign companies among their favoured list of repeat and established customers.

The market for British shipbuilders was consequently defined by the major outlet to British owners, supplemented by Dominion and Empire, Norwegian, French and Dutch owners. In all of these segments the shipbuilder followed a pattern of concentrating his sales efforts in a relatively few well-established markets, and with a core of well-established customary clients. The fundamental feature conditioning outlook and decisions of both shipbuilder and ship owner was clearly the symbiosis of British shipyards and British shipping lines. British shipbuilding and the British merchant marine had expanded in mutual interdependence, with British shipbuilders having an effective monopoly of the world's largest shipping market. Building British, and building for regular customers, inevitably led to the development of a strongly personalised connection between the chief executives of the shipbuilding and shipping companies. Marketing and sales were subsumed in these personalised links, and this dependence on relatively few builder–customer relationships meant that the preferences of a small number of regular customers effectively influenced each shipbuilder's product range. Construction was fundamentally to order from a few clients, and speculative building, while undertaken, was not common.[27]

Orders and construction were firmly rooted in this highly personalised contact network of strongly segmented markets, and it is this perspective which helps explain the general trends in production, and in changes in product and market shares. The pervading influence of builder–owner connections had the effect of making aggregate trends in the market of less significance to the shipbuilder than his expectations of whether one or more of his regular customers would be coming into the market to order new tonnage. Long experience had demonstrated that, except in the severest of depressions, shipbuilders could expect to receive orders through their client networks on a fairly regular basis. The shipbuilder's perspective on market trends and shares, and his calculation of future orders, was consequently specific, and partial, depending on customary arrangements. The general trends in supply and demand set the broad market environment, but they did not readily dominate the thinking of the individual shipbuilder.

The shipbuilder's perspective and expectations were consequently rooted in his builder–client contact network, and this had powerful implications for how the shipbuilders reacted to increasing competition, to increased capacity, and to the changes in products to motorships and tankers. The strong dependency on the British merchant marine, and the ingrained expectation that it would ultimately resume its long-established pattern of growth, induced British shipbuilders to treat foreign sales as a secondary, and for some a marginal market. In prolonged recession it also induced them to reduce British output in line with diminished demand from British owners, rather than to seek to cultivate new markets overseas. In part this reaction reflects the fact that orders for new ships were normally initiated by the ship owner seeking tenders from builders, and ship owners had their customary network, just as did the builders. The ship owners of overseas countries who extended their fleets between the wars were largely outside the customary British network, and since British shipbuilders had no developed system of seeking orders outside their customary links, foreign tenders for new tonnage did not flow routinely into British shipyards.

The dependency of UK builders on British owners, and the preferences of British shipping lines for particular tonnage types, were also significant in relation to the take-up of construction in motorships and tankers. The pre-eminence of British liner companies on the North Atlantic, and on the emigrant routes to Australasia, ensured that about one-quarter of the British order book by volume, and more by value, was concentrated in passenger liner production. Since the steam turbine was as yet unchallenged as a power source for this class of ship, this inevitably depressed the share and speed of uptake of the motorship in British order books. The fact that the major liner builders were also naval yards, where the turbine was again the main engine, reinforced the patterns of choice. Moreover, the widespread global tramp routes, and long hauls with established coaling stations, influenced British owners to persist with the reciprocating steam engine rather than switch quickly to the new diesel. Taking up the new tanker posed similar problems for the established builder–customer dependencies. As demand diminished in the naval and liner segments, the growth sector in tankers demanded both a switch to diesel engines, and the building of vessels with little fitting-out requirements. Neither choice was attractive to major builders whose expertise and investment favoured, and depended upon, expensive tonnage and the turbine. Similarly, as collier construction waned, the alternative of the tanker also confronted specialist builders with both the need to convert to a new technology, and the requirement to adjust to a much larger scale of vessel. The average collier constructed between the wars was around 2,000 gross tons, while the average tanker was in excess of 6,000 gross tons. Neither change was easily accomplished by, nor attractive to, the established collier and cargo builders. Britain's relative lag in motorship and tanker construction, and her declining share in exports and world ship production, all appear to be directly linked to these patterns of dependency, and to the power and nature of the builder–client relationships. The fact that these links were not powerful enough to prevent a loss of market share, and may even have hastened that outcome, ultimately pushed both shipbuilders and ship owners to confront the problem of cooperation, and of government support or intervention.

## Intervention

The First World War had brought about a necessary but unwelcome intervention by government in the affairs of shipbuilding and shipping. During that period there had been suggestions on two occasions that these industries should be nationalised,

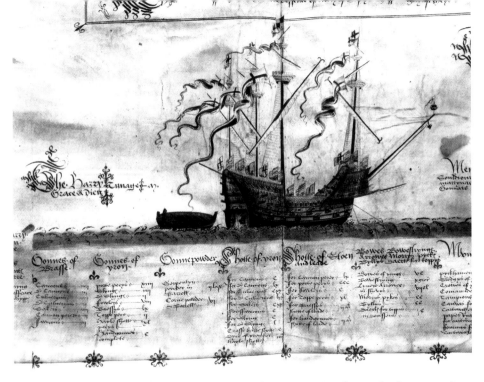

These illustrations show two of Henry VIII's great warships, commissioned soon after he came to the throne in 1509. Above, this near-contemporary illustration shows the *Great Harry* (also known as *Grace à Dieu*). This image is part of an ordnance inventory, and the ship's ordnance is listed beneath the image. The *Great Harry* was built at the Royal Dockyard at Woolwich.

Below: an artist's impression of the famous Tudor warship, the *Mary Rose*. The *Mary Rose* was built in Portsmouth but fitted out on the Thames. She was already quite an old vessel when she sank in the Solent in 1545. The remains of Henry VIII's flagship were raised in 1982.

This is a 1:48 scale model of the *Elizabeth Jonas*, *c*.1559, which was the first large English galleon to be built at the Royal Dockyard on the Thames at Deptford. The model is based on the draughts for the *Elizabeth Jonas* from papers known as 'Fragments of Ancient Shipwrightry' by Matthew Baker, collected by Samuel Pepys. Building warships of such scale and complexity was a huge undertaking in the sixteenth century, and the Royal Dockyards provided a major technological stimulus to the many crafts involved in building large wooden vessels.

A print of a herring buss, a type of fishing vessel developed from older designs by the Dutch. These were typical seventeenth-century fishing vessels and were built in huge numbers: one contemporary Dutch source claims that in the 1610s a fleet of a thousand busses would sail, with 20,000 sailors aboard. They would sail to Shetland each spring before starting to follow the shoals southward. In the early modern period, wooden vessels such as this were the mainstay of a myriad small shipyards around the North Sea coast and elsewhere.

In terms of technical sophistication, quality of equipment, and sheer scale, the Royal Dockyards were in the eighteenth century by far the most important centres of British shipbuilding. Here we see an aerial view by Joseph Farington of Chatham on the Medway in the late 1780s. The huge waterfront buildings on the right are the Anchor Wharf storehouses, with the 1,140-foot long ropery behind, within which is preserved a large proportion of the original rope-making equipment.

The Great Northern Coalfield around Newcastle was by far the largest and earliest of Europe's coalfields to develop into commercial significance. The principal market for the coal produced was London, and until the mid-nineteenth century vast quantities of coal were carried by wooden collier brigs of the type seen in this painting by Julius Caesar Ibbetson (c.1790). These vessels were strongly built, with flat bottoms to allow them to be grounded for unloading. Coal was a major stimulus of industrial development, and building colliers such as this was a major component of the North East's shipbuilding industry.

It was common practice to paint a single ship from three angles, as in this triple portrait of the East Indiaman *Royal Charlotte*, which worked in the 1760s. These armed merchantmen, many of which were actually built in India, carried goods and passengers, and were among the largest and most sophisticated commercial sailing vessels of the age. Despite their name, they were not generally owned by the East India Company, but were privately built and chartered to the company.

The Port of London was for centuries the largest and most important commercial shipping and trading centre in the British Isles, and during the age of wood and sail the Thames riverfront accommodated not only the Deptford Royal Dockyard but also a number of privately owned shipyards, drydocks and ship-repair facilities. Here the maritime artist Francis Holman depicts a typical late eighteenth-century riverfront shipyard, probably somewhere near Rotherhithe or the Isle of Dogs. The London shipbuilding industry atrophied in the nineteenth century as more and more of the industry transferred northward, to the Tyne, the Clyde, or Belfast.

© NATIONAL MARITIME MUSEUM, GREENWICH, LONDON, CAIRD COLLECTION

Perry's Blackwall shipyard on the Thames, *c.*1789. This was the largest private yard in Britain.

HMS *Victory* was launched at Chatham Dockyard in 1765 and rebuilt shortly before the Battle of Trafalgar in 1805. As can be seen by reference to the small collier near its stern, *Victory* was huge by the standards of the time: the majority of the British shipbuilding industry was concerned at this date with much more modest vessels.

A triple portrait of the brig *Studley*, a typical English merchant ship, *c*.1830.

A shipwright at work, fixing wooden pins into the hull of a late eighteenth-century vessel.

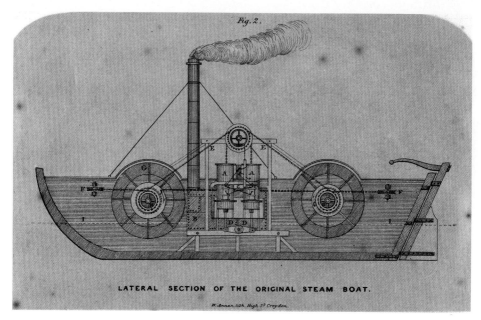

Fig. 2.

LATERAL SECTION OF THE ORIGINAL STEAM BOAT.

*W. Annan, lith. High St Croydon.*

Engraving by W. Annan of the double-hulled pleasure boat which featured the first marine steam engine. Patrick Miller, an Edinburgh banker, commissioned the mining engineer William Symington to build a steam engine to power this experimental craft by means of two paddle shafts by chains and ratchets, and propelled the steamboat on Dalswinton Loch, near Dumfries in Scotland, at five knots.

Coloured aquatint taken from Rudolph Ackermann's 'Repository of Arts' (1819), showing the *London Engineer*, a 70 horsepower paddle steamer built by Daniel Brent of Rotherhithe, with engines fitted by Maudslay, Sons & Field, at Lambeth. Built of wood, the vessel was designed for service between London and Margate. Note how much larger this vessel is than the *Comet* (opposite) of six years earlier.

Glasgow was an early centre of steamship development. Miller's demonstration of his paddle steamer in 1788 had proved the technology, and prominent among those seeking to develop the concept was the Scottish engineer Henry Bell (1767–1830). This oil painting by James Tannock shows Bell in 1826. Bell conceived the *Comet*, Europe's first passenger-carrying steamship (*below*). It was launched in 1812 and operated a regular service between Glasgow and Greenock.

Drawn by J.C.Bourne.    Published 1st July 1848.    C.F.Cheffins, Lithog.

Bell's *Comet* was a tiny craft of just 45 feet, and its engines developed only 3 or 4 horsepower. It is depicted passing Dumbarton Rock on the Clyde, 1812. Note the auxiliary sail on the tall smoke stack.

The side-lever engine for the *Comet* was built by John Robertson (1782–1868); it originally drove twin, 4-blade paddles on each side.

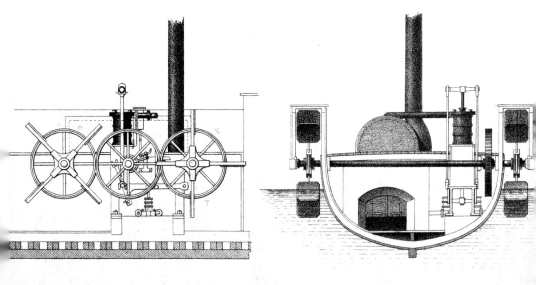

The most famous photograph (1857) of the Victorian age's most famous entrepreneur and engineer, Isambard Kingdom Brunel.

Brunel's wooden-hulled paddle steamer *Great Western* made its maiden voyage to New York in April 1838. She was built in Bristol and was the first purpose-built steamer for the lucrative Atlantic crossing.

Just a few years after the *Great Western* helped to inaugurate trans-Atlantic steam navigation, Brunel designed this, the SS *Great Britain*, a pioneering iron-hulled screw propeller liner, first introduced in 1844. At 322 feet she was 40 per cent longer than the *Great Western* and could carry almost twice as many passengers. The *Great Britain* was built in Bristol and displaced 3,675 tons.

SS *Great Eastern*, designed by Brunel and John Scott Russell for the Eastern Steam Navigation Co., was the largest vessel afloat until she was broken up in 1888. Built of iron on the riverbank at Millwall in 1853–58, this 'Leviathon' was 692 feet long, displaced 32,160 tons, and accommodated 4,000 passengers.

H.M. STEAM SLOOPS "RATTLER" AND "ALECTO" TOWING STERN TO STERN,
*for the purpose of testing the relative powers of the Screw Propeller and the Paddle Wheel*

'HM Steam Sloops *Rattler* and *Alecto* towing stern to stern': 'This Trial was made in the North Sea during a perfect Calm on the 3rd of April 1845, on which occasion the 'Rattler' towed the 'Alecto' sternforemost at the rate of Two Miles and Eight tenths p[er] hour … both Vessels exerting their full power in opposite directions.' The trial between two craft of equal power and size demonstrated the superior efficiency of the propeller.

The river Clyde was to become a major shipbuilding centre. This view of *c*.1860 shows the Govan yard of Robert Napier, 'the father of Clyde shipbuilding'.

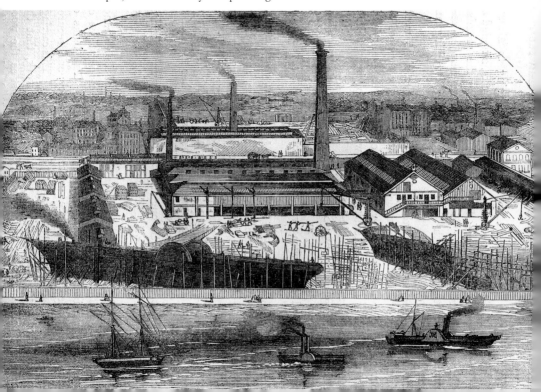

Beardmore's new yard at Dalmuir on the Clyde, 1908.

Large-scale shipbuilding , Barrow shipyard, 1890.

By the time that the artist Gerald Burn painted this depiction of launch of the *Fuji* at the Blackwall yard of the Thames Ironworks & Shipbuilding Company in March 1896, shipbuilding on the Thames was but a shadow of what it had once been, representing less than 3 per cent of iron tonnage launched in the British Isles.

Technical change: a specialised ship, HMS *Royal Sovereign*, which was converted to a turret ship in 1864.

Technical change: the SS *Glückauf*, built by Armstrong Mitchell at Wallsend on the Tyne in 1886. *Glückauf* was the first tanker into which oil could be pumped directly into the hold rather than into barrels or drums.

Technical change: MV *Jutlandia*, built by Barclay Curle in 1912, the first motorship to be built in Britain, photographed leaving the Clyde.

Technical change: Parsons' turbine-driven launch, *Turbinia*, photographed while sailing at speed in 1897. *Turbinia* was built in 1894 as an experimental craft, but her top speed of 34½ knots convincingly demonstrated the advantages of steam-turbine technology.

The Cunard Line's RMS *Mauretania* prior to launch in 1906. One of Swan Hunter & Wigham Richardson's most famous liners, and when she was launched the largest and fastest ship in the world. This vessel should not be confused with the later, 1938 *Mauretania*, which was built by Cammell Laird in Birkenhead.

Two Olympic-class liners built for the White Star Line by Harland & Wolff in Belfast: RMS *Olympic* (*left*), and the ill-fated *Titanic*. This photograph in February 1912 is the last showing both ships.

first in 1916, and again in November 1918.[28] On each occasion the proposals were rejected and, following the war, successive governments displayed little enthusiasm for involvement in the affairs of either industry. Both industries shared this lack of enthusiasm and held firmly to a philosophy of non-involvement throughout the 1920s. Richard Green, President of the Shipbuilding Employers Federation, declared that 'The Shipbuilding industry has always been opposed to State aid or interference of any kind',[29] while Sir William Currie, President of the Chamber of Shipping, made it clear that 'Hands off our shipping' should be the watchword of every government of this country, of whatever political persuasion.[30]

While intervention, or interference, was anathema to both industries, friendly support without strings attached was another matter, and the negotiation and implementation of support developed in three stages between the wars, driven by the twin problems of unemployment and foreign competition. By 1921 the problem of unemployed men and shipping had emerged quickly and dramatically, with the break of the post-war replenishment boom in 1920. Unemployment in shipbuilding, ship-repairing and marine-engineering rose abruptly from 3.8 per cent to 32.8 per cent of the workforce, nearly twice the intensity of unemployment in industry as a whole (Table 4.8), while 2.7 million tons of shipping, 14 per cent of the fleet, was laid up and out of work. At the same time, Germany formulated a reconstruction plan for rebuilding its flag fleet, France and Italy introduced aid for ship construction, as did Japan and the USA, who simultaneously reserved their coasting trade for national ships.[31]

Confronted by these developments, the sharp rise in unemployment, and the on-going problem of absorbing demobilised service men into the workforce, the government introduced its first support measure in the shape of the Trade Facilities Act of 1921. These provisions were not specific to shipbuilding or shipping, but were applicable across all industries. The initial sum set aside was £25 million, and was to be applied as a guarantee for loans for capital projects in Britain, or for the purchase of manufactured materials in Britain for use in capital projects overseas. The loans were to be raised by individual firms in the market, but guarantees providing extended repayment periods, were issued by the Board of Trade, backed by the Treasury. The provision was renewed annually until 1926, by which time £75 million had been set aside for guarantees, the period under which the support was available running to March 1927. The final sum guaranteed under the Act was £74.21 million of which £23.53 million was applied to shipping and shipbuilding companies, and a further £1.57 million to capital projects in harbour and docks facilities. In all, 31.7 per cent of the fund was obtained by shipbuilding and shipping, and a further 2.1 per cent by the harbour and dock companies. The guarantees of £23.53 million to shipping and shipbuilding provided £21.14 million directly in aid of ship construction, and provided for the building of 110 vessels of 850,000 gross tons, about 14 per cent of the tonnage launched in Britain between 1922 and 1927.

Table 4.8 Employment and unemployment in shipbuilding, ship repair and marine engineering (number of employees at July each year)

|  | Insured workforce, shipbuilding and ship repair | % unemployed | Insured workforce, marine engineering | % unemployed |
|---|---|---|---|---|
| 1920 | 338.8 | 3.7 | — | — |
| 1921 | 346.4 | 32.8 | — | — |
| 1923 | 269.9 | 43.2 | 65.5 | 22.2 |
| 1926 | 223.1 | 41.5 | 58.0 | 28.7 |
| 1929 | 204.5 | 23.0 | 58.4 | 8.9 |
| 1932 | 181.9 | 63.8 | 50.5 | 55.1 |
| 1935 | 157.2 | 42.6 | 45.6 | 26.4 |
| 1937 | 172.8 | 22.4 | 53.8 | 8.2 |
| 1939 | 176.0 | 18.6 | 59.9 | 6.6 |

Sources: Compiled from the *Ministry of Labour Gazette* and *Statistical Abstracts of the United Kingdom*.

The influence of the Acts was, however, more concentrated than this suggests. More than two-thirds of the money was provided for eight major shipping lines or groups, and Lord Kyslant's Royal Mail Group of companies attracted over 28 per cent. Nearly all the expenditure was granted to liner companies, and very little demand came from the tramp and general cargo owners. New tonnage, even with loan guarantees, was not attractive to ship owners, with at least five per cent of the flag fleet still laid up. It is also evident that nearly a quarter of the ships ordered under these provisions were motorships, where the cheaper credit available with a Trades Facilities guarantee, helped offset the initially higher costs in relation to an equivalent steamer.

The shipbuilders certainly regarded the Trade Facilities Acts as helpful instruments in maintaining orders and employment, but this view was shared by neither the government nor the ship owners at large. The ship owners broadly believed the Acts to be pernicious, encouraging the construction of tonnage that was not required, and adding to the problems of surplus tonnage. While the government had acted initially to try to support employment, it quickly came to share the ship owners' doubts. By the middle of 1923, Otto Neimeyer at the Treasury was arguing in a memorandum that 'a less suitable field to subsidise than shipbuilding can hardy be conceived. The world is overstocked with ships … [which] … are a drug in the market … the great need is to divert surplus men from shipbuilding to something else. Subsidy would do the precise opposite and encourage men to stay in an occupation in which they can never find permanent employment.'[32]

This hardening of attitude coincided with nearly half the workforce in shipbuilding being unemployed, and recognised that the problem of employment was a long-term structural issue. This view gained ground in the government, and in March 1924, after extensive discussion with Niemeyer, the Trade Facilities Advisory Committee decided to discourage all further applications for new shipping.[33] This withdrawal of support lasted for about six moths before the wisdom of withholding funds from shipping and shipbuilding began to be questioned. W.J. Sainsbury, Chairman of the Trade Facilities Advisory Committee, considered that the continued heavy unemployment threatened the survival of some yards. He noted that under the Dawes Plan, Germany would resume its competition, especially in the North Atlantic liner routes, and that loans were being raised to construct new vessels. He also believed that in the first two to three years of operation of the Acts, most benefit had gone to Northern Ireland, and British Shipbuilders had only had the support of about £7.5 million of the £13 million committed. In these circumstances the Committee believed 'that the dangers of permanent harm being done to the British shipbuilder is [sic] very serious'.[34] Hipwood, at the Board of Trade, and Niemeyer at the Treasury, both rejected this reasoning, arguing that support for shipbuilding went beyond the original minute of appointment of the committee, who were to satisfy themselves that any scheme supported would not support uneconomic trades, but would encourage general productive power and employment 'by increasing the means of production or reducing their costs, or otherwise to secure adequate benefit to the public in return for adequate assistance given'. Niemeyer argued that this object could not be achieved 'if you merely divert from Germany to England the building of a ship which is going to be built in any case. Your guarantee in that case is nothing more or less than a dole.'[35]

However, opinion was moving against retrenchment as the pressure of unemployment persisted. Lord St Davids, Chairman of the Unemployment Grants Committee, proposed that the government should cooperate with shipbuilders in financing the building of tramp steamers 'on speculation' to help maintain the trained personnel of shipyards who were otherwise likely to be dispersed.[36] Sir James Lithgow and Sir Andrew Duncan, representing the shipbuilders, also argued before the Committee on Civil Discord that there should be an extended use of Trade Facilities in granting guarantees for shipbuilding. Opinion in the Cabinet caught the immediate mood, and in December 1924 Baldwin agreed that the benefits of the Trade Facilities Act should be reopened to shipbuilding and shipping.

Guarantees were resumed on the same basis as before, but in face of mounting opposition from the ship owners. They sought to have a representative placed on the Trade Facilities Advisory Committee in an attempt to influence its decisions and to restrict the number of guarantees to shipbuilding. While they were not successful in this, the general improvement in trade between 1924 and 1927 favoured a reversal of policy on subsidy, and government declared its intention to end the Trade Facilities Act with effect from March 1927. The shipbuilders and the shipbuilding unions made a determined effort to retain the guarantee facility for shipbuilding. A joint deputation met with Baldwin and Churchill as Chancellor of the Exchequer in the House of Commons in February 1927 to make the case. They argued that in view of the continued high unemployment in shipbuilding, the Chancellor's view that the Act 'had exhausted its usefulness'[37] could hardly be applicable, and that it should be retained, even extended, for two purposes: first, to bring to British yards ships that would be built in any case, but would go elsewhere in the absence of credit guarantees; and, second, 'for building ships for special trades or routes such as ice-breakers, dredgers, trawlers, river craft, etc.'.[38] The deputation also pointed to the unfairness of the continuance of Trade Facilities Support in Northern Ireland, where the Act was used almost exclusively for the support of shipbuilding at the direction of the North of Ireland Government. The North of Ireland Government continued the measures through to 1940, by which time the Northern Ireland Guarantee Acts, 1922–38, had provided guarantees totalling £14.9 million.[39] The main beneficiary was Harland & Wolff which by a large margin was the leading yard in output in Britain between the wars.

Baldwin and Churchill received the deputation with politeness, even sympathy, but were not to be moved on the issue. The Prime Minister observed that 'most of us are opposed to Government interference on broad grounds', and that a guaranteed loan had the same effect on credit as a direct government loan issued to the public, leading directly to an increase in debt and a decrease of money available in the market. The government took the view that it was essential to reduce public expenditure and get the rate of interest down to help industry. Consequently, 'In the present financial situation of the county it is impossible to contemplate any further this scheme.' Moreover, the ship owners were 'very strongly opposed to any continuation'. He added that if Britain gave 'special facilities to a competitive industry there is no doubt that other countries will do the same'.[40] Churchill also argued that the shipbuilding industry had turned the corner, and that the position of shipbuilding had to be seen in the context of what the government had been trying to do for the nation as a whole. We had, as a nation, Churchill argued, 'been struggling back to the normal in spite of many difficulties and obstacles ... [and] ... in getting rid of the artificial support of industry through trade facilities we were taking a step to return to pre-war conditions. It is extremely important that we should do so.'[41]

With the government determined on reducing subsidy and intervention, the Trade Facilities Acts provision terminated in March 1927. For a time it appeared that the industry's fears had been misplaced, and that the government's confidence that conditions were improving had been well-founded. Between the announcement in April 1926 that the Acts would be discontinued, and mid-1929, general unemployment in Britain declined from over 14 per cent to under 10 per cent of the insured workforce, and in shipbuilding the rate diminished from the high of 41.5 per cent to 23 per cent, although that was still well over twice the national average. Tonnage under construction also doubled from the 760,000 tons in the year of the General Strike, to 1.56 million tons in 1929, while for the merchant marine, tonnage laid up contracted from 7.2 to 3.1 per cent of the fleet; the fleet itself had gained modestly in scale, by 800,000 tons to 20 million grt.

By the following year, however, the situation was deteriorating rapidly. In the aftermath of the autumn 1929 financial crisis, trade had slumped, freight rates had collapsed by one-third, and laid-up tonnage had more than doubled. Work under construction in the shipyards had dwindled from 1.56 million tons to 908,000 tons, while between 1930 and 1931 new tonnage actually commenced collapsed from 949,700 tons to a tiny 199,000. The order book had dried up, and that trend had been sharply evident from late 1929. In these changed circumstances the government received two deputations from different sides of the industry, each seeking support.

The first deputation was a large panel comprising a joint committee of the TUC General Council, the Executive of the Labour Party, and the Parliamentary Labour Party, which had formed a committee describing itself as the General Disarmament Committee, with a remit of dealing with problems arising from disarmament policy, especially those involving the displacement of labour, and unemployment. This group, headed by George Lathan MP, met with the new, now Labour Chancellor Philip Snowden on 24 July 1930.[42] The deputation wished to discuss, and ask for, a reintroduction of the Trade Facilities arrangements which, it noted, had been part of the Labour Party electoral programme in 1929, but had not been implemented since Snowden had opposed it on the grounds of subsidising inefficiency. The deputation argued that the serious loss of orders was often due to the provision of long-term credits favouring competitive nations over Britain, and that the situation was now so serious that the government had a choice of either finding money to guarantee orders and maintain work in the yards, or the less palatable option of dole money for men displaced and unemployed.[43]

Snowden was sympathetic but unhelpful. He paralleled Churchill's comments to earlier deputations, asking, 'what is the use of going on building new ships' when large tonnages were laid up and trade was at a low ebb. The deputation also suggested linking improved credit to a scheme for scrapping old tonnage, a proposal they believed to be already under discussion in the Board of Trade. Snowden was no less discouraging on this issue, indicating that some ship owners advocated selling old tonnage to rivals to encumber them with inefficient ships, rather than scrapping them. Moreover, he declared, all responses he had received from shipping interests indicated that no one in the industry wanted a scrapping scheme.[44] He made it clear that, in general terms, the government remained opposed to subsidy. He did, however, hold out some sugar to the disappointed delegation, intimating in confidence that Cunard's approach to government – for assistance in implementing its plans to build two great new liners to revolutionise services on the North Atlantic, and see off French and German competition – would not go unanswered. Since that implied that Cunard would be able to proceed with its plan, and sustain some employment, the hint of assistance was warmly received and approved. The outcome of even that degree of assistance was not immediate, since the Cunard request was caught up in merger discussions with the White Star Line, the terms of which would have materially affected the support required. The merger discussions foundered, and by the end of the year the government had agreed to cover any part of the marine risks insurance which Cunard could not place on the market.[45]

The other approach for assistance came from the Shipbuilding Employers Federation, who suggested a meeting with the Prime Minister, but were received by A.V. Alexander, First Lord of the Admiralty, on his behalf. The shipbuilders' deputation was led by their president, Amos Ayre, and met in the Admiralty on 8 December 1930. The seriousness of the situation was signposted by Ayre in his opening remarks when he said 'it was unique for his Federation to be approaching a Government Department for assistance as they had always preferred to work out their own salvation'.[46] The situation now, however, was so grave that they believed it their duty to set out the circumstances before the government and to 'ask for some steps to be taken by the Government to mitigate the position'. The shipbuilders believed that the already serious unemployment situation would become so much worse in 1931, 'that they felt justified in asking for acceleration of Government warship work'. With unemployment likely to affect one man in two in the industry in 1931, and with a complete absence of mercantile orders, since work in that side of the industry was extremely sensitive to trade cycles, Ayre and his group argued that 'it was a desirable principle that there should be an attempt on the part of the government to go as far as possible in an endeavour to flatten out the troughs in the trade cycle by a larger concentration of [naval] work in that period'.[47] The shipbuilders pressed the government to expedite the orders announced in the 1930 programme, and that as much as possible of the cycle of work be concentrated in 1931. The shipbuilders also reviewed all the possible objections to their proposal and sought to demonstrate that their needs could be met without breaching the terms of the London Naval Treaty of July 1930, or budgetary constraints, or the Admiralty's dislike for building blocks of vessels to one design when technical changes could be incorporated over a period of years, if the vessels were spread out in a sequence.

The detailed review of likely objections suggests the shipbuilders knew their appeal would be rejected, but that a case had to be made. In response the First Lord of the Admiralty confirmed that any departure from the advised and agreed programme of work under the London Naval Treaty would be regarded with grave suspicion and would prejudice future negotiations with France and Italy. Moreover, 'there was a large body of opinion in the House, which he thought had a solid backing in the country, who were opposed even to the extent to which the Government had gone in committing themselves to building'. The First Lord also added that any move to accelerate spending on the warship programme 'would be overwhelmed by public as well as House of Commons criticism to the effect that there were far better ways of spending money than on warship building'.[48]

Opposition to any increase in public expenditure, especially in the form of a subsidy to industry, combined with heroic attempts to maintain the balanced budget, meant that neither approach to the government for shipbuilding support was successful. Consequently, in 1931 unemployment reached 57 per cent of the workforce by June, and over 60 per cent by the end of the year. Even with the Fairplay price for a new 7,500 ton deadweight cargo steamer down to £37,500 from £48,750 in 1930, the industry could find little work, and by 1932 only 72,000 tons of ship construction was commenced in the entire industry.

The development of this calamity was signposted dramatically by the progress of Cunard's new express liner, Ship No. 534, being constructed at Clydebank. When John Browns finally received the contract for the liner in December 1930 the Clydebank yard had been without work for three months and all eight berths lay empty. The advance payment to Browns of £250,000, received on Boxing Day, prevented the Clydebank overdraft rising to £300,000, which would have been £100,000 above the usual limit.[49] The contract promised work for three to four years, and appeared to represent the stability all companies in the industry were seeking. Yet within 12 months, on 12 December 1931, all work on No. 534 had ceased. Sir Percy Bates, Cunard's chairman, informed Clydebank that 'the Discount Market is out of action and the Banks will not take its place. Neither the government nor the Bank of England will come to Cunard's aid.'[50] Clydebank had an average weekly employment of 3,554 men in 1931; by 1932 only 422 were employed on general yard maintenance.

Bates's explanation of the suspension of the work on No. 534 was that because of world trading conditions Cunard had been unable to earn sufficient income to enable it to cover annual depreciation on its existing ships. Since it was normal to finance new ships by raising bills on the market, discounting them to provide instalment payments to the builder, and then providing for repayment out of earnings set aside as depreciation, the failure to earn sufficient profit to continue this arrangement required Cunard to suspend work and payments on 534. This was undoubtedly the proximate cause of the suspension, but behind it lay the long-drawn-out negotiations by Cunard to acquire White Star, and to draw the government into helping pay for both the merger and the construction of the new liner. Bates had been seeking to involve the government in both directions since 1930 and was not above using the possible suspension of 534 as a lever. Within the Board of Trade and Treasury it was recognised that suspension of such a prestige project 'would be a serious shock to confidence here and abroad'.[51] Even so, the Governor of the Bank of England took the view that he could not press the banks to tie up money in Cunard in the present financial climate. Bates's view was that if the banks would not provide the necessary accommodation he was not prepared to lock up his own liquid resources; he had plans for these in the acquisition of White Star. On this, the government view was that, 'the recent attitude of Sir Percy Bates in regard to White Star can only be described as outrageous'. He was holding off any serious discussion in his belief 'that the White

Star Line would shortly fall into his hands at bankrupt prices, an event which is not going to be allowed to occur'.[52]

The government was determined that Bates would not have his way, not only because other ship owners such as Sir John Ellerman complained to Ramsay MacDonald regarding the iniquity of using funds supplied by taxation by one ship owner to assist another shipping line to compete against it, but because the government itself had a considerable financial stake in the Oceanic Navigation Company, the operating company of the White Star Line. Under the Trade Facilities Acts guarantees given to the Royal Mail Group in the 1920s, the Treasury, and the Northern Ireland Government held roughly a half interest in the Oceanic Steam Navigation Company, and both governments had a financial interest in the White Star Line approaching £3 million.[53] With the crash of the Royal Mail Group the government was not prepared to write off Trade Facilities loans, or provide further aid to Cunard, as the price for maintaining employment at Clydebank. As a consequence, the disagreement and manoeuvring continued, and the unfinished Hull of 534, the future *Queen Mary*, loomed over a silent Clydebank yard for 28 months, before work was resumed on 3 April 1934. The distaste for intervention and subsidy, sharpened by the battle of wills with Bates at Cunard, combined with the commitment to a very limited programme of naval construction under the London Naval Treaty, effectively withheld aid from government to shipbuilding, even in the crisis year of 1932 when unemployment climbed to a peak of 64.2 per cent in August. By then the employed workforce was down to 88,454 men, with 144,006 registered as out of work.

The plight of shipbuilding remained severe through 1932 and 1933, and the attitude of government to providing support only began to shift significantly in the wake of the abandonment of *laissez faire*. This involved the passing of the Import Duties Act, and the establishment of the Import Duties Advisory Committee in February 1932. Shipbuilding then gained some modest protection in that all materials imported for use in a registered shipyard were free of the basic 10 per cent *ad valorem* duty.[54] Continued attempts to persuade other countries to support a removal or reduction to barriers to trade demonstrably foundered by January 1933, when they were rejected by the World Monetary and Economic Conference in London. Thereafter, pressure mounted from ship owners, and shipbuilders alike, for assistance. By the end of the year the long-term saga of the on-off merger of Cunard and White Star had been resolved, and the terms of agreement between Cunard, White Star and the government were published on 18 December 1933. The government agreed to provide up to £3 million to complete 534, together with a further £1.5 million as working capital for the Merger Company. Provision was also made for a further £5 million toward the cost of construction of the second, sister ship. The North Atlantic Shipping Act introducing these arrangements was passed on 28 March 1934, and work recommenced at Clydebank on 30 April.

The merger agreement was critical to providing support for the resumption of work, and indicated how seriously government took the threat of foreign competition on the North Atlantic. But intervening to respond to competition on the Atlantic liner routes only added to pressure elsewhere, and in November 1933 the Tramp Shipping Committee of the Chamber of Shipping was approaching the government to provide temporary subsidies to tramp shipping to try to offset the competitive advantage foreign owners were alleged to enjoy due to subsidies, lower wage costs, and more sharply depreciated currencies.[55] A series of questions, discussions and debates on the matter occupied the House of Commons in the first half of 1934. The outcome was an unprecedented agreement by the Board of Trade to provide a one-year temporary subsidy of £2 million to offset foreign cost advantages, during which time the industry was required to draw up a scheme to ensure that the aid would be employed effectively in creating employment of British tonnage and seamen. Moreover, in order to act swiftly and try to adjust the supply of tonnage to help raise freight rates, the President of the Board of Trade advised that the government intended to provide Treasury loans in support of a scrapping and building scheme which would apply to all tramp tonnage, and to some categories of cargo liners.[56]

The industry responded swiftly with specific proposals which formed the basis of the British Shipping (Assistance) Bill which received Royal Assent on 26 February 1935. Part I of the Act made available a subsidy of £2 million in support of tramp voyages during 1935. The £2 million was held to represent the sum by which tramp earnings in 1934 had fallen below the level necessary to sustain depreciation at 5 per cent,[57] and was specifically intended to assist British owners to 'compete with foreign shipping in receipt of subsidies from foreign governments'.[58] The subsidy was to be reduced if the average level of freight rates rose above 92 per cent of the average level for 1929, and would cease if average freights rose above the level of 1929.[59] A Tramp Shipping Subsidy Committee was established to advise the Board of Trade on the operation of the scheme, and a Tramp Shipping Administrative Committee was also set up to promote the aims of minimising domestic shipping competition, and maximising the employment of British tonnage.[60]

Part II of the 1935 Act provided for Treasury loans of up to £10 million over two years, and repayable over 12 years at interest not to exceed 3 per cent. The aid was for British owners to build new vessels or modernise old tonnage. The proviso was that two tons of old tonnage had to be scrapped for each new ton constructed; the ratio was one to one for every ton to be modernised. The loans were to be in favour of the Treasury. Large passenger vessels, tankers and most refrigerated vessel tonnage were excluded from the Act whose focus was the tramp and general cargo fleet. Scrapping had to be carried out in Britain.

Under Part I of the Act, 378 shipping companies received subsidies to offset foreign competition during 1935. With £76,780 the Bank Line was the largest recipient. During 1936 the full sum of £2 million was again allocated, on this occasion across 426 shipping companies, the level of subsidy falling generally between £1,000 and £5,000. The application of the subsidy coincided with a general recovery of trade and freights, and UK tonnage laid up declined from 1.7 million tons at the end of 1934 to only 758,000 tons in 1936, and an insignificant 97,000 tons in 1937. By then freight rates had risen above the 1929 limit, the scheme was not utilised, and was indeed discontinued in 1938. This improved situation had partly been engineered by international cooperation through the International Shipping Conference which had achieved the introduction of agreed minimum freights in 1935 on Australian routes, and on trade to the St Lawrence, and the River Plate.[61]

This sharp turnaround of fortunes in tramp shipping had unfortunate repercussions for shipbuilding, for it meant that few ship owners were willing to scrap tonnage under the provisions of Part II of the Act. While £10 million was available for this purpose, only £3.5 million was taken up for new tonnage, and no use was made of the modernisation procedures. The Ships Replacement Committee received only 97 applications for scrapping, the total tonnage being 386,625 tons gross. The intention was that all such tonnage should be scrapped in Britain, but since scrap prices were higher abroad, the committee conceded sales of redundant tonnage for scrapping overseas. Consequently the committee's report of 1937 indicated that of 94 ships already scrapped, 55 had been broken up in Britain and 39 overseas.

Under the terms of the Scrap and Build Scheme, 50 new ships were built to replace old tonnage. Of these 27 were steamers and 23 motorships. Most of these ships, 34 of 145,000 tons, were built in the North East coast area, the home of the cargo ship. Scotland received orders for only nine small ships totalling 39,000 tons. Such a contribution to the recovery of the order books of British shipyards was generally held to be insignificant, and the scheme a failure. Tonnage commenced in British shipyards increased from 628,000 tons in 1935 to 1.08 million in 1936, and 1.06 million tons in 1937. The new tonnage commenced under the scheme was only 186,000 gross tons, which compares with the 85,000 tons of Cunard's second subsidised ship commenced at Clydebank in 1937 under the terms of the North Atlantic (Shipping) Act.

Even with these elements of intervention, the recovery in work was short-lived. The briefly buoyant freights of 1937 collapsed again in 1938, and new orders commenced in British yards plummeted to half the 1937 level, barely 505,000 tons. The short-term state assistance had been absorbed by both shipbuilding and shipping with little visible long-term effect. In effect the shipbuilding industry had to put its own house in order by other means. That involved unprecedented cooperation and the tackling of the problem of unused construction capacity through a scheme of rationalisation.

## Cooperation and rationalisation

The problems of weak demand and unused capacity dominated the thinking of British shipbuilders between the wars. The wartime increase in capacity had added 211 berths and 1.235 million tons of construction capability to the industry, lifting its theoretical annual capacity to 4.286 million tons. During the 1920s the regular surveys conducted by the Shipbuilding Employers Federation revealed that more than half the berths were regularly unoccupied, placing great strain on the industry. As a consequence 36 firms closed down between 1920 and 1930, eliminating 201 berths with a capacity of 379,500 tons. These were small companies unable to stand the strain from reserves, but their elimination left the capacity problem largely untouched.[62] The pressure was equally intense for the largest yards, especially since naval orders from the Admiralty had effectively vanished, and it was these yards who first edged, tentatively, toward cooperation. A preliminary meeting in 1925 proposed a three-year rota dealing with cruisers, but was not immediately accepted. Not until November 1926 was agreement reached to devise a rota covering one complete round of Admiralty orders, and this was activated a year later, beginning with a pooling arrangement for destroyers.[63] In fact, work was so scarce that the first rota did not actually achieve its objectives of sharing out orders to all members of the working group until 1934.

The involvement of the largest builders in a warship rota soon spread to discussion of cooperation in the hard-pressed merchant sector. Representatives of the main districts met in London in April 1927 to discuss the problem of prices for new contracts, and decided 'that shipbuilders should get closer together, in their common interests'.[64] An eight-member committee, consisting of three from each of the North East and Scotland, and two from the South of England and the West coasts were requested to review the matter and to 'formulate rules and regulations' which might form a basis for cooperation and mutual protection. Initial proposals for a tendering scheme to enable builders to recoup some expenditure on bidding for contracts did not gain full support, but by February 1928 the committee was asked to formulate a new scheme, a 'Shipbuilders Conference' to provide a protection scheme for builders against unfair conditions written into contracts by ship owners, brokers, or consultants; to negotiate with steelmakers for more reasonable prices; and to coordinate meetings with shipbuilding firms invited to tender by a ship owner who had normally placed orders with a specific builder.[65]

The committee reported progress to a general meeting of interested builders on 19 April 1928 at which the proposed rules and regulations, with minor amendments, were adopted unanimously. An executive committee of six, under the chairmanship of A.J. Campbell was elected, and the new body, the Shipbuilding Conference, was formed, initially with 27 member firms; the controller was John Barr. By 1930 membership was 51 firms controlling 60 establishments and 90 per cent of the output of the industry.[66] Membership was complete for builders of passenger vessels, tankers and warships, but diminished to 87 per cent for cargo builders and 60 per cent for small craft builders, in terms of output. The objectives were clear: to act on capacity to bring it into line with demand; to influence prices to obtain better returns on contracts in a buyers' market; to attempt to regulate competition to prevent builders taking contracts at a loss and thereby force down prices for all firms.

The new Shipbuilding Conference moved first on the problem of redundant berths, considering the issue on 21 November 1928. At that time the Shipbuilding Employers

Federation data showed 56 per cent of all berths idle. The principles of a scheme were drafted within three months and approved by the general meeting in March 1929. The purpose was to purchase redundant yards, sterilise them for all shipbuilding operations present and future, and to form a fund for the purpose by adding to tenders 'a sum calculated on an approved formula'.[67] Approaches were to be made to builders outside the Conference to seek their approval, and to encourage them to cooperate and join the Conference. Further details were left to the work of a special sub-committee approved by the AGM in July 1929, comprising Sir James Lithgow, Sir Alexander M. Kennedy, T.E. Thirlaway and A.L. Ayre.

The main problem was funding such a scheme in advance of monies flowing in from levies on contracts, and the Conference immediately opened a line of enquiry to the Bank of England. On 11 March 1929, immediately after the scheme had been approved in principle, the Conference had Sir Andrew Duncan write to the Governor of the Bank of England, Montagu Norman, on its behalf. Duncan had been the President of the Shipbuilding Employers Federation from 1920 to 1927, and had just been elected a director of the Court of the Bank of England, where he also acted as industrial advisor to the governor. Duncan advised Norman that the industry was proposing to organise a fund 'which could be used for this purpose of eliminating surplus berths. In order that the arrangements should work, banking facilities would need to be available to allow action to be taken even ahead of the fund itself being accumulated. I have been in close touch with the position and wanted to be sure whether the matter interested you before those guiding it raised it in any other quarter.'[68]

The governor was indeed interested, having the promotion of rationalisation schemes much in his mind, since so much of the banking system was heavily committed to the floundering staple industries. Six weeks later he, the deputy governor and the chief cashier, met Lithgow, Thirlaway, A.J. Campbell and the Conference controller John Barr, who outlined their proposals. They asked if Norman could assist in providing the planned holding company with capital, estimated to be in the order of £2 million. This, they stressed, would only be a first step in reducing capacity, and would be a preliminary 'to various schemes of amalgamation which it was hoped would put the industry on its feet'.[69]

Norman indicated that in principle the Bank favoured rationalisation, which he thought was proceeding much too slowly, and that he was prepared to assist provided that any capital 'should be on the basis of a business proposition'. The bank was not prepared to hold property as security. The scheme, moreover, would have to be approved by Whitehall, by which he meant that the scheme 'should not in fact eliminate healthy competition by the formation of ... one vast combine or trust'. As far as competition was concerned, Thirlaway assured the governor that, 'the worst competition they found had not come from abroad, but from uneconomic concerns which were being financed by the Banks', and the industry would appreciate it if he could use his influence to prevent any further bolstering up of such concerns. The governor, however, advised that the industry had to look to itself rather than to the banks to resolve the matter.

While declining to put pressure on the banks in their lending schemes it was clear that Thirlaway had a point. By the end of June the governor had collected information to the effect that 'of the 100 yards in the country which would be involved in the levy scheme, 30 are in five hands, and 40 in the hands of bankers'.[70] At the same time Norman received advice from J. Frater Taylor that 'there is not the slightest reason why the shipbuilding industry cannot be put on its feet if there is a live force behind the effort. … I strongly advise you to keep pounding at Lithgow.'[71] Lithgow was indeed emerging as the key negotiator within the industry. He made good initial progress save in the Sunderland district which remained aloof. This resistance was not easily overcome and only began to weaken in October 1929. By then the governor had made it clear that the Bank of England could not provide money in the form of a long-term advance, but was still prepared to help the industry get the £2 million it required.[72] The protracted negotiation on the funding of the scheme was in part due to the parallel developments within the Bank of England, as the governor and his advisers discussed the establishment of two agencies to promote and coordinate rationalisation schemes, namely Securities Management Trust (SMT) and the Bankers Industrial Development Company (BIDC).

While discussions with the bank progressed slowly, the shipbuilders incorporated their rationalisation company, National Shipbuilders Security Ltd (NSS) on 27 February 1930, which a capital of £100,000 in £1 shares 'for the purpose of purchasing redundant and obsolete shipyards, the dismantling and disposal of their contents, and the resale of the sites under restriction against further use for shipbuilding'.[73] Representatives of companies proposing to subscribe met in March and elected a board of ten members, leaving five vacancies to be filled by representatives of 'small builders' if they should join the scheme, together with representatives of the bank. At the first board meeting in April 1930, Sir James Lithgow was unanimously appointed Chairman.[74]

By June 1930 the NSS valuer, John Barr, had received written offers of sale for eight yards and verbal offers on another three. The board had also committed itself to purchase a 'northern establishment', Beardmore on the Clyde, for £200,000. In advance of any subscriptions or levies, the money was to be borrowed from the Bank of England against individual guarantees from member companies. Since the Bank of England had already provided £750,000 to Beardmore, held on its behalf by SMT in Debenture Stock, the prospect of a quick sale and recouping substantial funds for a concern with a scrap value of only £30,000, was clearly appealing.[75] E.H.D. Skinner, Montagu Norman's secretary noted that, 'Nothing like these terms would have been obtained for Beardmore's had it not been for the interest the Governor had taken in the Shipbuilding Scheme; this is one way in which Lithgow has shown his gratitude.'[76] The deal was concluded in November 1930, while the terms of the bank support, and the deeds of covenant to be signed by member companies were still being clarified.

On the terms finally agreed, the deeds of covenant required those signing to undertake 'for a period of ten years not to lay out or build new berths or new yards or to purchase or lease any yards not at present in operation'.[77] Members also agreed to pay a levy of one per cent of the contract or sale price of all vessels commenced after 1 November 1930.[78] The share capital of £1 million was finally offered for subscription as 5 per cent first mortgage debenture stock through the Bankers Industrial Development Company in January 1931. The prospectus named 46 companies as having signed deeds of covenant committing themselves to pay the one per cent levy, which on the basis of the contract or sale price of vessels completed by them between 1924 and 1930, would have delivered an annual levy of £293,100, a sum nearly five time larger than the £66,205 required each year for interest and the sinking fund. The Bank of England was satisfied that on these terms their loan 'is about as attractive as anything one can buy, while at the same time not preventing the company from being cleared up inside of 12 years'.[79]

By the time the loan was floated NSS had already purchased four yards (Table 4.9) and established an East Coast and a West Coast sales committee to expedite negotiations for yard purchase.[80] The NSS valuer, John Barr, had established that the industry had 144 berths suitable for liner and warship construction and 663 appropriate for cargo vessels. The outline intention was to cut capacity by one-third in each category: nominally some 50 liner and 120 cargo berths to be eliminated. Barr's basis of valuation was to take 'the pre-war cost of Establishments less ordinary depreciation for the age and condition of the assets'.[81] This valued the industry at £21 million; the purchase of one-third of the assets suggested a price of £7 million, but at Barr's suggestion NSS approved the formula for purchasing redundant yards to be that 'the price … should not exceed one half of their pre-war cost, less ordinary depreciation for age and condition, and making allowance for uneconomic features'. This gave an outline ceiling figure of £3.5 million, which adjusted for estimated scrap and sale value of assets indicated NSS would need to make an outlay of around £3 million to acquire one-third of the industry assets.

*Table 4.9*   National Shipbuilders Security Ltd; capacity sterilised, 1930–1939

| Year to end March | Yard | Location | Berths | Capacity, '000 gross tons | Purchase price (£) |
|---|---|---|---|---|---|
| 1931 | Beardmore | Clyde | 13 | 100 | |
| | Napier & Miller | Clyde | 5 | 40 | |
| | Ardrossan Dockyard (South Yard) | Clyde | 5 | 30 | |
| | John Chambers | Lowestoft | 4 | 4 | |
| | | | 27 | 174 | £302,520 |

| Year | Company | Location | | |
|---|---|---|---|---|
| 1932 | Charles Renoldson | Tyne | 4 | 6 |
| | Smiths Dock Co. | Tees | 4 | 45 |
| | Craig Taylor & Co. | Tees | 4 | 35 |
| | Renwick & Dalgliesh | Tyne | 4 | 45 |
| | Whitby SB Co. | Whitby | 8 | 5 |
| | Northumberland SB Co. (1927) | Tyne | 7 | 65 |
| | Cleveland Dockyard Co. | Tees | 7 | 40 |
| | Barclay Curle & Co. (West Yard) | Clyde | 5 | 50 |
| | Osbourne Graham & Co | Wear | 4 | 15 |
| | Arch. McMillan & Son | Clyde | 3 | 35 |
| | | | 53 | 366 | £310,660 |
| 1933 | Bow McLachlan | Clyde | 5 | 8 |
| | Earles SB Eng Co. | Hull | 4 | 30 |
| | Dunlop Bremner & Co. | Clyde | 4 | 25 |
| | | | 13 | 63 | £114,590 |
| 1934 | Ayrshire Dockyard Co. | Clyde | 6 | 45 |
| | Swan Hunter & Wigham Richardson, Southwick Yard | Wear | 4 | 30 |
| | Fairfield S & E Co. | Clyde | 4 | 40 |
| | | | 14 | 115 | £83,850 |
| 1935 | Palmers: Jarrow | Tyne | 8 | 75 |
| | Palmers: Hebburn | Tyne | 6 | 50 |
| | Palmers: Amble | Amble | 4 | 6 |
| | Sir N.G. Armstrong Whitworth: Walker | Tyne | 6 | 55 |
| | Dobson | Tyne | 3 | 35 |
| | Tyne Iron | Tyne | 3 | 25 |
| | Beardmore Engine Works | Clyde | — | — |
| | | | 30 | 246 | £710,460 |
| 1936 | Workman Clark & Co. (1928) | Belfast | 7 | 100 |
| | D. & W. Henderson & Co. | Clyde | 5 | 50 |
| | Caird & Co. | Clyde | 5 | 65 |
| | J. Crighton & Co.: Saltney& Connah's Quay | Chester | 26 | 6 |
| | | | 43 | 221 | £496,950 |

| Year | Company | Location | Berths | Tons | Value |
|---|---|---|---|---|---|
| 1937 | London & Montrose SB Co. | Montrose | 5 | 3.5 | |
| | Wm Gray & Co., Egis Yard | Tees | 4 | 40 | |
| | Graythorp Yard | Tees | 4 | 70 | |
| | Wivenhoe Shipyard | Wivenhoe | 3 | 3 | |
| | | | 11 | 116.5 | £108,980 |
| 1938 | Fairfield (S & E) Chepstow | Severn | 9 | 40 | |
| | Irvines S & E Co. | W. Hartlepool | 3 | 35 | |
| 1939 | Wood Skinner & Co. | Tyne | 8 | 35 | |
| | | | 20 | 110 | £81,400 |
| | Total (38 yards) | | 216 | 1,411.50 | £2,209,000 |

*Sources*: Data compiled from NSS Minutes and Files, National Maritime Museum, plus Bank of England Archives, SMT2/280, File 142/4.

The acquisition of redundant yards proceeded with remarkable speed; 38 yards were involved, most of them acquired by 1935. Some 216 berths were acquired, eliminating 1,411,500 tons of capacity, 35 per cent of the total in existence in 1930. The gross expenditure including fees and maintenance charges was £2,407,148. Against this was set revenue from sales of £918,230, income from the levies of £1,783,623, and income from investments of £55,185, a total of £2,757,038.[82] NSS had liquidated one-third of the capacity of the industry, made a profit, and was able to redeem the debenture issue in 1939, converting NSS into a private company wholly owned by the industry. In financial terms the self-pruning scheme had been a remarkable success.

The effect on the industry as a whole, however, is less easy to judge. The policy was self-designed and implemented, and consequently had to be even-handed among the different districts. Also, to be really effective, entire establishments had to be closed. In the first three years the Clyde and the North East shared the pain, 40 berths of 288,000 tons closing on the Clyde, 45 berths on the North East of 311,000 tons, comprising yards from Hull to Whitby (Table 4.9). However, by the end of 1932, the view within NSS was that if outstanding cargo offers were accepted, target rationalisation would practically be completed in the cargo sector, but warship and passenger capacity had yet to meet its target.[83] Moreover, it was also argued that 'rationalisation had, so far, only been carried out on the Clyde and Northeast Coast districts, and that if the West of England and Ireland did not come into line, further progress in those districts would be impeded'.[84]

The warship and passenger liner problem was the more pressing, and the board resolved to invite directors of warship and liner builders to meet with them to discuss surplus capacity.[85] A meeting with 18 representatives, five of whom were NSS directors, drawn from 12 firms, was held a month later. The outcome was an agreement to vary the standard purchasing practice of NSS. If it were not possible to acquire a whole establishment, Barr as valuer was empowered to negotiate in terms of either acquiring the shipbuilding rights of the site, or failing this to purchase groups of berths, or even a single berth.[86] The preference, however, remained the purchase of entire establishments. In the immediate aftermath of this meeting, Palmers' yards at Hebburn, Jarrow and Amble, became the object of negotiations between NSS and the liquidator, and Fairfields' West Yard also came up for consideration. Neither appeared to offer a simple purchase of a whole establishment.[87]

The Jarrow yard had been idle since 1931, and the receiver, Sir Harry Peat, was holding out for better than scrap prices; negotiations consequently were protracted. At the same time Fairfield was thrown into the picture through its own financial difficulties. By July 1932 the Bank of Scotland felt unable to extend its current overdraft facility of £280,000, and Fairfield was urgently seeking a further £200,000 to enable it to stay in operation. Norman, at the Bank of England, had been advised that Fairfield was a national asset and should not be scheduled for closure under the rationalisation scheme, Accordingly he was prepared to provide up to £200,000 on the same security as afforded to the Bank of Scotland.[88] In addition, however, Norman wanted the added security that if the company did not make good within two years, then NSS would guarantee to buy it. That was not immediately forthcoming, and in April 1933 Fairfield offered NSS its West Yard of four berths for £30,000. This was precisely the issue of a potential purchase that NSS was not anxious to enter into, but was caught up in the Fairfield funding negotiations with the Bank of England. The outcome was the first agreement to acquire part of a yard and as part of the security offered to the bank, Norman obtained Lithgows' personal annotation to the agreement indicating the possible purchase of Fairfield by NSS, 'should ultimate liquidation prove necessary'.[89] Some 40,000 tons of liner and warship capacity had been eliminated very cheaply. The large-scale capacity at Jarrow soon followed in April 1934, and with that acquisition, the backlog of liner and warship sterilisation was answered. More was soon to be added when Armstrong Whitworth & Co. offered their three yards at Walker, Dobson & Tyne Iron, to NSS for £120,000.[90] The final price was £126,985, and the NSS Board took on this purchase with a view to keeping on the large Walker Yard as a mothballed NSS company. It could be held on a 'care and maintenance basis until the Company was in a position to report purchases which would bring other districts more into line with rationalisation already affected on the Northeast coast. The threat of restoring a yard such as this could be used to make builders in other districts more likely to reduce their facilities.'[91] The Harland & Wolff yards at Greenock (Cairds) and Glasgow (D. & W. Henderson) were acquired in 1935 on the same basis, to be maintained as 'fighting units' to be operated to bring recalcitrant builders into line, and to be available as strategic units in the event of war.[92]

The outcome of such pressure was that NSS achieved its objective of district balance in the sterilisation of capacity. The Clyde, which usually built about one-third of UK tonnage, bore 35 per cent of the capacity sterilised; similarly the North East coast, which provided over half the annual tonnage, bore 52 per cent of the capacity sterilised. Only in the balance between naval and merchant capacity was there some deviation from the initial plan; 50 naval and liner berths had been targeted for closure while the final figure achieved was 41 berths of 350,000 tons capacity; the balance was made up of 175 cargo berths of 1.1 million tons.

When the sterilisation scheme was at the planning stage in 1929 and 1930 it was estimated that by closing only one yard in eight the resultant concentration of work in the other seven yards would more than offset the cost of the one per cent levy without an increase in the price of vessels built. By the end of 1938 one-third of berths and capacity had been eliminated and 64 per cent of all berths remaining were in use. NSS argued that if no berths had been eliminated, the 1938 order book would only have employed 44 per cent of capacity. The effect of the NSS sterilisation programme had consequently been to increase workload for surviving firms by about half, and that there was also a saving in cost of up to five per cent. That in itself had not closed the competitive gap between British and continental prices for new tonnage, but reckless price-cutting had been eliminated, and an improved climate of cooperation had been achieved.

The 'rationalisation' achieved by NSS was not simply in terms of reductions in physical capacity. The acquisition, sterilisation and re-sale policies of NSS also worked toward some combination and re-shaping of the shipbuilding firms in the main districts. The pool of warship builders was streamlined with the elimination of Beardmore, Palmers, part of Fairfield, and Swan Hunter & Wigham Richardson's Southwick yard. Shipbuilding in Northern Ireland had been concentrated by Harland & Wolff acquiring the Workman Clark facilities, but as a trade-off selling their Clyde yards of Cairds and D. & W. Henderson to NSS. Also on the Clyde, the Lithgow empire had been re-shaped, disposing of Dunlop Bremmer and the Adrossan Dockyard, while gaining control of the Fairfield company after the Anchor Line debacle forced its liquidation and reconstruction with the aid of the Bank of England. In the North East, while Palmers Jarrow facility was sterilised, the Hebburn facility was re-sold to Vickers for £85,000.[93] Vickers were prepared to offer £100,000 if they could keep two berths at Hebburn in addition to the Drydock, offering to close three berths at Walker in return, but NSS did not agree to the proposal.

These re-arrangements were a side-effect of the main drive to remove what NSS described as 'primary redundancy'. By 1938 it was believed that through its actions NSS had more or less equated the position of 'supply and demand ... in a practical, though not exact sense'.[94] The problem of severe cyclical fluctuation, however, remained. On this point the memorandum of association of NSS provided for the company 'to ... procure the closing ... temporarily of any works or business whether acquired by the Company or otherwise'. Consequently NSS began to consider ways of 'attaining temporary concentration' by way of offering an inducement to members to persuade them, temporarily, to close up to half their capacity. The resulting concentration of work would enable the remaining berths to operate at about half capacity even in times of severest depression.[95] Members could not reach agreement on the proposal, which was eventually dropped, but much more success was achieved with a range of other schemes directed to influence prices, competition, and sales. The Conference devised three main types of schemes to advance these ends, namely 'Tendering and Price Improvement Schemes; Subsidy Schemes, and "Segregation Schemes"'.

The problem of prices was essentially that of prices forced low in a buyers' market, the power of the ship owner being complemented by the indiscriminate price-cutting by builders desperate to obtain work. This issue was approached through the development of Price Improvement Schemes and Job Conferences, and had been the main purpose behind the creation of the Shipbuilding Conference in 1928, prior to the development of the sterilisation programme. Proposals for a trial scheme were invited from members in November 1931, and a special sub-committee was established in June 1932.[96] The outcome was agreement in March 1934 to form a Special Fund by means of compulsory contributions by members on the contract or sale price of vessels at the rate of half of one per cent. The fund was to raise up to £500,000 to be used to subsidise British builders to meet 'unfair' price competition from continental competitors. This was to assist in closing the gap between British and foreign bids, but was of limited help since no builder could apply for a sum in excess of two per cent of the contract price in normal circumstances. The Special Fund came into operation on 1 August 1934, applications being processed by a sub-committee chaired by Sir Alexander Kennedy of Fairfields. The scheme also included a small contribution, one-tenth of one per cent, to provide some reimbursement to companies invited to tender for contracts, but not gaining the orders.

This modest scheme was only one part of a much broader and more complex strategy of Price Improvement. The Conference established its 'Price Improvement Committee' in 1934,[97] which quickly produced a review and subsequent reports proposing two types of schemes of support, Scheme A and Scheme B. The first proposal set out scales to give guidance to members as minimum acceptable prices to tender for vessels based on length and deadweight. No member was to tender at less than the recommended price calculated in this way, although builders were left free to vary prices above this level in relation to variations in specification. This formula and scheme was first applied to cargo vessels in December 1936, and was subsequently extended to cover finishing vessels.[98]

By the time it was introduced the formula defined the direct and indirect outlays in production costs, to which was then added a minimum lump sum to cover establishment charges, depreciation and profit. The second scheme, B, was a more complex system to cope with the situation where builders were invited to tender for vessels for which owners stipulated complete, or near-complete, specifications with difficult technical requirements. Since estimates could vary widely in these circumstances, Scheme B provided for an averaging process among competing tenders. Companies advised their tender, confidentially, to the Conference Controller who reviewed the range of prices. The process involved raising the lowest tender price to the average, while the other tenders were adjusted upward proportionately from the new baseline to the highest tender and narrowed the range of prices among the others.

These schemes operated on the basis of Job Conferences which had formed in an informal way from 1928, and formally under the Shipbuilding Conference from 1933. Members tendering for contracts advised their invitation to tender to the Controller who then arranged a 'Job Conference' among all the builders who had been invited to tender for the same order. Voluntary agreements were then reached on minimum prices, acceptable contract conditions, and terms of payment. No builder would tender at less than the agreed minimum, the degree of solidarity being a counter-measure to ship owners attempting to load contracts with onerous conditions. Schemes for pooling and re-distributing tendering expenses were also implemented to help defray the tendering costs of unsuccessful bidders.

These job conference and price improvement schemes brought some order and cooperation into the highly fluid and competitive market for shipbuilders. A further step was to try to share out the available work in a more organised and systematic way, while minimising the scope of competition. This involved extending the familiar concept of 'rotas' of work in a more formal segregation scheme. Rotas were an effective means of allocating work by agreement and had been employed by the Warship Group since 1923. A similar rota among merchant builders bidding for Admiralty Auxiliary vessels was introduced in 1935. Developing from this the Conference had by 1936 devised a Segregation Scheme. This defined seven broad categories of vessels – small craft; dredging and harbour plant; special craft (for example, ice breakers); cargo vessels; tankers and whaling factories; passenger vessels; warship and other Admiralty vessels – which were further sub-divided to provide 73 ship categories.[99] Firms were allocated to categories where they had normally constructed vessels, and voluntarily agreed to confine their bids for orders to these categories. If any firm tendered outside permitted categories, the bid was subject to a 5 per cent addition as a handicap for attempting to gain orders in areas designated as the normal preserve of other types of companies. By 1938 some 63 companies had agreed to cooperate in the segregation scheme arrangements; this scheme, however, did not receive the formal support of all the members of the Conference and was consequently introduced on a purely voluntary basis.

The Shipbuilding Conference schemes of rationalisation, price support, job conferences, and segregation proposals were all exercises in self-help and cooperation in an industry wedded to strong independence and individualism. They were strategies aimed at reforming the supply side of the industry by controlling capacity, encouraging concentration and grouping of companies in formal and informal associations, and to modify competition and support price by collective agreement. The more difficult problem of demand was approached through deputations to the Admiralty to accelerate naval programmes, and pressure on the government to extend some form of trade facilities, and create arrangements to encourage the placing of new orders in British shipyards. The support for the 'scrap and build' scheme was consistent with the strategy of seeking support, but not intervention or interference from the government. All the schemes were aimed at putting the industry on its feet, and toward improving its longer term health and competitiveness. Under the influence of these diverse efforts the industry did slowly drag itself out of the crisis of the deep depression of 1931–33, and the shipbuilders did appear to have grounds for modest satisfaction. Largely through its own efforts the industry had survived the worst dislocation and depression in its history, albeit at a reduced scale, and by 1938 tonnage launched crept above the one million ton level for the first time since 1930. The improvement, however, was ephemeral, for by 1938 work was drying up, and only 505,096 tons of new work was commenced in British yards, compared to over one million tons on each of the two previous years. In 1939, it was only 630,000 tons, barely 25 per cent of the world total. In spite of heroic efforts of self-help, the industry was in a fragile state, and, confronted by this sharp relapse in fortune, the Shipbuilding Conference reviewed the situation and concluded that it had 'now gone beyond a stage at which it is possible for the industry to meet, by its own efforts, the ever growing competition from the continent'.[100] This was in the context of increasing national anxiety at the prospect of war reflected in a series of debates in the House of Commons on the adequacy of the merchant marine, and the sufficiency of British shipbuilding to meet an emergency. By July 1939 the government had published a White Paper proposing further subsidies for tramp operators over five years, and Board of Trade loans of up to £10 million for new tonnage without a scrapping requirement. Assistance was also to be provided for liner construction for the first time, and the government was also to seek to establish a national pool of reserve tonnage for use in emergency.[101]

The declaration of war on 3 September 1939 overtook these proposals, and the industry was swept onto a new footing, but the discarded measures had accurately reflected the pressure on the shipbuilding industry, and the deterioration in its position since 1914. A generation of intense difficulty had gnawed away at the layers of competitive advantage developed by the industry in the late nineteenth century, and left it weakened, though still the world leader. The international economic environment in terms of the number of effective competitors in shipbuilding had moved decisively against Britain, competition heightened by the effective closure of markets by protection, mainly in the USA, Germany and Japan. The network support to British shipbuilding, deriving from Britain's role as world financier and world carrier nation, had also weakened. Britain was displaced by the USA as world creditor, and, as the volume of world trade faltered, a flood of under-used shipping capacity depressed freights for the world merchant fleet, this most notably affecting the British fleet. As this monopoly market of British shipbuilders languished, the shipping and shipbuilding industries lost market shares and turned inward in a mutual, but more limited scale, of interdependence. The huge market advantage formerly delivered by the domestic fleet became, in its reduced scale, a ceiling on the perspectives and operations of British shipbuilders, encouraging retrenchment more than risk-taking.

The umbilical link of builders and ship owners in Britain also sustained the industry structure, company relationships, and supplier networks between the wars, but by standing still more than by progressive improvement and change. This constraint was notable in relation to the innovation of the motorship, and the ability of the self-teaching firms to accommodate the new development. Where before the war all the main shipbuilders with engine works had been steeped in the technology of steam, and passed it on by apprenticeships, shop-floor experience, and empirical adaptation, the familiarity with the technology of the motorship was far more limited. Eighty per cent of all motorship tonnage emanated from only 15 builders and half from only 5 builders between the wars. The foundation of technological competence and capability was much narrower with the diesel engine than it had been with all the pervasive marine steam engine, and the 'knowledge' base could not so readily be acquired on the job. The technological dominance of the marine engineering base had been weakened fundamentally, leaving the industry with one more previous layer of strength eroded. By the end of the 1930s, the international framework was less favourable for British builders; their technology leadership was diminished; two decades of slack demand had weakened the industry framework; and the dominant market position was under threat. The Second World War, consequently, impacted upon a still large industry, but one with eroding foundations.

CHAPTER FIVE

# War and recovery: 1939–1958

## The shipbuilding industry at war

The declaration of hostilities on 3 September 1939 abruptly transformed the prospects of British shipbuilding. The need to press for further government aid to stem the imminent closure of many yards evaporated, as the industry came under government control with the Restriction and Repair of Ships Order, 1939. Wartime needs quickly eliminated the problem of weak and unpredictable demand, and the long-standing burden of unused capacity and uneconomic prices rapidly receded. Full order books swiftly replaced two decades of scarce work, and the industry was launched into a twenty-year cycle which for the most part was a sellers' market, giving the shipbuilders unprecedented opportunities to reconstruct their depleted resources. The immediate price to be paid for the regeneration of activity was the loss of independence and the control by government of all aspects of the industry.

The transition to government control, and the scope of that regulation, was swifter, and greater, than had been the case in the First World War. As early as 1936 plans for the wartime control of merchant shipbuilding had been drafted by the Mercantile Marine Department of the Board of Trade, in consultation with the Admiralty and the Shipbuilding Conference.[1] As a consequence of this report a Merchant Shipbuilding Committee was established under the chairmanship of Sir Amos Ayre, chairman of the Shipbuilding Conference. He was also designated as the future director of 'Merchant Shipbuilding and Repairs', in the event of war. A 'War Scheme' for the allocation of work was also drafted, assigning yards to one of three categories: those which would be principally regarded as naval yards; those mainly to be operated as merchant yards, and, third, those which could be allocated both types of work in roughly equal measure. The plan was to control shipbuilding through a dual responsibility, the Admiralty for naval construction, and the Board of Trade for merchant tonnage.

The Reconstruction and Repair of Ships Order 1939 effectively transferred control of merchant shipbuilding to the government, and from October 1939 this was exercised through the new Ministry of Shipping.[2] Control was reinforced by the introduction of a system of licences for ship construction. The coordination of orders through Sir Amos Ayre as Director of Merchant Shipbuilding and Repair was accomplished informally until he took up his position in the new Ministry of Shipping in October 1939, but the division of control between the Ministry of Shipping and the Admiralty lasted only a few months. Pre-war plans had set a war-need target for merchant tonnage at an annual rate of 1.2 to 1.3 million gross tons,[3] but by January 1940 it was already clear that output would fall far short of that figure; merchant tonnage launched only reached 843,000 tons. The problem was not simply the physical capacity available on berths, but the competition between the Admiralty and Ministry of Shipping for materials, labour, engines, and boilers. Acutely aware of the dangers inherent in this, Churchill, as first Lord of the Admiralty, pressed the War Cabinet to bring the control of both naval and merchant construction under the Admiralty. This was accomplished on 1 February 1940, and Sir Amos Ayre's Directorate was significantly enlarged. A new position, Controller of Merchant Shipbuilding, was also created, to which Sir James Lithgow was appointed. Within the Ministry of Shipping, the Shipbuilding Division remained as a liaison unit, with the Directorate of Merchant Shipbuilding charged with advising the Admiralty on the new tonnage requirements of the numerous sections within the Ministry. Coordination with the Admiralty was also maintained through the continuation of the pre-war Merchant Shipbuilding Advisory Committee. Supervision of war needs was further refined in May 1941 by an Order in Council[4] which established the Ministry of War Transport to take over the previously separate functions of the Ministry of Shipping and the Ministry of Transport. These measures introduced an unprecedented level of control over shipbuilding, and it was later believed that the placing of all control under the Admiralty, within which the competing claims of Naval and Merchant tonnage had to be resolved, only worked effectively because of the personalities of Amos Ayre and James Lithgow, who were well able 'to contend with the weight of Navy tradition, the prestige of uniformed staff, and the efficient organisation of the Admiralty Technical Branches'.[5]

This system, so swiftly established, and effectively incorporating senior management shipbuilders within the naval establishment, worked well, and achieved a remarkable level of output (Table 5.1). Orders were placed for 1,649 ships of 7.18 million gross tons. Of these some 1,377 ships of 6.09 million tons were completed within the 70 months of war from September 1939 to June 1945.[6] This achievement, substantial as it was, represented only about half the shipbuilding output, for the demand for naval tonnage added construction of 1.7 million displacement tons, representing probably as much as 6.8 million tons of equivalent merchant construction in terms of engineering and work content. When converted in this way naval and merchant wartime construction combined totalled 12.9 million tons, giving an average of 2.2 million gross tons per year, a level not achieved even during peak performance of the industry in the First World War.

*Table 5.1*   UK wartime shipbuilding completions, 1939–1945

| | Merchant ships | | Warships | | Warship[3] × 4 tons | Total workload | |
|---|---|---|---|---|---|---|---|
| | No. | '000 grt | No. | '000 disp. ton | '000 grt | Total No. | '000 grt |
| 1939[1] | 76 | 246 | 57 | 94 | 376 | 133 | 622 |
| 1940 | 194 | 810 | 148 | 246 | 984 | 342 | 1,794 |
| 1941 | 236 | 1,158 | 236 | 236 | 1,460 | 472 | 2,616 |
| 1942 | 260 | 1,302 | 239 | 239 | 1,308 | 499 | 2,610 |
| 1943 | 236 | 1,202 | 222 | 304 | 1,216 | 458 | 2,418 |
| 1944 | 269 | 1,013 | 188 | 288 | 1,152 | 457 | 2,165 |
| 1945[2] | 106 | 361 | 58 | 81 | 324 | 164 | 685 |
| Total | 1,377 | 6,092 | 1,148 | 1,705 | 6,820 | 2,525 | 12,912 |

[1]  September–December 1939

[2]  January–June 1945

[3]  Gross register tons measure internal volume, while displacement tons measure mass (full load minus fuel section). During the First World War it was regularly assumed that one displacement ton was equivalent to 2.63 gross tons in terms of engineering and work content. With increasing complexity and sophistication of content the Shipbuilding Conference estimated one displacement ton as equivalent to 4 gross tons during the Second World War.

Sources:

[a]  Shipbuilding Conference: Statistical Summary June 1945

[b]  Statistical Digest of the War, HMSO, 1951

[c]  I.L. Buxton, *British Warship Building and Repair During World War II*, Table 1. Centre for Business History in Scotland, Research Monograph No. 2, 1984 (in his study Buxton allows a 5 gross ton equivalent for one displacement ton).

This enormous workload placed great stresses on the industry, not least in pushing private merchant tonnage off berths in favour of wartime needs for both merchant and naval tonnage. The Admiralty became the major customer. From the outbreak of war to the end of 1941, more than three-quarters of all merchant orders licensed were on behalf of the Admiralty Merchant Shipbuilding Department, and it was not until 1942 that orders for private owners were permitted to recover to about half the work licensed. Over the war years as a whole, orders for the Admiralty represented 52 per cent of all merchant tonnage placed, and 53 per cent of all completions. During the 70 months of war, merchant ship orders from the Admiralty were 52 per cent of all orders placed. When warship orders to the private yards are added, the Admiralty was the client for 1,951 of the 2,525 ships completed, over 77 per cent of the entire construction programme during the war.

This 'new work' programme was complemented, and in many ways constrained, by a huge burden of repair and conversion work. Up to two million tons of shipping could be undergoing repair at any one time at the peak of the battle for the Atlantic in 1942,[7] and in that year much labour was transferred from new work to repair and conversion as a first priority.[8] Estimates suggest that during 1942 and 1943 an average of 728,000 gross tons of merchant ships were repaired and returned to service each week. So critical was this work that it came under its own Director of Merchant Ship Repairs, Laurie Edwards of Middle Docks on the Tyne, and several repair facilities which had been closed for many years were reopened. The Jarrow Dry Dock, closed as part of the purchase of Palmers Hebburn yard by NSS Ltd in 1935, was reopened by permission of NSS in January 1941, to be put in order by Palmers, and 'to be used for urgent national purposes'.[9] In addition, three Admiralty floating docks were sent north to the Clyde, Fort William and Oban, to extend repair facilities on the west coast, as the convoys made for the western seaboard. These facilities coped with naval as well as merchant repairs, and the records demonstrate that the commercial repair yards handled 52,377 naval vessels between 1939 and 1945. While the majority of these were small craft – the larger naval vessel repaired normally being undertaken in the Royal Dockyards – some 1,959 destroyer repairs were also completed in the private yards.[10]

The undertaking of this wartime programme of new construction, conversion and repair work also transformed the employment situation in shipbuilding and marine engineering. At the end of 1938 the *Ministry of Labour Gazette* recorded an insured workforce of 175,000 in shipbuilding, ship repair and marine engineering, with an unemployment rate of 22.4 per cent. By October 1939 unemployment was reduced to 10 per cent, and was largely eliminated by 1940. The workforce averaged over 230,000, with the highest weekly employment reaching 249,115 in the week ending 9 June 1943. The overall pattern of employment as between new work and repair and conversion is shown in Table 5.2, with sixty per cent employed in new work. Within that total, about 60 per cent of the workforce on new construction was at work on naval orders. Female employment also increased substantially, from barely 4,000 in June 1939 to a peak of 41,060 in June 1944.[11]

The war effort clearly put the shipyards, engineering shops and repair establishments, back to full employment, and also gave the industry the chance to improve its finances. The total value of wartime shipbuilding output was placed at £551.1 million, while ship-repair contracts generated a sales value of £241.9 million to December 1944.[12] Warship construction represented 41.2 per cent of all work by value, while naval auxiliary craft and cargo ships for the Admiralty represented another 37.6 per cent; in effect the government supplied 78.8 per cent of the value of all work during the war years. Moreover, the priority given to war work meant that the group of warship builders dominated production. They built all warship tonnage, 26 per cent of all naval auxiliary work, and 25 per cent of all merchant work between September 1939 and December 1945. They also contributed 23 per cent of all repair work to December 1944.

*Table 5.2*   Shipbuilding and marine engineering average weekly employment, 1940–1945, in thousands[1]

| | Shipbuilding and engineering, new work | | | | Repair and conversion work | | | | Shipbuilding and engineering |
|---|---|---|---|---|---|---|---|---|---|
| | *Employment ('000)* | *% Naval* | *% Merchant* | *% Total* | *Employment ('000)* | *% Naval* | *% Merchant* | *% Total* | *Total Employment ('000)* |
| 1940 | 118.1 | 66.9 | 33.1 | 62.2 | 71.6 | 46.1 | 53.9 | 37.8 | 189.7 |
| 1941 | 129.5 | 63.3 | 36.7 | 62.8 | 76.4 | 46.7 | 53.3 | 37.1 | 205.9 |
| 1942 | 145 | 62.2 | 37.8 | 64.3 | 80.5 | 37.8 | 62.2 | 35.7 | 225.5 |
| 1943 | 150.8 | 62 | 38 | 64.5 | 83.1 | 41.3 | 58.7 | 35.5 | 233.9 |
| 1944 | 144.6 | 64 | 36 | 64 | 81.3 | 38.6 | 61.4 | 36 | 225.9 |
| 1945 | 134.3 | 58.2 | 41.8 | 63.3 | 77.9 | 37.2 | 62.8 | 36.7 | 212.2 |

[1] Average week in second quarter each year.

*Source*:  Shipbuilding Conference: Quarterly Statistical Summary, June 1945, pp. 20–2.

The total of value of war work was in the order of £793 million, £551 million for shipbuilding and marine engineering, £242 million for repair and conversion work. The profitability of this work is difficult to judge, for official returns clearly presented information in relation to Admiralty and Ministry of War Transport formulae, and may be expected to represent a minimum figure. On ship-repairing and conversion work, returns made to the Shipbuilding Conference show overall profitability declining form 8.8 per cent in 1939–40 to 5.9 per cent in 1944, the rate on private work averaging 13.4 per cent between 1939 and 1944 compared with under 5 per cent on Admiralty contracts. No such consolidated returns exist for shipbuilding and marine engineering, but individual company financial returns were made. These published returns, however, offer little real clue to the recovery in financial fortunes. The Fairfield Shipbuilding and Engineering Company in Glasgow, for example, returned net profits of £534,750 for the financial years 1 July 1939 to 30 June 1945. At the same time the profit and loss accounts recorded trading profits of £778,835 and £300,000 set aside for depreciation and a further £350,000 to contingency reserves. This contrasted with 1931 to 1936, when no depreciation or reserve had been set aside, and recorded profit was only £91,094.[13] Similarly in John Brown & Co. at Clydebank, where net profit was only £79,201 in 1935, it averaged £410,000 between 1939 and 1945. Moreover, the company accounts record that the average trading profit was at least double that figure, and that £500,000 had been placed as reserves, and £447,000 had been set aside for deprecation. Correspondence with the Admiralty in John Browns' papers reveals that in the first two years of war, profit levels up to 30 per cent had been attained in naval contracts, and that comparable figures had been attained by other main naval builders.[14] In the immediate circumstances of 1941 the Admiralty chose not to press the large profits made,[15] but in return the shipbuilders had to enter into discussion on a revised payment system which intended to establish turnover-to-capital ratios for each yard, and link these to a percentage profit. The builders resisted revealing their capital and turnover figures, but by 1943, a second cost investigation revealed average profit levels of around 12 per cent still prevailing.[16] The outcome was a new system of tendering which guaranteed a profit level of 7.5 per cent, this operative from the 1943 financial year.

The uncertainties and variations in accounting practices, and gaps in returns, make it impossible to estimate a general return to the industry in profit over the war years. However, the 7.5 per cent negotiated in 1943 was certainly a minimum figure, and most companies were able to make healthy surpluses, build up reserves. and provide for significant levels of depreciation, to repair the financial damage they had endured in the 1930s.

The resurgence of the industry in output, employment and financial return did not, as in the 1914–18 war, generate any significant new capacity in British shipbuilding. The 40 per cent of capacity still unused in 1938 provided an immediate shock absorber for rapidly escalating demand, and the recurring constraints on output were manpower and steel supplies. Moreover, NSS had placed three of its acquired yards on a care-and-maintenance basis, and maintained them against a wartime emergency: these were Armstrong Whitworth's Walker Yard on the Tyne, Cairds at Greenock on the Clyde, and William Gray's Egis Yard at Sunderland. By 1939, however, the plant in Cairds' and Grays' yards had been sold, as had part of the land at Cairds, and the West Harbour had been leased to the Admiralty.[17] However, by August 1942 no fewer than 24 yards formerly closed by NSS had been reopened for wartime work, the operators paying a £5 token sum as a waiver of the restrictions, the wartime use to be discontinued within three months of the ending of the hostilities. Most of the facilities were for steel fabrication for TLCs (tank landing craft), barges, and the repair work. The biggest yards reopened were Armstrong Whitworths' Walker Yard on the Tyne, and Swan Hunter & Wigham Richardsons' former Southwick establishment at Sunderland. In the negotiations to reopen the Walker Yard it was initially proposed that it should be 'for construction of all welded ships on the American plan',[18] but the problems of labour scarcity caused the proposal to be revised in favour of undertaking semi-fabricated hull assembly work.[19] While the NSS Board accepted this plan it simultaneously rejected a proposal to recognise a proposed patent for assembly-line shipyards submitted by a Dr John Tutin, who claimed his scheme was novel and revolutionary, and would enable ships to be built more rapidly and cheaply.

While most of the reopened yards were managed by steel fabricators, the reinstatement of large-scale construction at Walker and Southwick confronted the Shipbuilding Conference with the problem of how to manage the operations. This was resolved by creating a new company, the Shipbuilding Corporation, in December 1942. This organisation was owned by the Shipbuilding Conference, with an issued capital of £100,000 comprising 99,000 ordinary shares of £1 each and 20,000 deferred shares of 1 shilling each. Fifty-five shipbuilding and engine-building firms held 96,000 of the ordinary shares, while 30 companies, holding small blocks of 100 shares each, were represented through the creation of a nominee company, Birchin Lane Nominees Ltd, which also held the deferred shares.[20] Members of the Shipbuilding Corporation signed a deed of covenant committing them to pay to the Corporation a levy of 0.25 per cent of the value of ships completed to defray the anticipated loss to the company in opening old yards to produce ships in wartime. The industry agreed to take the step, and face the expense, the levy being offset against company tax bills by agreement with the Inland Revenue. While the motive was primarily to assist the war effort, the Conference also recognised that keeping the wartime facilities in the hands of industry had the effect of 'avoiding competition by admission to the industry of undesirable speculative interests, and that this had in part guided members in the way they had planned this mutual effort in the national interest'.[21] Under this arrangement the Walker Yard was operated as the Shipbuilding Corporation Ltd, Tyne Branch, and the Southwick Yard as the Wear Branch. As other yards were reopened they similarly became branches of the Shipbuilding Corporation. The Walker and Southwick yards remained the main new construction units, and by 1947 had completed 58 vessels for the Corporation, 37 at Walker and 21 and Swan Hunter, with a total deadweight of 277,000 tons.[22]

The stance taken by the Shipbuilding Conference and NSS Ltd in opening these redundant yards effectively prevented speculative investment in new capacity during the wartime emergency. As a consequence the Conference estimated that the expansion of plant and equipment during the war, together with the effect of improvement in design and productive methods, had added only 400,000 tons of productive capacity to the industry. Capacity in 1939 was reckoned at 2.555 million tons, and by 1948 was placed at 2.955 million tons, an increase of 15.6 per cent.[23] Moreover, whatever increase in capacity had taken place in Germany and Japan during the war was effectively removed by defeat, and as after the First World War the major wartime builder, the USA, ceased its emergency programme with the ending of hostilities. Its peak production of 11.4 million tons in 1943 was cut to 501,000 tons in 1946, and world production was below the 1939 level. The prolonged destabilisation arising from surplus capacity on a worldwide basis which emerged after the First World War was consequently not repeated, and British shipbuilding emerged from war in 1945 in a strengthened and advantageous condition in relation to its pre-war competitors.

# The expanding market, 1946–1958

The scale of war losses in merchant tonnage ensured that there would at least be a short-term post-war boom in orders and construction of new tonnage. Between 3 September 1939 and 2 September 1945, the British merchant marine lost by enemy action 2,539 ships of 11,831,410 gross tons, together with a further 226 ships of 633,000 gross tons as marine risk losses. The British fleet alone consequently lost 2,765 vessels of 12.46 million gross tons, representing about three-quarters of the pre-war deep-sea tramp fleet, and approximately half of both the pre-war liner and tanker tonnages.[24] At the end of the war the UK fleet was down to 12.659 million gross tons, more than 5 million tons below its 1939 level, although the government-owned merchant fleet comprised a further 3.4 million tons.[25] In addition, allied and neutral fleets suffered losses of 9.76 million gross tons, and enemy losses amounted to approximately a further 10 million tons.[26] The total tonnage loss as a consequence of the six years of general conflict was in the order of 32 million gross tons, about 14 years' output for world shipbuilding at the level prevailing in the 1920s and 1930s,[27] and at least five to seven years' work at the full capacity of the pre-war world shipbuilding industry. In global terms the world fleet had expanded by 11.5 million tons between 1939 and 1946, its tonnage of 72.9 million being achieved largely as a consequence of USA wartime production which temporarily drove the USA share of world merchant tonnage from 14.2 per cent in 1939 to 56.1 per cent in 1946. The wartime losses clearly created a large-scale and urgent need for new tonnage on a world-wide basis. In addition to this, other elements combined to convert an anticipated short-term replenishment boom into a decade of sustained expansion.

Immediately after the war there were problems of port congestion everywhere, but the situation was particularly serious in Europe and Britain where damaged and over-stretched port facilities were unable to turn ships around quickly. This problem is thought temporarily to have reduced the carrying efficiency of the world dry cargo fleet by about 20 per cent, and to have induced ship owners to add around 9.0 million gross tons to order books in an attempt to compensate. At the same time the European energy crisis placed huge demands on the American trans-Atlantic coal trade, and further added to new tonnage demands. More important, however, was the rapid recovery of world trade to pre-war levels. By 1948 the volume of world sea-borne trade had regained the 1938 level. This remarkable achievement in aggregate terms was largely an outcome of the very large volume of trade generated by the British export drive, which pushed British export values 147 per cent above pre-war levels by the end of 1948.[28] European foreign trade still languished below the 1938 level, but that deficiency was soon to be transformed by the impact of the Marshall Plan which pumped more than $13 billion dollars of aid into western Europe between 1948 and 1952. Another $2.6 billion of assistance was added to the middle of 1953.[29] Since the aid was largely in the form of commodities, grain, foodstuffs, and iron and steel products, the stimulus to trade was considerable. This injection was complemented by the acceleration of US demands for raw materials in the procurement and rearmament drive linked to the Korean War in 1950–52, and as a consequence world trade expanded almost without interruption to 1957. By 1955 world exports were 46 per cent above the 1937–38 level, and in value terms had increased 3.7 times.[30] Within this pattern of expansion, a new element in bulk trade grew by leaps and bounds. The international trade in oil, for example, grew at a rate of 7.5 per cent per year from 1950 to 1956, driven by the transition of the USA from exporter to net importer of oil, and the accelerating demands of European countries for crude oil as the oil majors began to transfer refining capacity from areas of production to the major industrial markets. World oil consumption had been 255 million tons in 1938, but reached 912 million tons in 1958.[31]

The combination of these market factors generated a huge order book for world shipbuilding in the decade or so from the ending of hostilities. By 1948 world orders stood at 8.0 million tons, and this nearly doubled, to 15.6 million tons, in 1952 (Table 5.3).[32] By then tankers represented two-thirds of the order book,[33] and from 1948 to 1958 tanker construction represented 48 per cent of all tonnage built in the world. The other notable trend in world construction was that the motorship modestly increased its total share of tonnage built to around 60 per cent of launchings between 1946 and 1958. With a market of such scale and buoyancy, shipbuilders found themselves in an exceptionally favourable environment. In effect the years from 1946 to 1958 were a sellers' market.

*Table 5.3*  World order books, 1948–1958[1]
('000 gross tons and percentage of world total)

| Year | World | UK | | Germany | | Sweden | | Japan | |
|---|---|---|---|---|---|---|---|---|---|
| | *Tons* | *Tons* | *%* | *Tons* | *%* | *Tons* | *%* | *Tons* | *%* |
| 1948 | 8,023 | 4,477 | (55.8) | | | | | | |
| 1950 | 7,894 | 3,312 | (41.2) | | | | | | |
| 1952 | 15,630 | 6,181 | (39.5) | 1,791 | (11.4) | 1,606 | (10.3) | 651 | (4.2) |
| 1954 | 11,249 | 3,947 | (35.1) | 1,417 | (12.4) | 1,392 | (12.4) | 787 | (7.0) |
| 1956 | 29,248 | 5,188 | (17.7) | 4,872 | (16.6) | 3,051 | (10.4) | 5,067 | (17.3) |
| 1957 | 34,511 | 5,734 | (16.6) | 5,425 | (15.7) | 3,759 | (10.9) | 5,080 | (14.7) |
| 1958 | 27,395 | 5,373 | (19.6) | 4,193 | (15.3) | 3,079 | (11.2) | 3,784 | (13.8) |

[1] Vessels of 1,000 grt and over at 31 December each year.

*Sources*: Shipbuilders Council of America, 1948; 1950. Shipbuilding Inquiry Committee, 1965–66. Cmnd. 2937, HMSO London, 1966: Appendix I, pp. 182–3.

# Supplying the demand

As British shipbuilders emerged from the high-pressure years of wartime work, they found themselves in the unique position of facing a tidal wave of orders from domestic and overseas clients for whom there was little alternative to Britain as a supplier. Germany and Japan, Britain's major competitors in the 1930s, were effectively removed from production by defeat, and by the restrictions imposed on their shipbuilding activities by the occupying forces. In both countries large parts of existing shipbuilding facilities were designated for reparations, and dismantled, and construction was sharply controlled by licensing. These restrictions were not eased significantly until 1949, in the case of Japan, and 1950 in Germany. Until then Britain enjoyed unchallenged world supremacy. As a consequence, between 1946 and 1948, British yards launched 3.488 million tons or 53.6 per cent of the world total, a share of world production not regularly enjoyed since before the First World War (Table 5.4). At the same time the British order book had climbed to 4.47 million tons, representing 55.8 per cent of world orders, and during these immediate post-war years the hard-pressed British yards also supplied about half of world exports of new tonnage. In the exceptional circumstances of the reconstruction period through to 1951 British shipbuilding re-established its dominance of the domestic market, since British ship owners were prohibited from placing orders abroad under the terms of the Exchange Control Act 1947, and the Contract of Borrowing Order 1947, and also extended Britain's share of the export market.

*Table 5.4*  UK and world tonnage launched, 1946–1958
('000 gross tons)

| Year | World | UK | % | USA | % | Sweden | % | Germany | % | Japan | % |
|------|-------|------|------|-----|------|--------|------|---------|------|--------|------|
| 1946 | 2,108[1] | 1,120 | 53.1 | 501 | 23.7 | 147 | 6.9 | | | 109[2] | 4.9 |
| 1947 | 2,093[1] | 1,192 | 56.9 | 163 | 7.8 | 223 | 10.6 | | | 112[2] | 5.1 |
| 1948 | 2,303[1] | 1,176 | 51.1 | 126 | 5.5 | 246 | 10.7 | | | 169[2] | 6.8 |
| 1949 | 3,126[1] | 1,267 | 40.5 | 633 | 20.2 | 323 | 10.3 | | | 148 | 4.7 |
| 1950 | 3,489[1] | 1,324 | 37.9 | 437 | 12.5 | 348 | 9.9 | 154[1] | 4.4 | 348 | 9.9 |
| 1952 | 4,394 | 1,302 | 29.6 | 467 | 10.6 | 456 | 10.3 | 520 | 11.8 | 608 | 13.8 |
| 1954 | 5,251 | 1,408 | 26.8 | 477 | 9.1 | 544 | 10.4 | 963 | 18.3 | 413 | 7.9 |
| 1956 | 6,670 | 1,383 | 20.7 | 169 | 2.5 | 484 | 7.3 | 1,000 | 15.0 | 1,746 | 26.2 |
| 1958 | 9,270 | 1,402 | 15.1 | 732 | 7.9 | 760 | 8.2 | 1,492 | 15.4 | 2,067 | 22.3 |

[1] Returns incomplete.  [2] Survey of Japanese Finance and Industry etc.

*Sources*: Lloyds Register of Shipping: Statistical Tables. Survey of Japanese Finance and Industry; Industrial Bank of Japan, vol. II, no. 4, April 1950.

This remarkable attainment was not to last. In 1950 Britain still held over 40 per cent of world orders, and of all tonnage under construction, but by 1958 both these shares had been cut in half. Britain then had 22 per cent of world tonnage under construction, and 20 per cent of the world order book (Table 5.3). Britain's loss of dominance was even more marked in tonnage launched, and in tonnage exported. In 1953 German output for foreign buyers equalled Britain's for the first time, and Germany displaced Britain as the leading builder for foreign flags in 1954. By 1958 Britain was supplying only 8.1 per cent of the world export markets (Table 5.5). In terms of tonnage launched, Japan edged Britain into second place in world launches in 1956, and in 1957 Germany pushed Britain into third place in the world ranking (Table 5.4). Britain's share of world output had crashed swiftly from 50 per cent in 1948 to 15 per cent a decade later. A century of world ascendancy in shipbuilding had been abruptly lost. Yet, even then, British shipbuilding retained the largest order book in the world (Table 5.3), but was clearly under increasing pressure from the other three major world shipbuilders, Germany, Sweden and Japan. Evidently Britain had lost out to her competitors in the expanding market conditions of the 1950s. The enigma is why British shipbuilding should have failed to capitalise on its immediate post-war supremacy?

*Table 5.5*   UK and world tonnage exports
('000 gross tons)

|      | UK exports | Foreign exports | World exports | % UK |
|------|------------|-----------------|---------------|------|
| 1951 | 602        | 636             | 1238          | 48.6 |
| 1955 | 539        | 1750            | 2289          | 23.5 |
| 1958 | 337        | 4146            | 4483          | 8.1  |

*Sources*: Lloyds Register of Shipping Annual Summaries.

## Failure to grow

The core of the answer to this question lies in the fact that, in the uniquely expanding market for new tonnage, and in the rapidly growing construction of new ships, Britain alone of all the main shipbuilding countries failed to increase its production. While world production doubled, from 2.1 million tons in 1946 to 4.4 million tons in 1952, and then more than doubled again to 9.3 million in 1958 (Table 5.4), British output held steady at between 1.2 and 1.4 million tons per year. In strong contrast to this stasis, the German industry reconstructed itself from virtually nil output before 1950, to 1.5 million tons in 1958. At the same time the Japanese industry regenerated from a few ships for domestic consumption in 1946 to over 2.4 million tons in 1957. These were staggering achievements in the space of a decade, while Sweden on a more modest scale increased output by more than a factor of three between 1948 and 1958. Uniquely Britain failed to respond to the rapidly growing world market: there was no increase in the scale of its industry, and as a consequence Britain's market share moved remorselessly downward from its post-war peak of nearly 57 per cent in 1947, to barely 15 per cent in 1958.

This evident circumstance of Britain's failure to expand output certainly explains the absolute loss of market share, and the relative shifts in shares of world output among the major shipbuilders; what is more difficult to answer is why the British industry should have behaved in this way. Throughout this period the industry itself consistently blamed government restrictions, and especially the limited allocations of steel, as major reasons for its failure to increase production. These were certainly real elements with which British shipbuilders had to contend: their effect, and the substance of the shipbuilders' complaints, deserve close examination.

One immediate post-war circumstance was that the complete wartime control of the industry was not quickly relaxed, although it was made plain by the new Labour government as early as December 1945, that shipbuilding did not figure in its plans for nationalistion.[34] With victory in sight, the government discontinued its wartime Shipbuilding Advisory Committee in November 1944, and replaced it with a new Shipbuilding Committee under the chairmanship of Sir Cyril Harcomb. The terms of reference of the committee were to advise on post-war priorities for construction of different classes of merchant ships, and how to share out shipbuilding berths among the competing claims of British, allied and neutral ship owners.[35] More broadly it was to advise on 'the promotion of cooperation between ship owners and shipbuilders in the ordering of new tonnage and to the arrangements most likely to contribute to the well being, efficiency and stability of the shipbuilding industry'. The most pressing issue was to assess the scale of the anticipated post-war demand for new tonnage from British, allied, and neutral owners, and to judge whether priorities among different owners would have to be enforced. In the absence of any hard evidence the committee adopted the rule-of-thumb already operating under wartime conditions, namely that British owners who had lost tonnage during the war would have first priority. Capacity would also be reserved to meet the needs of Allied governments who had lost tonnage in support of Britain during the war.

In order to regulate priorities among owners, the Shipbuilding Committee devised and introduced a system of permits for which owners wishing to construct a ship had to apply. These were issued through the Ministry of War Transport and detailed the type of vessel desired, the trade for which it was intended, and the provisional date indicated for keel-laying. The permits operated on an 18-month forward horizon, giving priority to tonnage intended to be built within that period. Applications were considered quarterly, and permits were issued in excess of available capacity to allow for withdrawals. This system was in addition to the Admiralty's statutory control of construction by its licensing system which also remained in force. The permit system in effect worked as a first screening of applicants for licences to construct, and it was rare for a building licence to be withheld after a permit enabling a ship owner to enter into negotiation with a shipbuilder had been granted.

This two-stage procedure was intended to enable the government to maintain control over shipbuilding output if there was an excessive flood of orders well beyond the capacity of the industry, or to take directive action if the flow of orders was seriously unbalanced in favour of particular districts or builders. Both these fears proved unfounded, and by June 1945 the committee was advising the government that permits could be issued to British owners who had no priority basis either on war losses or on tonnage obsolescence. This was acceded to, and almost immediately in July 1945 the Committee recommended that permits could now be issued to neutral owners. The 18-month forward horizon had given the government a good basis to judge owners' intentions, and to estimate the likely volume of work for up to two years ahead. The permit system ran from December 1944 until 30 April 1946, by which date the granting of permits was automatic and the procedure was then considered unnecessary and was consequently discontinued. The permit system in fact outlived Harcomb's Shipbuilding Committee by a month, it being itself superseded by yet another Shipbuilding Advisory Committee, in March 1946, chaired by Sir Graham Cunningham.[36] This had a much broader membership than the previous committee, adding union representation for seamen and for merchant navy officers to that of the shipbuilding unions, as well as incorporating industry representatives and departmental officers. The remit was also more general, and purely advisory on matters affecting efficiency, full employment, and war potential. As far as policy issues were concerned, it seems clear that the Shipbuilding Advisory Committee had little influence.

As during the war, the real supervision of the industry lay with the Admiralty and its licensing system, even though by late 1946 the licences themselves had become a formality. Behind the licences, however, the Admiralty exercised real control over the bulk allocation of materials to the yards, and on the priorities among the different classes of ships. The Ministry of Transport was in theory confined to advising the Admiralty on the material needs for particular ships, but its influence was significantly greater since the Licensing Officers in the major ports were all Ministry of Transport surveyors on loan to the Admiralty. Between them the Admiralty and Ministry of Transport effectively set ceilings on the volume of work and influenced the pattern and composition of construction through the licensing and bulk allocation procedures.

These regulations and restrictions clearly set parameters for British shipbuilders after the war, and the procedures for licensing continued throughout this period, as did the sanction of bulk allocations of timber, steel and other materials. In parallel to this, the freedom of action of British ship owners was also constrained by the Exchange Control Act 1945, and Control of Borrowing Order 1947, which jointly prohibited British owners from placing orders for tonnage abroad. This forced all

British orders into British shipyards between 1945 and 1950, though from 1951 permission was granted to build in European yards, and after 1956, orders could also be placed in Japan. For all practical purposes, however, British owners were effectively tied to British builders in this period, the restrictions enforcing a monopoly position of a closed market on the world's largest merchant fleet. Against this advantage, the Admiralty and Ministry of Transport controls were a bureaucratic burden that scarcely equalled the constraints laid upon German shipbuilding by the Allied Control Commission, or on Japan by the American Occupation Control. Yet in spite of much harsher controls which were relaxed in Japan from 1949, and more grudgingly and with more opposition in Germany in 1950–52, these industries were able to accelerate production beyond British levels in a remarkably few years. If there was a will to expand, bureaucratic controls could clearly be overcome. By inference, the controls exercised in Britain were unlikely, of themselves, to have enforced the non-growth of British shipbuilding in these years. If the bureaucratic framework is not a likely culprit, what of the shipbuilders' complaints about shortages of materials in general, and of steel in particular?

## Steel supplies

In the post-war reconstruction phase, and on into the 1950s, the pressure of demand on steel products was intense, and supply was regulated by allocations to all industries as recommended by the Materials Committee in relation to the export-earning potential of each industry. In the immediate post-war years shipbuilding was accorded some priority in supply, and, at least to 1948, steel deliveries to shipbuilding exceeded government allocations; the excess was 25 per cent in 1947 and 18 per cent in 1948.[37] While allocations were set at between 650,000 and 800,000 tons, deliveries topped 900,000 tons, and indeed varied little from that level between 1947 and 1958. The shipbuilders were in no doubt that this level of supply was a serious constraint on their ability to increase production and expedite deliveries. In 1948 the Shipbuilding Conference argued that, 'the inadequate supplies of steel … are primarily responsible for the post-war plan of the industry falling behind'. The Shipbuilding Advisory Committee accepted this view, and the chairman annotated a note to the First Lord of the Admiralty and the Minister of Transport to the effect that while the government might believe the industry's needs for steel had been met by the allocations, it had 'not been allocated enough to produce economically, let alone sufficient for their requirement'.[38]

That there was some truth in the shipbuilders' protests is evident in a memorandum reviewing the labour force required in the industry in mid-1948, which commented that the allocation of 800,000 tons of steel in 1948 would have the effect of restricting shipbuilding output to very little more than one million gross tons per annum.[39] Since little more than this level was delivered annually to the industry, and imports of heavy steel plates suitable for shipbuilding were modest, the steel supply received by the shipbuilders was certainly only at a level capable of maintaining output at 1.2 to 1.4 million tons per year. The tonnage delivered in 1945 was actually 930,000 tons, and the average between 1947 and 1958 was around 900,000 tons.

It is clear that steel supplies to the shipbuilders did not change significantly in these years, but it is not possible to argue from this to conclude that steel supply was the major factor limiting output. It is necessary to ask why the shipbuilders did not obtain more steel at a time when total steel output of finished products increased by 50 per cent, from 11.8 to 18.0 million tons, and when appropriate heavy steel plate production increased more sharply still, by 75 per cent. Part of the problem undoubtedly lay in the way in which the steel industry itself operated its steel-supply policies within the allocations set by the Ministry of Supply, diverting plates and sections to industries where extras and mark-ups gave steel makers better returns within the generally controlled prices. This, however, was not a major problem, and tended to affect the timing of deliveries more than total tonnage supplied. Moreover, if supplies were inadequate, the industry had been given leave to import foreign steel free of Import Duty from 1952, and the Admiralty confirmed that any steel imported in this way would not prejudice firms' allocations under the Ministry of Supply system.[40] However, when the Shipbuilding Conference made enquiries among member firms concerning supplementary supplies by import, it was noted that 'there was a general lack of interest in the proposal and the idea of collective purchase of foreign steel had been abandoned in the meantime'.[41] The fact that, under the price-control system administered by the Iron and Steel Board, the price of plates and angles in Britain was much cheaper than supplies from Germany, Austria or Japan, undoubtedly influenced the shipbuilders' decision. In 1953 the basic price of British ships' plate per ton was £30 6s. 6d. against quotations of £49 from Austria and, £43–£58 from Japan, depending on dimension. However, with a huge order book available, and fixed-price contracts not yet common, the reluctance to import steel certainly contributed to the materials problem, at a time when German and Japanese yards could clearly take contracts for ships at prices lower than those in the UK, and with earlier deliveries promised. The ceiling on Britain's output, while basically linked to the steel supply problem, was clearly also linked to other factors in the expectations and performance of British shipbuilders.

## Expectations

There is reason to believe that the modest output of British shipbuilding after the Second World War was also linked to market expectations as assumed by both the government and the industry. In both cases the projections were essentially pessimistic. On the government side, Sir Cyril Harcomb's short-lived Shipbuilding Committee was given the task, at the end of 1944, of estimating demand for new tonnage in the first ten years after the war, with a view to judging the scale of employment and activity likely in post-war shipbuilding. The study was completed by July 1945, and was based on assumptions that it would be desirable to restore the British merchant marine to 18.0 million gross tons at the earliest time compatible with trade and other considerations, and that every effort would be made to prevent the employment level in shipbuilding and marine engineering from falling below 90,000 in Shipbuilders Employers Federation firms, and a figure of around 120,000 for the industry as a whole.[42] The figure of 18.0 million gross tons for the post-war fleet, subsequently revised upward to a target of 18.5 million tons, effectively set the base level for projections for future work. By the end of December 1949 the UK fleet had recovered to 16.9 million tons, leaving a margin of 1.6 million tons of new shipping still to be acquired. The Admiralty and Ministry of Transport then projected orders for a Merchant Shipbuilding Programme for 1948 to 1955.[43] This set total orders for the eight-year period at 8.5 million tons, allowing 2.8 million tons for marine losses and scrapping, together with 1.6 million tons to replace sales of old tonnage, and 2.5 million tons for foreign orders. The projections for foreign orders were particularly pessimistic, assuming that the post-war boom would be satisfied by 1951–52, and that thereafter orders would diminish to pre-war levels of around 200,000 tons per year. These assumptions set the workload of the industry at only a little over 1.0 million tons per year, the largest part of this being dependent on British orders. It is clear that these projections were closely aligned to the level of steel supplies allocated to the industry, confirming its output at the projected level.

The industry, too, had limited expectations on the post-war development of its performance and output. The UK fleet target of 18.0 million tons had been recommended to the government by Sir Amos Ayre, and represented the view of the Shipbuilding Conference of the scale to be planned for, for the British fleet. This reflected the industry preference for a stable relationship between shipbuilding and the British fleet as the main source of orders; it also indicated the level of output the shipbuilders believed they could sustain with their existing capacity. The inter-war experience of large-scale unused capacity had profoundly influenced the mentality of its leaders, and embedded them in a philosophy of capacity reduction and control, rather than with a vision of expansion. At the end of the war the capacity of the industry was estimated to be 2.95 million tons, if the total capability of plant and berths were fully utilised for merchant tonnage and if there were no reductions in hours of work, or constraints on supplies of labour and materials. More realistically the industry believed the upper level of its post-war capability to be around 1.75 million tons,[44] and that it could readily expand output to this level provided steel supplies were increased by 50 per cent. Yet even when steel supplies were eased, and when allowance was made for changes in work practice involving more welding (with its consequent savings on steel required), the industry never approached this level of output. In 1953 the industry restated its belief that it could produce 1.75 million gross tons per year with a steel plate requirement of 900,000 tons.[45] That level of supply had been delivered previously, but output fell far below the projected level, and this again suggests that the real barriers to increased output lay in industry opposition to expansion of capacity beyond the prevailing anticipated level of orders for the British merchant marine.[46]

## No growth and modernisation

If there was a no-growth philosophy, or mentality, in British shipbuilding after 1945 – and the evidence on output, and the attitude to capacity strongly support this view – did this also constrain investment in the modernisation of yards and work practices, and did this in turn reinforce a low ceiling on the output of the industry?

The investment profile of the industry is hard to assess, but by the end of 1952, the *Financial Times* surveys of company financial results, included the published returns for 29 shipbuilding and ship-repair companies. These firms had accumulated capital and revenue reserves of £47.7 million against a total net working capital of £54.1 million. This suggests a cautious accumulation of resources rather than a vigorous programme of post-war investment. The statistical summaries of company returns made to the Shipbuilding Conference each quarter also include financial results, and these suggest that in the period 1946–1952 at least 70 per cent of net profit was being retained in the companies, of which up to one-third was being applied to depreciation and two-thirds to revenue and capital reserves. The industry appeared to be applying about £5 million per year to capital formation in this period, the emphasis being on modernisation of craneage and berths, rather than any extension of capacity. This level of £5 million per year compares with a value of output which averaged about £90 million per year between 1946 and 1950.[47] These are very modest levels of investment in the first post-war reconstruction period when the industry was working at full pace to cope with a swollen order book. The choice was to make do and keep going, rather than to plan for effective re-equipment and re-organisation which would have interfered with construction. It is difficult to believe that this strategy, and this level of capital formation, were adequate to maintain, far less to improve, the capital stock of the industry. After the decade of disinvestment in the 1930s, and the heavy wear and tear on already ageing plant and equipment during the war, this level of provision could hardly have done more than have allowed the industry to stand still; indeed, it is not improbable that there was further disinvestment in the industry as a whole, although some yards clearly made major efforts to modernise.

Some yards, mainly the larger liner and naval yards, had a head-start with newer facilities since Admiralty needs had contributed significant new investment during the war. At Belfast, for example, Harland & Wolff took over the welding shops, which had cost £317,508,[48] and also benefited from buildings and machinery installed by the Admiralty at their establishments at Scotstoun and at Liverpool. On the same foundation, Vickers-Armstrong embarked on a major modernisation programme at Barrow, reducing the berths from seven to four, and re-equipping them with eight new 40-ton capacity cranes, replacing the existing smaller 10–30 ton cranes. A new assembly shop with two large bays capable of handling prefabricated units of up to 40 tons was also constructed. Beginning in late 1944, the cost of the programme was in excess of £2 million, and at the time was the most extensive modernisation of production by any yard in Britain.[49] The most popular improvement was the reduction in the number of berths to cope with increased vessel size, and also to create space in cramped yards for new plate and welding shops and their associated storage areas. Berths were reduced on the Clyde at John Browns, Barclay Curle, Connels Denny, Lithgow and Scott's, and similarly on the Tyne at Swan Hunter and Hawthorn Leslie, Austin and Pickersgill and at J.L. Thompson on the Wear, Furness on the Tees, and Cammell Laird on the Mersey. All of these yards, and others, also improved the lifting capacity of their cranes.[50]

In the entire period 1946–58, however, there was only one new greenfield shipyard established in Britain, and that much against the views of the established companies who feared it would increase capacity and divert scarce steel supplies to an unwelcome newcomer. The Shipbuilding Conference also believed the proposed new yard would be under-capitalised. Approval in principle for construction was, however, given by government in January 1953, and plans were included in the capital investment programme announced by the Welsh Board for Industry. As the Conference observed, 'political and area-employment considerations were involved'.[51] The yard was constructed at Newport by the Atlantic Shipbuilding Company, and was intended for series construction of standard tankers and bulk carriers. In the event, industry suspicions of under-capitalisation proved correct, and due to lack of adequate funds the yard only ever produced small cargo ships.[52]

It is clear that the industry's 'no-growth' philosophy, while opposing capacity extension, did not exclude investment in modernisation. The small flow of funds of around £5 million per year from 1946 to 1950, increased to an average of £8 million each year between 1951 and 1956, and advanced again to £14 million in 1957 and £18.5 million in 1958, as a second phase of modernisation got under way from 1956.[53] But throughout the post-war period of full order books and British world market ascendancy, British shipbuilders did not plan for expansion, nor conceive of a systematic investment programme. Investment in cranes, berthage, welding shops and new plate shops, together with improvements to quays and storage areas were essentially piecemeal injections to cope with prevailing order books without interfering with regular production. In that sense investment was order-book driven rather than having a longer term expansionary horizon. This style of small-scale investment essentially maintained existing facilities and reinforced the low-output ceiling within which the shipbuilders operated.

## Competitiveness and market orientation

The inevitable outcome of this pattern of behaviour in maintaining output by adding new facilities to old establishments, rather than planning a large-scale re-design and modernisation of shipyard facilities, was progressively to expose and reinforce inherent weaknesses in British shipbuilding, weaknesses that had been emerging between the wars but which had receded in the wartime and reconstruction period. The dependence of British shipbuilders on orders from the British flag fleet was reinforced during the war, and compounded up to 1956, during which time British owners were not permitted to place orders overseas, though orders placed in European yards under licence were possible from 1951. In fact between 1952 and 1958 less than 10 per cent of all new tonnage registered in Britain was not supplied by British builders.[54] This long-standing link effectively harnessed British shipbuilders to customary clients whose fleet grew much more slowly than world trade, and whose preferences for new tonnage also diverged from world patterns.

Between 1939 and 1958 the world fleet increased from 68.5 million tons to over 118 million, a gain of 72 per cent. In contrast the British fleet added only 2.4 million tons, an increase of only 13 per cent. Even after allowing for the wartime and immediate post-war replacements, the world fleet added 38 million tons from 1948 to 1958, and while tonnage under the flags of all the other main mercantile nations grew rapidly (Table 5.6), Britain's fleet added little extra tonnage. The biggest growth segments for new tonnage were, in descending order, Liberia, followed by Norway, Japan, Germany, Italy, Netherlands, Panama, France, and Sweden. Of these only Japan and Germany were effectively closed markets, and the others represented expanding opportunities for British shipbuilders. However, even though export tonnage did represent a large share of British production in these years (Table 5.7) this was again mainly supported by a dependence on orders from well-established overseas clients. Between 1946 and 1950, when 31.6 per cent of British tonnage was built for overseas customers, three-quarters of the deliveries were to long-standing customers in Norway, the Netherlands, Portugal, France, Denmark, and Sweden. Indeed only two non-European markets were of any significance, the largest being the Argentine, which received 32 ships of 132,000 tons, and Panama with 13 ships of 91,000 tons. Over one-third of the export tonnage was for Norway alone. The pattern did begin to alter in the 1950s, but had the effect of narrowing the composition of the overseas order book. Between 1946 and 1950, Britain delivered new ships to 23 foreign countries, with 90 per cent of deliveries going to only eight markets; however, from 1951 to 1955, while orders were received from 29 countries, over half of all tonnage was delivered to one market, Norway, and nearly another quarter of foreign tonnage to Liberia, as an expanding flag-of-convenience fleet. In effect these two market areas absorbed nearly three-quarters of all British shipbuilding exports, and very few orders were taken from the rapidly growing fleets of Italy, Netherlands, France, and Sweden.[55] The market orientation of British shipbuilders consequently changed very little at a time when new flag fleets, not heavily linked to domestic shipbuilding industries, were becoming a rapid growth sector in the world shipbuilding market. The lack of any real attack by British shipbuilders in these markets was due not only to the customary client–builder links with domestic and a limited range of foreign owners, but because these established sources delivered an order book well beyond the needs of the British shipbuilding industry, which, committed as it was to no growth in capacity, let order books lengthen rather than invest heavily in new facilities. The success of this customary market orientation in filling the berths effectively underlined British shipbuilders' belief that the established scale of the industry was in line with market requirements. In positioning themselves in the market in this way, British shipbuilders effectively limited competition for the largest part of the order book to rivalry among British shipyards, and only faced emerging international competition in a very few overseas market areas, notably in Norway where preferential status was still strong, and in the flag-of-convenience fleets of Liberia and Panama, where customer links were much more volatile. Market orientation certainly contributed to maintaining the static overall scale of output of British shipbuilding, and this was reinforced by the product mix constructed in British yards.

*Table 5.6*  Main merchant fleets, 1939–1958
(millions of gross tons)

|  | 1939 | | 1948 | | 1958 | |
|---|---|---|---|---|---|---|
|  | mgt | % | mgt | % | mgt | % |
| UK | 17.9 | 26.1 | 18.0 | 22.4 | 20.3 | 17.2 |
| USA | 11.4 | 16.6 | 29.2 | 36.3 | 25.5 | 21.7 |
| Japan | 5.6 | 8.2 | 1.0 | 1.3 | 5.5 | 4.6 |
| Norway | 4.8 | 7.0 | 4.3 | 5.3 | 9.4 | 7.9 |
| Germany | 4.5 | 6.5 | — | — | 4.1 | 3.4 |
| Italy | 3.4 | 5.0 | 2.1 | 2.6 | 4.9 | 4.1 |
| France | 2.9 | 4.3 | 2.9 | 3.5 | 4.3 | 3.7 |
| Nlds | 2.9 | 4.3 | 2.7 | 3.4 | 4.6 | 3.9 |
| Panama | — | — | 2.7 | 3.4 | 4.3 | 3.7 |
| Liberia | — | — | — | — | 10.1 | 8.5 |
| Others | 15.7 | 22.9 | 17.4 | 21.7 | 25.0 | 21.2 |
| World | 68.5 | 100.0 | 80.3 | 100.0 | 118 | 100.0 |
| World, number of ships | 29,763 | | 29,340 | | 35,202 | |
| Average ship tonnage | 2,302 | | 2,736 | | 3,353 | |

*Source*: Lloyds Register of Shipping: Statistical Tables.

The dominant influence in construction after 1945 was that of the tanker, which quickly came to contribute nearly 50 per cent of annual world output. Launches of tanker tonnage grew almost four-fold, from 1.3 million tons in 1949 to 4.8 million in 1958, and during this decade tankers represented over half the UK order book, and over 60 per cent of world orders. This pattern presented a problem for British shipbuilders, who regarded this development as unbalancing the workload of British yards. Writing in the *Glasgow Herald* in January 1950, Charles Connell, then president of the Clyde Shipbuilders Association, observed that of all tonnage on berths or fitting out in British yards at the end of 1949, about 55 per cent was tanker tonnage; moreover, of orders still to be laid down, 70 per cent was for tankers, and of all foreign work ordered and under construction, 80 per cent was of tanker tonnage.[56] The problem was, he wrote, 'many yards have never built and are not designed or equipped to build tankers, although in the face of the great tanker demand some yards have undertaken this class of work for the first time'. The need was for orders for the many builders of small craft, coasters, colliers and specialised river and estuary vessels, to provide the diversified order book for which British shipbuilding traditionally catered.

*Table 5.7*   UK shipbuilding exports, 1947–1958

|         | *'000 tons launched* | *'000 tons exported* | *% exports* |
|---------|------------------:|------------------:|---------:|
| 1947–50 | 4,970            | 1,573            | 31.6     |
| 1951–54 | 5,370            | 1,863            | 34.7     |
| 1955–58 | 5,673            | 1,572            | 27.8     |

*Source*: Lloyds Register of Shipping.

In essence, tankers did not suit the majority of British yards. The smaller and medium-sized yards were not equipped to construct them, and the larger yards, save those such as Blythswood, Swan Hunter, and some others who only specialised in this type, preferred cargo-liner and liner construction to utilise their design facilities and skilled craftsmen and outfitters. Consequently, between 1946 and 1955, although tanker tonnage dominated world market trends, the British industry sought to preserve a more diversified building pattern. In the first five years after the war, liner and cargo tonnage contributed 62 per cent of UK tonnage launched and 45.7 per cent of the value of output, while tankers contributed only 21 per cent of value and 28 per cent of output. Even in the period 1951–55, when tankers dominated British order books and contributed 53.5 per cent of launched tonnage, the much smaller tonnage of liner and cargo vessels, 37.2 per cent, contributed a higher value of £278 million as against £267 million from the tankers.[57]

This surge of tanker construction in Britain partly reflected the rush of orders triggered by the Korean conflict and the rapid rise in freights, but it also stemmed from

US orders placed as part of American assistance to end the dollar shortage after the 1949 devaluation. But once this flood was through the order books, even though world orders for tankers rose strongly, British yards reverted to a less tanker-dominated production pattern. Tanker tonnage launched actually diminished sharply between 1955 and 1958, while tanker tonnage launched abroad more than doubled, from 1.7 million grt to 4.2 million grt. The product preferences of British shipbuilders, and the low level of modernisation investment undertaken to sustain that pattern in the first decade after the war, had not equipped British yards to cope with this rapidly growing sector. This was especially the case when the economics of oil transport, together with the first closure of the Suez Canal in 1956, triggered a very rapid increase in vessel size. In 1949 the three largest ships launched in the world, all between 21,800 and 24,000 gross tons, were liners built in Britain. Elsewhere in the world the largest ships launched, all tankers, came from the USA, and were all between 17,000 and 17,900 tons. By 1958 the four largest ships launched were built in Japan; all were tankers over 50,000 gross tons, the largest of 69,100 tons. In Britain the ten largest ships were also all tankers, but the largest, the *SS British Statesman*, built at Belfast, was only 27,800 tons. In contrast Germany had also launched the *SS Olympic Challenger* at 38,000 tons, and the Netherlands the *SS Rotterdam* of 37,000 tons. By 1958 Britain's shipbuilding market orientation, her product mix, building pattern and investment record, had combined to leave even the largest British yards ill equipped to build the new generation of larger tankers, and made it difficult for British builders to bid effectively in the most rapidly growing market area. The shipbuilders' preference for relying on British orders, and for liners, cargo-liner and other dry-cargo tonnage, focused the search for orders in the slowest growing area for new tonnage in the British fleet. Liner and dry-cargo tonnage in the British merchant marine actually declined by 10 per cent between 1939 and 1955, against an equivalent growth of 64 per cent in the world fleet. British liner and dry-cargo tonnage only recovered to 1939 levels by 1958. Moreover, while British tanker tonnage did nearly double to 1958, the world tanker fleet grew by a factor of three.

The continued dependence on the British flag fleet for most orders held British shipbuilders to the slowest growing market, one circumscribed by the slow growth of Britain's world trade and the relative competitiveness of the British fleet. The total volume of Britain's exports and imports had been 49.7 million tons in 1938, and had declined to 11.1 million tons by 1947; throughout the 1950s it averaged 33.9 million tons. As a consequence there was little demand to extend the dry cargo fleet, and the orders much desired by builders to give a better balance to production were scarce. Equally unfortunately for British builders was the poor competitiveness of British shipping in many routes and commodities. The liner companies reconstructed their fleets to ply the same mail and emigrant routes that had been their mainstay before the war. But as the cruise market began to develop, and aircraft began to impact on the North Atlantic passenger market, the British fleet was less well placed than the re-emerging French, Italian and German lines.[58] Similarly, the Rochdale Report considered the new cargo-liner tonnage ordered immediately after the war to be ill-suited to new market areas.[59] Moreover, British ship owners had expected ship prices to decline after a short post-war boom and had held off replacing tramp tonnage. Only 900,000 tons of new tramp tonnage was ordered between 1948 and 1956, and this had allowed foreign penetration of markets formerly served by Britain.[60] Finally, even in the fast-growing tanker market, British owners expanded tonnage only half as fast as foreign owners. Moreover, nearly three-quarters of the UK tanker fleet was owned by the large oil companies, the traditional British ship owner mainly turning his back on this new trade.[61] In all these ways the market dependence of British shipbuilders confirmed their pessimistic estimates of future orders, and supported their conviction that there should be no extension of capacity, and that output should be kept in line with domestic demand as the core market. While this continued to deliver full order books, for the most part, it provided no substitute market of any depth, and did not gear British shipbuilders to meet the new demands and expectations of non-British owners. One of these new expectations was a demand for quick and timely delivery, a requirement British shipbuilders also found difficult to meet.

## Building and delivery times

The most urgent problem at the interface between builder and ship owner was the issue of delivery. From the ship owners' position, early and prompt delivery had always been of prime concern, because of the desire to have new tonnage in service quickly enough to catch freight rates on the rise. From the shipbuilders' view, a rapid construction cycle and quick delivery kept orders moving, prevented a large backlog of frustrated customers, and enabled yards to offer quick start-up on, and earlier delivery of, new orders. Neither of these positions was attainable in the early post-war years when the worldwide demand for replacement, and additional tonnages, confronted a world shipbuilding industry reduced in capacity by the elimination of Japan and Germany as major shipbuilders, and constrained by universal shortages of steel and other materials. The consequence was the creation of very large order books, with very long delivery dates that were seldom met. By 1948 Britain held an order book of 4.47 million tons out of a world total of 8.02 million. In this swollen workload British yards were averaging nearly 22 months on berth and fitting-out, and this was marginally faster than times being achieved in foreign yards (Table 5.8). The shipbuilders were acutely conscious that the huge order book, in normal times a sign of health and buoyancy in the industry, 'was largely due to the fact that the inflow of orders for new ships was far in excess of the speed at which … they could be produced'. They were also certain that the situation had arisen from the circumstance that 'just at the time when demand for new ships was greatest, supplies of materials were most restricted', and had eventually led to 'a greatly congested order book and severe delays in anticipated delivery dates'.[62]

The depressing consequences of this combination of factors was reported to the Shipbuilding Advisory Committee in 1948 by the example of delays affecting one major British ship owner, Alfred Holt & Co. Holt had placed orders for twenty vessels in British yards since March 1945; in terms of the contracts, sixteen of these ships should have been delivered by the end of 1948, but by mid-1948 only seven had been completed, and a further one promised by the end of the year. A similar slippage was expected in the twelve remaining ships, and aggregate delays in delivery were then estimated to amount to 175 months, or 14.58 months for each vessel.[63]

*Table 5.8*  Comparative building times
all tonnage in months on berth and fitting out

|  | UK, months | Foreign builders, months | Foreign times UK ± |
|---|---|---|---|
| 1946 | 20.4 | 21.5 | −1.1 |
| 1947 | 21.7 | 23.8 | −2.1 |
| 1948 | 21.7 | 21.5 | +0.2 |
| 1949 | 18.9 | 15.5 | +4.4 |
| 1950 | 18.5 | 15.4 | +3.1 |
| 1951 | 19.8 | 17.1 | +2.7 |
| 1952 | 19.8 | 15.4 | +4.4 |
| 1953 | 19.8 | 13.1 | +6.1 |
| 1954 | 18.2 | 11.6 | +6.6 |
| 1955 | 17.5 | 12.8 | +4.7 |
| 1956 | 19.2 | 12.3 | +6.9 |
| 1957 | 18.6 | 11.8 | +6.8 |
| 1958 | 19.1 | 11.9 | +7.2 |

*Sources*: Calculated from Lloyds Register Annual Summaries of Tonnage Under Construction and Tonnage Launched.

Building time calculated by dividing tonnage on berth and fitting out (under construction) by tonnage launched.

As long as world tonnage remained in short supply, and freight rates remained buoyant, ship owners had little option but to wait resignedly in this long shipbuilding queue, a queue even longer than the average building times suggested, for it usually took at least a year between the signing of the contract and the commencement of work on the berths. As long as no one could do better, such long delays in delivery were not a significant factor in competition, but it was clearly recognised that this cushion could not be permanent, and delivery times would then become a major issue in placing orders. For while the total UK order book remained very large in this period

(Table 5.3) it concealed a considerable volatility in the ebb and flow of new orders linked to the movement of freight rates, and the exogenous shocks of war and political instability. Orders were boosted on three occasions: first, in the post-war replenishment boom from 1946 to 1948; second, in response to procurement and rearmament linked to the outbreak of the Korean War in 1951; and third, with the impact of the closure of the Suez Canal in 1956. Sharp contractions in the order book in 1949 and in 1953–54 were rapidly reversed as freights moved sharply upward in response to swift changes in demand for tonnage (Table 5.9). On the first of these occasions owners had little alternative but to place orders with British yards and accept the long delays, but by 1951 the situation was beginning to change. Restrictions on Japan and Germany building new tonnage had been eased significantly by 1951 allowing them to add their still small productive capacity to the market. British builders quickly noted that German yards were taking advantage of Britain's long delivery times by offering delivery 12 months earlier and, even though their base costs were lower, they were increasing prices accordingly to benefit from the sellers' market.[64] Japan was benefiting similarly, in spite of higher prices, because they could 'deliver new vessels within a third of the time taken by European and American builders'.[65] This initial loss of competitive edge on delivery to Europe was not so much due to a serious British gap in building times in 1951, a margin of less than three months (Table 5.8), but more to the fact that German and Japanese yards, lacking a backlog of orders, did not have a 12-month wait before contracts could be commenced.

*Table 5.9*   Index of tramp time charter freight rates

| Year | Index |
|------|-------|
| 1948 | 100 |
| 1949 | 82.3 |
| 1950 | 84.0 |
| 1951 | 173.7 |
| 1952 | 110.6 |
| 1952 | 100 |
| 1953 | 77.5 |
| 1954 | 86.1 |
| 1955 | 127.7 |
| 1956 | 157.0 |
| 1957 | 112.7 |
| 1958 | 67.1 |

Source: B.R. Mitchell and P. Deane, *Abstract of British Historical Statistics* (Cambridge: CUP, 1962), p. 540.

However, by the time the sharp surge in new orders preceding and linked to Suez came on stream, the building-time differentials had become a serious drawback to placing orders in British yards. From 1953 the average gap in building times between Britain and overseas yards widened to 6–7 months for all types of tonnage, and in the major growth market of tankers, British building times averaged 22 months, which was three times the building cycle in Sweden or Japan, and more than double the time taken in Germany or Holland.[66] Whereas in the late 1940s and early 1950s British builders had routinely explained their long delivery and construction times in terms of shortages of steel and poorly timed deliveries of steel within the gross allocations, that position was no longer tenable. Indeed, by 1956, British shipbuilders were admitting that the steel supply problem had eased, and in any case it had not been an exclusively British problem, since similar shortages had been experienced in West Germany, Scandinavia, and Japan.[67] Yet in spite of the fact that foreign builders had similar supply constraints, they had reduced their average berth and fitting-out time by half between 1948 and 1954, and had then gone on to maintain a 12-month building cycle, even though their order book had exploded from 8 million tons to 27 million tons between 1954 and 1957. In comparison the British builders had failed to make any significant improvement in delivery, and their order book and production times had remained relatively static. Britain's failure to reduce its building times in line with the achievement of competitors also acted to limit the overall output of the industry, and underwrote the failure of the industry to grow in expanding market conditions. UK shipbuilders consistently maintained that with their existing labour force they could produce 1.75 million gross tons per year, if steel supplies were adequate. Yet, even when steel supply was not a serious constraint from 1954, this target was never reached. The shortfall in output was always 300,000–400,000 tons.

If UK builders had been able to raise their launchings to 1.75 million tons in those years, this would have reduced their building and delivery times from around 19 months to an average of 15 months, and this would have kept British yards more closely in line with average building times on the Continent, if not in Japan. As it was, the failure to match improved building times in Europe and Japan progressively weakened Britain's hold on customers who were anxious for early and reliable delivery. The loss was first evident in export orders, for, as was noted in *Lloyds List and Shipping Gazette*, 'no foreign owner is going to come to this country if he thinks that strikes, disputes, and the likes are going to frustrate him when every other shipbuilding nation is offering him fixed delivery dates in addition to fixed prices'.[68] New elements in explaining Britain's poor delivery record are prominent here: the disruptive effects of labour disputes, and the attractions of fixed prices as well as earlier delivery. The new emphasis on labour issues at the root of competitiveness had been voiced sporadically in the early 1950s, and had become more evident from 1953–54.

By the mid-1950s the reports of the Shipbuilding Conference regularly reflect the view that the shipbuilders had been diligent in investing large sums in their industry, and that the modernisation programmes had placed British yards in a favourable position in equipment and organisation in relation to competitors. This view was succinctly expressed by R.W. Johnson, president of the Shipbuilders Employers Federation, at an informal meeting called between the Federation, the Shipbuilding Conference, and the Confederation of Shipbuilding and Engineering Unions in January 1959. The meeting was initiated by the shipbuilders, anxious to review with the unions the situation in the industry. Johnson reviewed the loss of leadership to Japan and Germany, which had so shaken British confidence, and asked 'if we have modern appliances, if we are in the van of research, and if we claim we are second to none in our methods of shipbuilding, why is our performance not very much better? Why is our output pegged to 1.4 million gross tons per annum when we have the capacity to turn out at least 1.75 million gross tons.' Since steel supply was no longer a constraint, and since there was an adequate supply of labour and skill, Johnson speculated that improvement depended upon cooperation with the labour force, and that while he would not suggest that 'all faults lie with our employees', he nevertheless felt that 'if we could find some way of avoiding the losses of productive time in our yards for whatever cause, we would go a long way towards matching not only the speed of output achieved by our competitors but also the reliability of the delivery dates quoted by them'. Failure to achieve these standards in previous years had meant that, 'It is a bitter fact that we have acquired among foreign ships owners a reputation for being an Industry which cannot always be relied upon to deliver ships on the date promised. Cases in which delivery dates are not kept are numerous, they receive wide publicity and do untold harm to our competitive position.'

While the loss of face and market allegiance was most strikingly seen in foreign orders, it was acknowledged that domestic ship owners could also be influenced by Britain's serious loss of competitiveness in delivery times. While the 1957–58 order book was protected, because the largest part of work was for long-standing British customers with substantial capital reserves, who would not readily leave their place in the order queue, if they were once enticed to leave the queue at Britain's yards and join it at 'some foreign yard, it will be very difficult to bring him back'.[69]

By the mid-1950s, the delivery problem had changed from being an outgrowth of immediate post-war constraints to being a reflection of the growing uncompetitiveness of British shipyards, and that weakening of competitive strength was being increasingly seen to rest, in the shipbuilders' analysis, on the poor response of the labour force to yard modernisation. Moreover, the productivity issue was inextricably linked to the other evident indicator of competitive weakness, Britain's deteriorating position on price.

## Productivity and prices

The persistent claim by British shipbuilders that they could produce at least 1.75 million gross tons per year with the available labour force, assuming adequate steel supplies, suggests, in the absence of achieving that target, that the industry made little advance in productivity in the 1940s and 1950s and that the investment programme had little effect in improving the pace of production. Unfortunately we have no systematic evidence on productivity in the industry at this time. At best we can make some tentative outline statements based on the tonnage completion rate of the men employed on new construction in the industry. This is a very crude measure, but the calculation suggests (Table 5.10) that the immediate post-war modernisation schemes, and the shake-out of some labour, raised output per man by about one-quarter between 1941 and 1950, but that thereafter there was no significant change. In contrast, on an entirely different basis of calculation, the Japanese shipyards achieved a 47 per cent reduction in man hours per gross ton worked between 1949 and 1956.[70] Similarly, employing an even broader measure of productivity, the average output in gross tons per yard, it has been calculated that in Britain the position was effectively static between 1950 and 1960, the tonnage produced increasing only marginally from 24,100 tons to 25,600 tons per yard; this is broadly in line with the tonnage per man trend outlined above.[71] By the same measure, however, Swedish yards more than doubled productivity, from 34,800 tons to 71,100 tons in the same period, and even French yards achieved a spectacular advance from a low level of 10,600 tons in 1950, to 39,600 tons in 1960, leaving British yards trailing behind.

*Table 5.10*   Tons produced per man UK shipbuilding, 1946–1957

| Year | Number employed in new merchant construction | tonnage completed (gross tons) | gross tons per man | Index |
|------|-----------------------------------|----------------------|--------------|-------|
| 1946 | 59,111 | 1,061,268 | 17.95 | 100 |
| 1948 | 68,024 | 1,212,618 | 17.82 | 99 |
| 1950 | 62,023 | 1,388,922 | 22.39 | 125 |
| 1952 | 57,660 | 1,263,804 | 21.92 | 122 |
| 1954 | 66,153 | 1,495,657 | 22.61 | 126 |
| 1957 | 62,710 | 1,420,659 | 22.65 | 126 |

*Source*: Shipbuilding Employers Federation Returns; Shipbuilding Conference, Quarterly Statistical Reviews.

Although these estimates are compiled in different ways, and all give rise to questions on their construction and interpretation, they nevertheless all point in the same direction. If there was any productivity gain in British shipbuilding in this period, it was in the period immediately after the war, and then it stagnated. Conversely, major competitors were recording much larger gains in productivity, and these must go some way to explaining the poor record of output and delivery recorded by Britain's shipbuilders in comparison to the rapid growth achieved by the other shipbuilding nations.

The explanation of this apparent productivity inertia is not simple. It clearly involves an element of workload factor, in that the coordination of ample orders and scarcer supplies of materials with available workforce, never achieved a recipe which would have delivered the target output of 1.75 million tons. Steel-supply constraints certainly imposed an absolute output level on the industry, but this ceiling was never pushed upward either by overcoming the steel-availability problem by importation or by accelerating the flow of work to raise volume output through productivity gains. The employers believed that the capital had been provided to enable productivity to improve, and there is some evidence of modest gains to 1950 or so, but that improvement was not sustained. The failure may be linked to two circumstances: either the investment programme pursued in the early 1950s was inadequate to meet the needs of construction for ever-larger tankers and ore carriers; or, gains in labour productivity were increasingly frustrated by a strike-prone and uncooperative workforce.

On the first proposition, the timing of the modernisation schemes suggests a slackening of investment in the early 1950s, picking up sharply from 1956 in the wake of the Suez crisis. The rapid growth in tanker and ore-carrier size appears to have taken British builders by surprise. In 1957 *Fairplay* notes that the general tendency for both dry-cargo bulk carriers and tankers to increase in size would make the problem of securing suitable berths in Britain increasingly acute, 'until builders' plans for the expansion and reorganisation of their yards are completed'.[72] The *Financial Times* was less circumspect in concluding that it was difficult to see how UK shipbuilders could overcome the advantages of continental and Japanese yards in quick construction without investment, and in this respect the industry's post-war expansion 'has been inadequate. The industry at present takes 45 years to write off investments.'[73] While the industry routinely rejected such criticism as ill-informed, and referred repeatedly to its £100 million investment programme, the outcome for the industry was a stagnation in output, a sharp loss of market share, and growing evidence of uncompetitiveness on delivery and price.

The responsibility of labour for the failings will be explored further below in relation to changes in technology and shipyard practices, but on the primary level of commitment to continuous working, the record is not flattering. The SEF records for shipbuilding establishments show 500 stoppages between 1946 and 1951, an average of over 83 per year, involving over one million man-days lost to the industry. In the next decade there were a further 745 main stoppages involving another 2.5 million days lost, making a total of 1,245 stoppages and the loss of 3.48 million man-days between 1946 and 1961.[74] Peaks of disruption occurred in 1947, 1953, and 1956–57, the concentration of workplace disturbance in the 1950s coinciding with the challenge of new competition from continental and Japanese producers. The loss of leadership in this period of hesitant investment and labour conflict is not solely or even directly due to these circumstances at that time, since the failure to commit to growth and a preference for stabilising capacity are rooted in the events of the 1930s. Nevertheless, the investment and labour issues are key elements in explaining the deterioration in price competitiveness which also began to erode Britain's market position at this time.

## Prices

Although Britain's shipbuilders had been steadily undercut on price by continental builders in the exceptional conditions of the 1930s, the Second World War effectively gave UK builders a fresh start on price competitiveness. Unlike the First World War, prices were more rigidly controlled in the second conflict, and by 1945 the average value per gross ton of ships built in Britain was £50.47 compared with £34.74 per ton in 1939, an advance of only 45 per cent. The USA was the only serious alternative source for large-scale tonnage supplies, and in 1945 the average unit cost of a standard cargo ship was $415 per gross ton compared with £42.0 per ton in Britain. Even had US prices not been three times higher, the chronic dollar shortage in Europe and elsewhere effectively ruled out large-scale acquisition of US tonnage.

With Germany and Japan excluded from large-scale ship production, Britain was effectively the main supplier of merchant ships for British and foreign fleets, and inherited a sellers' market in which obtaining delivery of new tonnage was more important than the price to be paid. Between 1946 and 1949 the average price paid per ton of all vessels built increased by 38 per cent to £87.1 (Table 5.11), and this was equalled by the delivered price rise for the standard Fairplay 9,500 dwt ton diesel cargo ship. The price per ton did move ahead more rapidly than either the cost of steel plates and angles, which until 1949 were subsidised by £3.0 per ton by the government, or earnings, which increased only modestly by 12 per cent under strong government control. This suggests that the builders did modestly exploit the sellers' market, not to the extent of setting prices at levels to test what the market would bear, but at least to guarantee good returns through escalation clauses built into contracts protecting them from movements in material and labour costs during the period of the contract. All contracts were also on a cost-plus basis, adding the long-established 8–10 per cent for profit. That prices were not pushed ahead faster was also due to the long-established builder–customer links; builders depended on repeat orders from customary ship owners, and any blatant exploitation of favourable seller conditions in the short run would have jeopardised longer term relationships which could deliver orders in less favourable circumstances.

The relatively modest rise in prices to 1949 was then accelerated by three shocks in a six-year period: the 1949 devaluation of the pound sterling; the rearmament boom of 1951–52 associated with the Korean War; and the effects of the Suez Crisis in 1956. Consequently between 1949 and 1958 the price of the standard Fairplay cargo ship doubled, although the advance on the price of all tonnage was more modest, at 60 per cent. It is in this period of rapidly rising prices that Britain began to lose ground on price, but the erosion was slow and not uniform in all categories of tonnage. Between 1949 and 1953, as Germany and Japan were reinserted into world markets as major producers, Germany certainly was able to build more cheaply than Britain. However, press comment suggests that while continental yards in general took advantage of the huge demand for new tonnage by offering earlier delivery times than Britain, they charged comparable prices to 'cash in' on the situation.[75] At the same time it was believed that Japan was still a higher cost producer than Britain, Japanese costs per ton for a 20,000 dwt tanker being in the range $175–$180, against equivalent British costs of $160–$165.[76]

*Table 5.11*   Price changes in British shipbuilding
(1946=100)

|      | 1 | 2 | 3 | 4 | 5 |
|------|-----|-----|-----|-----|-----|
| 1946 | 100 | 100 | 100 | 100 | 100 |
| 1949 | 138 | 138 | 126 | 110 | 112 |
| 1951 | 136 | 166 | 146 | 130 | 122 |
| 1953 | 150 | 214 | 171 | 182 | 148 |
| 1955 | 180 | 229 | 200 | 191 | 172 |
| 1958 | 225 | 276 | 244 | 262 | 195 |

*Sources*:

1. Average value per gross ton of ships launched. Calculated from Shipbuilding Conferences, Statistics of Merchant Tonnage Launched.

2. Fairplay Price of Standard 9,500 dwt diesel ship.

3. Chamber of Shipping price of deep-sea cargo liners and tramps built in UK yards for UK owners. Annual Report, 1958–59, Table 32.

4. Shipbuilding Conference; Prices of steel plates and sections.

5. Average Weekly Earnings; last pay week in April each year: *Ministry of Labour Gazette*.

In this situation real price competition was muted, but began to figure more prominently as British costs rose sharply after 1954, pushed upward by sharply increased costs of steel and accelerating wages. But even though steel prices did advance by 40 per cent, from £30 per ton in early 1953 to over £42 per ton by 1957, this was still significantly cheaper that the £50 per ton paid in Germany, £60 in Japan, and £65 per ton in Sweden. At the same time, however, wage rates in the UK industry had edged 10 per cent ahead of the Netherlands, and 20 per cent above Germany rates. Japanese rates were then only half the British level.[77] Allied to growing differentials in building and delivery times, these relative movements on steel and labour prices widened the price gap and pushed British builders into a weak position. By the middle of 1958, as the first serious post-war recession set in, information collected by the Shipbuilding Conference revealed Britain's deteriorating competitiveness on price. On insulated cargo liners of 10,800 dwt tons, the British price was 11 per cent higher than German quotations, 13 per cent above Swedish prices and 19 per cent higher than Danish builders. On a 9,000 dwt bulk carrier the British price was 5–10 per cent higher than those of Japan, France, Germany, and Italy. On passenger cargo vessels, a British speciality, Dutch prices were 26 per cent lower, and German prices 17 per cent below the lowest British tender.[78] These alarming differentials were more a sign of future problems than of past performance, for it seems clear that British costs and prices were not seriously adrift from those of major rivals through to 1954–55. However, as Germany and Japan quickly took leading shares of the world market, the competition for orders intensified. Where early delivery had been the main differential, it was now added to by the attraction of prices not only lower than available in Britain, but increasingly of fixed-price contracts which were also beginning to be backed up by preferential credit terms. The credit package consequently emerged as yet another factor in which Britain had made little progress in relation to competitor nations.

## Credit support

Financing ship construction normally required negotiation of financial arrangements between builder and ship owner in two ways. First, the costs of construction had to be provided for, and this was normally arranged in part by the shipbuilder drawing on his own resources, or by arranging bank loans, these advances being offset by the customer's deposit and instalment payments. This pattern of finance continued after the Second World War and did not normally present difficulty for the established British shipping lines with adequate capital reserves to provide for new tonnage. However, the second type of finance, post-delivery finance, began to figure more prominently in contract negotiations, the ship owner expecting to be financed for part of the price of the ship for a number of years after delivery. The security was normally in the form of a mortgage charge on the ship, the earnings of the ship being given as a pledge for the service of the loan. Since the demand for this type of facility increased notably after 1945, the Shipbuilding Conference responded by establishing in 1951 the Ship Mortgage Finance Company. The Conference members subscribed 25 per cent of the initial £1 million capital, later increased to £3 million, and also held a further £250,000 in debentures. The total resources of the company were £3 million in share capital and £2 million in debentures. The other partners in the company were The Industrial and Commercial Finance Corporation (ICFC) and about forty financial institutions and insurance companies. Between its establishment in 1951 and the end of 1958 the Ship Mortgage Finance Company had financed the purchase of 50 ships from British yards; it had lent out a total of £14 million, and placed a further £8.5 million with other institutions. The company usually offered a loan of 50 per cent of the delivery price repayable by instalments over five years.

While this was an important contribution by the industry to assist foreign buyers, it was small in scale and left most contracts to seek support by other means. Foreign purchasers could also benefit from credit guarantees under the Export Credit Guarantees Department, which offered facilities for credit insurance of up to 80 per cent of the contract price. If a credit-guarantee insurance policy was obtained the ship owner could then use it to raise loans from a bank, or other financial institutions, to meet a large part of the cost of the vessel. This provision, like that of the Ship Mortgage Finance Company, was normally for five years.

The underlying assumption in both these schemes was that export sales should be facilitated, but that domestic purchases would be adequately served by customary and private arrangements; for the first post-war decade that appeared to be the case. Indeed, as long as the inflow of new orders was vigorous, shipbuilders voiced little complaint or concern. But when the new competitive power of Germany and Japan coincided with a downturn in foreign enquiries, as it did in 1953, there was immediate pressure for better credit facilities backed by the government. In spite of continuous agitation by the Shipbuilding Conference for support in credit, the government was resistant. The scepticism of the wisdom of going down this path was voiced in the *Economist*, which condemned British manufacturers for tending to assume that more difficult export markets should entitle them to special or new credit facilities. A concession to the aircraft industry in 1953 did not open the door for the shipbuilders, even though examples of overseas orders being lost to foreign yards 'through lack of credit facilities' were alluded to.[79] The belief was that a more relaxed provision of export-credit support would tempt 'strong buyers to bargain for what they do not need; and ... would certainly increase the risk of a profitless "credit war" with Britain's competitors'. This remained the official attitude throughout the 1950s even in face of mounting evidence that more generous credit packages were being devised by major overseas rivals. Even so, there is little real evidence of any serious competitive edge being lost through inferior credit arrangements before the 1958 recession. Delivery time, followed by price, remained the major determinants, and even much more widespread and generous credit provision would not have compensated for the weakness developing in these two main areas of competitiveness. These in turn were related to the industry approach to technical and organisational change in the post-war years.

# Technological and organisational change

The war, and the period of rapid reconstruction and post-war expansion, hastened technical and organisational change in shipbuilding through innovations in the main inter-related areas of the construction, propulsion, and design of ships. In construction the nature of the process was fundamentally altered with the introduction of welding, burning, and prefabrication on a large scale. In propulsion, the innovation of heavy oil diesels with larger single shaft power, pushed harder against the steam turbine monopoly of providing power for larger vessels. In design, the scale economies inherent in prefabrication, together with the fuel and operational economies promised by larger bulk carrier hulls, triggered off a rapid growth in ship size. The response of British shipbuilders in each of these developments had direct consequences for the competitiveness of the industry in product mix and market orientation, and on the speed, efficiency and cost of construction and delivery.

## *Construction*

The construction of steel ships involved the assembly and joining of individual plates to frames on the berth by the process of riveting. Progress on the berth consequently set the productive capacity of the shipyard, irrespective of the capacity and efficiency of other facilities in the establishment.[80] The scale of individual berths also limited the impact of attempts to mechanise the construction process. Moreover, at the fitting-out and finishing stages, the opportunities for standardisation and mechanisation were even more restricted since the work depended on the individual working man operating in the confined spaces in the structure of the completed hull.

Construction on the berth, followed by difficult fitting-out procedures within a completed hull, consequently set ceilings on the volume and speed of output in the typical shipyard. The answer to breaking through these limitations had been demonstrated by the welding and prefabrication of ships on a factory basis during the Second World War. The Liberty and Victory ship programmes carried out by the American shipyards clearly demonstrated that unskilled labour could quickly be trained to use welding equipment, and could be organised to follow routine tasks for standard ship construction, much of the assembly taking place in plating sheds and assembly halls away from the berth, the completed prefabricated sections then being transported to the berth for assembly into more complex hull structures. The detailed construction records of the Liberty ship programme showed that for the 2,578 ships delivered, the man hours per vessel declined from a maximum of 3,159,000 hours to 219,000 hours; the maximum days for construction was 331, while the minimum achieved was 21 days. The evidence showed the learning curve based on construction of the Liberty ships in groups of ten. The very high average man hours taken to construct the first 10 ships had been cut in half after 60 vessels had been built; after 250 ships of the same design had been constructed, the average man hours was only one-third the time for the first batch. Even with more complex vessels, such as destroyers, the welding, prefabrication, and flow-line assembly techniques achieved dramatic savings. Of 348 destroyers delivered during the war, the average man hours taken to construct the first three vessels was 1,265,000; after 70 ships this had been cut to 584,000, and the minimum time taken fell as low as 396,000 man hours.[81]

In less dramatic circumstances, but employing similar techniques, the Eriksberg yard in Gothenburg achieved a reduction of 50 per cent in man hours required to construct 15,000 ton tankers as welding and prefabrication were steadily introduced between the late 1920s and the late 1940s.[82] Moreover, even in British yards, huge savings in time were realised in the wartime construction of B-type cargo ships through increased use of welding, and modest prefabrication. The average steel content of these ships was 2,500 tons, initially all riveted and assembled on the berth. By 1944 welding of prefabricated units was employed on just over half the steel tonnage (1,379 tons), and the time of construction was halved over that taken for ships where all the steel work was still riveted on berth.[83] All these applications also confirmed a significant saving on the weight of steel required for construction, varying from 7–10 per cent, depending on the type of ship.

The war-time experience seemed to show that the future of construction lay with the all-welded ship and extensive prefabrication, these steps delivering significant savings on steel and construction time over traditional methods. Immediately after the war, the USA and Sweden certainly committed themselves in this way, and between 1946 and 1949 data compiled at each April in the journal *Shipbuilder and Marine Enginebuilder* indicate a world production of 264 all-welded vessels totalling 1,511,721 gross tons, mainly produced in the USA and Sweden. In contrast, UK yards delivered only seven all welded ships of a modest 17,907 tons in this post-war period. Why, with the wartime evidence apparently so convincing on the benefits to be gained by wholesale adoption of the newer techniques, was there not a more rapid switch to all-welded and prefabricated construction in Britain?

Part of the answer lies in the mixed message portrayed by the reliability of the Liberty ships themselves. While production times had clearly been revolutionised, about 1,000 of the 2,710 ships built to the same basic design experienced problems, many, but not all, associated with poor workmanship, rather than with the inherent characteristics of the welding process.[84] Nevertheless, it had quickly become clear that the detailed design of a ship intended for construction by welding had to be different from that for riveting, the residual stress patterns created by joining plates by the two methods being very different. The problem of brittle fractures worried shipbuilders and ship owners, and caution was expressed by J.L. Adams, chief surveyor of the British Corporation Register of Shipping and Aircraft at a meeting held in the Institute of Welding in 1946. He argued that 'in our present state of ignorance all welded ships are not as safe as their riveted counterparts'.[85] At the same meeting the Director of Naval Construction, C.S. Lillicrop, warmly advocated a quick adoption of all-welded ships, but foresaw a 'national inertia' in the industry as a major problem.

In spite of these reservations, it is arguable that the lessons of war-time construction clearly pointed to the superiority in speed and economy of welding and prefabrication over riveting. However, that superiority had been best demonstrated for relatively simple and standard cargo ships, and the achievement of the benefits pointed to the need for a systematic reorganisation of the work process and a substantial investment in new plant and equipment. Moreover, reliable quality demanded careful pre-design of prefabrication and welding sequences, and close attention to the welding technique itself. There were therefore perceived obstacles in relation to applying the techniques to a wide and varied order book of ship types; to the scale of investment required to benefit from the technology; and from the organisation and control of labour in using the welding, burning, and prefabrication methods.

The first two problem areas – the ship types for which the technique was thought appropriate, and the scale of changes necessary in a yard to make welding effective – were closely linked. The American, and to a lesser extent the Swedish, experience showed the best returns being achieved with a high-volume throughout of ships produced in series or in batches. Series and batch production was the antithesis of British methods which exemplified customised production, even when repeat orders were involved. Moreover, the standardisation of work and design inherent in the simple cargo ship was felt to be inappropriate in yards routinely building a wide variety of ship types on adjacent berths. The preference was consequently to use welding as a complement to riveting, and apply it manually on the berth for much of the time.

The alternative, to apply welding systematically for most of the construction in prefabricated units, meant shifting away from a building technique based on the berth, to one where the balance of work took place in platers' sheds and assembly bays under cover within the yard. For that transition to be effective, berths had to be reduced in number and increased in size; extra space had to be created for sheds, bays, and handling preparation areas; and much also depended on improvements in overhead craneage and yard transportation systems.

Given these issues, only a very few yards in Britain contemplated such a large-scale re-organisation of work and facilities, notably the larger liner and naval yards such as Vickers at Barrow, Harland & Wolff at Belfast, and to a lesser extent, John Brown in their East Yard at Clydebank. The scale of reorganisation, and the depth of capital involved, conflicted with the pressures of post-war order books, inducing an *ad hoc* and piecemeal implementation of welding, rather than a systematic adoption and exploitation. Such a 'bolt-on' approach sacrificed a re-design of yard and yard practice in a production engineering sense, in favour of immediate profitability.

Even so, there was significant new investment in the first decade after the war, and there was clearly a steady extension in the use of welding in mixed construction with riveting in most yards. The number of welders employed on new merchant work doubled to over 1,700 men between 1942 and 1945, at which time they represented 5.8 per cent of the skilled workforce compared with 11.0 per cent being riveters. Riveters outnumbered welders by two to one, but by 1950, the two main groups had almost equalised, and by 1955 the balance had moved powerfully in favour of the welders. They then represented 10.7 per cent of the skilled men, and riveters only 6.3 per cent.[86] By 1960 welders outnumbered riveters in British shipbuilding by three to one. However, the piecemeal introduction of welding and prefabrication had clearly not delivered the gains in construction times and costs evident in Sweden, and even more so in Japan. The failure of the changes that had been introduced to accomplish significant savings seems also to be related to the third factor, the way in which welding and prefabrication labour was organised.

While the penetration of welding, as the major joining technology, was a feature of the post-war decade, the basis on which it was manned and organised in the workforce was set in the ten years from the mid-1930s. In that period the attempts of the shipbuilders to create a new grade of employment – 'ship welder' – which cut across established craft union job control, foundered on union opposition to what they believed were management attempts to de-skill and dilute a metal-working task. As the use of welding increased in the naval and liner yards in the 1930s, it was quickly clear to management that the welding function overlapped and touched on jobs currently being carried out by members of at least four major unions, the Boilermakers, the Blacksmiths Society, the Plumbers Association, and the Ship Contractors and Shipwrights Association. There was no established 'rate' for the job, and the interlocking interests of the unions opened up potentially damaging inter-craft demarcation issues.

Against this background the Shipbuilders Employers Federation considered two proposals generated in 1932 and 1933 as a basis for negotiation with the unions. The first proposal envisaged the designation of a new grade of employee, a 'ship-welder', entry to which would be by a two-year training programme, the qualified man to be paid at the national uniform rate for skilled trades, then 60 shillings (£3) per week.[87] In addition, a second more radical proposal envisaged reallocating the work involved in welding by eliminating the traditional squad system, in which the skilled men had monopoly control of all operations. In contrast, it was proposed to subdivide and simplify the procedures. Broadly, it was proposed that the platers should operate exclusively in the plating sheds, with pre-handling, straightening and mangling to be carried out by less skilled helpers. Moreover, transportation of welded plates to the berth could be undertaken by unskilled labour, and erection at the bay could be carried out by semi-skilled men. The SEF itself rejected this more radical reorganisation of work control, largely because it required a degree of managerial planning and quality control which only the largest yards were equipped to provide. Most smaller and medium yards lacked the managerial and technical infrastructure to adopt a production engineering system approach to welding and prefabrication, and essentially relied on the squad system for these functions.

Not surprisingly, even the modest proposals to coordinate the welding work in the new grade of ship welder, were rejected by the unions who were antagonistic to the removal of training from the apprenticeship system, and to the reduction in the period of time required for access to a skilled grade of labour. The control of this process by the employers rather than the union also proved to be a stumbling block. With the double rejection, employers attempted to introduce the ship welder scheme from 1934, but since only a few large yards had much interest in welding there was no systematic or coordinated employers' position. Consequently individual yards and companies confronted more coordinated union resistance, though even there the apparent concord was internally riven. While the four main unions had agreed in 1934 to support each other's members in opposition to employers attempting to introduce the ship-welder scheme, each in practice pursued independent strike action and agreed individual settlements with firms involved. The Boilermakers were particularly active and forced settlements on a piece-work rather than time-rate basis, even though the SEF scheme advocated time-rate payment.[88]

By being coordinated across all yards on a craft basis in this initial phase, the unions were more coherently organised than the employers, who lacked unity of purpose and were picked off yard by yard, conceding settlements on union terms. Among the unions 'force majeure' favoured the Boilermakers who by the early years of the Second World War had seen off the competition and achieved exclusive rights to arc welding in hull construction, and had done so on a piece-work basis, rather than on time rates. This was an extraordinary achievement by unions in a period of weak employment, when negotiating strength should have lain with employers, with up to half the workforce out of employment and anxiously seeking work. By inference, the employers lost control through their own failure to cooperate, placing self-interest above group coherence. The loss of control by management of welding and prefabrication to union squads, was repeated with the even less skilled tasks of automatic burning of plates to replace the older shearing and mangling techniques.[89] Under war-time pressures to maintain production, rights of operation were vested in the Boilermakers, thus maintaining these procedures as skilled operations when they were essentially unskilled tasks. The combination of these shifts to welding and burning moved craft control of the construction process on balance away from the berths where the Shipwrights prevailed, to the sheds and assembly bays, where the Boilermakers dominated, reinforcing their control of operations. Their effective closed shop, and craft control of welding, burning and prefabrication, were deeply embedded by the end of the Second World War, and dictated manning and operational usage as welding became more common in the shipyards after 1945. While craft control and job specification were protected by these arrangements, they imposed on the shipyards an organisation of welding processes and labour that could not deliver the savings of man hours gained in the Swedish and American yards. The rigidity inherent in the craft-squad system, of jobs exclusively allocated to particular craftsmen, inherently limited the benefits which could be gained from the investment and modernisation programmes, and goes some way to explain the weakening position of British yards in construction and delivery times, and the stagnation apparent in productivity.

## Propulsion and design

In the decade before the Second World War it was clear that demand in world shipping markets was moving strongly towards the motorship, bulk-cargo vessels and tankers. There is some evidence to suggest that while Britain, as the world's major shipbuilder, built more motor and tanker tonnages than any other country, her shipbuilders nevertheless moved more slowly into these market areas than builders in other countries. In the 1930s British yards constructed 45.9 per cent of their tonnage as motorships, while abroad the proportion was 63.7 per cent.[90] Similarly in tankers, one-third of tonnage by foreign builders was constructed as tankers in the 1930s compared to 24 per cent in Britain. While these trends were strongly linked to the different demand patterns of British owners *viz à viz* overseas ship owners, the tight linking of British builders and ship owners nevertheless meant that British builders were less and less favourably placed in adapting to meet the technical and design needs of the most rapidly expanding areas of demand.[91]

The war accelerated these trends in favour of the motorship and larger vessels, notably tankers, and in the unusual conditions after 1945 Britain's pattern of response closed the gap on foreign builders. Between 1946 and 1958, foreign builders launched 60 per cent of their tonnage as motorships, while in Britain the proportion was only slightly less at 58 per cent. Similarly in tanker construction, with emphasis on larger scale, Britain's output included 46 per cent as tanker tonnage, while overseas the proportion was again slightly higher at over 48 per cent.[92] While the overall performance in adapting to trends in propulsion and design were similar, the underlying trend was still of some deterioration in the British position. However, in the sharpest area of engineering competition, that of heavy oil diesels with superheating, challenging the use of steam turbines for larger vessels, Britain like the rest of the world built and designed around 70 per cent of its tanker tonnage as steam-turbine vessels. Only Sweden built mainly motor tankers by 1938, with 85 per cent of its vessels diesel-driven. Sweden, too, was the world leader on average size of tankers driven by diesel; in 1958 Sweden's average motorship tanker was 15,834 tons against the world average of only 5,345 tons. Most other countries relied on the turbine, where the average world steam-turbine engined tanker was 22,587 tons in 1958. It was in the scale of the tankers, rather than in their propulsion, that Britain was beginning to fall behind, the average British tanker being just over 18,000 tons.

None of these trends, individually, in ship size, choice of propulsion, or proportion of tonnage engined by diesel or steam turbine, suggests that British shipbuilders were being seriously outpaced by rival builders. But the small lag in every area cumulatively added to the other areas of weakness in building times, delivery, and cost, and edged

British shipbuilding more firmly out of world leadership in the 1950s. All suggest an industry moving less quickly than others to keep in touch with world trends. A degree of lethargy, if not inertia, was becoming apparent, and that lack of swift change was also evident in the organisation and structure of the industry itself.

As we have seen, there was no rapid extension of capacity during or after the Second World War, nor was there much interest in establishing greenfield sites, only the Newcroft yard being set up in 1953. Nor was there any significant change in organisational structure by merger, acquisition or closure. Between 1945 and 1958 the only significant mergers were the linkage of the Burntisland Shipbuilding Company on the Forth with the Aberdeen yards of Alex Hall & Co. and Hall Russell & Co. in 1951. There was also the linking of Austin and Pickersgill on the Wear, and of the specialist dredger yards of Simons and Lobnitz on the Clyde, both in 1957. The first merger was initiated by Scottish and Mercantile Investments, while the Austin and Pickersgill grouping was an acquisition by a consortium of London and Overseas Freighters, Lambeth Brothers, and Philip Higginson & Co.[93] The Simons and Lobnitz yards were both owned by the G. & J. Weir engineering group based at Cathcart on the south side of Glasgow.

Apart from these small groupings there was no restructuring of ownership or operation of British shipbuilding in the period 1938–58. There was also very little change in industrial concentration. Between the wars half of all tonnage launched was delivered by twelve yards, and one-quarter by four yards. Between 1946 and 1955, half of all output emanated from nine yards. Within this, there was very little change in the dominant builders; the top three of Harland & Wolff, Swan Hunter & Wigham Richardson, and Lithgows, were a constant, while in the top twelve only Laings and Hawthorn Leslie were newcomers in the 1950s. This stability also showed through in the scale of the larger yards in their average annual launched tonnage. Only Harland & Wolff and Vickers Armstrong launched in excess of 100,000 tons per year, and only one other British yard, Swan Hunter & Wigham Richardson, passed that level on one occasion in 1957. In contrast, by 1958, Japan had six yards regularly launching in excess of 100,000 tons per year and Germany had four, as had Sweden. The market for bigger ships was inexorably being tackled in the rapidly growing shipbuilding nations more strongly than in Britain.[94]

## The equilibrium trap

The underlying rationale dominating the investment decisions, product choices, and market positioning of British shipbuilders, was the link of their overall capacity and projections for orders and growth, to the replacement and new tonnage needs of the British merchant fleet. This symbiosis had driven the growth of shipbuilding throughout the steel and steam era, and into the age of the motorship. The outcome of this relationship had broadly been favourable for the shipbuilders. As long as world demands for new tonnage were dominated by the requirements for new ships by the British merchant fleet, the strategy ensured that British shipbuilders had a monopoly of the world's largest new tonnage market, and the industry was secure in its world leadership. The equilibrium position of holding British shipbuilding growth and capacity in line with the growth of the domestic fleet ensured world shipbuilding dominance.

This position of ascendancy depended, however, on the dynamic and leadership of the UK fleet in developing trades, and maintaining its position as the world's largest carrier. This position of leadership was already weakened in the inter-war years, and when the UK fleet ceased to grow between 1945 and 1958, after a rapid replacement of war losses, the equilibrium formula became a trap for British shipbuilders, locking them into a dependency on a stagnant sector in an expanding world shipping market. The dependencies binding builder to ship owner in this equilibrium trap worked both ways, but were of unequal strength. As world commodity trade expanded, and markets and shipping routes changed in the 1950s, competition in shipping accelerated faster than competition in shipbuilding, the need for new tonnage for a time outpacing the ability to supply it. Consequently, even though British shipping was losing market share, its orders were for a time still very tightly tied to British shipbuilders, and the relationship seemed secure. However, when the new shipbuilding capacity came on stream in the mid-1950s, the delivery and price advantage offered by Swedish, German, Dutch and Japanese shipbuilders offered British ship owners a way out of their increasing uncompetitiveness by replacing tonnage at lower prices, and more quickly, with foreign yards. It therefore became easier for British ship owners to find an alternative to their dependence on British shipbuilders, than it was for the shipbuilder, at prevailing British prices and deliveries, to find alternative clients once the builder–client link began to haemorrhage. With this development the equilibrium trap was sprung: the British ship owner had an escape route to alternative builders, but the British yards, long oriented to the British flag fleet, were left with a declining market sector which had steadily led them down a path of low investment and minimum change. By the end of the 1950s, in spite of a belated programme of modernisation, much of the British industry was falling behind European and Japanese competitors in technology, in work practice, and in shipyard organisation. While the margins of difference in product mix, price, and delivery were not yet large, the paths and pace of development of British and the main competitor shipbuilding industries were diverging rapidly.

British shipbuilding had enjoyed twenty years of opportunity for growth but had sought modernisation and stability in balance with the domestic flag fleet. That had created an equilibrium trap from which there was no obvious escape. The scene was set for the unprecedented and precipitous loss of market share that was now swiftly to follow.

CHAPTER SIX

# Deterioration: 1958–1963

## Recession

The rapid post-war expansion of world shipbuilding came to an abrupt halt in 1958. The rush to place tanker orders in the wake of the Suez Crisis had doubled the world order book, from 17.8 million gross tons in 1955 to 34.5 million tons in 1957,[1] and pushed world launchings to the record level of 9.269 million gross tons in 1958. Tonnage under construction world-wide reached 10.0 million tons, and completions also peaked at 9.059 million tons; by that time the world merchant fleet had reached 118.0 million tons, an advance of 26 per cent in the preceding five years, and world seaborne commodity trade had expanded from 655 million to 930 million tons.[2]

This hot-house advance first accelerated freights, then plunged them deeply downward. Tramp time-charter rates effectively doubled from the base of 1952 = 100 to 197 in the fourth quarter of 1956, before sliding steeply downward from 131 in mid 1957 to a low of 51 in mid-1958. Rates did not begin to climb steadily above that level until the second half of 1963.[3] The collapse of freights signposted an immediate problem of surplus shipping capacity which forced tonnage out of employment in a spectacular way. Shipping laid up through lack of employment advanced from 1.537 million tons in 1958 to 7.348 million in 1959 and was still 6.262 million in 1960.[4] This loss of momentum in the shipping industry inevitably brought in its wake five years of stagnation for world shipbuilding during which tonnage under construction, launchings and completions, all fell below the 1958 figures (Table 6.1). However, while the overall scale of world shipbuilding output was static, there were important changes in the relative positions of the major producers.

At first sight, on the evidence of launches and completions between 1958 and 1963, the shifts were slight. The West European shipbuilders, including the UK, had 64.1 per cent of world launches in 1958, and still 59.2 per cent in 1963, while the Japanese share had advanced from 22.3 per cent to 27.7 per cent. The European industry was still twice the scale of the Japanese. Similarly in completions, in 1958, the European industry delivered 64.6 per cent of the world tonnage with Japan a little less than 25.0

*Table 6.1*   World shipbuilding, 1958–1963
('000 gross tons)

|  | Launches | Completions | Order book |
|---|---|---|---|
| 1958 | 9,270 | 9,059 | 27,395 |
| 1961 | 7,940 | 8,058 | 18,656 |
| 1963 | 8,538 | 9,026 | 18,890 |

*Source*: Lloyds Register of Shipping.

per cent. Even in 1963 the relative positions were 61.2 per cent of completions from European yards, and 25.1 per cent from Japan. This stability, however, concealed a seriously deteriorating position for European shipbuilding as it lived on its legacy of a very large share of world orders from 1958, with over 68 per cent of the world total of 27.395 million tons. Japan then had a small order book of 3.478 million tons, much smaller than Britain's 5.373 million tons, and less than 14 per cent of the world total. Yet in the next five years, during which the world order book contracted by over 30 per cent to 18.89 million tons, Japan increased its share to 30.6 per cent, while the European builders suffered a loss of market share to just over half the order book (Table 6.2). In a period of intense competition for scarce orders Japan had bucked world trends by increasing its share of launches and completions, modestly, but more importantly in securing its immediate future by capturing the lion's share of a contracted and stagnant world market. The balance of shipbuilding power and world leadership had been shifted away decisively from Europe toward Japan. By 1963 the European industry was still larger than its Japanese rival, but the scales were tilting sharply against the European builders.

*Table 6.2*   Regional shares of world shipbuilding
and order books, 1958 and 1963

|  | Launches | | Completions | | Orders | |
|---|---|---|---|---|---|---|
|  | 1958 | 1963 | 1958 | 1963 | 1958 | 1963 |
| World totals ('000 grt) | 9,270 | 8,538 | 9,059 | 9,026 | 27,395 | 18,890 |
|  | % share | % share | % share | % share | % share | % share |
| Western Europe | 64.1 | 59.2 | 64.6 | 61.2 | 68.1 | 53.5 |
| Japan | 22.3 | 27.7 | 24.7 | 25.1 | 13.8 | 30.6 |
| Others | 13.6 | 13.0 | 10.7 | 13.6 | 18.1 | 15.9 |

*Source*: Lloyds Register of Shipping.

In this complex and fierce battle for leadership, and survival, the British shipbuilding industry suffered major reverses and its position deteriorated significantly, though not as sharply as some other European shipbuilders, performing notably better than the German and Dutch industries. Germany's share of world orders declined by over 60 per cent, and the Dutch by 75 per cent, against a fall of 56 per cent in Britain. Yet even as Britain retained the largest order book in Europe, until it was modestly surpassed by Sweden in 1968, and enjoyed a larger order book than Japan until 1961, the output performance of the British industry was weak. Launchings declined by nearly half a million tons from 1,402,000 tons in 1958, 15.1 per cent of the world total, to a poor 928,000 tons in 1963, a modest 10.9 per cent of world launches. Market share had been cut by more then 30 per cent in a five-year period.

This loss of market share was evident in both the domestic and overseas market. Domestically, the share of British tonnage launched going to the home flag fleet averaged nearly 82.0 per cent of total output, underlining the importance of the home market for orders. However, the total of new UK tonnage registered between 1958 and 1963, representing the scale of the domestic shipping market, was 8.579 million gross tons. British shipbuilders' share of this slipped steadily from nearly 79.0 per cent in 1958, to less than 60 per cent in 1963, indicating a significant penetration of the British market by foreign builders. The balance of trade in shipping exports and imports moved strongly against British shipbuilding from 1958, which was the last year in which tonnage exported exceeded imports. Thereafter Britain became a net importer of ships. Between 1958 and 1963 Britain imported 1.279 million tons of new ships, equal to an average year's output from British shipyards.

British export performance was also under stress in this difficult competitive environment. Tonnage launched for export in 1958 was 338,000 tons, some 24.1 per cent of output, but collapsed to 116,000 tons, a mere 8.4 per cent of production in 1959. By 1963 exports had recovered to 284,000 tons representing over 30 per cent of output. Yet when placed in the context of the world market for export tonnage, the British position showed a sharp deterioration. Britain had 10.6 per cent of world exports of 3.193 million tons in 1958, but only 6.4 per cent of a larger market of 4.424 million tons in 1963. Japan in contrast had doubled its export market share to 61.5 per cent, displacing the European shipbuilders from market leader. They had collectively held 68.8 per cent of exports in 1958, but only the balance of 38.5 per cent by 1963 (Table 6.3).

The deep recession from 1958 clearly held world shipbuilding in check for five years, output averaging only 8.5 million tons per year to 1963. In that static world framework, Britain regained second place in output behind Japan, delivering 14.2 per cent of all tonnage launched, against 13.0 per cent from Germany, and 23.2 per cent from Japan. This relative success reflected the benefit British builders gained from their customary control of the large home market, Britain's fleet at 21.56 million tons in 1963 still being second only in size to that of the USA, and more than twice

*Table 6.3*  Regional shares of world shipbuilding exports

|                                   | 1958    | 1960    | 1963    |
|-----------------------------------|---------|---------|---------|
| World exports ('000 gross tons)   | 3,193   | 3,016   | 4,424   |
|                                   | % share | % share | % share |
| UK                                | 10.6    | 4.8     | 6.4     |
| Western Europe (including UK)     | 58.1    | 64.6    | 32.1    |
| Japan                             | 31.2    | 30.6    | 61.5    |

*Source*:  Compiled from Lloyds Register of Shipping.

the size of the Japanese fleet of 9.9 million tons. But even with the advantage of the largest domestic market, and the status of the second-ranking world producer, the British shipbuilding industry showed serious signs of deterioration, with a declining share of world output, its weak penetration of world export markets, and its slackening hold on its own domestic market. The stagnation in output and loss of market share were immediately reflected in a serious loss of employment. The total workforce in shipbuilding and marine engineering declined by 65,000 between 1958 and 1963.[5] The largest decline in employment was in new merchant construction, which lost 29,700 men to reduce the workforce to 47,900 in 1963. Marine engineering lost 24,100 jobs, the labour force diminishing to 62,800. The other major signpost of deterioration was the closure of yards. In the post-war boom years to 1957, only nine small yards had ceased operation in Britain, but between 1958 and 1963 a further 18 closed, no fewer than 12 of these closing down in 1963.[6]

The years from 1958 and 1963 were clearly a critical period not only for British shipbuilding, but for the European industry as a whole. The British industry was significantly weakened in the environment of intense competition, which threw up problems of price competitiveness, access to credit support, reintroduced the problem of surplus capacity and sharpened the criticisms of the efficiency and productivity of both labour and management in Britain's shipyards. All of these issues are important in explaining Britain's reversals in the period, but as far as the industry itself was concerned the root problem was the reappearance of excess capacity.

## The capacity problem

During the post-war expansion of world shipbuilding there had been little concern in Britain with the inter-war preoccupation with surplus capacity. Indeed, the major anxiety was that British shipbuilding had consistently failed to work at its projected full capacity of 1.75 million tons of new shipping each year, this failure being regularly attributed to problems with the steel supply. In fact, as late as March 1958 the industry and its sponsoring government department, the Admiralty, were discussing proposals in the Shipbuilding Advisory Committee (SAC) to raise output to 2.0 million tons per year by 1960–61. It was believed that the completion of the modernisation plans in progress in British shipyards would make this target possible, although the Admiralty had calculated that the workforce would need to be expanded by about 11,000 men.[7] It was suggested that 4,000 of these would be needed on the Clyde, 3,700 on the North East coast and 1,200 on the Mersey. Both the union representatives and the shipbuilders on the SAC accepted the estimates, but believed the target could not be reached until 1961–62, and that the earliest evidence of increased output deriving from the modernisation programme would be seen in the launching figures for 1959.

This optimism was short-lived, fading quickly with the impact of the 1958 recession. Output and completions, far from showing the increase predicted on the basis of the modernisation schemes, each slumped irregularly from over 1.4 million tons in 1958 to lows of 928,000 tons launched in 1963, and 808,000 tons completed in 1964. The total order book similarly collapsed, from 4.07 million tons in 1958 to a low of 1.658 million tons in March 1963. Even worse, by September 1963 the industry only had 463,000 tons of orders on which work had not begun. The contraction of the order book had begun abruptly in late 1957, and by the end of 1958 the Policy Committee of the Shipbuilding Conference reported in a survey on the state of the industry that among twenty-one yards building the largest ships, only five had fewer than six ships to lay down, and were at that point relatively secure in workload and employment. However, of 12 yards building dry-cargo ships, only two yards had more than six ships that were firm orders, while of 43 yards building smaller and specialised ships, 18 had no work to lay down, 10 had only one ship, and three had only two ships still to commence.[8] By the spring of 1963, with only four months' work left to lay down for the industry as a whole, the Conference advised the Admiralty that 28 yards were already without work of any kind, or were completing their last ship with no further orders to commence.

The shock of this escalating deterioration in the position of the industry was profound. While in retrospect we can see the period of 1958–63 as a hesitation between two extended phases of rapid growth in world shipbuilding, the immediate impact of the decline in orders and output was to reawaken in British shipbuilders' dormant fears that any extension of capacity could only lead to increased competition, poor prices, and depressed conditions in the industry. The Conference conducted a wide-ranging review of the prospects for the industry at the end of 1958, setting it in the context of world trends in freights, the growth of the world fleet, and the capacity in world shipbuilding. The conclusion was that with world launchings at over 9.0 million tons in 1958, it would be possible to replace the world fleet in 11 years, and the tanker fleet in 8 years, against the normal expected lifespan of ships of 20 years. The implications led the Conference to ask if UK capacity was 'likely to be excessive in relation to foreseeable demand in any sector', and to speculate what the government's attitude might be to any suggested reduction in UK capacity.[9] The outcome of the deliberations of the Policy Committee was a report to the Executive Board in February 1959 which concluded that there was significant excess capacity in world shipbuilding and that it was 'indisputable that UK shipbuilding capacity is excessive in relation to the foreseeable overall demand'.[10] They believed the world-wide problem had developed from a drift towards various forms of subsidisation of shipbuilding abroad, leading to the establishment of unnecessary new capacity, linked to 'the cutting of prices to utterly uneconomic levels; and a tendency towards establishing a credit race'. The prospects for the future of British shipbuilding were conceived, as between the wars, almost exclusively in relation to the anticipated tonnage requirements of the British fleet. The Policy Committee had estimated that it was reasonable to assume an average future demand over the next few years of around 900,000 gross tons from British owners, and, more speculatively, 250,000 tons per year from foreign clients. Prospects of capturing a large share of orders from overseas were not given any particular consideration.

Confronted by the problems of recession, it is clear that British shipbuilding looked backward to inter-war thinking and inter-war strategy. This is evident in the reviews that the Shipbuilding Conference instituted into the work allocation and price-support schemes which they had developed in the 1930s.[11] Specific attention was focused on the 1930s Segregation Scheme from which it was concluded that 'one method of reducing costs and enhancing ability to compete for work might be by firms interested in certain type of ships forming a 'group'.[12] Implementation of such a scheme, however, would have to 'be a matter for individual firms' which could form a holding company to 'ensure a better distribution of work, reduction of overheads, and enable such a group, in effect, to do its own NSS'.[13] The 1930s' Scrap and Build scheme was also reviewed in the context that Japan was reported to be proposing such a measure, but the Conference believed the time was not ripe to approach the government on such a scheme. The advisability of pressing the government to bring forward warship work was also considered, but again the Conference believed that 'with the curtailment of defence expenditure there was little likelihood of additional warship work' being allocated.[14]

While the review was wide-ranging, the immediate outcome was that nothing was achieved in advancing naval work, and little real progress was made in cooperative coordination of work or voluntary grouping of firms. The inability to move in these areas to support the order book then reconfirmed the industry belief that its best plan for the future was to manage its capacity to keep it in balance with customary levels of demand from the home market. At the same time the British builders attempted to persuade their European neighbours that the reduction and control of capacity was in their best interest too. This issue was addressed through the meetings of the West European Shipbuilders Standing Committee, which agreed with the British delegates that 'the abnormally low level of shipbuilding prices had been caused primarily by the present unbalance between the volume of orders and the shipyards' production'.[15] However, there was no agreement to deal with capacity, merely a decision that each national association should consult with its members to undertake a study of the possibility of coordinated action to curtail each country's production 'in order to keep a more normal relation between the probable yearly volume of orders and the shipyards production'. There was no support in Britain for such a scheme; the problem as Britain saw it was not a temporary one subject to adjustment of output, but a permanent one caused by the uncontrolled expansion of shipbuilding capacity, a growth in which Britain had not shared. In Britain's view the real solution 'would be the pruning of capacity rather than production, and such pruning was more appropriate to those countries in which expansion has been so substantial'.[16] At this stage the Conference argued that, 'generally the size of the shipbuilding industry in the United Kingdom was not excessive', and that any capacity reduction should be made overseas.[17]

With the failure of this initiative, and with world capacity continuing to grow, the Conference was soon forced back to a consideration of capacity in Britain itself. By June 1962 it had before it a detailed memorandum on the structure and operation of the 1930s National Shipbuilders Security Scheme, which they believed could be the basis for any future rationalisation scheme.[18] The decision was that the Policy Committee should produce a scheme to be operated if circumstances made it necessary to purchase shipyards. The industry feared that, if firms were forced to close through lack of orders, there should be a scheme to purchase them to prevent them falling into the hands of speculators, an outcome which would be to the long-term detriment of the industry. It was proposed that the company owned by the Conference, the Shipbuilding Corporation, could be activated to operate the scheme in its initial phases. The Shipbuilding Corporation had been set up in December 1942 to manage NSS yards re-opened for war work. When its assets were added to those the Conference held in the Ship Mortgage Finance Co., it could have available to it immediate funds of £1.5 million. This compared to a view that the cost of even a limited redundancy scheme could be nearly £10 million.[19]

The draft proposals were advised to both the Board of Trade and Ministry of Transport and were received, the Conference believed, with 'favourable comment and the promise of every help in relation to other Government departments'.[20] However, by September the Board of Trade and the Ministry of Transport were seeking clarification of how the proposed redundancy scheme would affect construction, prices, and employment, in the shipyard districts, and also wanted more detail on the proportion of capacity to be eliminated, over what period the scheme would function, and which yards would be closed. Since the industry intended the scheme to be voluntary it could provide no satisfactory answers, though it indicated that the 'maximum amount of capacity which was intended to be eliminated [might be] a quarter or one third'.[21]

This hint was in fact significantly above the Conference estimates of surplus capacity in the industry, which placed the figure at 20 per cent.[22] The negotiations with the government were lengthy, but no approval was forthcoming, and the scheme foundered on the inability of the industry to specify the yards to be closed, and to come to an agreement on who would be responsible for redundancy payments for displaced workers. In the absence of any formal scheme the industry advised Ernest Marples, Minister of Transport, that 'it had continued with its own limited resources to provide means for shipyards to get out of business, and a few shipyards had in fact been dealt with through Shipbuilding Corporation'.[23] Just how many of the 18 yards which closed in 1963 had accepted assistance from the Conference is not known, but the sudden surge in closure suggests some connection with the renewed interest in capacity reduction as a Conference policy. The capacity eliminated between 1958 and 1963 represented an annual launching of around 176,000 tons, somewhere between 14 and 15 per cent of the annual average output of the industry in this period. This was a significant liquidation, but it is possible that the modernisation in the larger yards in part neutralised any benefit the industry might have anticipated. Most of the capacity eliminated in this period came from the Clyde, where the closure of Wm Hamilton & Co. at Port Glasgow, Harland & Wolff at Govan, and Denny at Dumbarton, took out around 100,000 tons of launch capacity. The only other larger yard to close was Wm Gray's at West Hartlepool, whose best post-war launchings were around 47,000 tons in any one year.

Leaving aside the unknown effects of modernisation on capacity, this reduction was not far from the 20 per cent the Conference had calculated as the immediate surplus hanging over the industry, so even in the absence of a formal rationalisation scheme there was some considerable movement toward implementing the industry policy of capacity reduction. The Conference continually expressed the conviction that only by reducing capacity could the problem of insufficient orders and poor prices be tackled effectively. The government agreed that a lack of orders, poor prices and slender profits were major problems, but did not share the shipbuilders' analysis as to the root cause of the difficulties. Ernest Marples argued that for the industry to seek to reduce capacity to come into line with the immediate needs of UK owners for new tonnage 'was not the correct approach,' for 'the first aim must be to reduce our shipbuilding costs, and if this entailed contraction of the industry, then this should be faced.' The brutal fact was that the British shipbuilding and marine engineering industries were not competitive with those in Sweden and Japan.[24]

The government view was that the problem lay in costs, rather than in capacity *per se*, and did not believe that capacity reduction of itself would resolve the problem of high costs and uncompetitive prices. The government took the view that if costs were reduced, more orders would be attracted, and the capacity issue would not be a major issue. Conversely the industry, steeped as it was in the experience of the 1930s, argued that it was excessive capacity in pursuit of too few orders that drove down prices, and only elimination of capacity would bring the industry back to balance. To reduce costs without reducing capacity was not productive.

There was indeed a good deal of truth in both arguments. A reduction of British capacity of itself, when worldwide capacity continued to grow, would not significantly have influenced British shipyard costs and prices. And with uncompetitive prices British builders could not expect to attract overseas orders, nor for long to hold on to the loyalty of British ship owners as customers. In that respect the government was right to put priority on reducing costs. Equally, however, cost reductions, with capacity spiralling out of control, simply meant a perpetuation of unbridled and uneconomic competition for orders. The shipbuilders' analysis highlighted this dilemma, and appeared to the minister to put the cart before the horse. It would be naïve to argue that the shipbuilders paid insufficient attention to the issue of costs. They simply saw the cost and capacity issues as inseparable, but gave their priority to the capacity problem. They did indeed pursue a number of policies in parallel with their capacity scheme, not least an extensive set of negotiations with the workforce to improve efficiency in an attempt to get their costs down and to improve construction and delivery times.

## Industrial relations

While the hardship of the inter-war period had set the minds of a generation of British shipbuilders in opposition to the concept of expanding capacity, and a concentration on survival rather than growth, the same experience of violent fluctuations, the collapse of demand, and the prolonged period of unemployment of men had reinforced the trade unions in their determination to protect jobs, and to control both employment and the organisation of work. Consequently, when the 1958 recession hit the industry, the employers were automatically concerned with issues of the control of capacity and the need to improve efficiency and competitiveness, while the labour unions were more concerned with the renewed threat of unemployment, and more specifically with the increasing insecurity of employment and the threat, real or imagined, to their wages and conditions of work. Although both sides of the industry were threatened by the decline in orders, there was little common ground in the immediate objectives of the employers and the employed. Since the industry also had a history of adversarial rather than cooperative industrial relations, and had largely neglected issues of labour organisation during the long expansion of the wartime and post-war boom, there were no established procedures for pursuing a thorough overhaul of working practices.

The opening initiative was taken jointly by the SEF and the Shipbuilding Conference in setting up an informal meeting with the CSEU in London in January 1959. The tentativeness of the employers' approach was evident in the opening remarks of R.W. Johnson, president of the SEF. Johnson explained that the shipbuilders were 'somewhat concerned about the future outlook of the industry', and 'felt that the present time, when there are no outstanding claims, was a most suitable one to meet' to discuss, informally, thoughts about the future.[25] He stressed the need for mutual confidence and goodwill, and to ensure that British yards were fully competitive with yards overseas. This issue of competitiveness was a recurring theme in his remarks, as was his stress on the view that the future of the industry depended on 'maximum efficiency, the ability to quote fixed prices, the ability to give speedy delivery'. He implied that the employers had done their part in investing in modernisation to secure these ends but that it was 'a great disappointment to us that we seem to be reaping so little by way of advantage from this expenditure, modernisation and reorganisation'. The agenda for the discussion was why this failure had occurred, and Johnson also delicately hinted that the shipbuilders thought the answer lay in 'finding some way of avoiding the losses of productive time in our yards for whatever cause'.[26] The CSEU agreed to a follow-up meeting to explore the issues and although that took place in February 1959 the approach and discussion went no further. Two years of deterioration in order books followed before another tentative meeting was arranged, in January 1961, when, at the settlement of a national wage claim, the unions again agreed to meet in committee with the SEF and SC to discuss steps to improve the competitive position of the industry. In the interval the Conference and the SEF had been active in collecting members' views on obstacles to maximum output in their yards. The list was long, ranging over failure to observe agreed procedures in relation to stoppages of work, absenteeism, embargoes on overtime, restrictive practices of all kinds, resistance to the introduction of improved techniques and new equipment, and manipulation of the piecework arrangements.[27] This essentially formed the informal agenda of issues reviewed by the president of the SEF at the meeting with the CSEU on 1 March 1961. On this occasion he openly declared that 'over the years there has grown up between us a mutual suspicion of each others' objectives', and that this was a factor which had to be 'frankly faced' in their negotiations.[28] He also added that the employers believed they had failed to convince the unions in the past that there were serious grounds for concern, and that it was not the desire of the employers to apportion blame for the industry's difficulties. The objective was to gain the full cooperation of the unions in making necessary changes, and to do so on the understanding that there was no intention to seek to lower wages or earnings, and in the knowledge that the talks with the CSEU should not interfere with the sovereignty of individual unions, to whom many of the problems would have to be referred for further consideration. Two further meetings took place, in March and July, during which the unions gave general assurances of cooperation, but from which no concrete proposals emerged. Talks then stalled when a fresh wage claim was presented, and negotiations were discontinued until the wage issue had been settled.

Under the pressure of changed market conditions, it is clear that the employers were moving swiftly to the conclusion that a radical shake-up of labour organisation was necessary in order to restore competitiveness. But what they had was a list of complaints rather than a policy for discussion with the unions. Not surprisingly, since the loose agenda of problems did not address directly the issues of security of employment and improved wages, the unions did not share the feeling of urgency that drove the employers. Since two direct industry-to-labour approaches had faltered, the third initiative was devised through the Minister of Labour, who convened a meeting of employers and unions under his chairmanship in December 1961. Clearly this was an attempt to place negotiations on changes and improvements in industrial relations and competitiveness in a more neutral forum than had been provided by the SEF and SC's first two approaches. Further meetings to discuss detailed aspects of the problems were agreed, the chairman to be Mr P.H. St John Wilson, the chief industrial commissioner of the Ministry of Labour. The preliminary meeting was scheduled for late January 1962, but the rejection of the CSEU's claim for increased wages and reduced hours of work by the employers on 4 January 1962, and the introduction of the government's 'Pay Pause', caused the unions to withdraw. The first joint meeting of representatives of the SEF and the CSEU did not take place until 25 May 1962, by which time the industry order book was down to only six months' work. The chairman, the Minister of Labour, John Hare, observed that the industry did not have a great deal of time to spare to resolve the problems facing the working party, but he thought that 'there seemed to be scope for a genuine industrial bargain which would bring to the employers' side the benefits of more efficient use of the industry's labour force, particularly of its skilled labour force, and to the unions the benefits of greater stability of employment for their members'.[29]

The possibility of a quick accord was remote, for, in response, two of the union representatives, Frank Foulkes and Dan McGarvey, respectively observed that there was a danger of the working party passing judgment on unions which were not represented, and that whatever conclusions might be reached by the working party on the union side, 'decisions on what action should eventually be taken would remain with the individual unions'. The representatives of the industry could have voiced similar cautions, for the formal structures of the employers' and union organisations, represented negotiating rather than executive powers. The shipbuilders were loosely coordinated in the Shipbuilders Employers Federation and the Shipbuilding Conference to represent, respectively, the interest of individual members in wages and conditions on the one hand, and commercial matters on the other. Beneath these national organisations there were district Shipbuilders Associations and the individual companies who negotiated their own interest at local level. On the workforce side, the craft basis of production in each yard was represented by up to 23 separate trades, organised in 18 main unions. While from 1936 they had been linked to the Confederation of Shipbuilding and Engineering Unions to negotiate major issues at national level, this was an overlay of limited responsibility which did not replace or subordinate traditional bargaining procedures, which were vested in specific unions from national down to district and individual yard level. The powers of the formal national organisations on both sides of the industry were only as effective as their individual members wished them to be. Consequently, while problems could be identified, and discussion meetings agreed by the formal national organisations, the steps necessary to agree policy, and then to implement it successfully, were in the hands of individual firms and unions. The lack of formal procedures to undertake such measures was bound to present another range of problems, and put constraints on the speed of movement.

In spite of these implicit constraints, a series of working party meetings was inaugurated, under chief industrial commissioner Wilson's chairmanship; each side had seven members, and the Ministry of Labour was represented by three officers. The industry organisations clearly made the running, and by July 1962 had tabled an outline scheme to reorganise the workforce into three main groups, comprising the metal trades, outfit trades and ancillary workers, the reorganisation to bring with it agreements on flexibility and interchangeability of labour and the replacement of the old apprenticeship system by a training scheme. Within the SEF a full scheme was drafted by October 1962, setting out and elaborating the proposals.[30] The composition of the proposed three-trade division of the workforce was spelt out in detail, as were the principles of flexibility and interchangeability. While these enabled all workers in the group to undertake the work of other groups in the trade, they maintained the existing craft specialisms in which workers as a general rule would continue to concentrate on the operations for which they had been trained. The details of the training scheme allowed for four years' training for youths commencing at age 16, and three years for those of 17 years and older. Provision was also made to train suitable workers from the ancillary trades to upgrade them to undertake the work of the metal or outfit trades. The period of training would be not less than two years, and on completion all schemes would provide a certificate of competence to each trainee. Each of the three groups of trades was to have its own clearly defined wage rate, which would be an all-inclusive piecework speed-hourly-rate, designed to ensure all employees would work at piecework speed during all working hours to ensure maximum output. The piecework prices were to be determined on accepted principles of method study and work measurement, and be paid on a strictly measured output basis. The reorganisation of the workforce and wage system was to be backed up by the establishment of formal procedures for dealing with conditions and hours of work, time keeping, overtime, weekend and holiday work, and nightshift. The plan also provided for formal procedures for dealing with demarcation, the avoidance of disputes, and termination of employment.

These radical proposals clearly placed recruitment, training and work control in the hands of management, and would have ended the control of the unions in these vital areas of concern. The wage proposals on piecework speed-time-rates would have ended a long process of wage drift in which the Boilermakers, followed by the other unions, had in an *ad hoc* manner managed to consolidate earnings into district rates. This had the result of creating guaranteed fall-back rates to be paid when piecework earnings could not be achieved, and effectively broke the basic principle of piecework, namely that earnings should be tied to output through payment by results.[31] It also placed wage settlements mainly on a yard and district level, while the SEF plan would have placed all wage settlements solely on a national level.

Such a departure from established arrangements was clearly of little appeal to the unions, but there was no immediate rejection. The media criticism of the industry, employers and unions, had been wide-ranging, and the unions were intent on demonstrating to the general public, and to the Ministry of Labour, that they were 'responsible' people.[32] Moreover, as McGoldrick makes plain, the Boilermakers, followed by the other unions, wanted to see how far the employers would go in paying for the concessions sought. Indeed, even though completely opposed to the scheme, the Boilermakers took the lead in negotiating each proposal in terms of a wage issue. The outcome was halting progress, considerable watering down of the initial proposals, and by September 1963, after eleven meetings stretching over 17 months, little had been agreed. Indeed by June 1963 the union representatives on the working party made explicit what was already known, that as a working group they were not in a position to negotiate an agreement on the subject. They advised the Federation to initiate separate discussions with the unions which organised and controlled the separated crafts which would be drawn together in the new groups proposed by the scheme. Nor were they prepared to support an agreement, undertaking merely to recommend that the individual unions concerned should 'enter into such early discussions in kindred groups which were mutually acceptable to them.[33] Separate meetings were initiated, but with little advance, and in September 1963 the Minister of Labour asked the Working Party to report back on progress made. A full plenary meeting of the employers and unions did take place on 20 November 1963, but at the end of it wide differences remained between the two sides.[34]

In reporting back to the central board of the SEF, the employers' representatives assumed that the working party would effectively be discontinued and took the view that, 'in any event it had not made any tangible contribution towards an improvement either in industrial relations or in the Industry's competitive ability', and that the only hope of progress lay in discussion with the various groups of unions.[35] Moreover, the effect of watering down the proposals in the protracted negotiations produced a backlash among the shipbuilders, some of whom were openly dissenting from the scheme as presented to the unions.[36] After two years of fruitless initial soundings between 1959 and 1960, and a further two years of structured negotiation under the auspices of the Ministry of Labour, the employers' attempts to get agreement to introduce a radical overhaul of the organisation of the workforce, its wage structure, and the procedures for training, disputes, and industrial relations, was to all intents and purposes a dead letter. The deep suspicions entertained by each side of the other in the industry, combined with the deeply ingrained individualism among the employers, and the equally deeply entrenched sectionalism among the unions, ensured that short-term views of individual advantage prevailed over any longer term rational assessment of the need for change in the industry. As a consequence the question of competitiveness was not answered, and the industry was left exposed to the pressures of a declining order book, which itself reflected underlying problems of prices, productivity, and credit.

## Prices, costs, and productivity

When the shipbuilders approached the unions in 1959 on the issue of competitiveness, the key to the problem was seen to lie in the inability of British yards to offer prices that were comparable with their major rivals. The shipbuilders' analysis was that labour costs were the main part of the equation in the cost of a ship that was wholly in their control. Consequently if labour costs could be reduced, prices could be improved, and this would be major step toward improving competitiveness. The price disadvantage for British builders had opened up alarmingly in 1958 as the recession set in, and as Japan cut prices aggressively to maintain market share. The *Financial Times* noted that Japanese contracts for tankers had been priced at around $250 per ton in 1956 and 1957, but that similar vessels in the 68–90,000 dwt range were being taken at $130–$140 per ton, and 15,000 gross ton freighters had declined from $290 per ton to $190 in the same time. Tanker tonnage prices were down by over 40 per cent, and cargo ships prices by one-third.[37] In Britain, in contrast, it was noted that contracts were still being offered with prices based on escalation clauses, and that prices were still rising by 7–8 per cent per year. The index price for British tonnage certainly rose by 9 per cent for deep cargo liners and tramps between 1956 and 1958, while tanker prices advanced 11 per cent.[38]

The outcome of these diverging trends was the alarming price differentials reported by the shipbuilders to the unions at their informal meeting in January 1959. The survey by the Shipbuilding Conference revealed that across a range of tonnage types British prices were frequently 20–25 per cent above comparable tenders from Danish, Dutch, German, Norwegian, and Swedish yards, and as much as 40 per cent higher than Japanese tanker prices.[39] In spite of these large competitive gaps, British prices did not begin to ease until 1962–63, when cargo liner prices were 16 per cent below the 1959 level, tramp prices 12 per cent down, and tanker prices 11 per cent below their peak levels which were only reached in 1962. Given this relative stability in British prices, it is not surprising that the investigation of costs and prices in British yards undertaken by the firm of accountants, Peat Marwick & Mitchell, in 1963, at the request of the Ministry of Transport and the Conference, revealed a continuing gap in competitiveness. In assessing tender prices for tankers in two size ranges – those of 50,000–60,000 tons deadweight and 60,000–70,000 tons deadweight – Peat Marwick and Mitchell found that on average British prices were £3.5 per ton above those of the main European builders, at least £5.0 per ton higher than Swedish prices and up to £10.0 per ton adrift from Japanese prices. On a 60,000 ton tanker this placed UK prices some £200,000 above average European prices, up to £300,000 above Swedish tenders, and a massive £600,000 more expensive than the average Japanese price of £2.16 million pounds. British prices, in the market sector where more than three-quarters of all new orders had been generated in 1962–63, were 7–10 per cent above European prices, 20 per cent dearer than in Sweden and up to 30 per cent higher than contracts taken in Japan.[40] The competitive disadvantage on bulk carriers up to 25,000 tons deadweight was not so severe, British prices averaging £54.9 per ton deadweight against Japanese prices of around £52.00, about a 5 per cent difference, but this widened in larger carriers in the 25,000–50,000 ton class, where the British price of £45.5 per ton faced Japanese prices of £38–£39.[41] The evidence on cargo ships was less clear, but this appeared to be a relatively small difference in price, British yards being broadly comparable with European and Japanese prices.

These comparisons were made on the basis of 54 orders taken between mid-1962 and September 1963 by 19 of the larger and medium yards in Britain, which with four exceptions represented all the new orders taken by these yards in this period. Since the output of these firms represented some 82 per cent of the annual production of the industry, the PMM survey may be taken to be substantially representative of conditions in British shipbuilding as a whole at this time. For these firms, and the industry as a whole, the problem was that in order to get these contracts, most had been accepted at prices estimated to make a loss. Of the 54 orders, 41 were expected to make an aggregate loss of 4.0 per cent, and only eight expected to return a profit of 0.2 per cent, another five expected to break even. The aggregate loss on the contracts was calculated by PMM to be some £3.29 million, after depreciation. None of the orders took account of possible unabsorbed charges, nor of additional costs arising from increases in materials prices and wages. Perhaps even more worrying was the opinion reported by PMM that there was no evidence to suggest that the Japanese were taking orders at a loss, although the Swedish yards were suspected of doing so in an effort to keep the Japanese out of their customary Norwegian market.

In retrospect this assessment was flawed, for it soon became clear that the Japanese had indeed been accepting some export orders at prices that were loss making, not so much from initial pricing below cost, but because the huge surge of orders obtained for export orders, 1.866 million tons in 1962, rising sharply to 4.375 million tons in 1963, temporarily placed tonnage beyond effective capacity. Also, the Japanese were for the first time taking orders for liquid petroleum gas carriers (LPG), high-speed cargo ships, and more specialised ship types in which they had little or no experience, and consequently earned almost no profit.[42] The Japanese were making a pronounced export drive in an overall weak market, and consequently drove down prices for all other builders. Profitability was consequently squeezed hard in all the major shipbuilding companies. In Britain a private financial survey of the industry by Hoare & Co. concluded that the profit to sales ratio had declined sharply, from 6.4 per cent in 1958 to 2.4 per cent in 1964. In Japan, reports made by the major shipbuilders under the Securities and Exchange Law, indicated that the profit to sales ratio had slipped from 5.2 per cent in the first half of 1962 to 3.6 per cent at the end of 1963, and to 2.7 per cent by the second half of 1964.[43] Similarly in Germany, where by 1963 prices were 10 to 15 per cent above Japanese levels, there had been a severe reversal of fortunes. Contracts taken up to 1959 had earned profits of 9–10 per cent, but those taken from 1959 were on average returning losses of 4.0 per cent by 1962 in large yards, but still breaking even in small yards building for local markets. By 1963 contracts taken in larger yards were being accepted at around 8 per cent below cost, a situation marginally poorer than in Britain.[44]

It is clear that the struggle to keep order books active in depressed market conditions forced world prices down to levels set by the Japanese. This offers some explanation for declining profitability, uneconomic prices, and loss-making contracts, but does not of itself explain why the costs of construction in Britain were so widely at variance with major competitors in the main ship types, especially in the tanker market. The PMM report attempted to analyse the cost difference by looking at the differentials as they arose in the main cost areas in the construction of ships (Table 6.4). On this assessment Britain was falling behind on price from a combination of dearer steel and hull equipment, and from higher labour costs, though not on this item in comparison with Sweden.

*Table 6.4* Price differentials per deadweight ton in tanker construction costs, 1962–1963

| | Price per dwt cheaper than UK price in | | |
| --- | --- | --- | --- |
| | *Western Europe* | *Sweden* | *Japan* |
| due to costs of: | | | |
| steel | £0.75 | £1.75 | £1.00 |
| hull equipment | £1.00 | £1.00 | £1.50 |
| labour | £1.50 | (£1.00)[1] | £5.00 |
| yard charges | | £0.50 | £0.50 |
| additional costs unaccounted for | £0.25 | £2.75 | £2.00 |
| Total differential | £3.50 | £5.00 | £10.00 |

[1] i.e. £1.00 more expensive than in the UK.

*Source*: Peat Marwick and Mitchell: Preliminary Report to the Minister of Transport on Shipbuilding Prices, Appendix X, p. 5.

The weakness and competitive disadvantage on steel was a new development, for in mid-1957 British steel plate was priced at £38 per ton, while the Dutch paid £45, the Germans £50, Sweden £65, and Japan £60.[45] *The Times* observed that this advantage should have enabled British builders to cut costs below those of competitors by as much as 5 per cent. By 1963, however, the position had been reversed dramatically, as European and Japanese steel production accelerated. UK prices had risen by over 10 per cent to £42.00 per ton, while builders in the European Coal and Steel Community countries could obtain steel plate at £37–£38 per ton, while the Japanese steel industry, under instructions from the government, was supplying steel for ship export orders at £38 and for domestic orders at £45 per ton.[46] UK shipbuilders had been offered supplies of Japanese Grade A steel plates at £38–£39 per ton delivered, but advised PMM that there were practical, but unspecified, difficulties in the way of making such purchases. Supplies from Europe were also apparently blocked by a cartel agreement between the British steel makers and the ECSC, which prevented the European makers offering steel for sale in the UK at below UK domestic price levels. Perhaps surprisingly in view of the price differential, British builders showed no great enthusiasm to seek new suppliers, nor to sever or adjust customary links with British producers.

The differential on labour costs was also a relatively recent development, UK wage rates having only pushed above the European builders, save Sweden, in the mid-1950s. By 1959 hourly labour costs in British shipbuilding were the highest among all the major European builders, except Sweden. The difference varied from 4 per cent above German rates to 12 per cent above Italian costs. By contrast, in Sweden hourly rates were 73 per cent higher than those in the UK. At this stage Japan was 20 per cent cheaper than Britain in hourly wage costs (Table 6.5). By 1962, however, the situation was reversed, and Britain had the lowest hourly rates, except for Italy and Japan. However, even allowing for this turnaround in hourly costs, the productivity differences still converted labour costs into an area of weakness for Britain. PMM assumed there was a 15 per cent gap in labour productivity between UK and European yards, and a 50 per cent gap between UK and Swedish and Japanese performance. They had made no separate study of productivity and could not imagine the deficiency was greater than 50 per cent in favour of Sweden and Japan. Their calculations consequently showed Sweden at a disadvantage in labour costs, and left price differences of £2.75 per ton and £2.00 per ton in Swedish and Japanese prices still to be explained. PMM had been unable to make calculations of differences in costs arising from machinery, which normally represented around one-third of the total cost of a vessel, compared to 22 per cent for steel and 27 per cent for direct labour and charges. They hazarded the view that the absence of information on machinery costs might well explain all the unattributable gap in their calculations; and doubtless there were differentials here, as well as in the other cost elements.

However, such slender evidence as there is suggests that the productivity gap between UK labour, and that in Sweden and Japan, was considerably larger than allowed for. Alexander and Jenkins estimated that between 1960 and 1965 the productivity of British shipbuilding – spreading this across the entire workforce rather than simply on steel workers – was 187 man hours per ton of steel output, compared with 82 hours in

Sweden and 70 in Japan.[47] On this basis Sweden was more than twice as efficient than the UK, and Japan more than two and half times more productive. These differentials would be more than sufficient to explain all the remaining gaps in PMM's cost calculation. The evidence of building and delivery times also suggests a much wider productivity gap. In 1958–59, the average delivery time in the UK was 19 months, but only half that in Sweden and Japan, indicating something like double the rate of productivity. Similarly, by 1963 Japan, Sweden and Germany still delivered ships in half the time taken by British yards, once more suggesting that PMM's productivity allowances were modest, and that labour costs and labour efficiency could have been responsible for a much larger portion of the differences in the prices quoted.

*Table 6.5*   Average hourly labour costs in shipbuilding
(US cents per hour)

|  | 1959 | Index | 1962 | Index | % change 1959/62 |
|---|---|---|---|---|---|
| UK | 82.3 | 100 | 96.4 | 100 | +17.1 |
| West Germany | 78.9 | 96 | 108.3 | 112 | +37.2 |
| Sweden | 142.4 | 173 | 169.2 | 175 | +18.9 |
| France | 77.0 | 94 | 124.0 | 128 | +61.0 |
| Italy | 72.9 | 88 | 84.4 | 87 | +15.7 |
| Holland | 75.5 | 92 | 100.2 | 104 | +32.7 |
| Denmark | 89.6 | 109 | 108.0 | 112 | +20.5 |
| Norway | 96.7 | 117 | 109.3 | 113 | +13.0 |
| Japan | 66.3 | 80 | 73.3 | 76 | +10.5 |

*Source*: (SRNA File J/1. Report on Japan: 1 November 1963)

The uncompetitiveness of British prices arising from these differences in steel, equipment and labour costs, would seem in themselves substantially to explain Britain's declining position in orders, launches and exports in this period. But as a report made by a representative of the Ministry of Transport made clear, in relation to comparing tender prices for European and Japanese builders, it was not wise to conclude too much from prices quoted, since the terms of payment and conditions of credit had come to play a large part in contract negotiations. This was the other main area of support that greatly exercised Britain's shipbuilders, who increasingly believed that they were losing orders, not so much on price alone, nor even on price and delivery, but more and more because they could not offer competitive terms on credit and terms of payment.

# Credit support

In Britain the standard arrangements for providing credit support to purchasers of ships was limited to 50 per cent of the delivery price over five years. This was for domestic buyers through the Ship Mortgage Finance Co., although foreign buyers could get export credit guarantees to support loans of 85 per cent over a similar period. The five-year period of extended payment was a convention, or gentleman's agreement, which the secretary of the Export Guarantee Department was confident was being observed by the main West European builders.[48] In spite of such assurances the shipbuilders were increasingly concerned over reports of more generous terms being negotiated, and met with the Ministry of Transport at the end of 1959 to pursue the matter. The MOT had only just had the departmental responsibility for shipbuilding transferred to it from the Admiralty in October. Five meetings took place in quick succession to April 1960, during which the Conference tabled evidence of more advantageous sources of finance being made available to foreign shipbuilders. They noted that Sweden was reported to be selling ships to Norway on seven-year terms, while in Germany three ship mortgage banks were said to be giving 40 per cent finance over 10 years at 7½ per cent. In the Netherlands, loans were thought to be negotiable up to 10 years, but as in Sweden without credit insurance provisions.[49] In Japan terms appeared to be available for 70 per cent credit over seven years, with no repayment for the first two years after delivery, or over 10 years with up to three years before the first payment.[50]

The Shipbuilding Conference sought to promote their case for government assistance through the influence of Lord Piercy, Chairman of Ship Mortgage Finance Co., since they believed that company would be the appropriate mechanism to manage a new and larger credit scheme for British shipbuilding. After discussions with the industry, Piercy sent a memorandum to the government outlining the scale of finance needed to guarantee orders on a revolving credit basis. On the assumption that orders and output should be sustained at the level of the previous five years, and to provide for 70 per cent credit over seven years to match Japan, with no repayment over the first two years, Piercy calculated that £228 million would be needed to provide cover for all export orders, and half of the expected domestic orders. This would keep the industry going at an output of around 1.4 million tons per year, but if output was set at 1.0 million gross tons, the financial support on the same basis would be reduced to £160 million, and to £108 million for a regular output of 750,000 tons.[51] The Conference stressed the urgent need for this kind of provision since their members were routinely reporting that, in contrast to previous experience, about 90 per cent of enquiries coming to them from brokers asked for credit, and almost all foreign enquiries expected it as part of the deal.

In spite of the sharp decline in new orders to around 500,000 tons per year the government, though expressing sympathy, was unmoved and was not inclined to support a credit race. The first modest easement of this position came early in 1962 when new arrangements for financing the export of ships through ECGD were introduced. While this reduced premiums and made finance easier to obtain, the low value of export business in British yards meant that this did not bring much relief to Britain's shipyards. The industry continuously applied pressure for more assistance, and ultimately in May 1963, when order books were reduced to less than six months' work for the entire industry, the government relented and made better credit support available. Even then it was not the rationale nor the weight of the shipbuilders' case that won the day, but rather the mounting unemployment in shipbuilding districts, with a general election due within a year. When the Shipbuilding Credit Scheme, known as the Marples Scheme, was set up in May 1963, the Minister of Transport made it explicit that it was a temporary measure for one year, and that it had the primary objective of promoting employment in the shipyards. The sum provided was initially £30 million and was to be available immediately, even though the scheme had not been to the House, and did not get its second reading until January 1964. By then its provision had been extended to £60 million in July 1963, and again to £75 million in October, the last increase to include cover for the new Cunarder that was to become *QE II*. The period and terms of cover were to be on a par with those available elsewhere, namely 70 per cent over seven years with up to two years before the first payment. The scheme was an instant success, and the drought of orders was dramatically ended. In the first two quarters of 1963, UK yards had taken only 235,000 tons in orders from UK owners, and 171,000 tons from overseas. In the second half of the year, domestic new orders which were covered by the new scheme, leaped to 1.037 million tons, while export orders, uncovered by the arrangement languished at 81,000 tons of new business. Some 1.523 million tons of new orders were taken against an average of only one-third that in the previous four or five years. Not all of the orders were of course covered by the new scheme. Its financial provision was entirely taken up by December 1963, by which time about 800,000 tons of new orders had been attracted by it.

When the full terms of the scheme were eventually published, in January 1964, cover was available up to a maximum of 80 per cent of contract price over 10 years for ships built in UK yards for UK owners. In addition the government accelerated the Admiralty programme, bringing forward new work worth about £50 million on an annual basis. The industry had been rescued from immediate crisis, but only by a temporary measure which bordered on a subsidy. The causes of the crisis in orders had not been resolved. World capacity in shipbuilding remained unchecked, and was indeed increasing as Japan brought new large building docks on stream. The hard issue of labour relations in British yards had stalled in extended discussion, and although the late 1950s' programme of investment in modernisation was nearing completion, the Patton Report on Productivity in Shipbuilding, prepared by the industry itself in 1962, revealed that improvement and modernisation were far from universal. The larger yards had made most progress, and the members of the Patton Committee believed their facilities were on a par with the best yards on the Continent.[52] However, even in the better British yards, production planning for steel work was highly variable; stocks of plate were found to be unnecessarily high; and the Committee itself could find no ground for recommending the use of standard plate, even though that was the practice in Japan and Sweden, where the committee had found it difficult to believe the claims on the throughput of steel. Even on their own revised figures, the largest Swedish yards were processing twice as much steel per man hour as the better British yards.[53] Most yards were also not using their prefabrication facilities to best effect, and too many obsolete machines were retained in use. As far as the smaller yards were concerned, the Patton Committee found that, although many had made some improvements, none had done so to the extent of the larger yards, and many had sites that were barely adequate in size, and had yard layouts that were not well arranged for modern shipbuilding methods.[54] Since neither the capacity issue, nor labour relations, nor modernisation schemes, had been completely or satisfactorily resolved, it is not surprising that British shipbuilding fell behind in productivity in this period. With unfavourable costs British shipbuilders could only quote prices that were simultaneously considerably higher than their rivals, but which were also at levels that bore little real relationship to costs, and committed the industry to rapidly deteriorating profitability.

The circumstance most frequently singled out as destabilising the industry was the 'Japanese Menace', a phase encapsulating criticism of unrestricted capacity extension, cheap labour, and unfair and uneconomic prices, based on suspected subsidy and government support. The hard fact of Japan's superior facilities and productivity was given less prominence, but was undoubtedly a major factor enabling the Japanese to capture the largest share of orders in the recession years, and to do so at prices, and on terms, which debilitated her competitors. Important as the Japanese intrusion into export markets was, Britain was also weakened by structural changes in the market which had nothing to do with Japan's new position. In the 1950s the ocean-liner market represented up to 20 per cent by value of the workload of the industry, and a much greater part of the work of the larger yards. But the impact of the long-range jet aircraft severely weakened the market from 1961. Home delivery of liner tonnage collapsed from 396,000 tons in 1961 to only 134,000 tons in 1964. Not only did orders in this sector weaken sharply, but liner tonnage in service in the UK fleet declined by 1.3 million gross tons between 1959 and 1964. Equally unsettling was the structural shift to fewer and larger tramp ships, with the number in the fleet contracting from 1,013 in 1959, of 3,416,000 grt, to only 806 ships of 3,365,000 tons in 1964. During that period the dry-cargo market as a whole had slipped from launchings of 879,000 gross tons in 1957 to 559,000 tons by 1963.

Traditional market segments were in decline, and the only growth sector for new tonnage on a large scale was the tanker market in which Japan, pushed hard by Sweden, was bidding to be supreme. The importance of attempting to capture orders in this shifting marketplace eventually led to some attempts at modest cooperation in marketing. From 1959 the Shipbuilding Conference had gathered information on export organisations developed by European builders, but had concluded that the setting up of such a 'group or groups in the UK, is unlikely generally to have any market advantage, personal contacts being regarded as much more important in most markets'.[55] By 1961, however, in deteriorating circumstances, the industry accepted 'that political pressure was again being exerted for an export drive' and that 'great value would accrue from the political and public relations angles, if the Industry did make some new step forward in the field of attempting to increase exports'.[56] Consequently in 1962 an Export Executive was appointed in the Shipbuilding Conference 'to supplement the efforts made by individual firms'. A team of three 'Export Directors' was soon in operation, making visits to countries such as Brazil, Mexico, Egypt, India and Pakistan, as well as to smaller emerging countries, to compile reports on market prospects.[57]

This was a largely ineffectual development and left the industry still tied to its dependence on the domestic market, which was itself now weakening, as British prices allowed unprecedented penetration to the core orders that had long sustained British shipbuilding in world leadership. Even that competitive advantage was decaying, and that left the industry in 1964 in the very uncomfortable position, that 'unless it could achieve substantial reductions in costs, then its future would be poor indeed, unless a direct subsidy were granted'.[58] This was Ernest Marples' view as he reviewed the effects of the Shipbuilding Credit Scheme. He found the industry resistant to his exhortations to consider bulk buying, and to explore the advantages of greater concentration of output by the grouping of firms. The alternative, he hinted, was that if the 'Labour Party was elected the Industry would face the threat of nationalisation'. Labour was indeed elected to power in 1964, and although that did not bring nationalisation, as predicted, it did inaugurate an extraordinary period of intervention by the State in the affairs of the British shipbuilding industry.

# CHAPTER SEVEN

# Intervention: 1964–1977

Emerging from the recession of 1958–63, world shipbuilding and shipping moved into more than a decade of exponential growth. The world order book grew more than sixfold to peak at 133 million gross tons (mgt) in 1974, and annual tonnage launched expanded by three and a half times to 35.8 mgt in 1975. The industry was then more than three times larger than it had been in 1964, drawn upward by demands from a world merchant fleet which more than doubled in scale to 342 mgt in 1975. What lay behind this expansion was the sustained growth in world seaborne trade, this more than doubling from 1,510 million metric tonnes (mmt) to 3,277 mmt in 1975. The main drivers of this expansion were the fast growth of tanker cargoes, and the trend to ever larger ships and longer hauls. The average tanker more than trebled in scale to 57,000 gross register tons (grt) by 1975, and in the boom of 1964–74 freight mileage in trade grew by 75 per cent to 16,387 million ton miles, and tanker cargoes nearly doubled to 10,621 million ton miles.[1]

## Growth and instability

While this was a period of very vigorous growth, it was also one of considerable instability. Between 1964–67, an 80 per cent increase in the world order book to 39 mgt was more than offset by the growth in shipbuilding capacity, leaving the industry at large with at best two years of work in hand. This weakness was abruptly transformed by the closure of the Suez Canal in 1967, which caused freight rates to surge upward by 20 per cent, and doubled the world order book to more than 78 mgt by 1970 (Table 7.1). However, the increase in tonnage delivered and afloat was so sharp that it outpaced the growth in trade, and caused the volume of laid-up tonnage to mushroom from a mere 600,000 grt in December 1970, to 4.8 mgt by mid-1972. Yet, before this could depress shipbuilding activity, the Yom Kippur War of 1973, and the ensuing oil crisis, reabsorbed the unemployed tonnage. This, however, merely concealed for a time the underlying problem of over-capacity in shipping. Indeed, this was then exacerbated as a frenzy of new building added 49 mgt to the world fleet between 1971 and 1975. By June 1976, laid-up tonnage had grown to 26.5 mgt, about 9 per cent of the world fleet.

*Table 7.1*   UK and world orders and launches
('000 gross register tons)

| | UK | | World | | UK share of world (%) | |
| --- | --- | --- | --- | --- | --- | --- |
| | *Orders* | *Launches* | *Orders* | *Launches* | *Orders* | *Launches* |
| 1964 | 2,472 | 1,042 | 21,840 | 10,263 | 11.3 | 10.2 |
| 1967 | 2,475 | 1,298 | 39,550 | 15,780 | 6.2 | 8.2 |
| 1970 | 5,027 | 1,237 | 78,503 | 21,689 | 6.4 | 5.7 |
| 1971 | 4,922 | 1,239 | 83,659 | 24,860 | 5.9 | 4.9 |
| 1972 | 4,216 | 1,233 | 86,498 | 27,714 | 4.9 | 4.6 |
| 1973 | 7,518 | 1,017 | 128,899 | 31,520 | 5.8 | 3.2 |
| 1974 | 6,133 | 1,281 | 120,704 | 34,624 | 5.1 | 3.7 |
| 1975 | 4,930 | 1,304 | 82,345 | 35,897 | 5.9 | 3.6 |
| 1976 | 4,230 | 1,341 | 62,425 | 31,047 | 6.8 | 4.3 |

*Sources*: Orders: Lloyds Register of Shipping, Quarterly Returns, 30 September each year.
Launches: Lloyds Register of Shipping: Annual Summary.

In this remarkable period of growth and instability, world shipbuilding, shipping and trade, were intertwined, their interaction leading to a structural crisis of surplus capacity in both shipping and shipbuilding. In 1965 world shipbuilding capacity was in the range of 12–14 mgt per year, with half of that still located in Western Europe, even though Japan individually was already the single largest producer. By 1970, world capacity was in excess of 20 mgt, and two-thirds of the expansion had taken place in Japan. Capacity then doubled to around 40 mgt by 1974. This was due not only to growth in Japan, but also to a determined expansion of capacity by European builders seeking to increase their market share. By then over half of world shipbuilding capacity lay in Japan, with 35 per cent in Western Europe, and another 12 per cent scattered among smaller builders. The main loser in both capacity and market share of output was Britain. In Britain, capacity was static at the never-attained potential of 1.75 mgt, with the consequence that as other nations expanded output, Britain's market share declined from around 10 per cent in 1964, to a mere 3.7 per cent a decade later. Britain's ranking in world output also slipped, from second to fifth place, behind Japan, Sweden, Germany and Spain. This remarkable deterioration in world position was the outcome of a stagnation in scale and in output during the most rapid expansion ever experienced in shipbuilding. And this decline was in spite of massive intervention by government, an intervention designed to support output, improve efficiency, and sustain employment in British yards.

By the middle of 1963, British yards had barely six months' work on hand, but an impending closure crisis was averted by the introduction of an emergency credit scheme. The support, introduced by the minister, Ernest Marples, quickly attracted new orders of over one million tons, though even with this infusion, the industry still had barely six to nine months of orders in reserve between 1963 and 1966. This weakness in the order book was underlined by the challenge of Japan which had captured half the total market, and contributed to Britain's poor output record. During the recession of 1958–62, British yards had launched an annual average of 1.38 mgt, but managed only 1.0 mgt annually between 1963 and 1966. The central problem was a poor rate of completions because of the collapse of orders from, and deliveries to, UK ship owners (Table 7.2). Not only was there a decline in building tonnage for domestic owners, but export performance was also poor. Britain attracted less than 4.0 per cent of world export orders between 1962–66, a total of only 1.014 mgt compared with the 12.5 mgt taken by Japan, some 47 per cent of the market.

At this time the fastest growing fleets were those of Norway, Liberia, Japan and Russia. Among these, Japan and Russia were effectively closed markets, and unavailable to Britain, while those of Norway and Liberia were completely open to competitive delivery of ships. In this scenario, nearly half of all British export tonnage went to Norway, with another 18 per cent going to Commonwealth countries. Liberia, which represented one-third of the market for new tonnage, took only 5.0 per cent of UK exports, as did both Greece and Panama. European fleets, Britain's closest neighbours, collectively took only 6.0 per cent of UK exports. This was partly due to the fact that the merchant fleets of France, Italy, West Germany and Spain were also mainly closed to foreign builders. Fragile and fluctuating order books, the weakening hold on the domestic market, and a poor export performance, all pressed hard on British shipbuilders in the first half of the 1960s. The main pressures came from the aggressive expansion of Japanese output, but even more from the price leadership the Japanese yards established in building large tankers and bulk carriers. Japan typically took orders at prices which barely covered their costs, thus ensuring that less efficient builders in Britain and Europe could only win orders for these larger ships at uneconomic prices. West European builders complained to their governments regularly about what they believed to be unfair Japanese competition. This was a central issue in the discussions of the 'OECD Working Party No. 5' in 1963–64, but in spite of this the governmental response to the shipbuilders' anxieties was cool. The British position was clearly conveyed to the industry by A.R. Titchner, Principal Secretary to the Board of Trade, who intimated that the government believed there was no evidence to support the claim that the Japanese were doing anything contrary to international agreements.[2] Moreover, the government believed it was not illegal for Japan to expand its capacity. On this issue the government thought that the shipbuilders should respond by increasing efficiency, rather than seeking to shelter behind subsidies and measures of credit support. This was in strong contrast to the belief of the builders that it was the huge increase in capacity by Japan which acted to depress prices, and created uneconomic conditions in the shipbuilding market.

*Table 7.2a*   Domestic and foreign built for UK registration
('000 grt)

|  | Total new UK registrations | Domestic built | Foreign built | % foreign |
|---|---|---|---|---|
| 1962–66 | 6,173 | 4,160 | 2,013 | 32.6 |
| 1967–71 | 12,589 | 3,555 | 9,034 | 71.8 |
| 1972–76 | 16,795 | 4,321 | 12,474 | 74.3 |

*Source*: Lloyds Register of Shipping: Annual Summary.

*Table 7.2b*   UK tonnage launched and exported

|  | Total tonnage in each five-year period | | |
|---|---|---|---|
|  | Total launched | Total exported | % exports |
| 1962–66 | 5,201 | 1,041 | 25.9 |
| 1967–71 | 5,711 | 2,157 | 37.8 |
| 1972–76 | 6,117 | 1,762 | 28.8 |

*Source*: Lloyds Register of Shipping: Annual Summary.

As this pressure mounted in 1964, the West European Shipbuilders (WES) agreed a joint statement to go to their respective governments. They argued that what had at first appeared to be a normal change in the market had, since 1962, developed into a deep crisis whose fundamental cause was 'to be found in the concentrated endeavours, fully backed by government support, which the Japanese builders are deliberately making to gain complete control of world shipbuilding'.[3] As evidence it was cited that while Japan had held only 15 per cent of world orders in 1957, half of all orders were taken by Japan by June 1964. This, for the first time, exceeded the combined order book of all the West European countries. Moreover, Japan had rejected all approaches to seek to establish quotas, and refused proposals which aimed to reduce the severity of competition in price, and on credit terms. In view of this intransigence, the WES concluded their statement by arguing that 'unless the pressure exerted on the market by the Japanese industry is eased, shipbuilding in Western Europe will shortly become so weakened that it will either cease to exist, or will have to rely increasingly on government support'. The WES then ended by asking their governments to make joint representations to the Japanese government 'whose support to its own expanding shipbuilding industry is the fundamental cause of the depression from which Western European shipbuilding now suffers'.[4] These were strong words which expressed deeply held convictions concerning the unfairness of Japanese practices. The European builders were certainly correct in believing that the Japanese had clear policies in support of their shipbuilding and shipping industries. The expansion of the Japanese fleet was explicitly encouraged to carry Japan's imports and exports in order to minimise strain on the balance of payments. Similarly, the 'Programmed Shipbuilding Schemes' set annual estimates of new tonnage required, and of the types of ships to be constructed. In addition, Japan advanced public funds to domestic owners at favourable rates for the building of new tonnage under the 'Interest Subsidy for Shipping Finance Scheme'.[5]

While these schemes did secure a base workload for Japanese yards, just as historically the orders from the British merchant marine had done in Britain, they do not of themselves explain the large Japanese lead in price and productivity. It was these advantages which were overwhelming British and European builders in the marketplace. What was conveniently ignored in the WES submissions to their governments was the massive investment which had been made in new facilities in Japan. Some £300 million had been invested in the decade to 1964, nearly £145 million of that in 1964 alone. Japan's consequent adoption of prefabrication and block building, together with the use of building docks and berth extensions, enabled their builders to double the productivity of steel throughput in the yards by 1956, and to make a further 20 per cent gain in efficiency by 1961. This was reflected in the annual value of sales per employee, which in 1965 was £5,500 in Japan, but was only £2,400 in Britain. This glaring gap in productivity was a more potent enabler of Japan's ability to capture world orders than the government support measures in themselves. The measures did, however, give direction and dynamic to Japanese shipbuilding in the years after 1957, at a time when British and European builders were struggling to complete modest modernisation programmes. In contrast, neither the UK nor the European governments had any explicit policy objectives or supports for their industries. In identifying this, the WES builders pinpointed a critical vacuum in policy which they claimed left them at a disadvantage in competing with Japan. They were not, however, successful in attracting government support at this stage, only Italy and France giving some direct aid to their small shipbuilding industries.

In Britain it was the election of Harold Wilson's Labour government in 1964 that brought some change in attitude to industrial policy. In shipbuilding, the government determined to investigate the condition of the industry. To begin with they decided to collect more information on prices and costs than had been obtained by the surveys in 1961 and 1963, which had been conducted by the accountancy firm Peat Marwick and Mitchell.[6] The government took this initiative not only in response to the complaints of unfair competition, but also due to mounting complaints by the shipbuilders that Development Area policy, which attracted newer industries to old industrial districts, was causing a shortage of skilled manpower in shipbuilding. Craftsmen, like joiners, electricians and welders, could find more secure employment in these incoming newer industries, where the jobs were also often better paid. As a consequence the shipbuilders also claimed that this was driving up wages in the industry, and that these constraints on the skilled labour supply exacerbated the problems of restrictive practices and labour indiscipline in the yards, and hence caused lengthy delays in delivering ships.[7]

This investigation was to be wide-ranging, and was to be conducted by the Shipbuilding Inquiry Committee (SIC). The chairman was Sir Reay Geddes, chairman of Dunlop: the report was to become known as the Geddes Report. Establishing the SIC was under consideration from November 1964, but it was not formally constituted until 16 February 1965. The SIC remit was 'to establish what changes are necessary in organisation, in methods of production, and any other factors affecting costs, to make the shipbuilding industry competitive in world markets'.[8] The SIC was only eight months into its investigation when the whole relationship of government and shipbuilding was abruptly and fundamentally altered by the impact of what was the first major post-war crisis in the industry. On 15 October 1965 the Fairfield Shipbuilding and Engineering Company, at Govan on the Clyde, was placed in receivership at the instigation of the Bank of Scotland. Given the sensitivity of the new Labour government to the issue of unemployment in the older industrial districts, the shock in political circles was profound.

## The Fairfield crisis

In 1964 the Fairfield yard had just completed a ten-year modernisation programme, at a cost of £5 million, and had subsequently taken on an additional 500 workers. In addition, it had attracted three new orders under the 1963 Credit Scheme, and its order book, valued at £32 million, was held to be sufficient to secure work in the yard for up to two years. However, under the pressure of Japanese competition, the orders had been taken at fixed prices, and subsequent increases in labour costs and delays in construction led to mounting losses on the contracts. The worst of these was reputed to be a loss of around £1 million arising from the delays on the *Nihli*, a floating hotel ship. In addition, later balance sheets showed a further provision of up to £560,000 to cover losses on other contracts.[9]

The Fairfield bankruptcy came in the wake of seven yard closures on the Clyde since 1960, and at the end of five years of increasing anxiety about the health of British shipbuilding. Between 1960 and 1961 there had been no fewer than four commissioned reports on aspects of the performance of the industry. In 1960 the Department of Scientific and Industrial Research (DSIR) reported on 'Research and Development Requirements of the Shipbuilding and Marine Engineering Industries'; this was followed in the same year by the report of a Joint Industry Committee under the chairmanship of James Patton. This was the Patton Report on 'Problems Relating to Productivity and Operational Research in Shipbuilding'. These were followed in 1961 by the Shipbuilding Advisory Committee (SAC) report on 'Prospects in the Shipbuilding Industry'. Finally, also in 1961, there was a survey of shipbuilding prices compiled by Peat Marwick and Mitchell, a report to the Minister of Transport on 'Shipbuilding Orders placed abroad by British ship owners'; this was supplemented in 1963 by a further, more detailed report on shipbuilding prices. These were all conducted for a Conservative administration which consistently and continuously urged the industry to improve its efficiency, and in particular to consider making economies of scale through grouping and merger. In contrast to this view, the industry favoured controlling and reducing capacity, and the closure of failed yards, as a means of stabilising costs and prices, and reducing competition.

Had the Fairfield failure been an isolated crisis, it is probable that the yard would have been closed. But with seven earlier closures all removing capacity from the Clyde, this was a difficult option for the government. This was especially the case as the government was awaiting the report of the SIC, and since it was politically vulnerable to union pressure to retain and protect jobs. Consequently, in an extraordinary period of 90 days, without consulting the industry, the failed Fairfield Company was translated from private ownership and bankruptcy into a new venture, Fairfields (Glasgow) Ltd. This was to be owned jointly by the government and a consortium of private and trade-union capital. The campaign to save the stricken yard was led by Iain Stewart, chairman of Thermotank Ltd, whose premises were near the Fairfield concern. Stewart was the immediate past-president of the Institution of Engineers and Shipbuilders in Scotland, and had long been an advocate of a new approach to work organisation and practice in Britain. His argument that Fairfield presented an ideal opportunity to save and reconstruct the company by implementing an agreed new system of management, industrial relations, work organisation and training, coincided with the Labour government's attempt to resolve industrial conflict through proposals embodied in their White Paper 'In Place of Strife'.

Stewart's proposals for Fairfield had the sympathetic ear and ultimate support of George Brown, the maverick deputy leader of the Labour Party, and the First Secretary of State. His enthusiasm committed the government to provide aid of £1 million to enable the yard to continue in operation immediately, and to provide time for discussions to progress. When, inevitably, news of these discussions leaked in early December, the Shipbuilding Conference was outraged, and had letters of protest hand-delivered to the Prime Minister, to the First Secretary of State, the President of the Board of Trade, and the Chancellor of the Exchequer. This intervention was rushed out early on 9 December in an attempt to forestall action before George Brown was due to make a statement to the House. The letters expressed keen regret that the industry had not been taken into the confidence of Her Majesty's Government, and that if the proposals were to be implemented without reference to, and in advance of the Geddes Report, then Fairfield would be placed in a privileged position. Moreover, if the leaks were correct that the intention was to carry out an experiment in labour relations, this could have serious consequences not only for the industry, but for the government's prices and incomes policy.[10]

Representatives of the industry finally had a meeting with George Brown on 15 December; it was not a success. The tone was set by Brown asserting that the industry had not been consulted, deliberately, since he regarded the crisis as a matter for the unions and the yard alone. The memorandum of the meeting, prepared by the Shipbuilding Conference representatives, recorded that their attempts to explain industry concerns were continually interrupted and that the interruptions became abusive.[11] Relations between the industry and the First Secretary of State could not have been more strained. This meeting was followed a week later by George Brown making a statement to the House on 22 December. In this he confirmed that 'we now have the foundation for a financial partnership between the Government, private enterprise and the Trade Unions, as a result of which the Shipyard can continue'.[12] He went on to say that the future of the yard was now in the hands of the men, whom the venture required 'to cooperate unreservedly in working the yard as efficiently as possible, and in particular achieving flexible manning arrangements and inter-changeability of workers [and] if cooperation was not forthcoming the whole scheme … would fall … and the yard would have to close.'

The unions were, in effect, required by Iain Stewart to tear up the rule book. At a subsequent mass-meeting of the workers he told them that the rescue package, involving public and private capital, would only be available if he accepted the chairmanship of the new company, and that he would only agree to that if the men gave the scheme their unanimous support. Faced with the choice of imminent closure of the yard and redundancy, or future concessions on working practices, the vote was overwhelmingly in favour of accepting Iain Stewart's proposals. In doing so, the men and unions accepted conditions that were far more radical than those which the unions had defeated through prolonged discussions in 1963, when the employers had sought to introduce labour reforms.

The assets of Fairfields (Glasgow) Ltd were purchased from the receiver for £1.06 million, half put up by the government, £400,000 provided by private sources, £150,000 from four unions, and another £50,000 as a loan at five per cent from the Electrical Trades Union, but without any equity holding. This package was not finally fully in place until October 1966, by which time the new venture had completed and launched the first of three new orders. Only two members of the new board of the company were established shipbuilders. These were John Lenaghan, previous general manager of the defunct company, and Oliver Blandford, who had been director of engineering in the neighbouring yard of Stephens of Linthouse. Responsibility for productivity services was entrusted to James Houston, recruited from the Singer Sewing Machine Company at Clydebank. He, together with Blandford, had the task of implementing, and making real, the proposed new techniques of work measurement and quality control, and for the evaluation, assessment and reporting procedures envisaged by Stewart.

The conception and birth of this bold experiment were moved by generous motives, and incorporated many of the ideas long desired by the industry at large.

While some in the industry acknowledged this, the way in which the Fairfield scheme was devised and introduced created considerable hostility among the shipbuilders, not only on the Clyde, but in the industry at large. The Fairfield rescue, involving unasked-for government intervention and participation, challenged the deepest convictions of the shipbuilders, namely that failed yards were a threat to other yards and should be closed, and that government should be kept at a distance. Further, government aid should only be undertaken on industry terms, and should not involve any direct intervention in industry affairs. In contrast, substantial public funds had been committed to Fairfield with no real assessment having been made of the true commercial condition of the yard. In addition, the new management team at Govan was considered to be an affront to professional shipbuilders. In promoting this scheme the self-respect and independence of the shipbuilders had been bludgeoned by George Brown, and this damage was to be a permanent wound in the relationship of the industry and the Labour government. The next assault on the self-perception of the shipbuilders was to come from the assessment of the Industry in the Report of the Shipbuilding Inquiry Committee in 1966.

## The Shipbuilding Inquiry Committee

The Shipbuilding Inquiry Committee reported on 24 March 1966. The report was welcomed by the industry, which undertook to study its conclusions in a positive and constructive spirit. The analysis of the report was both wide-ranging and succinct, and rested on two fundamental convictions. The first was that the only acceptable basis upon which British shipbuilding should continue as an industry was that it had to be competitive and profitable. Assumptions that it should be continued on grounds of 'defence, shipping, balance of payments or employment and social reasons' were not sufficient in themselves. The second conviction was that world shipbuilding was a growth industry, and that 'future world demand for ships offers a bright prospect for competitive shipbuilders'.[13] In this context the committee had set out to identify strengths and best practices, and to seek ways to reinforce and develop these throughout the industry.

The fundamental problem, as seen by Geddes, was that the British industry was not changing and developing fast enough to meet the challenge of new markets and growing international competition. The industry was hampered in responding and in innovating because of three basic weaknesses. First, because of its history of violent and unpredictable fluctuations in demand, and especially because of conditions between the wars, British shipbuilders had developed short-term attitudes to markets, men and money. Further, its structure of numerous small and medium firms, all fiercely independent, gave the industry no significant influence over its customers or suppliers. The implication was that, in buying and selling, the shipbuilders were essentially price takers rather than price makers. The third main weakness identified was that management and unions in the industry had failed in their attempts to negotiate constructively. The most damaging outcome of these characteristics was that the industry had made inadequate use of its resources and skills, and this was especially evident in weaknesses in marketing, purchasing, design and planning.

The general failure of British shipbuilding firms to base their policy on an appreciation of the market, and of the firms' role or objective in that market, meant that there had been poor coordination of design, production and sales promotion resources. Moreover, this in turn led to a situation in which the substantial outlay of investment capital had been made in an unfocused way, with little attempt to estimate the likely return in terms of efficiency, cost reductions or profits, and that even less attention had been devoted to attempting to assess the outcome. The investments had also been made without reference to whether the availability of skilled labour, or developments in the market, would enable the new plant and equipment to be effectively utilised once installed.[14] The large injections of capital had also been made in the absence of any projections of future cash flow to service the investments. The production, organisation, marketing and managerial weaknesses were clearly major elements in the contracting market share and poor competitiveness of British yards. It was not surprising then that Geddes found that, 'profits and cash flow of the companies within the industry are with few exceptions inadequate and would not at present allow the yards to be kept up to date'. Even the yards which had been extensively modernised, and were beginning to show higher than average levels of profitability and cash flow, were still found to be financially illiquid.[15] Geddes consequently recommended that there should be some urgent short-term support to enable changes with medium- and longer-term objectives to be introduced.

The main conclusion was that competitiveness and success in world markets required the British shipbuilding industry to redeploy and make more efficient use of its resources, rather than reduce its capacity. This was in line with the view regularly expressed by the previous Conservative administration and ran counter to the industry's preference for capacity reduction. The report argued that achieving competitiveness and profitability required far-reaching changes which would effectively amount to a fresh start being made by shareholders, management, men and unions. Recommendations to bring about such changes were made for action to be taken by employers, the trade unions, and government. The starting point in all areas had to be with the structure of the industry. As far as management was concerned, Geddes recommended specific action in four general areas. The industry should be rationalised by concentrating it into at least four large and compact building groups. The groups should select specific parts of the growth market and concentrate resources in these areas to permit individual yards to specialise and benefit from the advantages of short and simple lines of management and production control. The naval market should be concentrated in yards with management expertise in that area; three yards were thought to be sufficient for this purpose. Main engine production should also be rationalised into four units, and the groups should cooperate creatively in research and development and in commercial matters, as a means of presenting the industry more coherently and effectively to its customers and suppliers.[16]

Specific recommendations were also made which required action by employers and the trade unions acting together. The first change necessary was for employers and unions to set new standards of general efficiency and performance, linked to a wages structure based on work study methods. A second objective was to develop a new mood in industrial relations through urgent attention to improvements in working conditions, benefits, amenities and procedures, and also to improve communications within firms and unions. There was also a clear requirement to adhere to bargains in the spirit, and the letter, to introduce effective training of supervisors and shop stewards, and to improve the public relations, and public image, of the industry. Geddes also recommended that the unions should review their structure with a view to rationalising representation in five unions. It is striking how closely these recommendations mirrored the practices and changes then being attempted by Iain Stewart and his team in the resurrected company of Fairfields (Glasgow) Ltd.

Turning to the role of government, Geddes recommended the adoption of a positive policy which recognised shipbuilding as an important potential contributor to economic growth and to the balance of payments. As part of the policy, the government should adopt arrangements for giving relief from indirect taxation; place naval orders in ways to relieve stress on the industry order book; and give additional support for research and development. It should urge the steelmakers to reduce prices to mitigate a serious cost problem for the industry. The timetable recommended was tight, a period from March to June 1966 during which it was suggested that both management and labour should discuss the proposals at local level and advise their views to their respective central organisations. These, in turn, were to convey the views, and any reservations, to the government. If the responses by both sides of the industry, and by the steelmakers were positive, Geddes recommended that the government should then establish a new body, a Shipbuilding Industry Board (SIB) on a non-statutory basis.

The SIB, it was recommended, should be created for the five-year period that the Geddes Committee believed would be necessary to implement the changes it proposed. The SIB would be responsible for initiating, stimulating, and assessing the implementation of the action necessary to restructure the industry. It would be the agency which would administer and control government financial assistance. In addition it would monitor the prospects and performance of British shipbuilding firms, advise the government on these matters, and also on how British shipbuilders were affected by measures of assistance given to foreign shipbuilders.[17] Geddes also recommended that the SIB be provided with funds to finance restructuring loans. These were recommended for three purposes. First, to expedite grouping by buying out a reluctant company; the total available for this purpose not to exceed £5 million with a closing date for applications of 31 December 1969. Second, £25 million was to

First Sea Lord Admiral Fisher's design of an 'all big gun' battleship, HMS *Dreadnought*, built at the naval dockyard in Portsmouth in 1906.

Aerial view of the upper Clyde, 1930s. From bottom left: Govan Ferry, Fairfield shipyard, Stephens' Linthouse yard, King George V Dock. From bottom right: A. & J. Inglis's Pointhouse yard, Meadowbank and Merklands quays, Clydeholm shipbuilders, Barclay Curle's, Connell's, Blythswood shipbuilders, Yarrow's. Note how many empty berths there were during the Depression.

An evocative photograph by Edgar Tarry Adams of the slipway used to launch HMS *Cornwallis* into the river Thames at Blackwall, on 17 July, 1901.

© NATIONAL MEDIA MUSEUM / SCIENCE & SOCIETY PICTURE LIBRARY

Specialised ships: a torpedo boat destroyer, *c*.1900.

HMS *Hood*, the Navy's largest and most powerful battleship. Launched at John Brown's Clydebank yard, 1918; the engines were built at the company's Atlas Works in Sheffield.

© NATIONAL MARITIME MUSEUM

The Governor of the Bank of England, the dapper Montagu Norman, photographed in 1941.

John Brown & Co.'s ship number 534, the future *Queen Mary*. In this photograph we see the hull abandoned on the stocks, where no work was done between 1932 and 1934. *Queen Mary* was eventually launched in September 1934 and, powered by four Parsons' steam turbines, went on to win the Blue Riband for the fastest Atlantic crossing in 1938 at an average speed of 30.99 knots.

Unemployment in the Depression: the Jarrow Crusade, or Hunger March, October 1936.

Women at war work: moving baulks of timber at Palmers' Jarrow yard, 1917.

© IMPERIAL WAR MUSEUMS

As in the First, so in the Second World War women were recruited to work in the yards. Here women shipyard workers are photographed at a North East shipyard in 1943.

Women welders at a Greenock yard in 1943.

SS *Patrick Henry*: the first all welded Liberty Ship, 1941. *Patrick Henry* was the first ship built by Bethlehem-Fairfield Shipyards, Inc. of Maryland, one of the original nine emergency yards sponsored by the US government in 1940 to build tonnage for the war effort. *Patrick Henry* survived the war and was scrapped in 1958.

Vickers' Barrow-in-Furness yard: mass producing tankers in 1943.

SS *British Ambassador*, at the time of its construction in 1958 Britain's largest tanker, at 42,000 dwt.
Vickers, Barrow.

Vickers' Barrow yard before modernisation in 1947. All the berths are fully occupied in the post-war
boom.

The aircraft carriers HMS *Magnificent* and *Powerful* under construction at the yard of Harland & Wolff in Belfast, 1944.

Ernest Marples (*left*), Minister of Transport, 1961–64, with Richard Dimbleby.

Small, outdated British yards found it increasingly hard to compete with modern shipyards such as those in the Far East, particularly when the latter were able to offer more favourable credit terms and delivery times. This aerial photograph shows Denny of Dumbarton's Leven Shipyard prior to closure in 1963.

Some British yards did invest and were able to continue for a time. Here we see the Swan Hunter yard in 1964, with its improved berths and cranes. The tanker *Ottawa* is being launched.

Harland & Wolff's last large passenger ship, *Canberra*, was launched in March 1960. By this date air travel had completely displaced liner traffic as a means of transport, and large vessels such as *Canberra* were built as cruise ships. Here she is photographed in Majorca in 1976.

The modernised Fairfield yard at Govan, 1964.

The end of an era: the launch of the *Queen Elizabeth II* in 1967. This was Clydebank's and Britain's last great ocean liner. The *QEII* was built at the John Brown yard of Upper Clyde Shipbuilders, on the same site as other icons of British shipbuilding, including the *Lusitania*, *Aquitania*, *Queen Mary* and *Queen Elizabeth*.

For centuries British shipbuilding had provided a wide range of employment and training opportunities. Here, as late as 1981, a group of 125 apprentices pose in front of a tanker at Scott Lithgow's Kingston yard, Port Glasgow.

Vosper Thorneycroft's new yard at Portsmouth, which opened in 2003.
© John Oram

A view from Govan, showing BAE Systems' Scotstoun yard, with the covered berth and Daring-class destroyers.
© Donald Whannell

A Type 22 frigate, HMS *Sheffield*, built by Swan Hunter at Wallsend in 1986. This ship was named after the Type 42 destroyer of the same name destroyed in the Falklands conflict in 1982. Ten of the fourteen Type 22s were built at Yarrow's on the Clyde.

First of class, the Type 45 destroyer HMS *Daring*, which was launched at Scotstoun in 2006 and commissioned in 2009. The Type 45, of which six are planned, was designed to replace the Type 42s, the last of which was decommissioned in 2013.

Royal Fleet Auxiliary *Largs Bay*, which was launched by Swan Hunter in 2003. She entered service in 2006, but after just four years she was identified for disposal in the Strategic Defence and Security Review. She was sold to the Australian Navy.

Shipbuilders' skills can be transferred to other types of structure: this is the *Iolaire*, a sophisticated semi-submersible offshore platform, built by Scott Lithgow in 1981.

The P&O ferry *Pride of York* (until 2003 the *Norsea*), which was built by Govan Shipbuilders in 1987. She operates from Hull to Rotterdam and Zeebrugge.

The Swan Hunter yard is demolished in 2009 after almost 130 years of building commercial and naval ships.

An Astute-class hunter killer nuclear submarine, of which seven boats are planned. This is the first of class, HMS *Astute*, which was launched from Barrow-in-Furness in 2007 and commissioned in 2010.

Artist's impression of the 'Future Carrier'. Two of these Queen Elizabeth-class carriers are planned. The first, HMS *Elizabeth*, is being assembled at Rosyth Dockyard, and is due for launch in 2014. They are intended to carry Short Take-Off/Vertical Landing Lockheed Martin F-35B fighters.

Artist's impression of the 'Future Frigate', a Type 26 not intended to be in service until the late 2020s.

be set aside to meet working-capital needs arising out of the restructuring. Third, a further £15 million was earmarked to cover transitional costs of re-arranging facilities together with meeting costs of retraining labour in the new groups, where the costs could not be met under the terms of the 1964 Industrial Training Act. Another fund of £5 million was also recommended in the form of grants to meet transitional losses on resources that would not be fully utilised, or be duplicated, or be in process of running down during the reorganisation. On Geddes' calculations the programme of financial assistance totalled loans of £45 million and grants of £5 million together with £150,000 for commissioning consultancy reports on grouping proposals. The report also recommended a short-term provision of £30 million, and not more than £10 million in any twelve-month period, to provide Shipbuilding Credits to UK owners, on the same basis as credits already available to foreign owners building in UK yards. This was designed to ensure a steady order book during the period of restructuring, and would only operate between mid-1967 and the end of 1970. Geddes noted that the provision of assistance in these forms did not involve any subsidy to production, and was all related to the reorganisation of the industry. Moreover, the sums proposed were ceilings, not expenditure, and that they were subject to tight timetables and stringent conditions on the part of those applying for assistance.

The industry's initial welcome for the Geddes Report was followed by extensive local and national meetings, and the collective response to the Board of Trade was drafted by mid-June. Geddes had set out three scenarios for the future of the industry against which it was recommended that the shipbuilders and the unions should consider their reaction to the report. First, if the industry continued on its present path, the prospect was for a steady decline in market share, a stagnation of output at around 1.0 million gross tons, and a decline in employment in new construction from 51,000 in 1965, to a projected 30,000 by 1975. Alternatively, on a 'holding on' hypothesis, with modest changes in attitudes and structures, the industry could probably expect to work more fully to the potential existing capacity of 1.75 million tons per year, retain its present workforce of around 50,000, but essentially be progressively marginalised and always be on the defensive. The third prospect was to go for growth; to undertake the major restructuring proposed over a two- to three-year period, with the prospect of raising production to 2.25 million tons, and extending market share to perhaps 12.5 per cent as against one of only half that under the 'decline' hypothesis. This scenario assumed a stable workforce of around 50,000 on new building, but one delivering improved productivity and enjoying greater security of employment for the workers, and an attractive career prospect for young managers.

In formulating their response to the minister, Douglas Jay, the industry endorsed the concept of growth as the only practicable foundation for planning for the future. They noted that 'if our Industry is to survive and prosper there seems no alternative basis'.[18] The industry also supported Geddes' view that there would continue to be a large and growing share of the world market accessible to a competitive British shipbuilding industry, provided that inflation in the UK did not outpace that in competing countries, and that factor supplies were uninterrupted and competitively priced. The supply of steel at prices advantageous to the shipbuilders was held to be critical for the future prospects of the industry. On regrouping, the industry was, 'prepared to accept that to achieve viability and competitiveness, radical reorganisation of its structure must be carried through. There is broad agreement in principle for a wider measure of grouping and mergers of existing shipbuilding facilities into larger integrated units.' In order to progress this development the industry urged upon the government the urgent need to set up the Shipbuilding Industry Board as suggested in the Geddes timetable, that is from July 1966. This was a necessary step, as Geddes had argued, 'not only to assist firms with their financial problems arising from the reorganisation of the Industry, but also to provide guidance on the ways in which large groupings can best take place in the interests of the Industry as a whole'.[19] On the industrial-relations proposals there had been joint meetings of all the shipbuilding and marine engineering central organisations, with the Confederation of Shipbuilding and Engineering Unions (CSEU), and a joint conference of employers and unions at York. A 'Joint Industry Consultative Committee' had been established and considerable progress was made at a local level on agreements on demarcation, steel working, and better use of manpower, all with a view to satisfying the earnest commitments of intent and support required by the government before an agreement to accept the Geddes recommendations was likely. In conclusion, the industry expressed the hope that the government would without delay confirm its acceptance of the Geddes Report, and proceed immediately with the establishment of the Shipbuilding Industry Board, emphasising again the industry's opinion that the early availability of the SIB for consultation was essential if there were to be effective development of proposals for rationalisation and merger within the timetable set out, namely to establish the SIB from July 1966 and agree grouping proposals by December 1967.

In the political circumstances of 1966 it was never likely that this timetable would be met. The Geddes Committee presented its report to the President of the Board of Trade on 24 February 1966 as the General Election campaign was under way. It was published a month later, within a week of the election, and on the day before publication the government, through Douglas Jay as President of the Board of Trade, announced acceptance of the report as a basis for discussion on the future of the industry. After the election, and the return of the Labour government, a further announcement confirmed that the government expected the industry and unions to give their views by the end of June, as set out in the Geddes timetable. The response to these reports came on 9 August 1966 when Douglas Jay confirmed the government's willingness to involve itself in the reorganisation of the industry. He stopped short of establishing the SIB at that point, but announced that, when formed, the SIB chairman would be Mr William Swallow, who had been chairman and managing director of Vauxhall

Motors.[20] Consultations could begin on reorganisation, though the mechanism of the SIB and its funding had still to be set up.

In the meantime, pressure continued to mount on the industry, and support was given in two areas before the Geddes proposals could be set in motion. Harland & Wolff had been one of the 27 major companies included in the Geddes review, but before it became clear how it might relate to the Geddes proposals, the Northern Ireland government made £2 million available to the Belfast company in 1966 to avert an immediate threat of closure. In addition, the government took steps on the general issue of financial support for shipbuilders in the Finance Act 1966, which incorporated a Geddes proposal to provide a Shipbuilders Relief grant in the form of a 2 per cent rebate of the contract price on all ships delivered by UK builders after 12 September 1966.[21] As another step in this direction the Industrial Development Bill, August 1966, Section 5, provided for the Board of Trade to make grants for constructing a new ship, or converting an existing vessel, at a rate of 25 per cent of contract cost to cover the period from August 1966 to December 1967. The grants were available whether or not the ship was constructed in the UK, but it had to be British-registered. This helped produce orders, but the new beginning desired by the Geddes committee was taking shape only slowly, and did not gather momentum until the passing of the Shipbuilding Industry Bill in June 1967, about six months behind the initial Geddes schedule.

## Intervention and reorganisation

The reviews of the shipbuilding industry which had taken place between 1960 and 1965 had all, in some degree, advocated the need for some measure of concentration through grouping or merger. This was the central thrust of the Geddes Report, and it spoke the language which the Labour government understood and supported. The government was committed to restructuring British industry to improve its competitiveness, and in 1966 had established the Industrial Reorganisation Corporation (IRC) specifically with that purpose in mind. The industry had always resisted grouping, but on this occasion the lure of substantial funding overcame resistance, while the unions tacitly accepted it as an important step toward their preferred objective of public ownership. Their philosophy was that once the government was committed financially, any subsequent failure would precipitate further intervention, making nationalisation more likely.[22]

The acceptance of this strategy, however, was tantamount to policy making by omission, rather than policy choice by evaluation of a range of options. The Geddes remit had stressed making recommendations on organisational changes necessary to improve competitiveness, and that is what the Geddes Report formulated. But in advocating grouping, there was no questioning or assessment of the benefits that were assumed to flow from this change, nor any consideration of different kinds of linkage, say in vertical or horizontal integration to create diversified rather than specialised ship-production units. Moreover, government support and industry enthusiasm for the restructuring rested on the acceptance of Geddes' view that shipbuilding was a growth industry in world terms. This perspective was self-evident, but the British industry was not world-oriented; it was inward-looking to the UK flag fleet, and the belief that it could re-orient itself to world markets and increase in scale flew in the face of all the evidence and experience of the industry in the twentieth century. Resources were therefore to be committed to an industry which historically preferred individualism to cooperation, and its outlook was oriented more to survival than to growth. The acceptance by government that shipbuilders and unions were willing, and able, to make a fresh start involving fundamental changes in attitude and behaviour, was made without a shred of convincing evidence. Nevertheless, the passing of the Shipbuilding Industry Bill in June 1967 launched the industry into uncharted waters, but in an environment already significantly different from early 1965, when Geddes was set up. At that point the industry had been climbing out of recession, but by 1967 it had slipped back into a decline in order books, and in world market shares. The SIB restructuring was consequently facing a much more difficult market.

The Shipbuilding Industry Bill passed swiftly through the House and was generally supported by the Opposition. Its final form differed in four major ways from the Geddes proposals. Geddes had recommended that the Shipbuilding Industry Board should have power to administer a short-term credit scheme of £30 million, £10 million committed in any year, to even out the order book in the period of restructuring. However, the deterioration of work on hand from 1.07 million tons in 1965, to 781,000 tons in 1967, and the accelerating drift of UK orders going to foreign shipyards, 38 per cent of the tonnage placed in 1964, but 70 per cent by 1967, prompted the government to revise radically its views on credit. Section 7 of the Shipbuilding Industry Bill, 1967, introduced a new Shipbuilding Credit Scheme for domestic ship owners. Responsibility for the scheme was placed with the Ministry of Technology, which had taken over responsibility for shipbuilding from November 1966. The minister in charge was Tony Wedgwood Benn. On advice from the SIB he could recommend loans to ship owners building in UK yards, with funds of £200 million available at any one time. Loans were available for 80 per cent of the contract cost at 5½ per cent over eight years, and the scheme involved agreement to provide advances by both the English and Scottish clearing banks. This scheme at last answered years of pressure by the shipbuilders to place home owners on a level with foreign owners placing orders in British yards.

A second difference in the Bill affected Geddes' proposal that £5 million be set aside to cover transitional costs of loss of earnings on assets subject to restructuring, the funds to be on a tapering basis. Government accepted the principle, but the funds were provided on a fixed rather than tapering arrangement, and the scheme was consequently much simpler to operate. A simplification and enhanced flexibility were also introduced in the central provision of loans for working capital. The Geddes proposal had earmarked funds in different categories while the Bill permitted the SIB to apply the funds of £3.2 million at its discretion. The third and most radical departure from Geddes' recommendations in the Bill was that clause 6 permitted the SIB, with ministerial approval, to take a shareholding in a company instead of, or in addition to, making a direct loan. The Bill also provided for loans to be discharged by the issue of shares. This equity provision undoubtedly reflected the Fairfield experience, and the practice under the IRC. The general principle was that where substantial public funds were invested in an enterprise, the government should protect that provision by taking shares which would entitle its agencies to share in any future profits, and influence the management of the concern. The fourth change in the Bill was that while the Geddes Report had covered only the 27 major yards constructing vessels over 5,000 dwt, the Bill extended its coverage to include all yards building ships of 100 grt and over. This brought in more than 30 smaller yards whose business, and market, was far different from the larger yards. The rationale for this extension is not clear, for these yards did not operate in the world market, and their inclusion in any group could only mean closure. It is doubtful if there was any commercial ground for this step; rather, it probably reflected the government's view on the need to be seen to be even-handed, and to promote a public perception of fairness in providing access to public funds.

Geddes' approach to grouping had been pragmatically based on three principles. The yards incorporated in any group should be physically close to each other with not more than one hour's travel involved between them; the group should employ 8–10,000 men and have a capacity annually of 400,000 to 500,000 tons gross. Ideally the group should comprise four to six yards which incorporated a range of capabilities. Geddes also envisaged a specialisation of yards in three broad categories; 'S' yards, capable of building more specialist ships; 'M' yards focusing on multi-deck mixed cargo ships and 'B' yards constructing bulk carriers and tankers, ships without twin decks. On these principles Geddes considered that two major groups could be formed in the North East covering Tyne, Wear and Tees, and not more than two groups would be appropriate for the Clyde. Although not explicitly saying so, the form of words used in the report suggests the Geddes committee had a preference for a single group on the Clyde, but tacitly recognised that there were long-standing Upper Clyde and Lower Clyde shipbuilding environments. The committee also advanced the opinion that Harland & Wolff was more or less large enough to act as a group on its own, but that its linkage with another group should not be discounted. This was the extent of the guidance given, but it was sufficient to stimulate talks on the major rivers, for all the companies were experiencing problems of cash flow, while access to grants and loans through the SIB was conditional upon grouping.

The foundation for grouping was probably most advanced on the Tyne, where Swan Hunter had a tradition of takeover. It had owned Barclay Curle on the Clyde from 1912, and in 1965 had acquired the Grangemouth dockyard on the river Forth. In 1965 it also entered into merger discussions with Smiths Dock on the Tees, and this was accomplished in 1966 prior to Geddes. Acting on its own initiative in May

1967, the SIB proposed establishing a working group to promote a Tyne–Tees merger involving Swan Hunter, Hawthorn Leslie, John Readhead and Vickers on the Tyne, together with the Furness Shipbuilding Company yard at Haverton Hill on the Tees. This yard was owned by Sears Holdings, and was a serious loss maker. Within a month the four Tyne yards announced their intention to form a new group to be called Swan Hunter and Tyne Shipbuilders, with Sir John Hunter as chairman. The grouping would exclude Vickers' Barrow establishment, and would only involve the shipbuilding interests of the other companies. The status of John Readhead as a private company produced difficulties about its membership of a merger of public limited companies, and to overcome this Swan Hunter offered to acquire Readhead prior to grouping. Further negotiations produced a new grouping proposal in October 1967 which included the ship-repair interests of Readhead, as well as the shipbuilding assets. The group came into being on 1 January 1968 with Swan Hunter the major shareholder with 64 per cent, and Vickers and Hawthorne Leslie each with 18 per cent. The excluded Furness Shipbuilding Co. announced its intended closure shortly thereafter, but by September 1968, under pressure from SIB, Swan Hunter & Tyne Shipbuilders agreed to acquire Furness Shipbuilders, and the Ministry of Technology advance a grant of £1.0 million to make the takeover possible. This completed the first large group in the North East.

The second grouping in the North East involved the Wear shipbuilders, where three of the main companies had already merged as Doxford and Sunderland Shipbuilders in 1961. These were Sir James Laing & Co., John L. Thompson & Sons, and William Doxford & Sons, and each continued to operate relatively independently within the merged structure. In April 1967 it was announced that a working party involving the SIB would be set up to prepare proposals for a further merger of Doxford and Sunderland and with the other two Wear shipbuilders, Austin & Pickersgill and Bartram & Sons. The working party reported in September 1967, but the SIB rejected the proposal which involved the closure of Bartrams and of the Doxford yard, while offering no plan for expansion. Thereafter little progress was made, and in July 1968 the SIB advised the Wear companies that it would no longer recommend granting them credit guarantees for building ships under the Shipbuilding Industry Act, Section 7 provision. The embargo was unprecedented and amounted to coercion to form a group: it immediately affected five contracts and brought a quick protest from the firms to the Ministry of Technology. Following discussions, the credit facilities were restored, but the point had been made. Within a month Austin & Pickersgill and Bertrams merged, but without any assistance from the SIB, which remained frustrated in its attempt to create a larger group on the Wear.

The groupings undertaken on the Tyne and Wear involved full merger, and the emergence of a dominant partner in each group, Swan Hunter on the Tyne, and Austin & Pickersgill in the smaller Wear merger. The pattern that was to emerge on the Clyde had very different characteristics. The rapid closure of seven yards on the Clyde between 1960 and 1965, together with the Fairfield crisis, stimulated early interchanges on possible groupings. During 1966 talks took place between Stephens, Connells, Barclay Curle and Yarrow with a view to grouping, and Fairfields and John Brown also looked at a union; these initial exchanges were overtaken by the Geddes recommendations. By March 1967 Swallow as chairman of SIB had met the chairmen of Stephens, Connells, Yarrow, Fairfields and John Browns, and by the end of that month a working party had been established to formulate merger proposals. The chairman of the working party was Anthony Hepper, a board member of SIB and former chairman of Thomas Tilling & Co. There was disagreement from the outset, Fairfields, under Iain Stewart, advocating a full takeover of interest by one of the companies as the major party, the others favouring a merger of equals. It was also agreed from the outset that if a merger were agreed, the chairman of the group would have to be someone from outside the Clyde shipbuilding companies; such were the hostilities and tensions among the existing chief executives. The working party was asked to formulate proposals and to keep an open mind on absorbing the Lower Clyde yards, but that path was blocked by independent moves on the lower reaches.

In August 1967 it was announced that the four Upper Clyde merchant yards, Fairfield, Connell, Stephen and Brown's would form a group, with Yarrow expected to announce its position within a week. Yarrow did decide to join, but only on terms of retaining its own identity and operating as a self-contained, independent subsidiary. The working party had also recommended the new group acquire the Clydeholme yard of Barclay Curle, which Swan Hunter had put up for sale earlier in the year. The five yards proposing to merge rejected that option, and the SIB accepted the proposals in principle in December 1967, the new Upper Clyde Shipbuilders coming into operation in February 1968. The equity shares were John Brown & Co. at 30 per cent; Fairfields 35 per cent, and £350,000 in cash, Connell 5 per cent and up to £400,000 in cash; Stephen 10 per cent, and Yarrow 20 per cent and £1 million in cash. The issued capital was to be £4 million with a rights issue of 1 for 4 to raise £1 million in working capital. Some Fairfield shareholders did not take up the issue, and their shares were purchased by John Brown & Co., giving them and Fairfield each a 32.5 per cent holding. The merger was complex since not all the assets of the companies came into the new group. The non-shipbuilding interests of John Brown, Stephen and Yarrow were excluded, and UCS only had a 51 per cent share in Yarrow. Moreover, since the government already held 50 per cent of the equity in Fairfields, it became a holder of 17.5 per cent of UCS equity. The cash payments to three of the companies largely reflected the cost of buying out shareholders who opposed the merger, being unwilling to give up immediate earnings, small as they were, for a gamble on uncertain future returns. Sir Iain Stewart became deputy chairman of UCS, and Anthony Hepper resigned from the board of SIB to become chairman.

On the Lower Clyde, Lithgows and Scotts of Greenock began merger discussions and made a grouping proposal to SIB in September 1967. Negotiations were prolonged, for the Upper Clyde group working party argued that it was possible to harmonise the capital structures of the yards on both reaches of the river, and create a single large and diversified group. They particularly stressed the advantage of the Lower Clyde for building large tankers, and indicated that this would allow a single Clyde group to build across the whole range of ship types. They proposed that the Scott and Lithgow yards should function as an independent subsidiary, but that the Upper Clyde group should have a majority shareholding.

Scotts and Lithgow strongly resisted this and in 1968 effectively began to operate as a single company, even though no formal merger had been approved. Perhaps surprisingly SIB did not repeat its tactic of withdrawing credit support as it had done on the Wear. Moreover, since Geddes had recommended a concentration of naval building in only three yards, both Scotts and Lithgows, which then both had Admiralty orders, could have been subject to government pressure to accede to a unified group on the Clyde through threatening to remove them from the approved list of builders. This was apparently a serious prospect in August 1968, but in the end this was not pursued since the government stood apart from the grouping negotiations which were in SIB hands. The new Scott Lithgow group ultimately included the Greenock Dockyard in its merger which was not finalised until the end of 1969. SIB provided loans of £2.3 million and grants of £1.4 million for this grouping. Unlike the Upper Clyde, where most of the capital was absorbed in bringing the companies together, the capital on the Lower Clyde was for new facilities which extended and reinforced an apparently genuine merger of interests and activities.

Apart from these major groupings little else was achieved in concentrating activity. The tentative proposal that there might be an 'Irish Sea Group' linking Vickers at Barrow, Cammell Laird at Birkenhead, and Harland & Wolff at Belfast, evaporated when these companies could gain access to capital grants under the terms of the 1968 Industrial Expansion Act, which set aside £15 million for shipbuilding, and was available to applicants that were not part of groups. Smaller mergers did, however, take place, Vosper at Portsmouth, linked with Thorneycroft at Southampton in 1968, and in Scotland, Robb of Leith merged with Caledon of Dundee to form Robb Caledon. The only other small merger achieved with SIB assistance was the acquisition of Cochrane & Sons of Selby by the Drypool Engineering and Drydock Company of Hull in 1969.

The translation of the Geddes proposals into effective groups consequently succeeded in restructuring only a part of British shipbuilding. Four large companies controlling 40 per cent of UK capacity were uninvolved, three of them through their geographic isolation; Cammell Laird (7.0 per cent) Harland & Wolff (13.0 per cent); Vickers Barrow (7.0 per cent) and the reluctant Doxford and Sunderland Shipbuilders (13.0 per cent). Elsewhere, however, the effect of grouping was significant. On the Tyne, Swan Hunter and Tyne Shipbuilders emerged as the largest group in the UK with 16.5 per cent of capacity. On the Upper Clyde, UCS was nearly as large with about 15.0 per cent of capacity, and was probably the most varied group in its yard and ship types. The Scott Lithgow group on the Lower Clyde produced a tighter group with 11.0 per cent of capacity. Twenty-seven major yards reviewed by Geddes had been reformed in a period of two years into three new and large groups, together with a number of smaller mergers, and four larger independent companies. Seven shipbuilding entities effectively controlled UK capacity in 1969, where 27 had done so just three years earlier. To that extent the achievement was remarkable, but even with this degree of concentration the UK groups were significantly smaller than their Japanese equivalents. The Swan Hunter group was less than half the size of the two largest Japanese consortia, while it and the other larger units, UCS, Scott Lithgow, Doxford and Sunderland, and Harland & Wolff were roughly comparable in scale to the major European builders, and equivalent to the smaller Japanese establishments.

Geddes had also recommended a rationalisation and concentration of the marine-engine building sector, but progress there was poor. These were often the more profitable parts of the independent shipbuilding concerns and had largely been separated off prior to grouping. Thus the John Brown and Alexander Stephen engineering companies were outside the UCS group, as was Swan Hunters Wallsend Slipway Company. That sector remained over-populated by many relatively small firms, and suffered from considerable excess capacity. The only significant SIB assistance was given to the merger of George Clark and NEM on Tyneside. The restructuring achievement, even though less than the optimum aspired to by Geddes, was still a remarkable reshaping of British shipbuilding in a short space of time. The objective, however, had not been to create larger units as an end it itself, but to do so in such a way as to lay the foundation for a transformation of management, a fresh start for labour relations, and the achievement of greater efficiency and competitiveness. These aspirations were to be cruelly dashed.

## Deceptive improvement

Ever since the recession of 1958–63, the central problem for Britain's shipbuilders had been a scarcity of orders, and a weak order book. After 1966, to some extent, this appeared to have been resolved. The establishment of the SIB and the flow of capital into restructuring the industry were welcome developments, but it was resolving the cash-flow deficiencies of the companies that was the critical boost to confidence in the industry. This stimulus coincided with both the devaluation of Sterling by about 14 per cent against the dollar, and the impact of the Six Day War. The devaluation improved the competitiveness of British prices, while the Six Day War caused the closure of the Suez Canal for what proved to be a protracted period of eight years. The closure of the short route to the oil states in the Gulf, and the disruption of shipping, caused time charter rates to rise sharply, and induced a rush of new orders. World order books which had been sluggish since 1958 more than doubled to 83.6 mgt in 1971. Orders were plentiful and British yards kept pace with world trends, doubling orders from 2.47

mgt to 4.92 mgt in 1971 (Table 7.1). Where previously the Industry had had less than two years' work on hand, this influx stretched the work available to four or five years.

While this was a welcome relief, it did not resolve the underlying weaknesses in the industry which had been exposed in the many reports in the early 1960s. Although world output of merchant tonnage increased from 14.3 mgt in 1966 to 24.9 mgt in 1971, UK output remained static at between 1.08 mgt and 1.23 mgt. Consequently, as the world industry expanded, the UK market share declined sharply from 7.6 per cent to 4.9 per cent. This deterioration was exposed most worryingly in the increased foreign penetration of the UK shipping market, as measured by the volume of new tonnage registered by British ship owners. Between 1962 and 1966, British owners annually registered some 1.2 mgt of new ships, but doubled this accretion to 2.5 mgt each year from 1967 to 1971. However, as UK owners doubled their demand for new tonnage, British shipbuilders continued to supply them with around 800,000 grt each year, thus allowing foreign builders to drive up their share of the British market from 32.6 per cent to 71.8 per cent by 1971 (Table 7.2). The failure to expand output essentially gifted the expanding domestic shipping market – long a British shipbuilding monopoly – to foreign builders. Ironically, while losing domestic market share, UK builders held on to about 4.0 per cent of world exports, which had doubled to 53.9 mgt in 1971.

However, even as export orders appeared to be stabilising, world market trends were shifting quite rapidly. In the five years to 1971, world registrations of new tonnage totalled 98.5 mgt, but 29.2 mgt of this was closed to competition in the protected markets of Japan, France, Italy, Spain and the USA. Another 23.0 mgt was absorbed by the open markets of the flag-of-convenience fleets of Liberia, Greece and Panama, who, lacking shipbuilding industries, imported all their tonnage. The balance of 33.0 mgt was in the competitive flag fleet and shipbuilding markets of Britain, West Germany, the Netherlands, Denmark, Sweden and Norway.[23] Yet even with these restrictions, the doubling of world tonnage exports to 53.9 mgt in 1971, indicated that the world shipping market was becoming truly global.

In Britain the response to this expanding market was that UK shipbuilders continued to rely on three main market outlets, Norway, the flag-of-convenience fleets, and the Commonwealth countries. Between 1962 and 1966 these took 80 per cent of all UK exports, while half of all tonnage went to Norway alone. In the next five years, to 1971, these markets took two-thirds of UK tonnage exports, but the UK share of the Norwegian market slipped from 48 per cent to less than 29 per cent. At the same time, dependence on Liberia, Greece and Panama increased from 14 per cent to 33 per cent, and exceptionally the traditional Commonwealth market almost vanished, slipping down from 18 per cent to only 3 per cent by 1971. This loss was offset by what proved to be a one-off capture of orders from West Germany which moved out of the closed market group, and took 15 per cent of UK export tonnage. Ominously, in this shifting and volatile market, UK builders struggled to win orders in the main West European markets. Sweden, Denmark, the Netherlands and France, collectively took only 4 per cent of UK export tonnage. This outcome underlined the influence of problems identified in Geddes, and other reports, namely that of increasing price differentials between the UK and its main competitors, and even more, the issue of the poor performance of British yards in the speed of construction and delivery of orders. In this highly competitive market some 39 per cent of all UK deliveries of new tonnage were one or more months late, while some 9 per cent of orders were more than six months behind schedule.[24] A more positive interpretation of the delivery performance between 1967 and 1971 would be to argue that 61 per cent of all deliveries were less than one month late. That, however, was not how British deliveries were increasingly perceived by ship owners.

The relatively poor performance of British shipbuilding, and the shifts in its market, were in part due to the product preferences of UK builders, which showed marked differences from world industry patterns. Between 1967 and 1971, orders for tankers and bulk carriers took up three-quarters of the world market, and were over 83 per cent of the Japanese order book. In Japan these were divided between 44.5 per cent as tankers and 39.0 per cent for bulk carriers. In Britain in contrast, these two categories took up only 69 per cent of the order book. The preference in Britain was for ore and bulk carriers, these providing 45.6 per cent of orders, while oil tankers represented less than one-quarter of output. Again in comparison with world patterns, general cargo tonnage took 22.0 per cent of UK output, well above the 12.0 per cent in Japan, and the world average of 17.6 per cent in that market sector. Britain's pattern of construction also differed in the size of tonnage built. In its traditional specialism of general cargo ships, Britain built vessels well above world averages. British cargo ships averaged 10,000 grt compared to a world figure of 7,726 grt, and a Japanese average of only 6,394 grt. Elsewhere, however, Britain built smaller ships than other major builders. The largest differential was in oil tankers, the UK average tanker of 15,755 grt being only half the world figure of 31.456 grt, and even further behind the Japanese tanker of 35,128 grt. The only sector in which Britain more or less kept pace with the increase in scale was in ore and bulk carriers, the UK average of 24,364 grt only slightly smaller than the world average of 27,000 grt.

In spite of these differences, and the slippage in world ranking, the infusion of SIB funds enabled the industry to retain a 6.0 per cent share of world orders. The SIB advanced £42.9 million in grants and loans to UK shipbuilders between 1967 and 1971, and cash grants of 25.0 per cent of the cost of building a ship were also made available to UK ship owners. Under Section 5 of the 1966 Industrial Development Act, grants amounting to £870.9 million were approved, and £196.8 million of these had already been paid out by 1971. A further source of credit support for UK ship owners was created through Section 7 of the Shipbuilding Industry Bill, which provided guarantees of 80.0 per cent of the cost of a ship, the loan being at 5½ per cent over eight years. The initial provision was a fund of £200 million in support of new orders, although this was increased to £400 million in 1969, and again, to £700 million, in

1971.[25] These measures were a significant boost to UK shipping and shipbuilding, and delivered 6.33 mgt of new orders to the industry between July 1967 and December 1971, more than twice the level of the previous five years. By the time the new Conservative government of Edward Heath dissolved the SIB on 31 December 1971, it had guaranteed loans for 488 new ships with a contract value of £1,095 million.[26]

On the face of it, this infusion of financial support, and the rejuvenation of the order book, should have returned the post-Geddes restructured shipbuilding industry to health and prosperity. Order books were full, but they turned out to be far from profitable. The Geddes mergers had brought together many companies which joined the new groups with a backlog of uneconomic orders. In addition, in the rush to take orders in the expanding market, British yards found themselves being increasingly marginalised. In the booming buyers' market, fierce price competition forced British builders to fill their order books with contracts which were only available on a fixed-price basis. Thereafter, inflation in the UK trebled from 2.0 per cent to more than 6.0 per cent between 1966 and 1970, forcing up the costs of materials and labour. Average weekly earnings in shipbuilding and marine engineering rose sharply from £16.18 in 1963 to £37.13 in 1971.[27] The combination of inflation, rising costs and the need to make heavy penalty payments because of delivery delays, all contributed to mounting losses in the industry. This malign conjunction surfaced in three main crises which, collectively, seriously distorted the profitability of the industry at large. These emerging pressure points focused on Cammell Laird at Birkenhead, Govan Shipbuilders and the parent Upper Clyde Shipbuilders (UCS), and in Harland & Wolff at Belfast. Of these three, only Govan/UCS emerged from the Geddes rationalisation mergers; the others had retained their independent stand-alone status.

At Harland & Wolff the haemorrhage on contracts began as early as 1962 in a cash-flow crisis. This arose from losses on the liner *Canberra*, together with the costs of modernising the Musgrave yard, and the under-performance of subsidiaries on the Clyde at Govan, at Finnieston, and at the Clyde Foundry.[28] By 1965 the company was reporting anticipated losses of £1.25 million, these associated with two tankers under construction for Shell UK. This was eventually reduced to £1.0 million through Shell agreeing to cancel the contract for one of the vessels.[29] Harland & Wolff was finally to declare a net loss of £1.9 million after tax and depreciation in 1965. In this fragile condition Harland & Wolff felt threatened by the implications of the Geddes Report which made access to financial support conditional upon company reorganisation involving, wherever possible, amalgamation and merger. This spectre took real form late in 1965 when Cammell Laird made tentative approaches concerning the possibility of a merger. Harland & Wolff's position was further complicated through a worsening of its cash-flow problem in 1966, and by the threat of a takeover by the Greek ship owner, Aristotle Onasis, who had a substantial shareholding in the company. Considering neither the Cammell Laird nor the Onasis approaches palatable, Harland & Wolff then approached the Northern Ireland Minister of Commerce to inquire what support might be available to sustain the yard as an independent employer in Belfast. It also simultaneously opened tentative merger discussions with Vickers Armstrong at their Barrow-in-Furness yard.[30]

Among these approaches, it was the discussion with the Northern Ireland Ministry of Commerce that bore fruit. In September 1966 the Ministry made Harland & Wolff an offer of a guaranteed loan of £1.5 million, this to be raised from the Northern Bank and the Belfast Banking Co. This provision was to extend for up to nine months, and was to be replaced as soon as legislation could be passed which would enable the Ministry of Commerce to provide a longer term loan of £3.5 million. The offer, however, came with strings attached. The Ministry required that Harland & Wolff's chairman, Dr Rebbeck, should stand down and be replaced by their appointee, John Mallabar. He was the senior partner of J.F. Mallabar & Co., chartered accountants. These changes meant that by November 1966, the effective control of Harland & Wolff had passed into the hands of the Northern Ireland Ministry of Commerce.[31]

When Mallabar took over as chairman, he inherited a difficult situation with losses deteriorating to £4.14 million, and a management widely regarded as conservative and inward-looking. Finding that orders were scarce for the type of ships traditionally built at Belfast, Mallabar revived a previously shelved proposal that the company should seek to enter the market for large ships. This was to involve investing in the construction of a very large dry dock, as was common in Japan. One of the yard's regular customers, Esso, was sufficiently supportive of the scheme to take the step of writing a letter of intent for an order of two large tankers for delivery in 1970, these to be the first part of a four-ship project.[32] The estimated cost of building the giant dock was put at £13.5 million. This was to be covered by a grant-in-aid of £5.5 million from the Government of Northern Ireland, the balance of £8.0 million to be raised by Harland & Wolff from its own resources. By January 1968 the company had negotiated a loan of £3.0 million from the SIB, this to cover anticipated costs of reorganisation as the works progressed. It then provided the remaining £8.0 million by creating loan capital secured by a floating charge on its own assets, completing this step in 1969.[33]

The decision to build a huge new dry dock was a massive undertaking. Designed to be 557 metres long, 93 metres wide, and with a depth of 8.4 metres at mean high water in Spring, it was then to be the largest in the world, capable of floating out a tanker of one million deadweight tons (dwt). Perhaps inevitably, the project suffered delays and was well behind schedule at the end of 1969, the estimated cost having then risen to £16.0 million. The partial completion of the dock, and the consequent disruption of other yard facilities, also had serious knock-on effects on the programme of ship construction. The first of the two tankers for Esso, and two other orders, were delayed with inevitable financial penalties for the yard.

These, apparently, were teething problems, for on a more positive note, the availability of the recently modernised Musgrave yard, together with the new dock coming on stream, gave Harland & Wolff, alone among UK yards, the capacity to take orders for the largest ships afloat. With this advantage the yard secured orders in 1969 for five large bulk carriers and two super-tankers. The ability to take on such a volume of work also demanded that Harland & Wolff had to raise its annual steelwork capacity from 120,000 tons to 200,000 tons.[34] While winning these orders were highlights of 1969, the year was to prove a particularly difficult one. Losses in the yard rose to £2.06 million, and total company losses reached £8.3 million. This financial morass was compounded by extensive labour problems in the yard, these being exacerbated by growing civil unrest in the province, and from June 1970 the beginning of a bombing campaign by the Provisional IRA.[35] Consequently, even with the completion of the dock in March 1970, and a healthy order book, shipyard losses rose to £3.28 million, and a new cash-flow crisis engulfed the firm.

The situation of Harland & Wolff was not improved by the return of the new Conservative government at Westminster in June 1970. The administration was openly unsympathetic to the continuation of financial support for the UK shipbuilding industry, and at this critical juncture it was politics, not economics, which came to the rescue of the company. The combination of civil strife, the bombing campaign, and the fear of yet more unrest if there were to be large-scale unemployment in Belfast, proved to be a powerful solvent of government resistance to providing financial aid. This heady and dangerous cocktail persuaded the Edward Heath government to treat Harland & Wolff as a special case; a further loan of £3.5 million was approved through the SIB, with additional assistance being guaranteed through to 1974.[36] Nevertheless, given the huge financial burden Harland & Wolff imposed on both the Westminster and Northern Ireland governments, it is not surprising that the Heath administration soon actively encouraged moves to reduce the liability. During 1970 the government was involved in confused and competing discussions with both Aristotle Onasis and Fred Olsen. The first involved discussions with Onasis to take out a leasehold on the company, while the Olsen negotiations involved a proposal to acquire a half share in Harland & Wolff. Both proposals involved the government in writing off large losses, and in guaranteeing long-term support. The costs to the government were large and rather open-ended, and the discussions with both suitors were ultimately abandoned in favour of direct state support to enable the company to continue as an independent concern. This outcome was profoundly influenced by the turmoil of continuing civil unrest in Northern Ireland, and the feared consequences if Harland & Wolff were to be forced into closure like Upper Clyde Shipbuilders.

Between 1967 and 1971 the Harland & Wolff yard accumulated losses before tax and depreciation of £8.3 million. When losses at the engine works are added, the total loss at Belfast was £9.25 million at the end of 1970. This dismal outcome was in spite of the company having received huge financial support. The SIB had provided loans of £15.0 million, and other government aid amounted to £36.6 million. This was a transfusion of £51.6 million within the five years to 1971. Of this large injection of aid, only 41.0 per cent was devoted to capital expenditure, the balance of £30.5

million going to offset losses on unprofitable contracts. As the main employer in Belfast, Harland & Wolff received nearly one-fifth of all government assistance to UK shipbuilding between 1967 and 1971. The company was in every sense 'a special case'. The other major recipient of public funds at this time was Upper Clyde Shipbuilders.

The post-Geddes grouping on the Upper Clyde brought together one naval yard, Yarrows, two purely merchant yards, Barclay Curle and Connells, and three yards which could build both naval and merchant ships, Fairfields, Stephens, and John Browns. This combination known as Upper Clyde Shipbuilders (UCS), illustrates better than any other of the Geddes mergers the failure of that initiative to achieve coherent working units. In UCS there were six yards with entirely different cultures, equipment, and working practices. Yarrows insisted on working independently on its own terms, and four of the others were entirely hostile to Fairfields and the 1965 experiment. The UCS merger also had to cope with relating to fifteen different unions and wage grades across the yards. All the companies were also insolvent. The new chairman, Anthony Hepper, claimed that the overall deficiency in August 1967 was £2.5 million. This was given in evidence to the Expenditure Committee of the House of Commons, following the liquidation of the company in 1971. However, in his report to the liquidator, Robert C. Smith, the accountant Professor David Flint stated that the overall deficiency had already doubled to £5.0 million by the time the merger was concluded in August 1968.[37]

The central problem for the new UCS management was that it had inherited bankrupt yards, loss-making contracts, and a desperate need of capital for both modernisation and day-to-day operation. On taking over, the new board estimated that, given enough financial support, it would take between two and four years to return to profitability. To do so would also require improvements in productivity of between 33 per cent and 70 per cent, the range reflecting the differentials to be overcome among the separate yards. If this could be achieved, the board claimed that it would be able to return the group to profitability in the financial year 1972-73. With this as their objective the directors applied to the SIB for a grant or loan of £10.8 million, some £1.75 million of this to cover cash payments to constituent companies for the acquisition by UCS of their shares. Of the remainder, the board specified a need for £3.7 million for capital expenditure, and £4.7 million for working capital. The SIB response was to offer UCS loans of £5.5 million, half the requested sum. Within this the SIB allowed only £2.0 million for each of capital expenditure and working capital, and £1.5 million toward the cost of acquiring the shares. UCS consequently began in business with known deficiencies of capital for both fixed investment and working needs. This response by SIB was to characterise its attitude to the group throughout the life of UCS. The provision of capital was always less than requested, and usually sanctioned later than required.

With cash flow a constant worry, Hepper and his directors plunged into the market to acquire orders whose initial and stage payments could be drawn on to contribute to working capital outlays. By May 1968 UCS had taken on new orders of £60.0 million, while still encumbered with inherited loss-making contracts. These included the *QE11* at John Browns in Clydebank, and the OCL container ship, *Jervis Bay*, at Fairfield's Govan yard. The new orders were taken at a rush, not only to supply some working capital, but to sustain employment in the yards. These contracts were ultimately to saddle UCS with losses of £9.8 million.[38] Serious as these were, they were soon to be overwhelmed by other losses arising from the inherited contracts. These eventually recorded losses of £12.0 million for UCS.[39]

Since the SIB loan had allocated only £2.0 million for working capital, the UCS Board then authorised a share issue to raise a further £1.0 million to supplement it. Even with this increment the board noted that the £3.0 million available for working capital would only cover day-to-day needs until the end of 1968. By November 1968 the company cash forecast for 1969 predicted borrowings rising to £6.9 million by August. When the final accounts for the trading year 1968–69 were signed in August 1969, they showed a consolidated trading loss of £9.6 million.[40] Within a year of the formation of UCS, the Minutes of the Directors meeting of 13 February 1969, noted that 'there [is] an immediate need for cash ... and the situation was now acute, and the total additional cash necessary to see the Company through the year was in the order of £5.0 million.'[41] In addition, the forecasts for cash flow for the year to 16 January 1970, estimated a peak borrowing of £8.0 million by the end of August 1969, this falling to £6.0 million by January 1970.

Confronted with these forecasts, the board again approached the SIB seeking a loan of £6.1 million, this to include £3.0 million to cover transitional losses, and £1.7 million for under recovery of full costs on new orders. The SIB response was, predictably, unsympathetic. After examining UCS draft accounts, SIB concluded that the results projected by the company led it to doubt that further financial assistance was justified. Rejecting the application for £6.1 million, SIB then offered a grant of £2.5 million, since it had already paid UCS another £500,000 on an emergency basis.[42] The UCS board replied that this offer was not acceptable to it. The directors, however, were prevailed upon to accept this reduced funding by the direct intervention of the Minister of Technology, Tony Wedgwood Benn. At this juncture it was he who urged on SIB that UCS should not be put into liquidation.[43]

Throughout this roller-coaster year, the board of UCS was struggling to produce a corporate plan that would be acceptable to the SIB. Having been persuaded to accept the reduced SIB grant, which they regarded as inadequate for the longer-term continuation of UCS, the chairman, Anthony Hepper, wrote to the chairman of SIB on 9 April 1969 to set out the concerns of his board. He advised that UCS would exhaust its working capital by May 1969, and could not survive financially until June 1969 without further assistance. He stated that survival depended upon UCS being able to acquire further new orders which were likely to return a profit. However, unless UCS had assurances that it would have sufficient finance to complete and deliver such orders, he could not go into the marketplace, and if this were to be the situation, his Board saw no point in continuing to draft a corporate plan.[44]

Notwithstanding this warning and evaluation of UCS prospects, the board did deliver a draft corporate plan to the SIB. This contained a call for a financial injection of £10.0 million, a call immediately rejected by SIB. Despite this, negotiations continued, and at the end of May 1969, a third draft of the corporate plan asked for aid of £7–£8 million. In response the SIB offered £5.0 million, £2.0 million as a grant and £3.0 million as a loan. On this occasion SIB stipulated that if UCS accepted the provision, then 'no financial assistance of any nature whatever beyond what is offered in this letter will be provided by us [SIB] to you [UCS]'.[45] Since this offer still left UCS short of £3.0 million in working capital, and having no means of bridging the gap, Hepper advised the SIB on 16 June 1969, that his board could not take up the offer of £5.0 million. And, as a consequence, his board had no option but to apply to the court for the winding up of the company, and for the appointment of a provisional liquidator.

The implication of such a step for employment on the Clyde induced a second direct intervention by the Minister of Technology, Tony Wedgwood Benn. This resulted in the SIB recanting on its stipulation that no further funds would be available to UCS if the offer of £5.0 million were accepted. Encouraged by this modest relaxation in the conditions of the loan, UCS then accepted the SIB finance, the first tranche of £2.0 million being advance in July. Further negotiation with SIB resulted in the UCS affair being discussed at a Cabinet meeting in October 1969. The upshot of this high-level intervention was that UCS received an additional loan of £7.0 million. This was jointly provided from the resources of the Treasury and the Ministry of Technology.[46] This Cabinet involvement also led to the suggestion to the UCS board, that the company cash-flow problem could be eased if UCS were to dispose of its 51 per cent shareholding in Yarrow Shipbuilders. Since UCS losses were projected to rise to £12.39 million by August 1970, the board took the hint and instructed the joint auditors of UCS-Yarrow to report on the implications for both parties if UCS were to sell its share in Yarrows.[47] The acquisition of this 51 per cent holding had cost UCS £1.8 million at the time of the merger, but in April 1970, the auditors valued the holding at only £568,000. Yarrow Shipbuilders simultaneously reported a trading loss of £1.148 million.

In the meantime, UCS had begun to show some improved results. The arrival of Ken Douglas as managing director in May 1969 proved to be a breath of fresh air. Douglas was able quickly to work through the remaining loss-making contracts and began to rationalise production across the yards. He did so by introducing two basic ship designs to standardise the output of the yards, drawing on his experience of his time at Austin and Pickersgill and his work on the SD14. The two ships were to be based on the Cardiff-class bulk carrier of 28,000 tons deadweight (dwt), and new Clyde Class of general cargo ship of 18,000 dwt. He also revolutionised steel processing by re-opening the plate yard at the adjacent premises of Stephen at Linthouse. These measures began to see some improvement in productivity, and this so impressed the board that in its forecast outcome for the year to July 1971 it projected a profit of £1.454 million. This also encouraged Hepper to send an upbeat progress report to SIB, in the expectation that the improvement would ensure continued financial support while the Douglas reforms began to work through the company.

This hope, however, was to be dashed in a most unexpected and unforeseen way. At the board meeting in July 1970, at which these more favourable projections had been made, the SIB-appointed director, A.I. MacKenzie, had expressed doubt that these projections could be achieved. Subsequently, during a routine visit to the Department of Trade and Industry (DTI) in October, MacKenzie voiced his reservations on the ability of UCS to achieve the productivity gains necessary to generate the level of profit the board was forecasting. These reservations reached the ear of John Davies, the new Conservative Secretary of State, who had only taken up office on 15 October. Then, without reference to the UCS Board, Davies decided 'not to provide further guarantees under the Shipbuilding Industry Act', thus effectively making it impossible for UCS to undertake new orders. Finding the minister adamant in this, the UCS Board then wrote to Davies in December 1970, advising that in the absence of guarantees, UCS would be unable to continue trading.

Davies' quick rejection of further aid to UCS was completely in line with the determination of the new Conservative administration that it should not support industrial 'lame ducks'. This was also the attitude of other shipbuilders on the Clyde and in the North East of England, who were hostile to a competitor company, UCS, being kept in business by public monies. Nevertheless, when faced with the consequences of liquidation, especially for employment, the SIB in collaboration with the DTI, proposed a compromise. The government would agree to resume financial guarantees on orders if UCS could raise an additional £3.0 million to support its working-capital requirements. If UCS accepted this, it would also have to agree to sell its holding in Yarrow Shipbuilders. With the promise of resumed financial guarantees for its orders, UCS was able to persuade some of its clients to agree to price increases amounting to £2.8 million. With the negotiation of this extra income in place, the government resumed financial guarantees for UCS, though this was still conditional on the disposal of Yarrows, a move finally accomplished on 9 February. If this sale had been concluded when the auditors had reported in mid-1970, the sale would have generated £500,000 for UCS. However, by February of 1971 the earlier valuation was worthless. In the intervening months losses on Yarrow contracts had risen from £1.148 million to £4.5 million, and the company was on the verge of closure through lack of liquidity. Since Yarrows then had a negative asset value, UCS had to sell its 51 per cent holding to the new Yarrow Shipbuilding Company Ltd for a nominal payment of £1. To make matters worse, UCS still had to provide cover for all the guarantees it had given on behalf of Yarrow contracts, the Yarrow overdraft, and other guarantees made to the SIB on its loans to Yarrow as part of the UCS group. This was a costly exercise for UCS, but Yarrow came out of it extremely well. In order to protect its naval work at Yarrows, the MoD agreed to help the company with a loan of £4.5 million. In addition, Yarrows was able to take ownership of the new covered berth which UCS had financed at an outlay in excess of £1.0 million.

The outcome for UCS was much less favourable. The period without order guarantees from October 1970 to February 1971 severely undermined the company projections on profit and on cash flow. By mid-April, the directors noted a serious deterioration in the UCS cash position. In order to try to sustain their cash flow, the board had resorted, increasingly, to delaying payments due to creditors. By early May 1971 these had accumulated to unpaid debts of £5.98 million. These were projected to rise to £6.5 million in June, and to over £8.0 million early in July.[48] Coinciding with this, a three-week slippage in the ship-construction programme meant there was a delay in UCS receiving contract instalment payments from the ship owners, exacerbating the cash problem. This deteriorating situation was the object of a financial review which was considered by the board at its meeting on 7 June 1971. The review estimated that UCS would have a net asset deficiency of £4.0 million at the end of August 1971. This was before making provision for loans from the SIB, the Ministry of Technology, and other sources. In addition, the cash-flow forecast showed overdue sums owing to creditors, and on overdraft, rising to £9.8 million by 17 December 1971. This was three times the estimate of £3.1 million which had been made in February. Following this gloomy prognosis, the board made further approaches for assistance to both SIB and the DTI. When these were rejected, the directors resolved on 14 June 1971, to petition the court for the appointment of a provisional liquidator.

The liquidator appointed was Robert Courtney Smith. Initially he devoted his energies to try to keep work going on existing contracts, his longer-term objective being to recover as much as possible from the wreckage to make some return to creditors and investors. By 4 October 1974, when he sent the Secretary of State his commissioned report on UCS, prepared by Professor David Flint, a Labour government was again in power, and Tony Wedgwood Benn was again the responsible minister. Robert Smith's accompanying letter to the minister noted that at the time of his appointment as liquidator in June 1971, the realisable assets of UCS were estimated to fall short of the full claims of the creditors by some £28.0 million, though by 1974 this had improved modestly to a deficiency of £24.3 million, of which the government was the major creditor for £13.9 million.[49]

While these were very large sums, they represented only the tip of the iceberg of UCS debt. In its short life from February 1968 to June 1971, a period of forty months, the SIB annual reports reveal that UCS, and its successor Govan Shipbuilders, had received £12.792 million in grants and loans. The later 1972 report by Booz-Allen and Hamilton on British shipbuilding, revealed that additional assistance totalling £52.3 million had been provided, and that the total support to UCS had come to £65.0 million. This was some 40 per cent of all government assistance to the shipbuilding industry between 1967 and mid-1972.[50] UCS, together with Harland & Wolff, consumed £116.8 million of public monies, 83 per cent of all aid to British shipbuilding in these years.

The third large-scale beneficiary of government aid in this first phase of post-Geddes intervention, was the Cammell Laird company at Birkenhead on the Mersey. By early 1970, Cammell Laird, like UCS, was in financial crisis, following heavy losses on fixed-price contracts. It was also incurring extensive penalty payments because of lengthy delays in delivering orders. Cammell Laird did approach the SIB seeking aid, but since the yard was mainly a warship-building enterprise, SIB concluded that the request lay beyond its powers, which were in support of merchant shipbuilding. In face of the rejection, Cammell Laird then made application for aid directly to the government. This was in May 1970, on the eve of the general election which was to bring Edward Heath's Conservative administration to power. However, the out-going Labour government had responded swiftly to the Cammell Laird appeal. It acted through the Industrial Re-organisation Corporation (IRC), to approve loans to the company of up to £6.0 million. This was conditional upon the shipbuilding business of Cammell Laird being separated out of the larger Laird Group of companies. The outcome of this arrangement was that the government acquired a 51 per cent shareholding in Cammell Laird Shipbuilders for an outlay of £1.5 million. The incoming Heath administration agreed to honour this public equity holding, the shares to be held on behalf of the Ministry of Technology by a public trustee. In honouring the departing Labour government's action, the new Conservative administration not only inherited a half share in Cammell Laird, but also its losses on twelve contracts which amounted to £12.0 million by the end of 1971. By the middle of 1972, the company had received a total of £21.5 million in aid, about two-thirds of this devoted to capital expenditure on modernising the yard. This contrasted strongly with UCS where only 19 per cent of funds received went on capital investment, and with the 41 per cent of aid devoted to capital spend by Harland & Wolff. These three crisis companies collectively absorbed £138 million in public funds between 1967 and 1972, over 86 per cent of all aid to the industry. The remaining firms received only modest assistance. Scott Lithgow on the Lower Clyde, and Swan Hunter on the Tyne, each received in excess of £5.0 million, while Yarrow had £6.0 million, most of these provisions going to offset accumulated losses on contracts.

In contrast to the crisis companies, some of the other yards remained in profit for all or most of these years. The Apledore Company, and Austin and Pickersgill, both regularly recorded profits between 1967 and 1971, while Doxford and Sunderland Shipbuilders only slipped into the red in 1970, as did Scott Lithgow and Swan Hunter. The much smaller Robb Caledon merger also began to record some losses from 1969. In all the firms, increasing inflation brought rising costs of sub-contracted materials, these on occasion being by as much as 50 per cent. This was a threat to profitability, but it was the growing problem of late deliveries and the consequent penalty payments that were mainly responsible for eating up the narrow profit margin on the fixed-price contracts, and converting them into serious loss makers throughout the industry.

In this aggressively competitive world industry, most British shipbuilders were slipping into debt, and in the logic of the free market the companies should have faced closure. In Northern Ireland, the political situation and civil unrest precluded that outcome in 1971. In mainland Britain it was the liquidation of UCS and the union-led work-in, together with massive and largely peaceful public demonstrations and marches in support of the workers which ultimately induced the Heath government to draw back from allowing the logic of the market to dispose of its 'lame ducks'. This evocatively named 'u-turn' in the closure philosophy of the Heath government was soon to ignite and initiate a second and much more costly phase of intervention from 1972.

## The path to nationalisation

The Heath 'u-turn' on the closure of UCS was a critical event for both the industry and the government. Under pressure, John Davies' initial refusal to support the illiquid UCS was soon modified through his appointment of an emergency committee. This was to advise on the implications of the collapse, and to report on what reconstruction, if any, could be attempted from the UCS wreckage. The committee comprised Sir Alexander MacDonald, chairman of Distillers, David MacDonald, a director of Hill Samuel, Sir Alexander Glen of Glen Line Shipping, and Lord Robins, former chairman of the National Coal Board. Dubbed the 'four wise men', they presented a very brief report on 29 July 1971. This proposed forming a new company based on the adjacent Govan and Linthouse yards, together with selling off the Clydebank and Scotstoun facilities. These measures, if adopted, would drastically cut the UCS workforce from around 8,500 to about 2,500 employees.[51] The threat of such widespread redundancy produced a novel reaction from the workforce. Instead of the traditional resort to strike action, the workers participated in cleverly conceived 'work-in'. This involved the men, especially at closure-threatened Clydebank, in an occupation of the yard where they carried on working under the eyes of the liquidator, who had his temporary office there. The 'work-in' was a seemingly spontaneous reaction, and largely outside the control of the formal union organisations. As such it was unpredictable as to its actions, activities, and outcome.

The public reaction on Clydeside was also unexpected. The plan to close so much of the UCS facilities was widely seen as the near ending of any significant merchant shipbuilding on the upper reaches of the river. What then occurred was widespread demonstrations and high-profile public support for the men and the work-in. While the mass demonstrations and marches in Glasgow were noisy, they were serious in intent and largely peaceful in conduct. Yet such was the official concern at the possibility of these developing into widespread unrest, that it raised in some quarters the spectre of a

Belfast situation of civil unrest on the streets of Glasgow and in the Clyde shipbuilding towns. A report to the Cabinet from the chief constable of Strathclyde voiced this prospect, and is held to have been a significant catalyst in dissolving the resolve of the government to allow 'lame ducks' to go to the wall. Moreover, the government had already acted to nationalise Rolls Royce in March 1971, after it collapsed largely due to problems in developing the RB211 jet engine. The close conjunction of these pressures persuaded the government to accept the recommendations of the report of its 'four wise men', and to propose a scheme to reconstruct part of UCS on the basis of wholly owned state company to be known as Govan Shipbuilders. It also acted to defuse the situation at the heart of the work-in at the Clydebank yard, by agreeing to seek a purchaser for the business. At the Govan yard, funds of £35.0 million were made available to cover anticipated losses during the first three years of the reconstruction of the new Govan Shipbuilders. And at Clydebank the situation was eventually resolved by the middle of 1972 through the sale of the yard to the Marathon Oil Company of the USA. The yard was sold for £1.5 million, but the understanding was that Marathon Oil would receive around £12.0 million in government aid to help develop the Clydebank yard for the construction of oil rigs.

While this intervention stemmed the crisis on Clydeside, the industry at large was bombarding the government with increasing and ever more pressing pleas for assistance. In particular it was seeking improved investment grants, a shipbuilders' subsidy on contract prices, and an economic risk guarantee on contract prices. This last was to protect the builder from the effect of inflation on the contract price during the period of construction.[52] The increasingly embattled administration of Edward Heath responded to these pressures by introducing the 1972 Industry Act. Part III of this Act specifically related to the shipbuilding industry. In moves designed to relieve some of the immediate pressures on the industry, the Act extended government guarantees on shipbuilding credits for UK ship owners, and also introduced a short-term temporary scheme of construction grants on a tapering basis. It also confirmed the allocation of the £35.0 million in aid to Govan Shipbuilders, and extended further support to Cammell Liard at Birkenhead. These were all emergency, short-term provisions, and before committing to any longer-term support, the government resorted to the commission of yet another report on the industry. This was contracted to the American consultants firm of Booz-Allen and Hamilton. While awaiting the preparation of this report, the Ministry of Industrial Development employed Section 7 of the 1972 Industry Act to sanction additional selective support for the three yards in which the government had equity. Consequently, by the end of 1972 the government had come to own all of Govan Shipbuilders, 51 per cent of Cammell Laird, and 47.6 per cent of Harland & Wolff.

The Report on British Shipbuilding by Booz-Allen and Hamilton was published in February 1973, and the conclusions on the condition of the Industry were strikingly reminiscent of those of the Geddes Report of 1966. As such they identified issues and problems which were very different from the analysis of the situation as identified by the industry's leaders. The shipbuilders stressed that their industry problems arose from the lack of protection in the marketplace, and from excessive and unfair competition, especially from the state-supported Japanese shipbuilders. In addition their poor productivity was linked to long-standing restrictive practices imposed by the unions. And last, the major reason for its difficulties was that excess capacity generated by foreign builders had enforced uneconomic prices on the UK industry.

In strong contrast to this analysis, the Booz-Allen Report, like Geddes before it, argued that the poor performance of the industry was linked to deficient management, to serious failings in the reliability of construction and in the delivery of contracts, and to the poor competitiveness of British prices. In view of these persistent and endemic weaknesses in British shipbuilding, Booz-Allen concluded that 'despite growing world demand for shipbuilding, the UK will be faced with increasing competition which it is ill-equipped to meet'.[53] The report's review of market trends suggested that world demand for new tonnage was likely to weaken in the second half of the 1970s, and in such a declining market the endemic weaknesses in British shipbuilding would mean there would be a continuous contraction in Britain's market share.

These conclusions were unambiguous and highly unfavourable on the prospects of the industry. As such, they should have initiated a significant re-appraisal of how the industry now viewed its future, and of how government policy for the industry might be developed. For in 1972, the prospects for British shipbuilding did indeed appear to be bleak. Orders won by the industry had plunged from 1.7 mgt in 1970, to less than half that at 839,000 grt in 1972, which was barely enough for nine months' work. The seriousness of this downward trend was, however, obscured and abruptly reversed by the Yom Kippur war of 6–24 October 1973, together with the effects of the oil embargo and curtailment of production imposed by the OPEC group between October 1973 and March 1974. These events in turn had a dramatic effect on oil prices, on freight rates, and on demand for new tonnage. In 1972 the price of crude oil was around $3 dollars a barrel, but was nearing $12 dollars by the end of 1974. In freight rates, the tramp time-charter index, taken as 100 in 1971, first declined to 76 in 1972 before escalating to 278 in the fourth quarter of 1973, and then averaged around 220 through to 1975. In the frantic rush to get new tonnage into this rising market, the world order book exploded from 86.8 mgt in 1972 to reach 128.9 mgt at the end of 1973, and was still as high as 120.7 mgt in 1974 (Table 7.1). In the peak of the ordering boom in 1973, a huge total of 73.0 mgt of new orders was placed world-wide. And in Britain, despite all its weaknesses, 4.35 mgt of new orders were attracted, pushing the industry order book to 7.5 mgt by September 1973. At the average output of the industry, that should have been a workload stretching forward for six or seven years.

Encouraged, and made complacent, by this exceptional infusion of new orders, Britain's shipbuilders roundly rejected the warning and pessimism of the Booz-Allen analysis, which forecast a downturn of orders in the second half of the 1970s. On behalf of its members, the Shipbuilders and Repairers National Association, successor to The Shipbuilding Conference, argued that, 'in contra-distinction to the Report's forecast, the Council's view was that in the next decade, the shipbuilding demand was more likely to show further growth than otherwise, and that the aim of the UK shipbuilding industry could, and must, be to regain an increased share of the market'.[54] With this injection of optimism there was a surge of investment in modernising and in reconstruction in many companies, which in three cases involved a significant partnership with shipping concerns. These were the association of the Court Line with Appledore Shipbuilders, and with Doxford and Sunderland Shipbuilders; the linkage of Maritime Fruit Carriers (MFC), with Swan Hunter; and third, that of London and Overseas Freighters (LOF) with Austin and Pickersgill.

The involvement of the Court Line in shipbuilding had begun as early as 1964. It had then acquired the small yard of P.K. Harris & Sons at Appledore in Devon, where in 1970 it built a new, modern yard. The Court Line interest was extended in the same year with the purchase of North East Coast Shipbuilders, then the main ship-repair group in the UK. Two years later, in January 1973, Court Line again extended its shipbuilding interests with the acquisition of Doxford and Sunderland Shipbuilders on the Wear. This was then renamed as Sunderland Shipbuilders. At Appledore, Court Line had created a covered building facility where it developed the assembly of ship sections in a ship factory process. It had considerable success with this, and at Sunderland decided to develop the new technique on a larger scale. Court Line presented its plans to redevelop the old Pallion yard in this way to the Department of Trade and Industry (DTI) in January 1973. Agreement to proceed with the first phase of the Pallion project was reached speedily in February, the cost estimated to be £21.0 million.[55] Reconstruction began in October, with the first ship being floated out of the new building dock in June 1975. By then, however, Court Line was in liquidation. In the intervening years Court Line had involved itself extensively in the hotel, leisure and holiday businesses. As a major provider of air travel to Clarksons Travel Group, Court Line had been obliged to take the group over to prevent its collapse in 1973. But in doing so it inherited a Clarkson debt of £7.0 million. When this obligation added to the cost of modernising Pallion, and was then followed by the collapse of the world shipping market, the conjunction threatened the continued operation of the company which had large commitments to tens of thousand of holiday makers through its Travel and Air Charter interest. In a last-ditch attempt to avoid liquidation, Court Line approached the government for aid amounting to £33.0 million. If granted, Court Line offered then to sell off its shipbuilding assets as well as its ship-repair business. The initial response from the DTI was an offer of £11.0 million, but after further negotiation the government acquired all these assets from Court Line for £16.0 million.[56] The Secretary of State, Tony Wedgwood Benn, commended this acquisition to the House of Commons on 26 June 1974, announcing that by this intervention the government had saved 9,000 jobs and orders worth £48.0 million.[57] This relief ensured only a brief continuation of the holiday and air-charter business of the Court Line Group, which went into voluntary liquidation on 16 August 1974.

Formal and informal links among shipbuilders and ship owners had been common since the nineteenth century, but had waned in significance from the 1930s, only picking up again from the end of the 1960s. On the Tyne, Swan Hunter established this link with Maritime Fruit Carriers (MFC), but this association was to result in serious damage to Britain's largest shipbuilding group. Emerging from the post-Geddes mergers, Swan Hunter had yards on the Tyne, Tees and Humber, and also on the Forth in Scotland. Collectively, the Swan Hunter group yards accounted for 18 per cent of all new-build capacity in the UK. As such, Swan Hunter was a full-range builder, capable of constructing all types of ships from small cargo ships to large tankers. It also had a stake in building warships. After the merger, the group had moved into the very large cargo ship market. It created the capacity by combining two of its existing berths in its Wallsend yard, and by investing in building container ships at its Walker yard.[58] The company had been in the red to the tune of £9.0 million in 1969–70, but had edged into a modest profit of £540,000 by 1971.[59] Even so, it was struggling to attract orders, and a way out of this scarcity seemed to be offered through establishing a connection with MFC, an Israel-based shipping company. In the 1960s MFC had diversified into operating refrigerated ships, and by 1973 operated 46 ships, of which 35 were reefers, refrigerated container ships.[60] MFC had also begun to operate both gas carriers and oil tankers, all types of ships that Swan Hunter could build.

The public announcement of the MFC association with Swan Hunter came in January 1973, with MFC intimating that it was placing an order with Swan Hunter for six tankers, each of 313,000 dwt. This was followed in February by a second statement, revealing that Swan Hunter was to build twenty ships for MFC. These were estimated to have a contract value of £150.0 million. An even more dizzying prospect was that there could be orders for a further thirty vessels, these including oil tankers, LPG product tankers, and OBOs, ore-bulk-oil carriers.[61]

To enable it to cope with work of this proposed scale, Swan Hunter and MFC set up a new company, Swan Hunter Maritime Ltd. Swan Hunter had a 25 per cent share valued at £2.5 million. The function of this company was to sell, charter and operate the ships to be built in the Swan Hunter yards. This was a hugely ambitious programme, and in order to manage it Swan Hunter had to set aside its traditional pattern of diversified shipbuilding. It also had to abandon its emphasis on building high-quality, high-value specialised container ships and naval vessels. In reversing its historic building strategy, Swan Hunter now had to concentrate on building simpler, but larger and more standardised, ships. This change in direction also required Swan Hunter to invest £11.0 million of its own resources in enlarging facilities at Wallsend, and also at the Hebburn building dock.

The prospects for the success of this bold venture were, like those of Court Line, shattered by the abrupt collapse of the tanker market in 1974, and the following collapse of MFC itself. Such was the entanglement involved between Swan Hunter and MFC that the shipbuilder was only able to extricate itself from the venture in 1976. This involved Swan Hunter selling its 25 per cent holding in Swan Hunter Maritime to a surviving associated concern of MFC for £1.9 million. The immediate consequence of the collapse of MFC was that Swan Hunter suffered large-scale cancellations of the projected orders, and had to cover the costs of liabilities incurred to sub-contractors. Beyond these penalties, a consequence of tying itself so closely to MFC was that Swan Hunter had not tried to win orders from other clients during the boom in 1973. As a result it was seriously short of work as the shipping markets turned sharply downward form 1974.

The third venture linking North East shipbuilders with a shipping concern was the association of Austin & Pickersgill (A&P) with London Overseas Freighters (LOF). This link extended as far back as 1957, but LOF did not achieve full ownership of A&P until 1970. It had also taken over another Sunderland shipbuilder, Bartram & Co., in 1968. The attraction of A&P for the shipping company was its success in designing the standard cargo ship known as the SD14 (standing for single-deck 14,000 dwt ship). This had been selected from over thirty competing designs for a standard cargo ship submitted for approval to the Shipbuilders and Repairers National Association in 1966. British shipbuilders were then seeking a design to replace the ageing fleet of wartime Liberty ships. The first SD14 was launched by A&P in 1969. The SD14 had been designed to attract volume orders, and the potential was not lost on LOF, which moved quickly to gain full ownership of the company. LOF was controlled by two Greek shipping families, the Mavroleans and the Kulukindis. Under their ownership A&P's Southwick yard was modernised and devoted to the serial production of SD14s. This was backed up by LOF offering financial packages to attract orders and support construction.[62] The initial responsibility for introducing the SD14 lay with an innovating manager, Ken Douglas. He was managing director at A&P from 1957 to 1969, then leaving to join UCS on the Clyde. The SD14 was so successful that the Southwick yard had to be further extended and improved from 1973, the cost of this rising to £39.0 million by September 1974.[63] Unlike the Court Line and MFC ventures with shipbuilders in the North East, this was a successful collaboration.

Such success in British shipbuilding was rare at this time, as was evidenced on the Clyde where both the reconstructed Govan Shipbuilders and Scott Lithgow were experiencing increasing difficulties. At Govan, Ken Douglas continued the standardisation of products he had begun under UCS, refocusing the yard on the two standard ship designs of the Cardiff-class bulk carriers, and the Clyde Class of dry-cargo ship. He pushed this forward until he left the company in 1974. His innovations did bear fruit, for between 1973 and 1977 Govan Shipbuilders launched sixteen Cardiff-class bulk carriers, and ten Clyde-class cargo ships, these mainly for the Kuwait Shipping Line. Yet, even with such a regular workload the company continued to need support from the government. The initial start up grant of £35.0

million had increased to £37.5 million by June 1975, at which point the yard needed a further injection of £6.9 million. This was to allow it to complete a modernisation programme. It then swallowed another £10.3 million in aid to cover anticipated losses on contracts through to 1977.[64] Government aid to Govan Shipbuilders between 1972 and 1977 accumulated to £54.7 million.

Meanwhile, on the Lower Clyde, the merged Scott and Lithgow concerns continued to function as mainly separate enterprises. Both yards experienced continuous shortages of skilled labour, a situation which hampered their modernisation plans. These plans proposed to develop the Kingston yard at Port Glasgow to move into the building of large tankers, while at Scott's in Greenock the objective was to retain its involvement in naval work, particularly with the Oberon Class of conventional submarines. At the Kingston yard delays with the improvements were such that it was not until the end of 1971 that Scott Lithgow was able to complete the construction of its new large concrete-building mat. Only then could it begin work on its first order for a very large cargo carrier (VLCC) ship. This was the *Naess Clansman* of 259,000 dwt, subsequently renamed as the *Nordic Clansman*. It was built in two halves on the mat, then floated off and joined up afloat. When launched in 1973 it was two months late in delivery.[65] Scott Lithgow's effort to break into the VLCC market was protracted, and was late in coming on stream. Tragically, it was quickly to be overtaken by the calamity of the OPEC oil price rises, and the collapse of the tanker market from 1974. This resulted in the cancellation of orders for two large tankers, and at the same time the collapse of MFC left the yard with another tanker under construction, and steel already cut for a second MFC ship. While it was Swan Hunter that bore the brunt of the collapse of MFC, Scott Lithgow was also hard hit, as were other yards, since in 1974 about one-third of all orders in British yards had been placed by the failed MFC company. Scott Lithgow was later able to complete both MFC tankers, but was only able to sell them at a considerable loss in the glutted tanker market.

Following the collapse of the VLCC strategy, Scott Lithgow turned to the offshore oil and gas market, a source of work that had long been avoided and neglected by British shipbuilders. Somewhat surprisingly, Scott Lithgow quickly won two orders for Offshore Supply Vessels (OSVs) from Seaforth Marine, the contracts worth £3.6 million.[66] This apparent success led the yard to take another order by venturing into what was a new and complex market for Scott Lithgow. This was an order for a sophisticated, dynamically positioned drill ship. This contract of £16.0 million was followed by another two even more expensive orders totalling £50.0 million, all from the Norwegian group of Abe Jensen of Bergen.[67] These were risky moves into untried areas, and the steepness of the learning curves encountered, and the transitional costs involved, forced Scott Lithgow to make provision for anticipated losses on a spectacular scale. The fixed-price contracts resulted in losses of £1.44 million in 1971, while estimated losses on those for delivery between 1972 and 1974 were put at £5.0 million.[68] Bad as this was, Scott Lithgow was also hit by damaging and protracted strikes by boilermakers and engineers in 1972, these pushing the projected losses up to £7.5 million. The company was also running into difficulty in Greenock. Scott's found itself facing serious problems on four contracts for the Oberon-class submarines. These involved delivery delays and expensive remedial work. Two of these boats were for the Chilean Navy, the other two for the Royal Australian Navy. These problems helped push up anticipated group losses to £9.0 million by the end of 1975.[69] Compounding this, problems also began to emerge from the decision to enter the offshore market. The drill ship *Ben Ocean Lancer* was three months late when launched in 1976, and another drill ship, *Pac Norse 1*, was similarly delayed when launched in 1977.

These deepening problems on the Clyde were mirrored elsewhere in the industry. At Cammell Laird the aid of £14.0 million provided in 1972 soon vanished, and by March 1976 the yard had absorbed a further £13.4 million in loans which had been made available under the provision of Section 7 of the 1972 Industry Act. Early in 1977, this had to be supplemented by another £6.0 million to keep the company afloat during the protracted struggle to nationalise the industry. In a similar fashion, Harland & Wolff at Belfast also continued to absorb government aid, responsibility for the yard having passed to Westminster following the collapse of the Northern Ireland Executive in July 1974.[70] Contracts taken for delivery between 1974 and 1979 had, in February 1974, been estimated to return a profit of £10.0 million. Five months later this was revised to forecast losses, and it was estimated that 'the negative net worth of the Company was nearly £32.0 million'.[71] It was this calamity in the context of the political situation in Northern Ireland – with 10,000 jobs depending on the yard – which precipitated the new Labour government at Westminster into nationalising the company fully. Only this step, it was argued, could protect jobs, provide emergency aid, and complete the modernisation programme.[72] An order, approved by the House of Commons on 8 May 1975, provided aid to a maximum of £40.0 million. Then, under the terms of the Shipbuilding Industry (No. 2) Northern Ireland Order 1975, this was extended to £60.0 million in August, the provision to run to March 1979. In advising the House of Commons, the minister also noted that Harland & Wolff had not made a profit in the last decade, and that from 1966 to March 1975 it had received government assistance in excess of £81.0 million.

In June 1974, as the Heath government gave way to the Wilson administration, it was evident that the British shipbuilding industry was in dire straits, and that the world industry was entering on a serious downturn. The world order book, which in 1974 had peaked at over 133.0 mgt, had by 1977 shrunk to only 36.7 mgt. In the tanker market, orders slumped from 76.0 mgt in 1973, to only 523,000 gt in 1976. Laid-up tanker tonnage exploded from a mere 103,000 gt in June 1974, to reach 22.0 mgt in June 1976. In the dry cargo market laid-up tonnage swelled from 573,000 gt to 4.3 mgt. In all, by June 1976, over 26.5 mgt of shipping was laid up and unemployed, signalling a massive structural over-supply in world shipping markets. For all shipbuilders this also signalled a dismal outlook for new orders. In the UK this disastrous reversal caused the order book to decline sharply from its peak of 8.5 mgt in 1973, to 4.2 mgt in 1976, with further contraction to 2.9 mgt in 1977. The severity of the situation was revealed more starkly in the level of new orders placed in British yards; these had reached 4.355 mgt in 1973, but totalled only 67,000 gt in 1975.[73] In this environment the industry was once again confronting familiar problems of unused capacity and a downward spiral of unemployed men and capital. On this occasion these problems coincided with the election of a Labour government which had already declared its intention to nationalise the industry. When the representatives of the industry met with the new Secretary of State for Industry in April 1974, they were advised by Tony Wedgwood Benn that he had already instructed a departmental inquiry into the means by which the principles of the nationalisation proposal could be implemented.[74]

Although the industry had expected this, coming as it did at the end of a decade of increasing intervention, this rapid move by the minority Labour government confronted the shipbuilders with a dilemma of how to respond. It was clear to the Shipbuilders and Repairers National Association (SRNA) that 'any detailed discussion [with the government] would inevitably reveal that the Industry is not united'.[75] The official position of the industry, as represented by the SRNA, was that it was opposed to nationalisation. Indeed, despite much internal disagreement, the industry opposed nationalisation vigorously. The SRNA argued that shipbuilding did not need public ownership. What it did need were 'short-term measures to promote orders and thereby reduce the serious damage ... and heavy unemployment', which would otherwise emerge in the period of uncertainty over the future ownership and future long-term policy for the industry.[76] In adopting this tactic of declaring opposition to nationalisation, while at the same time asking for short-term aid, the industry sought to delay progress on the part of the government, in the hope that Wilson's minority administration would be unable to get sufficient support to pass the legislation. In that eventuality, the industry believed that Harold Wilson would have to go to the country again, with the prospect, and hope, that a Conservative government would then be returned. On behalf of the industry, the SRNA then pursued a holding strategy in which it drew up a draft of the measures to which industry would be prepared to agree, in order to ensure its continuance and survival within the private sector. In their document called 'A possible policy for a Conservative Government: The Present Situation',[77] the SRNA asked that a Conservative administration should act to control inflation, and provide grants 'for further capital [to be] invested for the long-term future which [the industry] cannot self generate'. In addition, the industry asked for 'short-term support to maintain order books and employment'. Beyond this the SRNA argued that if the industry were to have a long-term future, there would need to be a commitment by government 'to a more continuous national policy [for shipbuilding] ... and [government action] to secure home [shipping] orders for domestic shipyards'. Only such a scenario, of long-term government commitment and support, it was argued, could provide the industry with the opportunity and means to deal with 'the deterioration in industrial relations, and therefore in productivity [which was in part due] to the expectations of worker power encouraged by the proposals of Nationalisation'.[78]

The SRNA then set out what the industry would undertake to do, if a Conservative government were to favour such measures. The industry would first commit to participate in collaborative market research to identify which ship types it should concentrate on producing in the next ten years. Such collaboration had been urged on the industry for at least fifteen years, but had always been resisted since the shipbuilders did not believe they had anything to learn from marketing.[79] In addition, to ensure that this proposal would succeed, individual shipbuilding companies 'would collaborate with the plan by an accepted and agreed specialisation by yard'.[80] This type of cooperation had been implicit in the segregation scheme outlined, and briefly considered, by the Shipbuilding Conference in the 1930s, and something similar had been urged on the industry in the 1960s, not least by its own association. Nothing had come of these overtures, and it was certainly only the threat of imminent nationalisation that forced the industry to consider adopting such long-neglected measures of cooperation. In the same document the SRNA declared that its members were 'ready and willing to accept the degree of restriction on individual freedom within the framework of a national policy in which they participate'.[81] This also committed the industry to undertake changes in management which were necessary and required 'as a condition of financial support'. Apart form this, however, management would continue to be free 'to design, sell and build ships without central bureaucratic controls'.[82] Major efforts would also be made to secure employee participation at all levels of decision taking and planning, with the aim of increasing productivity by 50 per cent.[83]

Given the historic commitment of the shipbuilders to individualism, and to keeping government out of the industry, this document spelled out a remarkable shift in thinking, and gave an indication that they were 'willing to examine any alternative to outright nationalisation'.[84] Nevertheless, the willingness to embrace change was less than whole-hearted, being contingent upon 'the government's acceptance of a substantial shipbuilding industry on terms of equality with its major competitors', in terms of getting access to government aid.[85]

It is clear that as the industry slipped into crisis in 1975, it had no strategy to deal with its manifest problems. The industry commitment to capacity control had been displaced by government support for restructuring, which had not secured the hoped-for future of growth and prosperity. In the decade to 1975 the competitiveness of the industry had weakened significantly, and in this context the SRNA proposals amounted more to an industry wish-list than to realistic policies which might have appealed to a Conservative government. By 1975, the industry dependence on government financial support was a *sine qua non*, a complete reversal of the principles of independence and self-help which had long sustained it. Even if a Conservative government had been returned to power, it is unlikely that the industry wish-list would have received support. At it was, the return of the Labour administration consigned these aspirations to pipe-dreams.

The critical condition of British shipbuilding in the wake of the market collapse in 1974 was set out for the Labour government in a confidential report at the end of 1976.[86] This was a joint report from unions, the Labour Party, and appointees on the organising committee for the proposed nationalised industry. It argued that 'if no new orders are received, the Industry will run out of work, except in one case, by the latter half of 1978'.[87] Moreover, in view of the industry's record in attracting orders, the report concluded that 'unless special measures are taken, there is a very serious risk that the major part of the UK shipbuilding industry will collapse shortly after nationalisation, simply from lack of work, resulting in massive unemployment and loss of the greater part of our shipbuilding capacity'.[88] Consequently it concluded that 'without government help most of the shipbuilding industry is unlikely to survive'.[89]

Understandably the shipbuilders did not accept this prognosis. In response they argued that 'it is not a question of shipbuilders collapsing; they have survived crises before and most will doubtless survive this one; it is a question of yards closing and men losing jobs'.[90] Historically, in facing cyclical depressions, the industry had always sought to bring capacity back into balance with domestic demand. This had involved reducing capacity through allowing uneconomic yards to close, and by easing the financial pressure on companies by letting men and capital assets fall out of employment for a time. The shipbuilders firmly believed that their long commitment to rationalisation of capacity had kept companies alive from the 1930s, and that with a similar policy they could weather the storm, even in the heavily over-supplied market conditions of the 1970s. The commitment of the shipbuilders was to the preservation of capital and private ownership. In contrast, the growing intervention of government from the early 1960s had had the objective of supporting employment. In this respect, industry and government objectives were in fundamental opposition. And with a Labour government in power, support for the industry was essentially employment-driven, and further aid would now only be available through full state ownership. By the 1970s, the long stagnation and relative decline of British shipbuilding, arguably an outcome of private-sector commitment to capacity control and stable state output, had brought the sometime world leader in shipbuilding to the point where its continued operation required financial support that could only be accessed by ending private ownership. Nationalisation then came to replace capacity rationalisation as the policy intended to sustain the industry, this resulting in the creation of British Shipbuilders in the grim economic circumstances of 1977.

# CHAPTER EIGHT

# End game: 1978–2010

## World shipbuilding

From the end of the Second World War, shipbuilding experienced two sharply contrasting thirty-year cycles of production. Between 1945 and 1975 the industry enjoyed a long and sustained expansion, with only a minor hesitation in growth between 1958 and 1963. During these three decades world launchings increased from 2.1 mgt in 1946 to 36.4 mgt in 1974. At the same time the world merchant fleet grew over five-fold from 80.3 mgt in 1948 to a post-boom peak of 424.7 mgt in 1982. This long growth cycle was halted abruptly by the effects of oil-price increases in 1973, and again in 1979, which precipitated the advanced economies into a deep and lengthy recession. These events in turn plunged world shipbuilding and shipping into deep depressions. World trade volumes peaked later in 1979 at 3.7 billion tons, a level not surpassed for the next decade. The collapse in trade volumes and freight rates led to dramatic increases in laid-up ship tonnage. By 1978, 29.9 mgt of shipping was unemployed, this deteriorating to 50.3 mgt in 1983, nearly 12 per cent of the world fleet.

The abrupt puncturing of this long expansion in ship construction consequently flooded the shipping market with a huge over-supply of carrying capacity. There followed a sharp decline in the demand for new tonnage. From the peak world launching of 36.4 mgt in 1974, it took twenty-seven years before the industry regained that level of output. Within these years, world output was less than half of the 1974 level for fifteen years from 1978 to 1991, and did not begin to grown consistently until 1989–90, this recovery ironically coinciding with the final dissolution and privatisation of British Shipbuilders. This long depression of activity was also clearly mirrored in the world order book. This had peaked at 133.4 mgt in 1974, but it was not until 2004 that this was finally exceeded, with orders at that date of 146.2 mgt.

Surplus capacity hung heavily over the world industry for more than two decades, creating a structural problem affecting both demand and supply. These factors could only be brought back to some semblance of balance by a combination of reductions in shipbuilding capacity, disposals of older tonnage, and some recovery in trade volumes. Trade activity only regained its 1979 level a decade later, by which time there had been disposals of 165.8 mgt of shipping, over 102 mgt of this going in a surge of disposals between 1982 and 1987. Moreover, between 1976 and 1989, Japan had reduced its building capacity by some 33–40 per cent, while in Europe the 1975 capacity had been cut in half. This combination of recovering trade, tonnage disposals and the reduction of capacity in the two main shipbuilding regions was sufficient to initiate the long-hoped-for recovery in demand for new tonnage. World new orders, which had languished at an average of 15.0 mgt annually in the 1980s, rose to 21.0 mgt between 1991 and 1994, then increasing to 28.0 mgt in 1999. This upward trend escalated to 52.0 mgt per year between 2000 and 2004 before peaking at 164.8 mgt in 2007 (Table 8.1). World shipbuilding was again buoyant from the mid-1990s, but the link between demand and supply was not stable. This was because the reductions in capacity achieved by builders in Japan and Western Europe were more than offset by new players, who expanded capacity aggressively, and in doing so profoundly changed the focus of the world's main shipbuilding regions (Table 8.2).

At the end of the first thirty-year cycle of expansion, in 1975, Japan had come to dominate world shipbuilding, capturing half the market, while Western Europe occupied a strong second place in production with nearly 40 per cent. As late as 1995, Japan and Europe were still in first and second place in production, but the challenge of South Korea was accelerating, with the capture of over 20 per cent of the market. This aggressive market challenge had catapulted South Korea to first place in the world rankings by 2003, with 37 per cent of the market. Japan then still held second place, but the emerging Chinese industry, with over 10 per cent of the market, had pushed the Western European industry down into fourth place (Table 8.2). By the end of the boom in 2009, China had exploded into prominence, with over 28 per cent of the market, to take second place behind South Korea, with Japan declining into third position.

This huge expansion of capacity was supported by another wave of disposals of 1970s' tonnage, some 147.8 mgt of shipping being scrapped between 1993 and 2003. This removal of old tonnage was paralleled by a vigorous growth in trade, with world trade volumes more than doubling to 7.7 billion tons between 1989 and 2010, a growth rate which expanded the world merchant fleet from 404.9 mgt to 830.7 mgt between 1986 and 2008. At the conclusion of this great bubble of expansion, the European shipbuilding industry had been overwhelmed and marginalised, its market share tumbling from nearly one-quarter in 1999 to a mere 3.5 per cent ten years later. European shipbuilders then completed only 2.6 mgt of ships, and held only 288,000 tons of new orders, less than one per cent of the world order book in 2009.

In the first decade of the twenty-first century, the efforts made by Japan and Europe to balance supply and demand by cutting capacity were overwhelmed by the state-supported growth of shipbuilding in South Korea and China. The hard lessons of

*Table 8.1a* World shipbuilding, 1975–2009, launches, completions and orders
(millions of gross tons, quinquennial averages)

|  | World new orders | Total order book | World launches | World completions |
|---|---|---|---|---|
| 1975–79 | 12.7 | 62.2 | 23.6 | |
| 1980–84 | 16.4 | 32.5 | 16.2 | |
| 1985–89 | 14.1 | 25.1 | 13.4 | |
| 1990–94 | 20.9 | 41.1 | | 17.9 |
| 1995–99 | 28.2 | 53.3 | | 25.4 |
| 2000–04 | 52.5 | 96.0 | | 27.3 |
| 2005-09 | 88.7 | 274.2 | | 60.2 |

*Table 8.1b* Annual new orders and completions, 1999–2009
(millions of gross tons)

|  | World new orders | Completions |
|---|---|---|
| 1999 | 28.9 | 27.8 |
| 2000 | 46.1 | 31.7 |
| 2001 | 38.5 | 31.3 |
| 2002 | 28.2 | 33.4 |
| 2003 | 74.0 | 36.1 |
| 2004 | 77.2 | 40.2 |
| 2005 | 60.0 | 46.9 |
| 2006 | 99.6 | 52.1 |
| 2007 | 164.8 | 57.3 |
| 2008 | 86.4 | 67.7 |
| 2009 | 32.5 | 76.9 |

*Sources*: Launches: Lloyds Register Annual Summary. Completions: Lloyds Register World Fleet Statistics. Orders: Lloyds Register World Shipbuilding Statistics.

*Table 8.2*  World market shares by main shipbuilding regions
% share of tonnage launched/completed

|  | 1975 | 1995 | 1999 | 2003 | 2009 |
|---|---|---|---|---|---|
| Japan | 50.1 | 39.0 | 34.6 | 35.1 | 24.6 |
| Association of West European Shipbuilders | 27.2 | 25.9 | 23.4 | 9.0 | 3.5 |
| Other European builders | 12.5 | | | | |
| South Korea | 1.2 | 21.6 | 29.4 | 37.1 | 37.6 |
| China | | c 4.0 | c 6.0 | 10.4 | 28.4 |
| Total launched/completed (mgt) | 35.9[1] | 22.6[2] | 27.8[2] | 36.1[2] | 76.9[2] |

[1]  Launches in million gross registered tons

[2]  1995–2009; Completions, millions of gross tons.

*Sources*: 1975: Lloyds Register Annual Summary; 1995–2009: Lloyds Register: World Fleet Statistics.

the consequences of the boom of the early 1970s and the subsequent long depression arising from over-capacity were ignored, and the relentless expansion of capacity by the new players ultimately took the industry to the brink of a new crisis. In 2008 this was initiated by the world crises in finance and credit. This quickly demonstrated that the violence of boom and slump, which had historically haunted this cyclical capital-goods industry, had not been diminished by decades of government support and intervention. Rather, the amplitude of boom and collapse had been intensified, and the frequency of its occurrence accelerated by it. It is at the beginning of this dramatic second post-war thirty-year cycle that British Shipbuilders was created as a nationalised corporation, in which for a time government assistance aimed to help British shipbuilding to survive in a hazardous market, one typified by scare orders, uneconomic prices, and deepening depression.

## British Shipbuilders, 1977–1989

The demand to nationalise British shipyards had long been voiced by the labour movement, and the industry had indeed been included, initially, in the nationalisation plans of the post-war Labour government, only later to be removed from the agenda. The labour movement's desire for shipbuilding to be publicly owned did not disappear, however, and it re-emerged when the deepening problems of the industry led to piecemeal government aid and intervention in the 1960s. This growing intent culminated in the preparation of a draft proposal for nationalisation in July 1973.[1] This was a report drawn up by a joint working party of the Labour Party, the Trade

Union Council, and the Confederation of the Shipbuilding and Engineering Unions (CSEU). As such it fed into the policy agenda of the new Labour government, returned as a minority administration in February 1974, and then with a small majority in October of the same year. The government thus moved quickly to propose the nationalisation of the shipbuilding and aircraft industries, presenting the Aircraft and Shipbuilding Industries Bill to the House of Commons in April 1975.[2] A platform for public ownership in shipbuilding had, of course, already been established by the state take-overs of UCS, Cammell Laird and Harland & Wolff, as well as the shipbuilding interests rescued from the failure of the Court Line.

When first presented, the Bill proposed the nationalisation of all the major merchant and naval shipbuilding enterprises, their related training companies, the manufacturers of slow-speed diesel engines, and the major ship-repair companies. These proposals were strenuously opposed by the industry through its Shipbuilders and Repairers National Association (SRNA). As developed in 1974, the SRNA case against nationalisation insisted that the industry was experiencing a revival, had full order books, and only yards such as Govan Shipbuilders were losing money.[3] Their case for the industry recommended a corporate approach through the establishment of a Shipbuilding Council. In such a forum it was proposed that the unions and the industry could cooperate to develop a national shipbuilding policy. However, any hope of moving in this direction was soon sidelined by the dramatic deterioration in world shipbuilding between 1974 and 1975. This savage reversal was captured in an article in the *Economist*, which concluded that, 'if nationalise we must, let it indeed move fast. A world crisis in shipbuilding is on the way.'[4] This plea was to fall on deaf ears for, in spite of the looming crisis, the opposition to nationalisation was fierce, led in the House of Commons by the Conservative Party. The tactics were ruthless and inventive, and succeeded in stopping the first attempt to pass the Bill over the confused issue of 'hybridity'. This involved a complex disagreement over what constituted a ship and shipyard in terms of the facilities to be nationalised. This bizarre technicality effectively delayed nationalisation by two years. Only a late concession by government, in deleting ship repairers from the Bill, finally enabled it to pass and receive the Royal Assent on 17 March 1977, with vesting day specified as 1 July 1977.[5] Between the first presentation to the House in April 1975, and its final passing in March 1977, the Bill had suffered an amazing catalogue of delays, obstructions, filibusters, and amendments. It set a record for being 58 days in the committee stage, while on the floor of the House it became a battleground not of economic consideration or social consequences, but of opposing and mutually hostile political ideologies.

The delay of two years between the presentation and the passing of the Bill saw world and British shipbuilding topple from the peaks of production and optimism of 1974 into the first stage of prolonged depression in the shipping and shipbuilding markets. For British shipbuilding delay and infighting ultimately generated a climate of friction and disillusionment among the members of the 'organising committee'. This had been set up in December 1974 to plan for the operation of the new nationalised corporation. When the Bill failed to pass at the end of 1976, the deputy chairman and chief executive-elect for British Shipbuilders, J. Graham Day, resigned. His letter of resignation to Eric Varley, the Secretary of State for Industry, was blunt and uncompromising. He wrote, 'My experience on the Organising Committee … has been such as to confirm the fears I expressed before my appointment. … That in the public sector I could not operate in a way which would allow me to be a fully effective manager.' He went on to note that he considered that, 'the delay in carrying through nationalisation has meant that opportunities that were available for restructuring and stabilising particularly the shipbuilding industry are now gone. As a result the tasks now required to be prospectively undertaken by a Chief Executive of British Shipbuilders are substantially different, and not such as I ever contemplated undertaking.'

Just how damaging the two-year delay in nationalising the industry had been for the industry's prospects is difficult to judge. Graham Day was later to maintain that the delay had no damaging effect. His opinion was that, 'It would only have done damage if there had been a strategy which was late in being delivered. Since there was no strategy, it didn't matter at all.'[6] It was the lack of any government strategy that was the root source of Graham Day's disillusion with the nationalisation proposal. At a meeting with Gerald Kaufman in 1976, Minister of State for Industry, Day had tried to persuade him that the shipbuilding industry needed fundamental change and restructuring. This was necessary, he believed, since the OPEC price rises had changed the whole nature of world shipbuilding. In contrast, Kaufman reiterated government opinion that the problem facing the industry was simply that of another familiar cyclical downturn.[7] Given such differences in opinion and conviction, Graham Day's resignation was inevitable. This also triggered the resignation of all the other experienced members of the organising committee, their departure taking with them all the preparatory ideas and plans for running the new corporation.

This exodus left in post only the chairman, Admiral Anthony Griffin, and, after some persuasion, the trade union member, Ken Griffin. These two were soon joined by a seconded civil servant, Michael Casey, an under secretary in the Department of Industry who had recently been the head of the Shipbuilding Policy Division. Casey was to become the chief executive of the new corporation, British Shipbuilders, with Admiral Griffin remaining as chairman. British Shipbuilders came into being as world shipbuilding contracted, and with the inherited companies on the brink of collapse. The initial responsibility for organising the corporation, and coping with the fragile and deteriorating situation, fell to a board whose chairman and chief executive were experienced administrators but who had no managerial experience of the industry. The three full-time members of the board, Admiral Griffin, Michael Casey and Ken Griffin, were soon joined by the appointment of seven part-time members, four from the industry, and three with backgrounds as full-time trade-union officials.

When formed on vesting day, British Shipbuilders acquired ownership of 27 shipbuilding, marine engineering, and training companies. Almost immediately the six ship-repair companies, excluded from the nationalisation Bill, were voluntarily taken into public ownership. As a consequence the corporation began life as a holding company for 131 registered companies, of which 80 were actively trading. Initially these were grouped in 26 profit centres which included 32 shipyards, 19 ship-repair yards, and six general engineering works.[8] The terms of the Bill had excluded 34 small yards capable of building ships of up to 5,000 dwt which remained in private ownership, as did some ship-repair facilities. With these small exceptions, British Shipbuilders controlled 97 per cent of all merchant shipbuilding, 99 per cent of all warship construction, and about half of all British ship-repair facilities. In Belfast the publicly owned Harland & Wolff remained outside British Shipbuilders. These businesses brought some 86,000 employees into the corporation. Of these, 64,000 were at work in shipbuilding, 38,800 on merchant work, and 25,200 on warship building. Among the shipbuilding regions, 24,000 worked in Scotland, 33,000 in the North East of England, and 19,000 in the North West district from the Mersey to Barrow-in-Furness. The remaining 10,000 were employed in many facilities outside the main districts.[9]

The companies absorbed into the corporation had net assets at 31 March 1977 with a book value of £136 million, and a turnover of £713 million in the year to March 1977. The pre-tax profit of these concerns was £9.0 million, after taking credit for government grants and subventions.[10] The cost of bringing these assets into public ownership was £70 million. While some of the smaller shipbuilding companies earned modest profits from the order boom, an assessment of the financial condition of the companies acquired showed that 15 of the major companies were loss makers and substantially insolvent. These casualties included Sunderland Shipbuilders, Cammell Laird, Hawthorne Leslie, Scott Lithgow, Barclay Curle, Ailsa Shipbuilders, Robb Caledon, Smiths Dock, Swan Hunter and Tyne Ship Repair.[11]

This was the raw material from which the inexperienced board of British Shipbuilders was expected to create an efficient organisation. The nationalisation Bill required the board to achieve four main outcomes. Operationally the corporation had to promote the 'efficient and economic design, production, sale, repair and maintenance of ships and slow-speed diesel engines'. Strategically, the board had to have full regard to the requirements of national defence in taking its decisions. More generally, the board was required actively to promote industrial democracy, and, fourthly, administratively and in terms of accountability, the board had to produce an annual corporate plan together with annual reports and accounts. To prepare a corporate plan and accounts, and to negotiate with unions to promote industrial democracy, were duties which in their several ways were to prove equally difficult and challenging. As a first step the board devised an organisational structure to enable it to begin to manage the business of the corporation.

The corporation was initially organised in four main sectors, namely merchant shipbuilding including offshore work, naval shipbuilding, ship repairing, and marine engineering. There was also a small general engineering sector. The merchant shipbuilding sector was also subdivided on the basis of the building capacity of the yards and allocated to groups as 'large', 'medium' and 'small' yards. The 'large' yards were identified as the 'core' facilities in the corporation. This gave administrative form to the complex holding company that was British Shipbuilders. The board at the corporation headquarters retained control of finance and policy, while operational and management responsibility was devolved to the subsidiary companies. While this had the appearance of a standard holding-company organisation, British Shipbuilders did not function as effectively as a holding company in the private sector. As a public corporation, British Shipbuilders' board and headquarters staff were not independent in policy making nor in decision taking. In matters of finance the chief executive and board made proposals up the chain of command to the Department of Industry and the Treasury, and beyond them, also to the European Commission in Brussels. The minutes of the board meetings make it clear that this was a clumsy, vexatious and time-consuming procedure. At the fourth board meeting in November 1977, it was noted that in trying to forecast the financial position of the Corporation for the nine months to 31 March 1978, 'insufficient money had been made available from the Intervention Fund to cover the Polish Deal [and] the shortfall had been increased by delay in the Treasury's granting permission to sell dollars forward'.[12] Two years later the board again noted that 'British Shipbuilders continues to experience severe delays in obtaining Intervention Fund approval from the Department of Industry.[13]

Problems with finance also developed down the chain of communication and control from the board to the executive officers in the subsidiary companies. When trying to prepare consolidated accounts and financial detail for the corporate plan, the board member for finance, Mr Elderfield, reported 'that the financial control of the majority of the yards had been of a very low calibre, that the basis of the budgets submitted for 1978–79 was extremely suspect, and [consequently] he was in no position to give any indication of the current years trading prospects, [or] to monitor operations or to progress preparation of the Corporate Plan'.[14]

The lack of board autonomy was also evident in the conduct of wage negotiations. At its third meeting, on 23 September 1977, it was recorded that the board had serious concerns about the effects that the government's handling of the mechanics of wage negotiations were having on the workforce and management, on production and productivity, and on British Shipbuilders' headquarters. A year later concern with the same issues caused the board to cooperate with the officials of the CSEU to draft a joint letter to the Secretary of State. This protested that the corporation 'had effectively been prevented from engaging in direct wage negotiations with its employees by the restrictions placed upon it by government, and by the confusion that surrounded apparently conflicting ministerial statements as to whether the limit on pay increases is 8½ per cent or 10 per cent'.[15] All of this was felt to undermine the credibility of the corporation and company management, and of the trade-union officials. The malaise and general feeling in the board was expressed by E.K. Griffin as deputy chairman. He noted that 'the industry had been fraught with difficulties during its first months of operation, and to a certain degree the Board had been discredited through government policy which was outwith the Corporation's control'.[16]

These tensions were constant concerns and made for a climate of high uncertainty in which the board had to develop its first corporate plan while trying to win orders and bring some coherence to the operation of the new corporation. Confronted as the board was by the world-wide surplus of shipbuilding capacity and a sharply declining demand for new tonnage, the preparation of its corporate plan was made extremely difficult. The board had to make assumptions about the trend and volume of new orders, the share of these that the corporation might expect to attract, and, even more difficult, at what point in the future could the board anticipate that demand would begin to recover. On the timing of the expected upturn in the market, all available projections appeared to suggest that the beginnings of a recovery might be discernible between 1980 and 1982, to be followed by a progressive pick-up through to 1985. If this were a reasonable scenario on timing, the next assumption for the board to make was what share of new orders the corporation might attract. The recent market share of world new orders for British Shipbuilding had been only 2.8 per cent. If this were to be maintained then the corporation calculated that it could expect that its tonnage launched of 679,000 grt in 1978 would decline and bottom out at 388,000 grt in 1980, before beginning to recover from 1982 to reach 604,000 grt in 1985. However, even these modest assumptions depended on how the corporation could win orders in prevailing market conditions, and if it failed to maintain its current market share, or if world trends in trade and demand did not live up to the projection, what fall-back planning could the board make? In this climate of extreme uncertainty the Intervention Fund, which had been introduced as an emergency measure in February 1976 to subsidise orders, was a critical element. In the absence of the Shipbuilding Intervention Fund (SIF), British Shipbuilders had no prospect of bridging the price gap of 30–35 per cent between British and Japanese yards, nor of competing effectively with Sweden and Germany.

In considering what and how to plan for its four main sectors, and subsidiary general engineering, in the five-year plan period to 1983, the board saw no real problems for the warship yards. The three main yards had good order books from the Ministry of Defence (MoD). Similarly in general engineering the board considered that prospects for orders, and for diversifying activity, were satisfactory. The main problem areas were consequently identified as merchant shipbuilding, engine building, and ship repair.[17] At this stage the board also knew that a second tranche of the SIF had been approved by the European Commission, this to run to the end of 1978 at an annual rate of £85 million. The caveat was, however, that any further extension of SIF would be conditional upon the board producing an acceptable corporate plan by December 1978. Critically, too, this plan would have to include proposals for restructuring merchant shipbuilding, and would have to specify what reduction in capacity would be planned for.[18] This was a real dilemma, for the board knew that in the depressed market and low price conditions of 1978, any prospect of gaining enough orders to occupy the capacity of the merchant yards fully would need SIF support in the order of £250–£300 million each year to offset the British price disadvantage. The board also knew that this was not a realistic expectation, and consequently the corporate plan would have to propose some reduction in the current merchant capacity, which the board estimated to be 632,000 compensated gross registered tons (cgrt).[19]

Weighing all these elements in the balance, the board considered four options on which it could plan the forward corporate strategy. Option 1 assumed retaining the current capacity of 632,000 cgrt and employment of 33,300 personnel. To be effective this required SIF support of £250–£300 million per year, which over the five-year plan period would require the government to provide subsidies of £1,250–£1,650 million. Given market forecasts, this was considered to be impractical. Option 2 took as its base line a capacity of 430,000 cgrt being attained by 1980–81, this requiring an SIF of £440 million over the plan period. Activity at this level would, however, incur losses on contracts, and manpower would need to be cut to 21,000 by 1982–83. Option 3 assumed a yet deeper cut in capacity, to 330,000 cgrt. This would require an SIF of £390 million, but the workforce would have to be slashed to 13,000, and the corporation would still incur significant trading losses. The final Option, 4, was conceived as a doomsday scenario. It assumed no gain on the low level of orders current in 1979, which would cut capacity to 250,000 cgrt, and a labour force reduced to 9,000. This would mean the progressive closure of all but two of the large yards. This was rejected as an impossible scenario in which 'the social consequences would be alarming, and the possibility of any controlled contraction utterly remote'.[20]

On this diagnosis the board considered that only Option 2 seemed able to provide a framework for forward planning. This required an SIF of £110 million per year, and this was taken as the baseline for drafting the corporate plan. In adopting this, the board minutes cautioned that it was 'important that in presenting [the plan] it should properly present the Corporation's positive approach to the future, and should not leave the impression of a plan simply designed to run down the industry'.[21] What lay behind this caution was the deep anxiety the board had over asking for SIF support of £110 million annually, for this was the critical input necessary to make Option 2 feasible. They had earlier noted that if an SIF of £110 million were rejected, then a continuation of the existing SIF limit of £85 million 'would reduce the ability to acquire work to 330,000 cgrt, forcing the Corporation to adopt Option 3, which would inevitably involve the closure of major profit centres'.

The corporate plan based on Option 2 was presented to the Department of Industry at the end of December 1978, although the minister had earlier been advised of the strategic options being considered, and of the board preference for proceeding with Option 2. A committee of ministers, chaired by the Minister of State for Industry, Gerald Kaufman, was set up to consider the future strategy for the corporation. However, with a general election pending, no statement of intent was made to the House until 4 April 1979. This vaguely declared a preference for the corporation to proceed by a step-by-step approach to the rationalisation of the industry, and significantly avoided giving support to the restructuring proposals inherent in adopting Option 2. Indeed, instead of giving any commitment to restructuring, the government required the corporation to make no announcement of any redundancies during the election campaign. Consequently, after having had the plan before it for five months, no government decision in support of the board was forthcoming.[22]

In the political circumstances of 1978–79, with the government confronted by waves of strikes, often unofficial in the 'winter of discontent', the momentum given to managing the new corporation stalled. Consequently when the new Conservative administration was elected on 3 May 1979, British Shipbuilders had to re-start the planning process with a less sympathetic Margaret Thatcher government. It was not until 23 July 1979 that the new administration announced its position in relation to the corporation and the industry. While broadly accepting the objectives set out in Option 2, the minister declared that the government doubted that the corporation would be able to obtain the volume of orders required to sustain the Option 2 capacity of 430,000 cgrt. This caveat produced some refinement of the plan to produce Option 2A. This agreed to make explicit the scale of planned redundancies, and when they were expected to be implemented. Moreover, the board's ability to plan for reconstruction of the industry was destabilised by the uncertainty created by the Conservative manifesto commitment to return parts of British Shipbuilders to private enterprise. More immediately serious was the undermining of the declared support of the revised Option 2A, by the government dramatically cutting back on the level of SIF support. While the corporate plan asked for an annual SIF of £110 million, the government set support at only £120 million to cover the two-year period from July 1979 to July 1981. Confronted with this drastic reduction in subsidy the board advised that the 'Executive would now asses implications and identify the volume of business the new Invention Fund could support. It would identify core yards, and the inevitable corollary would be the closure of certain merchant yards and the reduction of labour in others.'[23] By the end of August the board had estimated that the reduced SIF implied reducing capacity to between 400,000 and 420,000 cgrt by 1980–81, and a cut back in the workforce to 18,000–19,000 by 1980.[24] A month later the board agreed the target capacity at 400,000 cgrt per year.[25]

During its first two years of existence to July 1979, the corporation was hindered by delays in decision taking, as well as uncertainty and inadequacy in its funding. Neither the timeframe of information and decision taking, nor the scale of its financial provision, allowed for coherent management or planning. Yet, in spite of this, the corporation did make some progress with piecemeal restructuring and with redundancies. These had been made inevitable when yards ran out of work, or were making substantial losses. Four yards had been closed, Redheads, South Dock, Burntisland and Haverton Hill, as had Scott Lithgow Dry Docks. With some slimming down in other establishments 5,675 redundancies had been implemented. This was in line with the objectives of the revised Option 2A plan which sought to reduce the July 1977 work force of 38,730 to only 18,000 by June 1980. The actual employment then was in fact lower, at 17,626, by which time a total of 36 building berths had been closed.[26]

By the time the stewardship of Admiral Griffin and Michael Casey came to an end in March 1980, employment in the merchant sector had been cut by more than 47 per cent, from 38,770 in July 1977 to 20,428 at March 1980. The severity of this reduction was offset in part by the transfer of 7,000 of these men to work on naval contracts in the mixed yards. Employment there had more than doubled to 13,724 in March 1980. There was also a considerable switch of men into employment in offshore activities. Employment there in March 1977 was only 220 men, but had expanded to 2,296 employees by March 1980. These swings and balances eventually saw a 20 per cent reduction in employment in the merchant and mixed yards, a loss of 9,039 jobs over 33 months. In contrast, employment in the warship sector was broadly stable at around 19,500. However, employment in ship repair and engine building suffered cuts of a half and a quarter, with losses of 3,981 jobs and 4,636 posts respectively. In the small general engineering sector, employment did better, edging up marginally by 284 men to a total of 7,266 employees. When taken together the total workforce in British Shipbuilders had declined from the 84,437 on vesting day to 72,700 at the end of March 1980, a cut back of nearly 17 per cent.

The context in which these changes took place was the extraordinarily difficult market which saw the world order book contact from 133.4 mgt in 1974 to an annual average of just over 31 mgt between 1977 and 1980 (Table 8.1). Additions of new orders were less than 13 mgt each year between 1975 and 1979, and from this market Britain won only 275,000 tons of orders annually. This was barely a 2.0 per cent share, and caused the corporation order book to contract from 1.5 mgt in 1977 to only one-third of that in 1980. Since UK tonnage completions that year were 422,000 gt, the order book was barely equal to one year's production.

Within this hostile environment the board found that it was constantly fire-fighting a myriad crisis situations. Under pressure from the government British Shipbuilders had acquired a number of ship-repairing companies in the North East, at Falmouth, and on the Thames.[27] These proved to be problematic acquisitions to the extent that it was noted at the board meeting in January 1979 that the ship-repair sector, representing barely seven per cent of turnover, was responsible for half the forecast loss of the entire corporation.[28] At the same meeting losses at the Haverton Hill yard were reported to be running at £4.0 million annually, and the yard was earmarked for closure. Serious problems also emerged in the engine-building sector. The board soon discovered that poor levels of investment since 1945 had left the companies so far behind foreign competitors in slow-speed diesels that it was now too late to try to catch up, and that by mid-1980, the main Doxford establishment was virtually out of work.[29]

While these problems congregated in the North East of England, the Clyde was also in difficulty. In reviewing the operation of Govan Shipbuilders, the board minuted that 'there appears to be a complete lack of control at the top level'.[30] The situation was so serious that, in December 1979, the board approved the removal of the Govan chairman and appointed E.D. Mackie as his replacement.[31] Meanwhile, down river at Scott Lithgow, ship 1192, the *World Scholar*, was well behind schedule and due for delivery at the end of December 1979. If not handed over on time the customer, Dexters, had the option of outright refusal to take delivery, with the best compromise for Scott Lithgow likely to be a compensation payment of between £6 million and £10 million. This was a large oil tanker of 126,239 grt. Together with other problems, this calamity saw Scott Lithgow post losses of £41.7 million for the year to March 1980. This was nearly 44 per cent of the total trading loss of £95.7 million in the merchant-shipbuilding sector. In the first two full trading years, from April 1978 to March 1980, British Shipbuilders accumulated a trading loss of £159.3 million, of which merchant shipbuilding was responsible for £123.5 million, some 77 per cent of the total.

This alarming scale of the on-going drain on public resources confronted the new Conservative administration in May 1979. It was quick to note that, while the merchant sector had generated huge losses in its first year of operation, the warship sector had, in contrast, made a profit of £20.86 million. This contrast clearly encouraged the government to look toward fulfilling its manifesto commitment to return at least part of British Shipbuilders to private ownership. The first step was to terminate the contracts of Admiral Griffin as chairman, and Michael Casey as chief executive. They were replaced by the single appointment of Robert Atkinson as chairman and chief executive with effect from 1 July 1980. Immediately he set about dismantling the organisation of industrial sectors, and instead introduced a divisional structure. He established five trading divisions: merchant shipbuilding; warship building; engineering; ship repairing; and offshore construction. Each division was to have its own managing director and local board. Atkinson also established a separate technology department, bringing together the British Shipbuilding Research Association, British Shipbuilding Hydrodynamics, and the industry Research and Development Team. The headquarters or conceptual design team was also included in the new grouping. In addition, Atkinson created British Shipbuilding (Training, Education and Safety), charged with developing a common policy across the firms in the corporation.

While Atkinson believed his restructuring of British Shipbuilding would lead to improved performance, he also had to act to reduce costs and make savings. He moved quickly to dispose of the Walker and Hebburn yards on the Tyne, the Pallion yard on the Wear at Sunderland, Scotstoun Marine on the Clyde, and Thames Ship

Repair. Further disposals, of Caledon at Dundee, and the Southwick and Hartlepool facilities, followed quickly in 1981. Dry docks at Jarrow, South Shields and Hull were disposed of the following year. All of this was re-active and piece-meal rationalisation, and though not part of a planned strategy, was initially remarkably successful in reducing losses. The trading loss of £109.9 million for 1979–81 was reduced to £41.4 million the following year, and again to only £19.8 million in 1981–82. Unfortunately this considerable achievement was to be negated by the huge loss of £117.5 million in Atkinson's final year of 1982–83. The causes of this lay first in the unrelenting poor performance of the merchant-shipbuilding division, and second in the disastrous performance of his innovation of the offshore division.

In merchant shipbuilding, the forecasts that the market would begin to pick up by 1982 proved to be unfounded. Indeed in 1982 the world market contracted sharply to generate only 11.2 mgt of new orders, and averaged only around 16.0 mgt over the five years to 1984 (Table 8.1). In such a poor market Britain found it hard to compete with the SIF cutback from £65 million in 1979, to £55 million for 1980–81, and reduced again to a poor £45 million in 1981–82. The reduction in SIF was not the only problem, for small as the support level was, British Shipbuilders found it increasingly difficult to draw funds from it. This was because there was a reduction in the proportion of the ship selling price which could be offset by the Intervention Fund. In 1979, up to 30 per cent of the selling price of a vessel could be offset by the SIF, but this was reduced to 23 per cent for 1980–81, then further reduced to only 15 per cent between 1982 and 1984. While the SIF had funds of £154 million available between 1980 and 1983, British Shipbuilders was only able to draw down £113.3 million. This reflected their difficulty in getting orders at the prices they could quote with the support of the declining offset rate imposed by the SIF. With British prices lagging 30 per cent behind those of Japan and South Korea, the subsidies available from the SIF could not bridge the price gap. Indeed, the only way British Shipbuilders could get orders was to quote a price that was known to be below cost, and certain to be loss making. Constrained in this way, the corporation's share of world new orders slipped from 2.0 per cent to 1.2 per cent between 1980 and 1983, while its share of world tonnage completed declined from 3.0 per cent to 2.0 per cent. Indeed, in this period British completions of 900,000 cgrt outran new orders placed of 802,000 cgrt. The industry was in constant danger of running out of work, with serious consequences for under-utilisation of labour, for the need to adopt short-time working, and for a deepening loss of profitability in the merchant-shipbuilding division. Losses of £48.04 million for 1980–81 escalated to £54.17 million in 1982–83 and to £84.01 million 1981–82. The total merchant division loss of £186.3 million contrasted strongly with the profit of £142.2 million generated in the warship division. While the performance of the two shipbuilding divisions almost balanced the books, that of the new offshore division was a spectacular failure.

The creation of the separate offshore division had been a clear response to the upsurge in demand for oilrigs following the oil price increases in 1979, and the consequent boom in rig charter rates. Within the new offshore division, the lead yard was designated as Scott Lithgow at Port Glasgow. The Cammell Laird yard at Birkenhead was then added to the division. This re-designation of work for Scott Lithgow and Cammell Laird was to remove them from merchant shipbuilding, and from seeking SIF support for their contracts, since after allowing for a transition period in completing existing work, the yards were to concentrate solely on offshore work. A third component added to this new division was VO Ltd (Vickers Offshore) at Barrow-in-Furness. In contemplating moving into offshore work as early as 1978, British Shipbuilders had appreciated it lacked the skilled personnel to do so. The solution had been to purchase from Vickers its existing team of engineers in their Vickers Offshore (Project and Development) unit. This was approved by the Secretary of State in January 1979.[32]

Of the two construction companies allocated to the division, Scott Lithgow had had some previous experience in offshore contracts. It had built two drill ships, *Ben Ocean Lancer* in 1976, and *Pac Norse I* in 1977. Prospects for orders in the buoyant offshore market seemed bright, and it was Cammell Laird who attracted the first major contract. In June 1981 the Birkenhead firm signed a £60 million order with Dome Petroleum of Canada for a semi-submersible platform. It could have been no coincidence that Graham Day, sometime managing director of Cammell Laird was then a senior executive with Dome Petroleum. Scott Lithgow was also quickly into the new market. In 1981 it took orders for HMS *Challenger*, an SOV (seabed operation vessel), and an £80 million order for a semi-submersible platform from Ben-Odeco and the British National Oil Corporation. This was to become the *Ocean Alliance*.[33] Scott Lithgow also won the order for the *Iolaire*, an ESV (emergency support vessel). A further contract for a semi-submersible, the *Sea Explorer*, was taken in 1983. Each of the orders, for the *Ocean Alliance*, the *Iolaire*, and *Sea Explorer*, took Scott Lithgow a further step up the league of technically difficult and advanced construction. These were far different from the assembly of tankers and bulk carriers which had been the previous staples of the yard. These were worrying ventures, for Scott Lithgow had already shown that it lacked adequate skilled manpower when undertaking earlier contracts, notably in the case of the *World Scholar*. It was also known that, as a group, Scott Lithgow lacked planning staff. In March 1980 the executive committee of British Shipbuilders' board had noted that 'the position of Scott Lithgow is deeply worrying. There were problems of production management and organisation ... also there were severe work load problems.'[34] The committee also noted 'the unbearable financial strain that Scott Lithgow currently represented. In particular to get the ESV project back on track and properly managed.' Under pressure, the Scott Lithgow managing director, Ross Belch, retired. The new chief executive of Scott Lithgow was Cameron Parker, taking up the post from 1 June 1980.

However, not even a new management could readily overcome the record of poor industrial relations and strikes at Scott Lithgow. In 1981 there were no fewer than fifteen unofficial disputes at the yard. Going public, the new chief executive, Cameron Parker, complained in an interview with the *Greenock Telegraph* that absenteeism was twice the average of that in British Shipbuilders nationally, and the Scott Lithgow group had poor productivity, and the worst industrial relations in the corporation.[35] This public pillorying of the workforce simply added to the volatile hostility in the yard, and made the challenge of adjusting to the new technology more difficult. The failure to rise to this challenge essentially proved to be destructive to the group reputation. The ESV, *Iolaire*, was nearly two years late when finally accepted in March 1983, this delay costing Scott Lithgow a penalty payment of £6.0 million on top of other production losses. In November 1983, the *Ocean Alliance* was only 30 per cent built, already then eighteen months late, and consequently cancelled by BP. The *Sea Explorer* was also finally a year late in delivery. These were calamities which caused Scott Lithgow to accumulate losses of £95.37 million between 1981 and 1983. At the same time, the other offshore yard, Cammell Laird, accumulated further losses of £19.0 million. Atkinson's innovation of the offshore division had generated losses of £107.8 million, some 60 per cent of corporation losses in his period as chairman and chief executive. Atkinson blamed Scott Lithgow for the failures, commenting that not only did the group have a history of losses and late deliveries, high absenteeism and poor industrial relations, but that Scott Lithgow had let down 'British Shipbuilders, the nation, and themselves'.[36]

Reflecting on the Scott Lithgow and offshore fiasco in an interview in 1992, the then deputy chairman of British Shipbuilders, Ken Griffin, commented on a broader management failure in the corporation. Of British Shipbuilders' board, he said, 'At Scott Lithgow we did not face up to the fact that to change from building merchant ships to building oilrigs was a very costly change. ... We as a Board made them do something, and when they didn't do the impossible, we blamed them for not succeeding.'[37] In a similar vein, Maurice Phelps, the board member for personnel and industrial relations commented on 'the arrogance of our attitude in getting into the offshore business. Actually we believed that in Scott Lithgow and Cammell Laird we could actually transfer from building commercial ships to building offshore rigs with much greater and higher technological requirements, and dealing with contract negotiations with totally different perspectives. We were taken to the cleaners in terms of the contracts we ended up signing, believing we could build when we simply lacked the experience and training.'[38]

During his three years as chairman and chief executive, Robert Atkinson was embattled with a government which mainly believed he was not pursuing cuts and closures vigorously enough. The government wanted to meet its manifesto commitment to privatise at least part of the industry, but Atkinson stoutly resisted this. He made it plain that he was willing to dispose of ship repairing, but that he was determined to retain both merchant and warship building within British Shipbuilders. The balancing of their respective losses and profits made both divisions essential to his strategy for the shipbuilding industry. On this strategy he met with total indifference from the government. Atkinson recalled that Sir Peter Carey, Permanent Secretary, told him explicitly that, 'Margaret wants rid of shipbuilding'.[39] He also found that Norman Lamont, Secretary of State for Industry, was totally unsympathetic to his vision for the industry, believing that, 'Lamont only seemed happy when I had closed down a yard or laid off 500 men'.[40]

Faced with such official intransigence, and personally opposed to privatisation, Atkinson intimated his resignation in June 1983. He left the corporation at the end of August, even though his contract could have run the end of December 1983. By the time he left office, the pressure on British Shipbuilders had resulted in the closure of another seven yards; the disposal of four dry dock facilities, and a number of ship-repair companies. In spite of this, the overall workforce had only been cut by 11 per cent, from 72,700 in 1980 to around 64,400 in 1983. His rearguard fight to retain employment certainly irritated ministers. His efforts kept employment in warship building relatively stable, losing only 1,900 jobs to a total of 23,845 in March 1983. He was less successful in the merchant division, where the workforce declined from 34,245 to 22,573. Proportionately bigger losses were sustained in the smaller engineering and ship-repair divisions, with respective reductions of 47 per cent to 70 per cent to workforces of 3,192 men and 2,625 employees by March 1983.

As Robert Atkinson tendered his resignation in June 1983, the industry was on the brink of dramatic change. The Conservatives were returned to power under Margaret Thatcher on 9 June 1983. They had an increased majority and were determined to push ahead with privatisation. A month later the government passed a new British Shipbuilders Act 1983. This amended and revised the duties which had been set out for the corporation in 1977. The 1983 Act gave the Secretary of State the power to instruct British Shipbuilders to discontinue or reduce its activities, and to instruct the disposal of any facilities of the wholly owned subsidiaries of British Shipbuilders. The 1983 Act effectively introduced legislation which enabled privatisation to take place. This was intended, initially, to implement the return of the warship builders to private ownership, but it also cleared the way for the sale of the merchant yards.

These steps, together with the appointment of Graham Day to succeed Robert Atkinson, signalled a distinct toughening of the government attitude to the corporation. Within a month of returning to power, Norman Lamont as Minister for the Department of Trade and Industry, confirmed the government's intention to privatise the warship yards, and added that the merchant yards would also have to improve their competitiveness.[41] In making this statement to the House, Lamont was clearly spelling out the terms of Graham Day's appointment. Day was later to confirm that he had 'agreed through a two-page letter and a timetable, privatisation plans with the government'.[42] Since Day had resigned as chief executive-elect in 1977, his appointment surprised many, but the out-going deputy chairman of the corporation, Ken Griffin, claimed he had been instrumental in proposing Day, since he had been anxious 'that the next Chairman should be one to give the Industry a chance'.[43] In retrospect, however, Griffin believed that Graham Day had proved to be 'a political innocent, and had no-one to act as [a] political advisor. He took the ministerial line and put it into operation, and that meant savage cuts.'[44] Conversely, G.H. Fuller, the board member for warship building believed it was only with Graham Day's appointment that British Shipbuilders' management began to get a grip on things.[45] Similarly, the board member for personnel and industrial relations believed, 'Day was a breath of fresh air in that he did not conceal where he stood. He told the unions the warship builders were to be privatised, and that was his job.'[46]

When Day took up his post in July 1983, he inherited the developing fiasco of the losses in the offshore division, and began immediately to dismantle it. At the end of the financial year to March 1984, the corporation reported its worst ever trading loss of £161.9 million, £101.3 million of which came from the offshore division. Day was to find that in the four-year life of the offshore division, it had generated losses of £209.2 million, 60 per cent the entire losses of the corporation between 1981 and 1984. Consequently, although the 1983 Act had cleared the way for the privatisation of the warship yards, Day's first act of emergency surgery on the corporation, was to be the privatisation of the offshore yard of Scott Lithgow.

The event triggering this decision was the cancellation by Britoil of the £86 million order for a drilling rig which was already two years late at the end of 1983. An immediate consequence was the announcement of 800 redundancies at Scott Lithgow on 17 January 1984, together with plans to implement a further 2,200 redundancies by March, this then leaving fewer than 1,000 jobs in the yard.[47] In confirming these measures, Graham Day reprised that Scott Lithgow had recorded a loss of £260 million since 1975, and stated that British Shipbuilders was not prepared to ask the government to fund further losses. Day also announced that the corporation planned to sell VO (Vickers Offshore), its offshore technology design company to John Brown Engineering. The disposal of Scott Lithgow followed quickly in March 1984. It was sold to Trafalgar House for a reported £12 million, though the net cost of the disposal to British Shipbuilders came to £71 million. This was said to be roughly what it would have cost the corporation to close the yard. The purchase of Scott Lithgow by Trafalgar House was part of moves it had been making to get into the offshore construction industry. During 1984, Trafalgar House spent around £100 million in purchasing a stake in the B.P. Forties oilfield in the North Sea, and in a UK oil company, Candecca. It had also negotiated a £15 million takeover of RGC Offshore from the British Oil Corporation.

While the privatisation of Scott Lithgow was an *ad hoc* decision, the government moved quickly to set up a coherent framework for the disposal of the warship division. Not only were the core yards of Vickers, Vosper Thorneycroft and Yarrows to be sold, but the corporation was also instructed to sell the smaller warship yards of Hall Russell and Brooke Marine. In addition, the mixed and composite yard of Swan Hunter was to be sold, as was the offshore yard of Cammell Laird, which had previously been a composite builder. The timetable demanded substantial progress in sales to be made between July 1984 and March 1985, with privatisation to be completed by 31 March 1986.[48] It was also confirmed that the loss-making ship-repair yards were to be sold, and that henceforth British Shipbuilders would concentrate on its core business of merchant shipbuilding and the manufacture of marine diesel engines.

As chairman and chief executive, Graham Day was entirely committed to this strategy, believing that 'unless we [British Shipbuilders] could break out some of the businesses that were likely to survive, then [the Corporation] was likely to lose them all'.[49] With the timetable set, Day's implementation of the process was both rapid and ruthless. The small Brooke Marine yard at Lowestoft was the first to go, to a management buy-out, concluded on 9 May 1985. The much larger core business of Yarrows at Scotstoun on the Clyde was next, sold to GEC on 27 June 1985 in a deal costing £34 million. Vosper Thorneycroft at Southampton was the third disposal, again to a management buy-out, on 1 November 1985. There was then a brief pause in activity until Swan Hunter went to another management buy-out on 20 January 1986. With the deadline for privatisation fast approaching, Hall Russell was sold to a consortium, Aberdeen Shipbuilders Ltd, on 14 March 1986, and finally, on 27 March 1986, the process was concluded with the sale of Vickers Shipbuilding and Engineering (VSEL) at Barrow, together with its linked facility of Cammell Laird at Birkenhead. This disposal was to an employee consortium, and was completed only four days before the deadline set out by the Secretary of State in June 1984. Graham Day had delivered the privatisation programme to the letter, and to the day, an extraordinary achievement in such a short timescale.

This piecemeal and rapid disposal was achieved at a loss of £248 million to British Shipbuilders, the selling prices apparently reflecting the market view of the future trading prospects of the companies.[50] The disposals also involved a massive transfer of employment of 30,400 personnel from the public corporation to the books of private firms. This left British Shipbuilders as a rump organisation comprising the merchant yards and some engine builders. The corporation workforce, which had been 40,785 on 1 April 1985, was abruptly cut to 10,013 by 31 March 1986. In addition to manpower lost in transfer, another 372 jobs were lost in the final disposal of ship repairing and general engineering, and in the reduction in headquarters staff.

Such a rapid and dramatic dismemberment of British Shipbuilders could not be accomplished without some disruption and impairment of the management and performance of the corporation. This was inescapable since the privatisation was forced through while the world shipbuilding market remained deeply depressed, and still burdened with over-capacity of between 30 and 40 per cent. World new orders reached only 15.6 mgt in 1984, 12.9 mgt in 1985, and 12.7 mgt in 1986. In this environment the beleaguered British Shipbuilders attracted only 363,000 cgrt of new orders between 1983 and 1986. So intense was competition, and prices so low, that between July 1984 and December 1986 British Shipbuilders was able to take only SIF support of £21.4 million, even though funds of £100 million had been approved. By March 1986 the corporation order book had only 196,000 cgt on hand, a tonnage well below its annual output capability. Such a weak order book inevitably led to gaps appearing in the production programmes of the yards, to impaired levels of productivity, and escalating losses through the under-utilisation of the workforce and of yard facilities. These circumstances are reported to have cost British Shipbuilders some £52 million in the trading year to March 1986, and a further £39 million the following year.[51] The consequences for productivity were also serious. The average annual production rate in compensated gross tons (cgt) per man employed, peaked at 20.6 cgt in 1980–81. It had then fluctuated erratically from a nadir of 12.8 cgt in 1981–82, to reach 16.3 cgt in 1984 and 16.4 cgt in 1986. The comparative performance for Japan was 32.6 cgt per man, double the level for British Shipbuilders.[52] These productivity figures in British Shipbuilders were indeed lower than those prevailing in the industry in the last years before nationalisation. The consequences were also evident in the cost per compensated gross ton produced. In 1984 the cost per cgt in British Shipbuilders was £490; this compared with a cost of £349 per cgt in Japan and of £220 per cgt in South Korea.[53] These huge differentials in productivity and in costs clearly identified the scale of the disadvantage under which British Shipbuilders laboured in trying to win orders in the poor market conditions of the time. This also goes some way to explain government disillusionment with the industry.

With the privatisation programme completed, Graham Day resigned and was replaced as chairman by his deputy, Philip Hares. He then presided over a severely truncated organisation comprising four merchant companies, Govan Shipbuilders and Ferguson-Ailsa on the Clyde, NESL on the Wear, and Appledore Shipbuilders in Devon. There were in addition residual engine building at two sites, at Wallsend, and at Greenock. These were to become Clark-Kincaid Ltd. Three support organisations also remained in the corporation, Sunderland Forge Services at Pallion on the Wear, and Marine Design Consultants with offices at Pallion, and at the Caledon yard in Dundee. The training organisation, British Shipbuilders Training Ltd, survived and remained at Glasgow. Among these facilities, Smiths Dock, part of NESL, was to close, as was the Wallsend establishment and the Troon yard of Ferguson-Ailsa. Consequently, as Philip Hares took over at British Shipbuilders, his organisation had 3,107 employees in the NESL group comprising yards at Pallion, Deptford and North Sands, another 2,349 employees at Govan Shipbuilders, and 348 men at the Ferguson yard at Newark in Port Glasgow. The small Appledore yard employed 638. The three yards scheduled for closure had employed 2,183 men, and when those were gone, British Shipbuilding workforce was reduced to around 6,500.

This geographically dispersed rump organisation was then restructured in three new divisions. First was the 'merchant companies' comprising Govan Shipbuilders, NESL, and the 'small yards'. Next was 'ship technology' dealing with marine design, building technology and estimates analyses. The third division was 'engine builders and regional services' comprising Clark-Kincaid and Sunderland Forge Services. In the new merchant companies division, NESL (North East Shipbuilders) was reincarnated in March 1986 by the integration of Austin and Pickersgill, and Sunderland Shipbuilders together with Smiths Dock, which was scheduled for closure. The small Appledore yard in Devon, and the Ferguson yard on the Clyde were to be operated as a joint unit within the 'small yards' group. Under Philip Hares British Shipbuilders was a small-scale company with its regionally dispersed yards divorced from its former linkage to the profitable warship yards. In this form British Shipbuilders was a marginal and highly vulnerable organisation in the crisis-ridden world of merchant shipbuilding. In effect, privatisation had destroyed critical mass in British Shipbuilders. The decision to transfer the composite or mixed yards into the warships group for privatisation had denied British Shipbuilders the ability to compete for business in a range of niche markets, especially in those for Royal Navy fleet auxiliary supply vessels. The Swan Hunter and Vickers yards could have contributed this capacity. Graham Day initially seemed to have that as an option for the post-privatised British Shipbuilders; in the end that did not happen, and the composite yards were included in those to be returned to private ownership.

This decision reflected not only the antipathy of the warship builders to being included in the nationalised industry, but the determination of the government to retain the maximum possible spread of yards competing for MoD business. The MoD attitude to maintaining competition among the warship-building companies had indeed prevented British Shipbuilders from attempting to rationalise capacity in the warship sector. In pursuit of maintaining competition, MoD continued to relate to each warship yard as a separate entity, as it had done prior to nationalisation. This went as far as MoD delivering tender requests directly to the individual yards, without British Shipbuilders' headquarters having any knowledge of the details. Correspondingly the warship builders regarded the government in the shape of the MoD and the DTI as quite distinct agencies. To a large degree the warship builders saw the DTI as irrelevant and quite separate from their real customer, the MoD.[54] The warship builders consequently saw nationalisation as introducing an irritating layer of bureaucracy which interfered with 'business as usual' with the MoD. Privatisation consequently signalled a return to normal business for the warship builders: a cosy relationship which guaranteed them a protected niche market. While the warship builders saw themselves as special and successful organisations, that was not a universal opinion. Graham Day indeed thought them to be 'probably the least competitive firms, the least efficient, and the most over-manned, and the worst managed'.[55]

This issue of how to maintain competitiveness and improve efficiency in quasi-monopoly organisations also concerned the Conservative administration in relation to the Royal Dockyards. In the 1980s they too were under pressure and in decline. Only Devonport and Plymouth on the south coast, and Rosyth on the Forth in Scotland remained as the main operational dockyards. Collectively they undertook about four-fifths of the maintenance and refitting work required by the Royal Navy fleet, though the major work was that of re-fitting and re-fuelling Britain's nuclear submarines. The Polaris submarines were at that time serviced exclusively at Rosyth, providing work for 6,000 employees, while at Devonport the workforce was as large as 13,000. The remaining one-fifth of work involved auxiliary vessels and small warships, and was open to competitive tender from the privatised warship yards, as had been the case when they were part of British Shipbuilders.

Therefore, in line with the philosophy of maintaining competition for MoD orders, the government was determined to introduce a framework of 'commercial management' through which there would be initiated a four-year cycle of invited competitive bids to undertake the management of each Royal Dockyard. With this as an objective, Michael Heseltine, Secretary of State for Industry, announced in the House on 23 July 1985, that 'contractorisation' was to be the preferred option for the future management of the dockyards. Bidding documents were issued in April 1986 with closing dates of 1 August for Rosyth, and 29 August for Devonport. The Rosyth contract was awarded to a consortium operated by Babcock International and Thorn EMI. At Devonport the contract was awarded to a management team formed as a new company called Devonport Management Ltd (DML). At Rosyth, the new management initially retained the monopoly of refitting the nuclear submarine fleet for the Royal Navy, but in 1993 the government switched this role to Devonport, and announced its plans to privatise the Rosyth Dockyard. The sole bidder was Babcock International who had earlier bought out the Thorn EMI share in the consortium. Rosyth was finally acquired by Babcock International in January 1997. Meanwhile, DML at Devonport inherited the monopoly of servicing the nuclear submarine fleet, and it currently maintains and services the Trident fleet. This specialisation has resulted in the Devonport workforce steadily being reduced to around 4,000 employees in the first decade of the twenty-first century. Consequently by 1987, in seeking to avoid perceived dangers from a monopoly supply from a public corporation, the government had successfully privatised all the warship builders, and moved the Royal Dockyards onto a commercial footing. What remained beyond this privatisation drive was the rump of merchant yards in British Shipbuilders, and across the Irish Sea, the hugely unprofitable enterprise of Harland & Wolff.

After the departure of Graham Day, his successor Philip Hares, quickly found that his emasculated corporation still confronted a highly competitive world market and a scarcity of orders, in which his merchant yards were continuously on the edge of running out of work. At Govan Shipbuilders the yard was nearing completion of a North Sea Ferry order for P&O. It had no other work to follow, although it was trying to attract orders for container ships for China. Similarly at NESL the company was completing two offshore supply vessels for the Stena Line of Sweden, and was in urgent need of new orders.[56] Unfortunately, the ability of British Shipbuilders to win new orders had been rendered more difficult through the introduction in 1985 of the device of the 'Contract Supply Limit'. This stipulated that if orders gained with the SIF, which was supposed to subsidise orders to make them at least break even, made losses, then in the following year access to the SIF subsidy for subsequent orders would be automatically restricted to compensate for the earlier losses. In this deteriorating market the need for new tonnage was also suddenly diminished in 1986 with the failure of the shipping lines of Sanko of Japan and C.H. Tung of Hong Kong. When they were forced into the hands of their bankers many of their ships were off-loaded cheaply onto the already saturated shipping market. British Shipbuilders' chairman, Philip Hares, was unable to respond to this setback, suffering a heart attack at the end of 1986. He was replaced on an interim basis by Maurice Phelps, the personnel director, who acted as chairman until the appointment of John Lister in April 1987.

In spite of this management upset, the board under Hares decided to try to escape from the over-supplied mass market by initiating the development of three specific ship types designed to compete in niche markets. These innovations were to be designs for a multi-cargo products carrier, a refrigerated cargo ship, and a scientific research vessel. These were sophisticated products where the competition for orders would come primarily from neighbouring European shipbuilders, rather than from the mass producers of Japan and South Korea.[57] With these first steps into niche market products, British Shipbuilders began to extend the strategy by beginning work on a new generation of designs for containerships and Ro-Ro vehicle ferries. This shift in market focus was accompanied by a drastic cut in capacity from 200,000 cgt in 1986 to 120,000 cgt in 1987. This was a decision to match British Shipbuilders production capacity to a realistic assessment of its likely market prospects.

These were bold initiatives, but they were not an immediate solution to the need for additional orders. Some easement of these pressures seemed to have been achieved at NESL with the signing of a contract for up to twenty-five Danish ferries, but this in the end proved to be the source of its demise. At Govan Shipbuilders some improvement of the workload was achieved by orders for two containerships for China, although this still left the yard with up to 20 per cent unused capacity. Encouraged by these developments, the new chairman, John Lister, was initially optimistic that he and the board would be able to stabilise the corporation by exploiting these niche markets. This was an optimism also based on the fact that from 1988 there at long last seemed to be some signs of revival in the world order book (Table 8.1). Such hopes were, however, to be frustrated, first by the growing insistence of the government that the merchant yards should be sold, and second by the continuing poor performance of the yards. Between 1986 and 1988 the Govan yard suffered losses of £73.9 million, while NESL turned in a massive loss of £153.5 million. The small yards also made significant losses, the joint operation of Appledore-Ferguson recording a loss of £26.3 million. For the corporation as a whole, losses ran at £168.4 million for 1986–87.[58]

This poor performance coincided with the return of the third Conservative government in June 1987, and seems likely to have been the last straw convincing the government to seek buyers for the remaining yards. Yet, if these loss-making businesses were to attract buyers, then at least in the short run the government had to support them as going concerns. To do this there was an urgent need to increase British Shipbuilders' borrowing powers, and this was done through the 1987 Shipbuilders (Borrowing Powers) Bill. This raised the existing limit from £1,400 million to £1,500 million, with provision for a further increase to £1,800 million. In presenting the Bill to the House, Kenneth Clarke, the new minster responsible for shipbuilding, noted that there was no serious prospect of an upturn in world demand for shipping before 1990. He also observed that in the long crisis that had affected shipbuilding since 1975, the French industry had been reduced to one yard, and that Sweden had abandoned merchant building completely. These allusions to withdrawals from shipbuilding were probably early hints of what was to come in Britain. Referring to the parlous condition of British Shipbuilders, Clarke advised the House that in the trading year 1987–88, the corporation would have to operate within an external finance limit of £118 million, 'and its survival depended on its ability to improve its performance and to reduce its costs'.[59]

With this renewed support British Shipbuilders did win new orders of 244,000 cgt in 1987–88, but neither performance nor costs were improved. Losses reached £110 million, and this was the breaking-point for the government. In April 1988 Kenneth Clarke advised the House that British Shipbuilders was in negotiation with Kvaerner Industries of Sweden for the sale of Govan Shipbuilders, and that another party had expressed interest in the Appledore yard. He also intimated that the government would welcome any serious approach for the purchase of NESL.[60] From this point on, the disintegration and disposal of British Shipbuilders was swift. In May Clarke was able to tell the House there was interest in the Ferguson yard at Port Glasgow, and in the Clark-Kincaid engine works at Greenock. He was adamant that the return of the yards to private ownership was 'the realistic way to secure their long-term future'.[61] These moves were taken in direct opposition to the British Shipbuilders' chairman, John Lister. In giving evidence to the Trade and Industry Committee on 14 June 1988, Lister confirmed that he had been instructed to sell the Govan yard, and that, in his view, British Shipbuilders had little prospect of operating effectively without that yard, and would subsequently disappear.[62] Two weeks later Clarke announced the sale of Govan to Kvaerner Industries for £6.0 million, although other costs including liability for redundancy payments would cost the corporation £19.0 million. Kvaerner not only acquired a very modern yard for little outlay, but in doing so also gained access to Intervention Fund grants for merchant ship orders. Kvaerner, in return, undertook to place orders with Govan for two gas tankers, with an option for a further two. Kvaerner also declared its intent to make Govan its lead facility for the development of gas ship technology. The sale of the Ferguson yard at Port Glasgow followed in December 1988. This was purchased by the HLD Group at a cost to British Shipbuilders of £3.8 million, while the Appledore yard went to Langham Industries at a cost to the corporation of £3.4 million.[63]

At the end of 1988 only NESL was still in British Shipbuilders' hands, and it was in great difficulty with its contracts for the Danish ferries. These had been negotiated very quickly between April and July 1986, the main agent being a Sunderland-based Danish naval architect. He was acting on behalf of a Danish property developer, Henrik Johansson. The deal, signed finally on 18 July 1986, was for twenty-four ferries, all to be delivered to companies controlled by Johansson. These orders seemed likely to secure work for 1,650 men, more than half the NESL workforce, for up to three years, the last ferry being due for delivery in December 1989. However, what should have been a lifeline for NESL soon ran into difficulties. In the autumn of 1986, the first of the ferries for the Stena Line failed to satisfy on a number of technical systems while on trial. This problem coincided with a client, ITM, going into receivership, leaving the contract for a barge in NESL's hands.[64] The ferry was then delivered to Stena Line, but the problems recurred and persisted. The outcome was that in October 1987 Johansson refused to accept further ships. This dispute dragged on until February 1988, at which point British Shipbuilders offered to reschedule the due stage payments in an attempt to re-open negotiations. Receiving no response, British Shipbuilders then cancelled most of the contracts, again hoping to force Johansson to negotiate. This step plunged the corporation into complex and protracted legal wrangling which left NESL in a precarious position.

Stalled on the Danish orders, NESL then attempted to secure an order from Cuba for ten container ships, business valued at £100 million. This, however, was dependent on NESL gaining access to SIF support of £28 million, which the government withheld. The government made it clear that these funds would only be approved if NESL were sold to private enterprise. This resulted in a stalemate in which the government initiated a bidding process for the sale of the yards. On 30 September 1988, it was reported in *The Times* that four bids had been received. Any brief optimism for the future of NESL was soon stilled, for in October Tony Newton, as successor to Kenneth Clarke, reported to the House that, on evaluation, none of the bids had been judged viable or acceptable. On this evidence the government therefore saw no prospect of maintaining NESL in its present form. He had then decided that the yards would be closed progressively as their current orders were completed. In amelioration of the effects of closure, he advised the House that with aid from the EEC, a new enterprise zone would be established in Sunderland.[65] By December 1988 the government had agreed to accept counterpart funding from the EEC to establish the enterprise zone. Since such EEC funding was always a *quid pro quo* for an undertaking to rationalise and reduce capacity, there were local suspicions that, in its desire to escape from the burden of British Shipbuilders' losses, the government had agreed to close NESL to achieve the reduction in capacity required by the EEC as a condition of approving the grant. With the closure of NESL British Shipbuilders then concluded the sale of Clark-Kincaid, Sunderland Forge, and British Shipbuilders Training. These were disposed of in April 1989, and, while residual elements of British Shipbuilders were not sold off until 1991, the corporation had effectively ceased to exist by Easter 1989. Between 1978 and 1988, British Shipbuilders had received total public subsides of £1.27 billion.

## Harland & Wolff

Having successfully sold off the last of British Shipbuilders' yards, the government not surprisingly then turned its attention to the continuing haemorrhage of capital at Harland & Wolff. The support of £60 million sanctioned by the Shipbuilding Industry (No. 2) Northern Ireland Order, 1975, had prevented imminent closure of the now fully nationalised yard, but did not resolve the cancer of loss-making orders. These orders for bulk carriers and tankers continued to dominate yard business between 1975 and 1978. There were eight launches of 1.095 mgt, of which six were supertankers, the others a bulk carrier and a products carrier. In the same period the yard had cancellation of two bulk carriers and three supertankers, all save one being due to the failure of Maritime Fruit Carriers. Even with such setbacks the yard converted a loss of £4.88 million in 1975 to a small profit of £2.59 million the following year. This was to be the last profit the yard was to make. With the tanker orders completed, and new work scarce, losses began to accumulate from 1978 when they surged to £25.45 million. By the end of 1980 they had accumulated to £104.9 million.[66] The yard was then effectively at a standstill, delivering launches of only two small passenger car ferries for Sea Link UK. These totalled only 14,105 gt, the lowest launch tonnage in the history of the yard.

The lack of orders available in the depressed ship market had forced Harland & Wolff to accept orders for smaller but more complex vessels including car ferries and gas carriers. The transition proved to be costly and technically difficult for the yard, and most of the contracts ran badly behind delivery dates. Two product tankers ordered by Furness Withy for delivery in 1978 were only delivered in June and October 1979. Sea Link ferries due in Spring 1979 were not delivered until April and October 1980, both over a year late. Delivery of the more complex LPG carriers was even further delayed. The first due in April 1980 was not delivered until the end of April 1982. It had been the first LPG order placed by Shell in a UK yard for many years, and the long over-run was seriously damaging to Harland & Wolff's reputation. A second LPG carrier was even later in delivery in October 1982.[67]

These deepening problems and the poor record of the yard forced a reduction in the workforce from 9,675 employees when nationalised in 1975 to 7,034 men at 31 March 1982. The loss of large ship business also dramatically reduced the scale of construction activity in the yard. Between 1975 and 1979, twelve ships of 1.2 mgt had been launched, but in the next six years, 1980–85, the eleven launches totalled only 260,169 gt. While these did include two small oil tankers and one bulk carrier, the remainder comprised two passenger car ferries, two LPG carriers and four refrigerated cargo ships. All were more complex ships than Harland & Wolff had previously constructed.

The responsibility for pushing forward with this new direction lay mainly with a new managing director, John Parker, recruited from the board of British Shipbuilders in November 1982, to take up office in February 1983.[68] Parker also succeeded in taking Harland & Wolff back into the naval market. In March 1984 he gained a £30 million order from the MoD for the conversion of a container ship into an aircraft training ship.[69] This was launched in March 1987, and was the first naval ship launched at Belfast for seventeen years.[70] This was followed by controversy when the MoD awarded the yard an order for a new Auxiliary Oiler Replenishment Vessel (AOR) in April 1986. The design had been developed by Swan Hunter as the lead design yard, and they had expected to receive the order for the first-of-class ship. These were considerable successes for Parker, but as early as September 1980 he conceded that even with an order book worth £300 million, the yard was desperate for orders. The workforce had already been cut back to 5,000, and all were facing redundancy if no new orders were forthcoming. In November 1986, Parker confirmed redundancy for 600 full-time and 200 temporary workers with effect from early 1987, with another 500 jobs expected to go during the year. The run-down in employment accelerated in 1988 when the workforce was down to 3,800 by October, with another 500 redundancies forecast. By then Harland & Wolff had accumulated trading losses of £343.7 million between 1978 and 1988, and had consumed £532.7 million in public funds.[71]

As had been the case with British Shipbuilders, the government had had enough, announcing that Harland & Wolff should be sold to private ownership. The first serious approach for the yard came in June 1988 from Mr Ravi Tikkoo, chairman of the Tikkoo Cruise Line. His proposal to the Northern Ireland Department of Economic Development was to acquire the yard to build a lavish cruise liner to be named, somewhat grandiosely, the *Ultimate Dream*. In the course of the negotiations Tikkoo was offered the yard for a nominal sum. If this were to be accepted and followed up with an order for the proposed liner, the government offered then to write off more than £500 million of accumulated losses. In addition it would provide some £17 million in subsidy toward the £287 million cost of the cruise ship. Generous as this was the negotiations collapsed on 19 October 1988.[72] John Parker's response to this disappointment was to propose a management-employee buy-out for the yard. By the end of the month the Parker consortium and two others, Bulk Transport Shipping, a London-based bulk-carrier operation, and UM Holdings, a Turkish tanker concern, were bidding for the company.

The negotiations with three bidders were protracted and indecisive, and it was not until the late entry of the Norwegian ship owner, Fred Olsen, as a backer for the

Parker buy-out, that an agreement in principle was agreed for the sale of Harland & Wolff to the management and employee consortium. The deal announced on 22 March 1989 proposed the sale of the assets of the yard for £6.0 million.[73] In return Olsen was expected to place orders for three 150,000 dwt tankers, work that would provide employment for most of the 2,700 strong workforce for three years. The buy-out was finally concluded on 8 September 1989. By then around 80 per cent of the workforce had applied for shares. They could individually apply for between 400 and 900 £1 shares to help generate the £2.35 million that the workforce had been asked to contribute to the £15.0 million cost of the purchase.[74] The managers were intended to provide £500,000 personally and raise another £2.5 million in loans from banks in Northern Ireland. Fred Olsen's contribution was to be £12.0 million. If these contributions were met, the government undertook to write off the accumulated losses, and then contribute £38.75 million toward the costs of rationalisation, and to cover continuing liabilities of £26.0 million. The government also agreed to provide an advance of £60.0 million of loan stock, this to be repaid when the yard returned to profit.[75] The government also had to pick up the penalty costs of having awarded the first AOR contract to Harland & Wolff, in spite of its lack of experience in building naval vessels, and against the expectations of Swan Hunter. On the sale of the yard the AOR ship had to be transferred for completion to Cammell Laird, and the government had to pay £53.0 million in compensation.[76] This link-up with Fred Olsen took Harland & Wolff back into the tanker market, a market it had struggled to leave behind. The sale of Harland & Wolff also took the last British merchant yard back into private ownership, and with this deal the Conservative government had eventually succeeded in disposing of its unwanted and unloved shipbuilding industry.

## Merchant disintegration

When the remaining merchant yards of Govan, Ailsa, Ferguson, Appledore and Harland & Wolff were privatised by the end of 1989, they were cast adrift as individual marginal producers in a market that was about to embark on two decades of explosive growth. World new orders, which stood at 19.3 mgt in 1989, more than doubled to 46.1 mgt in 2000, and then more than trebled to a peak load of 164.8 mgt in 2007 (Table 8.1). The expansion in ship completions was also dramatic, growing from 13.0 mgt in 1989 to 76.9 mgt twenty years later. With such an abundance of work available, it is a bitter irony that the surviving British yards still struggled with poor order books. They were squeezed into taking marginal orders by the cut-throat prices and quick deliveries of competitors, and especially by the South Koreans. To make matters worse, Britain's ability to compete on price was further weakened as the EEC reduced SIF support to 13 per cent of the ship's cost, and then to only 9 per cent in 1991, before phasing out all subsidy support at the end of 2000. Prospects for survival were consequently poor.

Of the small yards, Appledore was acquired by North East Shipbuilders Ltd and linked to its Austin and Pickersgill yard, to form A & P Appledore International, to specialise in ship repair. Its success led to a re-branding in 1995 as the A & P Group. By 2010 it had become the largest UK ship-repair and conversion company. It operated in three divisions as A & P Tyne at Hebburn, A & P Tees at Middlesbrough, and A & P Falmouth, the largest ship-repair facility in the UK. The other small yards were both on the Clyde, Ailsa at Troon, and Ferguson at Port Glasgow. Neither was a player in the main large ship market, but rather niche producers of small and more specialised ships. Ailsa was bought in 1986 by the West Australian Perth Corporation. It operated between 1986 and 1996 as Ailsa Perth, building its last ship in 1988. It then survived on repair work until placed in receivership in 1996. The premises were then acquired by the Cathelco Group, a specialist in seawater pipe work and anti-fouling protection systems. Under Cathelco, the Ailsa yard re-entered shipbuilding with an order for a ferry, and some landing craft work for the MoD. Cathelco then withdrew from this work in 2000, and closed the yard.[77] Unable to sell the premises, Cathelco agreed a fifty-year lease of the yard to Associated British Ports in 2002.[78] ABP took this up as a convenient extension to their fast ferry service operating from Troon to Northern Ireland. Two years later ABP sub-let the yard dry dock to Greenock-based Garvel Clyde who used it to expand their capacity for repairs, re-fits and conversions. Like Appledore, Ailsa found the repair and re-fit market more secure than shipbuilding.

The only small yard not to slip quickly into ship repair was Ferguson at Port Glasgow. Privatised in 1989 as part of the sale of Clark-Kincaid, the Greenock-based engine builder, it passed into the hands of the HLD Group, which in turn sold a majority shareholding to the Norwegian Kvaerner Industries Group in January 1990. Since Kvaerner had also acquired the large Govan yard, Ferguson did not fit into its plans. It then sold Ferguson in March 1991 to a consortium, Ferguson Marine PLC, for £225,000. A further change of ownership followed in July 1995 when the Ferguson Marine shareholders accepted a bid of £4.9 million from Holland House, itself controlled by the Dunnet family.

In spite of these frequent changes in ownership the Ferguson yard was successful in developing its niche market for small, higher-quality ships, notably in oil-rig supply vessels, fishery protection cruisers, small ferries and mini-bulk carriers. Its weakness was that it was a very small-scale operation whose steel throughput was only around 1,800 tonnes annually. It had no economies of scale available to it and found that it was progressively under-cut by the uneconomic prices offered by cut-throat competitors, notably from Poland and the Far East. Its last ship was completed in 2007, since when the yard has sought work in ship repair, re-fits and refurbishments. It also maintained a small management service, and in February 2010 it won a £3.2 million order to re-fit an accommodation ship for the offshore oil industry.[79] This diversification has sustained a small workforce of around 100, and keeps open the possibility of a re-entry to shipbuilding if circumstances were to improve.

Unlike the privatised small yards, Govan on the Clyde, and Harland & Wolff at Belfast were players in the main shipbuilding markets, though neither had been able to fill their order books. When rescued from closure by being acquired by Kvaerner Industries in June 1988, the cost to Kvaerner was £6.0 million, although the final cost of disposal to British Shipbuilders for contract liabilities and redundancies was between £19 million and £26 million.[80] Govan's workload was initially sustained by Kvaerner transferring two orders for gas tankers from its own Norwegian yard. To meet its undertaking to develop Govan as its main centre for specialist chemical and gas carrier ships, Kvaerner then embarked on a £30 million improvement plan at Govan, involving the construction of a large covered indoor assembly shed, and reducing the operational slipways from three to one. Transfers of two further orders for LPG tankers followed, and by the end of 1991 the re-badged yard of Kvaerner-Govan won another four orders for chemical carriers. Three were for National Chemical Carriers of Saudi Arabia, the other for the Norwegian Sarli Group. These were the first orders not coming from within the Kvaerner group itself. These contracts were concluded with haste to beat the deadline date before the EEC reduced the SIF subsidy limit from 13 per cent to 9 per cent.[81]

Kvaerner was to claim that its modernisation programmes at Govan dramatically reduced the time ships spent on the slipway. When constructed in the open air, hulls spent an average of eighteen months on the slipway. Once the yard moved to the assembly of sections in the covered hall, time on the berth was reduced to twenty weeks. This was said to have achieved a 40 per cent improvement in productivity over the levels common in the yard when it had been acquired in 1988.[82] Even with these improvements Govan made losses in its first two years under Kvaerner, and achieved only a small profit in 1993. By then it had an order book for seven ships, enough to guarantee work through to the end of 1995. Initial job losses of 500 men had been recovered to give a core workforce of 1,700, together with another 300 temporary contract workers. This modestly promising beginning was, however, not to be sustained. Orders proved elusive and at prices forced ever lower by the South Koreans to levels that mainly failed to cover the costs of materials in European and British yards. Consequently, by late 1998, only a decade after being rescued by Kvaerner, Govan was again running out of work, all current contracts likely to be completed by May 1999. The problem was not Govan's alone, for the setback affected the whole Kvaerner Group, which announced pre-tax losses of £100 million for 1998. Expansion had greatly over-extended the group in engineering, shipping and shipbuilding activities, and caused Kvaerner to embark on a major restructuring, involving a complete withdrawal from its shipbuilding activities. Following this announcement of intent in April 1999, the Govan yard was put up for sale. The workforce had by then been reduced to a core of 850 permanent and 250 contract workers, and all were expected to lose their jobs as work on the contracts was completed by the autumn.[83]

Negotiation for the sale of the yard extended over six months, finally being concluded in October by a sale to GEC-Marconi. They agreed to pay £6.0 million for the assets and goodwill, with Kvaerner retaining responsibility for the completion of the last two orders, and for redundancy costs. Just as Kvaerner had saved Govan from closure in 1989 by transferring work from its own Norwegian yards, so too did GEC-Marconi. It quickly transferred work on two naval supply vessels from its VSEL yard at Barrow-in-Furness. A third transfer followed giving Govan immediate work on parts of two amphibious assault vessels, and on the hull of an auxiliary oiler ship.[84] With this change in ownership, Govan was withdrawn from merchant shipbuilding to become part of the Marconi-Marine warship group. This had yards at Yarrows at Scotstoun on the Clyde specialising in frigates, and at Barrow-in-Furness, specialising in nuclear submarines. With Govan now part of this group, only Harland & Wolff remained as the sole surviving large merchant shipyard in the UK.

At Belfast Fred Olsen fulfilled his commitment to kick-start work in the yard by placing the promised orders for three 150,000 dwt tankers. Although the large tanker market was still over-supplied with tonnage, Olsen was on record saying he believed Harland & Wolff could be turned into a profitable builder of small to medium tankers, by leaving the giant producers of Japan and South Korea to fight over the supertanker and large bulk carrier business.[85] This strategy flew in the face of received wisdom among European shipbuilders who were uniformly trying to diversify out of the over-supplied tanker sector. Olsen's confidence in his strategy seemed justified when the result for the first sixteen months of operation of the Belfast yard achieved a small pre-tax profit of £11.7 million.[86] This initial success was followed by the yard securing orders for four bulk carriers, all to Harland & Wolff's own design for Cape Size vessels.[87] These were all of 162,000 dwt, designed to take the Cape route carrying cargoes of coal and iron ore. This flow of orders seemed sufficient to secure employment for the workforce of 2,500 until the end of 1995. Disappointingly, however, the contracts led to losses of £16.9 million in the 1994–95 tax year.[88]

This setback, and the persistence of low prices in the tanker market, led Harland & Wolff to revise its initial Olsen strategy, and try instead to diversify into building higher-value products. Specifically Harland & Wolff began to seek orders in the construction of deep-water floating production platforms and vessels for the oil industry. In the 1980s such a strategy had killed off Scott Lithgow and Cammell Laird, but this does not appear to have deterred Harland & Wolff, and they had early success in gaining a £400 million order from BP for a floating platform and off-loading vessel. The demands these made on the yard for specialist labour and unfamiliar work programmes persuaded Harland & Wolff to sign a two-year contract with Ronstadt, Europe's largest employment services company. Under this arrangement Ronstadt contracted to supply skilled labour for specific tasks, and if Harland & Wolff employees were temporarily laid off, Ronstadt could seek to find them employment elsewhere in

Europe.[89] This initiative allowed Harland & Wolff to rationalise its workforce to a core of 1,750 permanent jobs and another 500 on sub-contracts.

The BP order was followed by two more complex orders from Global Marine, a company based in Houston, Texas. The contracts were initially priced at £180 million each. In order to undertake this work the yard had to increase its workforce to 1,800 permanent and 1,500 contract employees. As had earlier been the case with Scott Lithgow and Cammell Liard, Harland & Wolff found that complex changes made in design during construction, and the extra time involved, led to huge cost over-runs. As a consequence Harland & Wolff sought £120 million in compensation from Global Marine in 1999. This request was complicated when Global Marine refused to make a final stage payment of £23.0 million on the second rig. In response, Harland & Wolff increased its compensation claim to £133 million to cover excess costs on both rigs, but an arbitration award only delivered the company £21.9 million, approximately the sum of the last unpaid instalment on the second contract.[90]

As this disaster was unfolding, Harland & Wolff had bid for, but failed to win, the Cunard order to build what was to become the luxury cruise ship, *Queen Mary II*.[91] This failure meant the yard had no work on hand beyond June 2000. The core workforce, already reduced to 1,200, was then forced to be cut in half by September 2000. This was an emergency strategy to try to match employment to the declining workload in the yard. Both rigs for Global Marine were in fact delivered in 2000, but the huge losses involved, together with the lack of orders, forced the workforce down to only 386 in October 2002. These were at work completing a Ro-Ro ferry for the MoD. This was the MV *Anvil Point*, built on sub-contract for a German yard, and was the last ship to be built in Belfast. It was launched in 2003, after which Harland & Wolff sought to re-deploy into design and service work for renewable energy products, and also into ship repairing. The parent company, Fred Olsen Energy, then renamed the company Harland & Wolff Heavy Industries Ltd. Like all the other privatised merchant yards, Harland & Wolff had finally exited from merchant shipbuilding, and sought a new role in related fields of activity. As with the small Ferguson yard, the strategy did not exclude a future resumption of ship construction, and by 2010 it had secured employment for 500 at Belfast.

The major yards of Govan and Harland & Wolff were effectively out of merchant shipbuilding by 2000. The loss of these left the UK shipbuilding industry with no major merchant builders. This caused the Shipbuilders and Repairers National Association (SRNA), the industry pressure group, to reform and rename itself the Shipbuilders and Ship Repairers Association. The SSA claimed that, although the main yards had gone by 2000, there remained in operation around 50 small yards working at about half capacity, and producing about 25 small ships each year. The consequences of the withdrawal of Govan and Harland & Wolff for the industry are clearly seen in Lloyds Register data on world fleet statistics. In 2003, as Harland & Wolff launched its last ship, Lloyds Register recorded that the UK launched only 13 ships of over 100 gt, a total of 33,000 gt against a world industry output of 36.1 mgt. By 2007, when the Ferguson yard launched its last vessel, the UK industry is recorded as having completed only three ships of 1,000 gt. Small-scale boat building and yacht building will clearly continue in many small yards, but what remains of Britain's former prowess in shipbuilding is now only to be found in the warship-building sector.

## Warship rationalisation

The privatisation of the warship builders between 1985 and 1986 returned seven shipyards to private ownership in a niche market that was about to experience declining defence expenditure with the end of the Cold War following the fall of the Berlin Wall in 1989. The outcome for the companies was fierce competition for orders in a sector burdened by over-capacity, inefficiency and declining demand. Of the seven yards two were small, Brooke Marine at Lowestoft and Hall Russell at Aberdeen. Neither survived in the warship sector. Brooke Marine withdrew from warships work to re-name itself as Brooke Yachts, a company which traded between 1985 and 1992, before going into receivership in 1993. It re-emerged briefly as Brooke Marine Yachts Ltd from 1996 to 2000, and then failed at that time. Hall Russell was also privatised in 1985 and survived for three years, going into receivership in November 1988 with debts of £10.0 million. At that point it had one order under construction, a ferry for St Helena on behalf of the Overseas Development Administration.[92] The yard was then acquired by A & P Appledore who were to complete work on the ferry.[93] After completion in 1990, the yard limped on for two years with some repair work, finally closing in 1992. The A & P Group retained the Hall Russell Dry Dock and operated it under the name River Dee Ship Repairers.

The early elimination of Brooke Marine and Hall Russell left five significant yards in the warship sector. The most complicated of these privatisations was the Vickers yard at Barrow-in-Furness, which had been linked to the failed offshore yard of Cammell Laird for the purposes of the sale, owing to its previous experience in building diesel-electric submarines. This corporation became known as VSEL Ltd. The other yards were those of Vosper Thorneycroft at Southampton, Yarrows at Scotstoun on the Clyde, and the Swan Hunter establishment on the Tyne. Of these, both Cammell Laird and Swan Hunter were to fail between 1990 and 1993. Their path to failure developed from the complex interplay of defence cutbacks, MoD procurement and order placements, and consolidation and rationalisation in the sector. This rationalisation stemmed from the competition among the rival firms of GEC-Marconi, British Aerospace (BAe), and Vickers Shipbuilding and Engineering Limited (VSEL).

When the warship yards were privatised, all save Yarrow and Hall Russell were acquired by management or management-employee consortia. Hall Russell went to a local business group, while Yarrows was acquired by GEC, Britain's largest electronics and communications company. GEC had no previous experience of shipbuilding, but in acquiring the electronics firm of Marconi in 1968, had deployed its GEC-Marconi division in developing defence-related business. The acquisition of Yarrows in June 1985, a specialist frigate yard, consequently took GEC-Marconi into MoD warship business. By 1990 GEC-Marconi had also acquired Plessey and Ferranti, enabling it to move ambitiously into the defence electronics field.

While Yarrows became part of a large and growing electronics and defence corporation, Swan Hunter, in contrast, remained independent and resumed its customary role as a warship builder to the Royal Navy. Between its privatisation in January 1986 and 1990, Swan Hunter was almost completely dependent upon MoD orders. In this period the yard completed the building and fitting out of three Type 22 frigates, *Sheffield*, *Coventry* and *Chatham*. Swan Hunter was also allocated the order for the second first-of-class, Royal Fleet auxiliary (RFA) ship, the *Fort George*, and a batch of Type 23 frigate orders in 1989. Their only non-naval order was for a specialist cable laying vessel for Cable and Wireless, an order obtained in August 1987. These orders provided the yards with work through to 1993, but with the workload on the Type 23 frigates past its peak by August 1992, Swan Hunter had to announce redundancies for more than 1,400 of its 3,600 workforce.[94] The yard's hope of survival then depended on being successful in competition with VSEL for the order for a helicopter carrier, this to be HMS *Ocean*. Swan Hunter's bid to the MoD was £210.6 million, while that tendered by VSEL was £71.0 million lower at £139.5 million. MoD awarded the contract to VSEL on 11 May 1998, and two days later Swan Hunter called in Price Waterhouse as receivers. Not only did MoD reject the Swan Hunter bid, but it also refused to pay the yard £20.0 million it had claimed for additional costs incurred in building the *Fort George*. This had left Swan Hunter without orders, and unable to secure any further working-capital facilities.[95] When Price Waterhouse met with the shareholders they reported that Swan Hunter had debts of more than £40 million. Against this, the book value of the assets was given as £39.2 million, though as receivers they estimated that a sale would at best realise only £6.3 million.

The receivers then negotiated with the MoD to complete the fitting out of the three Type 23 frigates, but even with this work, the workforce had fallen to 700 employed by September 1993.[96] A brief hope of resuscitation was kindled when, though in receivership, the yard was allowed to bid for the order for the re-fit of HMS *Belvedere*. This prospect was linked to the possibility of the purchase of the company by the French group, Construction Mecaniques de Normandie (CMN). This hope was extinguished when MoD awarded the *Belvedere* contract to Rosyth Dockyard whose bid price was £10 million below that of Swan Hunter.[97] In the absence of any new work, the Swan Hunter design team was made redundant in November 1994, at which point the last frigate had delivered. Price Waterhouse had by then achieved the sale of the Neptune yard to A. & P. Appledore, and of the Hebburn yard to Tees Dock Yard. The Wallsend yard was still unsold, but this first re-incarnation of Swan

Hunter had ended in failure within a decade of its re-birth. This was an outcome to which the MoD certainly contributed through its policy of drip-feed order allocation among too many firms, the policy of keeping as many firms in operation as possible to keep competition meaningful in the warship market.

The failure of Swan Hunter left Yarrows as the remaining big player in surface warship building. Vosper Thorneycroft at Southampton was at that time concentrating on the smaller and more specialised mine-hunter market. The other big player in the naval market was VSEL in submarines, with its yards at Barrow, and in Birkenhead with Cammell Liard. When privatised in March 1986, VSEL at Barrow employed around 11,600 and had another 500 at work at Cammell Laird. At Barrow, VSEL had work in hand on the last three of the seven Trafalgar-class nuclear submarines. These were able to provide some work through to 1990, and all were commissioned in 1991. In parallel with this work, VSEL was also building the first of the Upholder Class of conventional diesel-electric submarines. HMS *Upholder* was laid down in 1983, launched in December 1986, but not commissioned until June 1990.

This workload was supplemented through contracts for the four Vanguard-class Trident nuclear submarines. The first three were launched between 1992 and 1995, the last, HMS *Vengeance*, not being launched until September 1998, and then commissioned in November 1999. However, although VSEL's monopoly of nuclear-submarine construction guaranteed some work, it did not ensure either smoothness or continuity in employment. As construction passed its peak demand for labour, VSEL encountered frequent problems in retaining its workforce. In an effort to compensate, VSEL made a serious bid in 1987 to gain orders to build nuclear submarines for the Canadian Navy. In spite of detailed and lengthy negotiations, the Canadian government withdrew in 1989, deciding to remain with conventional submarines.[98] The pressure on work continuity began to emerge seriously during 1990 as work was completed on the Trafalgar-class submarines, and was passing its peak on the Vanguards. The outcome was that VSEL announced planned redundancies for 500 employees in August, and for another 1,500 redundancies from November 1990.[99]

While these workload problems emerged at Barrow-in-Furness, VSEL also faced growing anxiety with the performance of its Cammell Laird yard at Birkenhead. Orders for another three Upholder-class submarines had been awarded in 1986, and VSEL had placed these with Cammell Laird. The first of these three was launched in November 1989, but on the remaining two boats, delays in construction and cost over-runs were escalating. These were so serious that in October 1990 VSEL declared its intention to sell its Birkenhead subsidiary. Cammell Laird then employed 1,900 whose future was then uncertain, though the slow work on the submarines was expected to sustain some employment through to 1993. The situation did not improve, and in December 1992 VSEL announced it planned to close the yard with the loss of the remaining 900 jobs when the orders were completed in 1993.[100] The rundown of employment also accelerated at the main plant in Barrow-in-Furness where redundancies pushed employment below 8,000 by January 1993. Beyond that, as the workload declined on the remaining Vanguard submarines, employment was expected to contract to a workforce of around 6,000 by May 1994, less than half the employment at the peak of work on the nuclear submarine contracts.

At this juncture, the best hope for future employment in VSEL lay with plans for the next class of hunter-killer nuclear boats. Studies to define the nature of this replacement were initiated in 1991, but it was not until July 1994 that the formal bid phase for the project was approved. The work was expected to cost in the region of £2–£2.5 billion. The lure of such a valuable contract attracted the interest of both GEC-Marconi and BAe into what had always been the monopoly preserve of VSEL. GEC-Marconi had a firm foothold in the surface warship market through its ownership of Yarrows, but BAe was an entirely new player in the naval market, though long-established in aviation. BAe had been formed in April 1977 in the nationalisation of the British Aircraft Corporation, Hawker-Siddeley and Scottish Aviation. Fully privatised by 1989 it began a restructuring of its activities. One development in August 1991 involved a joint venture with the French SEMA group to cooperate in bidding for large defence contracts in Europe and in the Middle and Far East.[101] The resulting company, BAe-SEMA, was a fifty-fifty venture with BAe, paying SEMA £9.8 million for its share. This SEMA Group included YARD, the Yarrow spin-off design operation in naval architecture and warships. It was this link that gave BAe a basis for bidding for the work that would come in a contract to build the new class of hunter-killer submarines. Initial collaborative approaches from BAe to VSEL led to a formal bid to acquire VSEL in October 1994. GEC-Marconi responded with a similar bid. The opening bid for VSEL by BAe was for £478.5 million.[102] Two weeks later GEC-Marconi countered with a bid of £532 million.[103]

Inevitably these bids produced an expression of concern over the consequences for competition in the warship sector which caused the Office for Fair Trading (OFT) to refer both bids to the Monopolies and Merger Commission in December 1994.[104] It was not until six months later, in May 1995, that the Secretary of State for Trade and Industry, Michael Heseltine, allowed both bids to be resumed.[105] BAe returned quickly with a bid of £17.7 per share, but was beaten off by a GEC-Marconi counter offer of £21.5 per share, which valued VSEL at £835 million, some 75 per cent higher than the initial offer by BAe.[106] Acquiring VSEL meant that by the end of 1995, GEC-Marconi had emerged as the dominant force in Britain's naval sector, owning both the Yarrow yard on the Clyde and the VSEL submarine complex at Barrow-in-Furness. With this development GEC-Marconi came to control not only the fitting-out work of the third Vanguard Trident missile submarines, but the building and fitting-out of the fourth boat, HMS *Vengeance*. GEC-Marconi was then in pole position to win the contract to build the successor hunter-killer submarines. These were to be called the Astute Class, and the contract for the first three submarines, valued at £2–£2.5 billion, was placed with GEC-Marconi on 26 March 1997.[107]

Although GEC-Marconi's victory over BAe in 1995 excluded the latter from the warship market, the next five years created new opportunities through dramatic changes which affected not only UK defence contracting, but also internationally in America and Europe. The ending of the Cold War after 1990, and the reduction in defence spending in both the USA and Europe, produced a marked re-appraisal of defence strategies and future equipment needs. In this context governments began to encourage moves to rationalise their industries and to reduce capacity. In 1995 the US merger of Lockheed-Martin created the world's largest defence contractor, and this was quickly emulated in 1997 in the merger of Boeing and McDonnell Douglas. These giant corporations dwarfed the UK and European defence firms, and made it clear that similar consolidation would be necessary to enable British and European defence contractors to withstand US competition.

The setback that BAe experienced in failing to acquire VSEL merely encouraged it to broaden its defence-contracting capabilities in other ways. It had not abandoned its plan to be recognised as a prime contractor capable of managing large and complex defence contracts. The European reaction to the US mergers was first to encourage cross-border initiatives to bring about a unified European aerospace and defence company. In 1995 BAe and its German counterpart, Daimler-Chrysler Aerospace (DASA), began to explore this possibility, though formal merger discussions did not begin until July 1998.[108] By then BAe had taken over the UK assets of Siemens-Plessey, and acquired a 49 per cent stake in STN Atlas of Germany, greatly extending its scope and strength in defence electronics and telecommunications. Also, in September 1998 BAe paid SEMA £77 million to buy out its share in the BAe-SEMA venture. All these moves were designed to enhance BAe's position and demonstrate that it could be regarded as a viable prime contractor for both aircraft and naval defence system projects.[109]

The merger discussion between BAe and DASA reached an agreement in principle in December 1998, but this was to be overtaken by changes within GEC. At the end of 1997 the GEC chairman, Lord Weinstock, had retired, to be replaced as chairman by George Simpson. Simpson had been deputy chief executive of BAe from 1991 to 1993, and his appointment was seen by many as an indication of GEC's ambition to absorb BAe. Simpson did embark on a major review and restructuring of GEC which particularly emphasised the desire to increase GEC presence in the USA. With this in mind, GEC acquired the US Tracor Corporation in 1998, a major US defence company. This was brought within GEC as part of Marconi Electronic Systems (MES), the new name for GEC-Marconi. This significant penetration of the US defence market did, however, carry with it the possibility of an American countermove to take over MES. In a move to prevent any such danger, and simultaneously being opposed to any trans-national defence merger in Europe, GEC began to look for a stronger partner for MES by putting it up for sale in December 1998. The obvious partner to keep MES as part of a British operation was BAe, and discussions were opened on this possibility. With this opportunity in its sights, BAe quickly disengaged from the proposed merger with DASA. Just as quickly, agreement was reached in January 1999 with GEC to acquire its MES division for £7.8 billion. This merger instantly elevated BAe to the rank of the third largest defence and aerospace group in the world after Boeing and Lockheed-Martin.[110] European Union approval for the merger was obtained in June, and US acceptance followed in November 1999. By this time GEC-Marconi had also acquired the Govan yard from Kvaerner. Since in agreeing the merger GEC had retained the Marconi name, the new group was named BAE Systems (BAES). With this merger, BAES became the dominant producer and contractor in the UK naval market. It had inherited from MES the Yarrow and Govan establishments on the Clyde, and the large VSEL submarine complex in Barrow-in-Furness. The only players in the warship sector still independent of BAES were Southampton-based Vosper Thorneycroft, the Naval Dockyards at Rosyth and Portsmouth, and a briefly resurrected Swan Hunter on the Tyne.

The competitive challenge from the re-born Swan Hunter did not seriously concern BAES; nor did it last for long. In the liquidation of Swan Hunter in 1994, the Wallsend yard was acquired initially by the Hartlepool-based THC fabrication group, which was then taken over by the Dutch Heerema Group, controlled by Jaap Kroesse. He first deployed the Wallsend yard in ship conversion, but then embarked on a £38 million modernisation programme which included building a large floating dock and a covered assembly hall. These facilities attracted the interest of the MoD which, always eager to encourage competition in the warship sector, allocated Swan Hunter two orders for the new Bay-class Alternative Landing Ship Logistics (ALCS). Swan Hunter was, indeed, designated the lead yard for the design of the ships. The two orders, each valued at £80 million, were for the *Largs Bay* and the *Lyme Bay*. Swan Hunter also received an additional sum of £62 million to cover its lead-yard services. The orders were placed in December 2000 for delivery in 2004. These complex ships were allocated to Swan Hunter, which had not built any ships since 1993, and the project was to prove fatal for the company. The *Largs Bay* was launched in July 2003, but not commissioned until December 2006, suffering hugely rising costs. The second ship, *Lyme Bay*, was not launched until August 2005 and was then transferred by the MoD to Govan for completion, where two other Bay-class ships had already been built.[111] Costs for both ships at Swan Hunter had by then risen to £309 million, and the yard was then disqualified from bidding for further MoD work. The yard then reverted to ship breaking, and was soon put up for sale by Jaap Kroesse. The equipment at Wallsend was subsequently purchased by an Indian concern, the Bharate Shipyard, in April 2007. The cranes, the floating dock, and other equipment were dismantled and transferred to India by the end of 2007. The site at Wallsend was then taken over by North Tyneside Council and One North East, and what remained of the company was renamed Swan Hunter (NE) Limited. It was to concentrate on providing management support and engineering-design services for shipbuilding and offshore activities.

While the competition from Swan Hunter quickly failed, that from Vosper Thorneycroft was to be much more robust. Between its privatisation in 1985, and 1995, Vosper Thorneycroft operated almost exclusively as a specialist builder of glass reinforced plastic (GPR)-hulled mine sweepers. Its main orders came from the MoD for the Royal Navy, and from export contracts from the Gulf States, especially Saudi Arabia. The product was Vosper Thorneycroft's design of the Sandown Class of mine-hunters. Although concentrating on these vessels, Vosper Thorneycroft twice bid for orders for Type 23 frigates, but lost out on both occasions, in 1992 and 1995, to Yarrows. These bids signalled an attempt to diversify out of their specialist niche market, for even there Vosper Thorneycroft had begun to feel the consequences of the peace divided in the mid-1990s. Diminishing demand there left the yard with only two years' work on the books by 1998. This situation effectively pushed Vosper Thorneycroft into trying to get a share of the work in what was to become the Type 45 destroyer (Daring-class) contracts. To equip itself to build this large ship, the company initially planned to invest £10 million in extending and modernising its Woolston yard at Southampton.[112] This ambition inevitably took the small concern of Vosper Thorneycroft into direct competition with GEC-Marconi, then the dominant producer, who was confirmed as prime contractor for the Type 45 project in November 1999.[113] Since the BAe and MES merger was also concluded in November, it was BAES who became the prime contractor.

While the MoD confirmed BAES as prime contractor and design authority for the Type 45, it also acted to sustain competition for the orders by allocating the second of the first three Type 45 orders to Vosper Thorneycroft. This success then prompted Vosper Thorneycroft to put aside its plans to modernise its Woolston yard in favour of moving its business from Southampton to a larger site within the Devonport Dockyard at Portsmouth, where it planned to build a new, modern yard.[114] MoD's action in sharing out work on the Type 45 infuriated BAEs chief executive, John Weston, who publicly argued that BAES could not meet MoD price targets if part of the work went to Vosper Thorneycroft. The war of words intensified when MoD announced in July 2001 that it would place another three orders for the Type 45, and that it still planned to fulfil the project plan of building twelve Type 45s. In an attempt to squeeze out Vosper Thorneycroft, BAES offered to build all twelve ships at advantageous prices. If this were accepted, the consequences for Vosper Thorneycroft would have been disastrous, since the cost of building the new yard at Portsmouth made it vital to have access to the Type 45 programme. The acrimony generated by BAES's tactics did not help its cause, and Geoff Hoon as Secretary of State resisted BAES's claims and confirmed the allocation of work to Vosper Thorneycroft.[115] The steel for the first-of-class Type 45, HMS *Daring*, was not cut until March 2003, by which time the arrangement for sharing the work had changed. As construction began, all the ships were to be built in blocks in each of BAES's Clyde yards and in Vosper Thorneycroft's (now known as VT) new yard in Portsmouth which opened in spring 2003. VT was to be responsible for blocks

E/F, the bridge to bow sections and for the funnels and masts. These were then to be taken by barge to the Clyde to be joined to the other blocks in the Govan yard. The MoD had also decided that for ships 2–6, all the blocks from VT and BAES would be assembled at the VSEL complex in Barrow-in-Furness. The increased costs of this allocation later caused BAES to transfer assembly back to the Clyde, since the Barrow workforce did not match the Govan performance on the Type 45s.

Important as the Type 45 contracts were, the main objective of the competing firms post-2000 was to gain a share of work in the project for the future carrier (CVF) programme. The 1998 Strategic Defence Review had focused on the nation's need to create deployable expeditionary forces which would have full operational capabilities, effective at considerable distances from the UK home base.[116] One decision in support of this strategy was the plan to build two new aircraft carriers. These were to be designed as mobile airbases and able to enhance UK strategic sea and air capabilities.[117]

Competing project teams were set up by BAES, and an emerging rival Thales UK, a British division of a French defence corporation. The newly ambitious VT had some involvement in both project teams. The design competition for the CVF was concluded in November 2002, by which time the MoD had decided that the scale of the project was beyond the capability of any single company. This conclusion coincided in 2002 with the publication of the government's Defence Industrial Policy (DIP), a precursor of what was to be the more influential Defence Industrial Strategy (DIS) published in 2005. The DIP aimed to establish links between government and industry to provide a clearer framework for the defence procurement process. It also made it clear that it was necessary for the government to act in ways to sustain the UK defence industry. This objective was made more explicit in the 2005 DIS, which set out industrial capabilities which government believed were necessary to ensure national security. In the maritime field this was to encourage the development of an MoD–industry partnership. The nature of the partnership was to be such as to maintain a full national capability from concept through design to construction, delivery and support, together with regular upgrade through to eventual disposal. The concept of maintaining 'appropriate sovereignty' in defence contracts was to be a key element in the development of the DIS.[118] The evolution of thinking between the publication of the DIP and DIS was to inform and guide the MoD strategy in developing the future carrier programme. After the publication of the DIP in 2002, the MoD required BAES and Thales UK to work as an alliance in moving the project forward. Under considerable pressure from the government, the Future Carrier Alliance was painfully pieced together during 2003. In this collaboration BAES, as preferred prime contractor, was responsible for project management and shipbuilding, while Thales Naval Ltd was responsible for whole ship design. In addition, representing MoD, the Defence Procurement Agency acted both as a partner in the alliance and as the client. Relationships in this enforced alliance were never easy, the MoD de-selecting BAES as the preferred prime contractor in April 2004, and adding another partner to the group the following February. This was Kellog Brown and Root (KBR) a subsidiary of the US Haliburton Defence Group. KBR was said to be experienced in alliancing, and in coordinating complex defence projects, and was brought in specifically to manage the demonstration phase of the project which was planned to run from February 2005 to June 2007. This MoD addition to the alliance was followed by another in December 2005, this time the inclusion of the VT group and Babcock Marine as full partners.

As the alliance progressed, and the future volume of warship-building work became clearer, the government and the MoD came to believe that their strategy in this sector would be best served through the MoD dealing with one main company as prime contractor and partner. Consequently, pressure began to be exerted on BAES and VT to consider a merger. Since neither was keen seriously to consider such a move, the MoD ultimately made it clear that it would not sign contracts for the carrier programme until it could deal with a single firm. The first serious step towards this came on 25 July 2007 when BAES, VT and MoD signed non-binding heads of agreement on how to consolidate the surface-warship sector. The accompanying Terms of Business Agreement, subsequently set out provision for a fifteen-year partnership agreement designed to set out a defined workload of design, build, and through-life support between MoD and the planned merger company.[119] However, while MoD had pressured BAES and VT by intimating a refusal to sign contracts pending a merger, in their turn BAES and VT made it clear that the merger would only go ahead once a firm offer of contracts was given. This counter-move, and growing public concern over the cost of the budget, coincided with considerable opposition in the House, and delayed progress on the merger for a year. It was not until 11 June 2008 that MoD, BAES and VT finally signed the legally binding agreement initiating the fifteen-year partnership, substantially as set out in 2007. It was only then that BAES and VT agreed to a merger, which created BVT Surface Fleet Ltd, on 1 July 2008. Two days later contracts for two new aircraft carriers were signed in Portsmouth on board HMS *Ark Royal*, then the aircraft carrier and flagship of the fleet.[120]

The contracts allocated work worth £3.0 billion to firms in the aircraft-carrier alliance. One worth £1.325 billion was allocated for the construction of giant blocks for both carriers by BVT Surface Fleet in its yards at Govan and Portsmouth. Another contract for £300 million went to BAES's yard at Barrow-in-Furness, also for construction of large blocks of the carriers. A third contract of £675 million went to Babcock Marine at Rosyth Dockyard for the construction of bow sections and for final assembly of the ships, while Thales UK had £425 million to cover design and engineering work. Last, a contract of £275 million went to a BAES subsidiary, Integrated Systems Technology (Insyte), for the supply of mission systems. KBR, the other partner, had left the alliance at the conclusion of the demonstration phase of the project in July 2007. The carrot of these huge contracts generated in the carrier project had finally produced a significant rationalisation of the UK surface-warship sector through the creation of BVT Surface Fleet in June 2008. That merger was on the basis of a 55 per cent holding by BAES, and a 45 per cent share by VT group. However, in signing up for this, VT had included an exit clause which could be exercised within three years by selling out to BAES. BVT Surface Fleet was barely a year old when VT exercised this option to sell its 45 per cent share to BAES. The sum involved was £340 million, but once VT had met obligations on cost over-runs on patrol-boat contracts for Oman and Trinidad, together with settling inter-company balances and share-dividend repayments, the net sum payable to VT was £298.3 million. The sale was finally concluded by the end of October 2009.[121]

In withdrawing from warships building VT planned to concentrate on developing a broader-based support-services and out-sourcing group, a strategy it had been developing from the mid-1990s. Freed from BVT, VT then attempted to take over the Mouchel Company, an engineering design and business services group, but withdrew from negotiations in March 2000 to try to fight off a merger bid from Babcock International. They were unsuccessful in this and agreed a merger with Babcock on 23 March 2010 in a deal worth £1.3 billion, which created a defence and support services group with sales of more than £3 billion.[122] This move by Babcock followed their earlier acquisition of Development Management Ltd (DML) in June 2007, DML then becoming part of Babcock Marine Services. This acquisition also included DML Appledore, the small specialised shipyard which was then renamed Babcock Marine Appledore. With the acquisition of DML, Babcock regained the refitting and maintenance work for the RN fleet of nuclear submarines, work which the MoD had transferred from Babcock at Rosyth to Devonport in 1993. With these merger moves, and the consequent rationalisation of firms, the MoD substantially achieved its objective of establishing a partnership with one principal contractor. With effect from 2008 this was implemented through the link of MoD and BAES Surface Ships for warship work, and through MoD and BAES Submarine Solutions for submarine work. With these partnerships BAES had also achieved its objective of becoming the prime contractor for UK defence contracts.

Considering the always difficult, and often hostile relationship between BAES and the MoD, this was a remarkable outcome. Tensions and disagreements had constantly been in evidence in both of the main on-going MoD-BAES contracts, those for the Type 45 destroyers, and for the Astute Class of new hunter-killer submarines. At the root of the hostility was constant government and MoD complaints over deficient project management by BAES, while for its part BAES regularly complained over the inequities of MoD procurement policy, and the iniquity of MoD fixed-price contracts. There was indeed much that was true on both sides of the complaints.

On the Type 45s it is clear that the MoD had imposed changes in work allocation, and the switching of assembly work from Govan to Barrow-in-Furness had involved both BAES and Vosper Thorneycroft in delays in construction and in cost increases. In addition, government cut-backs in previously planned expenditure, reflected in the 2003 Defence White Paper, 'Delivering Security in a changing World: Future

Capabilities', had reduced the number of Type 45s to be built from twelve to eight. This was subsequently further reduced to six, involving for a time uncertainty over whether boats seven and eight would be built. This reduction was first rumoured in December 2006,[123] but not confirmed officially by the Minister for the Armed Forces, Bob Ainsworth, until July 2008.

In this tense and unhappy relationship, BAES responded in 2004 by threatening to sell both its warship and submarine yards, claiming that the yards made insufficient returns from the work obtained from the MoD. This dissatisfaction was made public in April 2004, BAES revealing that the warship and submarine division, each with a turnover of around £400 million a year, were small-scale units within the BAES group, which had sales of £12 billion, the naval work contributing only around seven per cent of annual group sales.[124] This threat sparked a very public row between BAES Chief Executive, Mike Turner, and the Secretary of State, Geoff Hoon. He responded by informing BAES officially that, on grounds of national security, the government had the right to veto any attempt by BAES to sell is naval businesses.

The Type 45 Destroyer programme proved to be a protracted and costly project. The first-of-class ship, HMS *Daring*, only had its steel cut in March 2003, and while launched in February 2006, was not commissioned until July 2009, entering service in August 2010. It then suffered damage in collision with a tug in September, only five weeks after entering service. The last of the six built, HMS *Duncan*, was not launched until 11 October 2010. The fiasco of the Type 45 contracts was reviewed in detail by the Public Accounts Committee in 2009. Its report was severely critical of the delays and escalating costs, and was particularly critical of the role of the MoD.[125] It noted, 'the problems of the Type 45 project result from the Department's failure to take sufficient account of the technical risks involved in such a complex project, in its estimates of the likely costs and timescales to deliver, and in the commercial contract which it agreed, which led to a poor relationship with industry'. These failures led to a detailed review of the project and a renegotiation of the contract in 2007, in an attempt to stabilise costs. The PAC also found BAES was at fault in that 'project management arrangements on the Type 45 project were poor, and allowed the culture of optimism to persist for too long'. The outcome of these deficiencies was that when the first-of-class, HMS *Daring*, entered service it was two years late, and in 2009 the project was already £1.5 billion over the original budget.

The Public Accounts Committee report also recommended that the lessons learnt from the Type 45 business should be applied to the Future Carrier project, with particular regard to pricing the contract, and in considering how best to manage it. BVT also drew on that experience when considering the implications for the company arising from the future workload in building warships. The BVT Surface Fleet chief executive, Alan Johnstone, drafted a memorandum to the MoD outlining his thoughts on what the prospects were for work in the warship sector after the completion of the two aircraft carriers. He observed that while these contracts would keep some of BVT capacity employed to 2015 or 2016, there was a renewed uncertainty beyond that. Addressing this probability he suggested that future MoD requirements could be met from a single BVT facility, implying the closure of two of their three surface-warship yards. The memo was leaked on 30 June 2009, and the political response, to what Johnstone then claimed was only 'a worst case scenario', was entirely predictable in the shipbuilding constituencies. It raised a furore over employment fears, a pressure on government to the advantage of BVT. The fears were soon quieted, however, when BVT and the MoD did signed the agreement for the fifteen-year partnership to regulate work, and to begin the planning for the prospective building of the Future Surface Combatant ship, the Type 26 frigate. The Type 26 was to be the planned replacement for the Type 23 frigates, phasing in from 2020. The agreement to sign a fifteen-year partnership deal to build between eighteen and twenty-six frigates at a cost of £3.5 billion was announced by the MoD on 27 October 2010.[126] Under this agreement MoD undertook to provide BAES Surface Ships, the successor to BVT, with a minimum of £230 million each year to generate work for the yards in Portsmouth and on the Clyde. The row over the leaked memo had accelerated the implementation of yet another extended guarantee of work for BAES Surface Ships.

While this appeared to guarantee some longer-term security for the warship yards, a similar guarantee for the submarine facility at Barrow-in-Furness was still out of reach. At Barrow, the Astute-class submarine programme was exhibiting even greater delays and cost increases than the Type 45 programme. The initial contract placed for three Astute-class submarines in 1997 had been priced at £2.5 billion. BAES inherited this contract from GEC-Marconi, and quickly ran into problems. The first-of-class boat, HMS *Astute*, was first laid down at the end of January 2001, but progress was slow, largely because the attempt to use three dimensional computer-aided-design blueprints to detail the work requirements proved to be too complex and were largely incomprehensible to the workmen. By January 2003 BAE reported the programme was in difficulty and already £800 million over budget.[127] An impending impasse between BAe and the MoD was avoided by an agreement in February by which MoD provided £430 million, and BAE another £250 million to tackle the technical problems. Part of the investigation to try to solve the problems involved a contract with the US Navy enabling BAE to draw on the experience and advice of the US company, General Dynamics Electric Boat. This arrangement ran for three years from 2004 to 2007, at which point an increase of £580 million was agreed to cover the additional costs arising from improving the design.

In spite of these expensive delays and technical difficulties, BAE received the contract for the fourth Astute-class boat, HMS *Audacious*, in May 2007, and progress on the contracts was scrutinised by the House of Commons Defence Committee review of Defence Equipment in February 2010. The evidence presented to the committee revealed that the initial contract cost for the first three Astute-class boats was £2.57 billion, but that this was expected to rise to £3.93 billion by March 2010, some £1.35

billion over budget and 57 months late.[128] Despite this calamitous performance, BAES was given the go-ahead for both boats five and six in March 2010.[129] Beyond that the government commitment to build all seven Astutes was confirmed in the Strategic Defence and Security Review in October 2010. The Defence Committee review, while critical of BAES over-runs, did concede that the long delay between the completion of the Vanguard programme, and the commencement of the Astute-class project had involved a serious run-down in employment, and had made it difficult for BAES to re-establish the skill and management base necessary for the Astute contracts. BAES nevertheless secured contracts for all seven of the hunter-killer submarines, and in addition MoD confirmed that BAES Submarine Solutions at Barrow would be the base for the Future Submarines Integrated Projects Team. This was to begin to plan the design for the ballistic-missile submarines eventually to replace the Vanguard Trident missile boats. This team also involved the collaboration of Rolls Royce and Babcock Marine, although cut-backs from the 2010 Defence Review has delayed the timing of this project by five years. This implies that the first replacement ballistic-missile submarine would not be in service until around 2028.[130]

The guarantee on the seven-boat Astute-class programme provides work for 3,500 employees at Barrow-in-Furness and for another 1,500 jobs at other locations. In addition, the lead role for BAES Surface Ships (BAESS) in the Queen Elizabeth-class aircraft-carrier programme, secured employment for some 4,000 in the two Clyde yards, and for another 3,000 at Portsmouth. These combined programmes support some 12,000 jobs, and the work is clearly very important for the UK economy. In November 2009 the Fraser of Allender Institute at Strathclyde University published a report examining the importance of the warship work undertaken by BAESS. In the 2008–09 financial year BAESS had a turnover of £1.12 billion, while that of the entire group exceeded £18.5 billion, the warship contribution being some six per cent of the total. Globally BAES group employed 105,000, of which the warship yards provided employment for 7,000, about 6.6 per cent of the total. The combined warship and submarine divisions employed some 12,000, just over 11 per cent of the global workforce. While these warship and submarine activities of BAES are critical to UK national security, and to the livelihood of local concentrations of employees on the Clyde, in Cumbria, and at Portsmouth, they are not so significant in the context of the global activities of BAES itself.

Given the partnership agreements covering the aircraft-carrier programme, and the projected Type 26 frigate plans, work and employment in BAES seem secure in the short to medium term, certainly to 2014–15. However, the leaked memo on potential future rationalisation of warship capacity has been given a new credibility in the decisions to slow down the carrier programme, and to sell or mothball one of the carriers after only three years in service, and not to equip the remaining carrier with aircraft until at least 2020. The additional delay to planning for the replacement ballistic-missile submarines also adds to the uncertainty. Moreover, the cut-backs announced in the 2010 Defence Review will result in a significant reduction in future workloads and replacements. In 1988–89 the Royal Navy had a fleet of 108 major ships, that is of submarines, carriers, escort and major supply ships. By 2008-09 this had been reduced to 57 major ships, and the 8 per cent cuts imposed across the defence budget in October 2010 could see this reduced further to about 45 major ships in the next four years.[131] The present core fleet of 23 ships has to be reduced to 19 ships comprising six Type 45 destroyers and thirteen Type 23 frigates, the *Ark Royal* having been decommissioned early. In view of these dramatic reductions, and the continuous pressure on government departments to reduce costs and make savings in expenditure, the existing partnership agreements between the MoD and BAES can give no lasting guarantee of work volumes or employment in the decade ahead. It seems certain there will be a further enforced reduction in surface warship building capacity involving the closure of one or two yards. Closure of the Portsmouth yard would clearly improve workloads and efficiency on the Clyde at Govan and Scotstoun. Equally if a Clyde yard were closed and Portsmouth retained, there would be a loss of critical mass on the Clyde, and it is unlikely that a single Clyde yard would long survive. In this forthcoming calculus of capacity, cost and efficiency, the odds may well favour the Clyde with a two yard work load flexibility. Nevertheless a core facility at Portsmouth for surface ships linked to the servicing of the nuclear submarine fleet there could be a workable option, especially if there is to be a severe cut in surface warship construction capacity. This option would also need to be linked to Barrow for submarine construction, and to the Babcock facility at Rosyth for large-scale ship-assembly capacity.

These are the probable scenarios with which BAES, the MoD and government, will have to grapple post-2010. When British Shipbuilders concluded the enforced privatisation of its warship division in 1986, it transferred a workforce in excess of 30,000 into the private warship yards. By 2010 protracted rationalisation has reduced this to barely 12,000. Given the Defence Industrial Strategy commitment to the principle of maintaining national sovereignty in UK defence procurement, one issue for both government and BAES is how much further can the core shipbuilding employment be reduced while still maintaining a national capacity and capability in naval construction. The Defence Review of 2010 and its raft of cut-backs may well be the trigger setting off the end game in the warship sector. That end game was reached for merchant shipbuilding in the UK in 2000. It is not impossible that the end game for a major part of existing warship capacity will be reached between 2015 and 2020, that bringing to a sad end to five centuries of merchant and naval building as major industries in Britain.

# CHAPTER NINE

# Epilogue

In the five centuries since 1500 the life cycle of shipbuilding in Britain has come full circle. In Tudor times it was the emphasis on building ships of war that was the main influence in establishing an identifiable shipbuilding industry. Today, warship building remains as the surviving sector of Britain's once great shipbuilding industry. In the intervening 500 years Britain emerged as the major maritime nation in the world. In the development of the wood and sail industry, war and state protection saw off competition from the Dutch and French, and rivalry from the newly independent United States pushed British builders to revolutionise the design and scale of its ships to drive the traditional craft industry to an apogee of efficiency in the 1870s.

However, it was not the traditional industry in wood and sail that laid the foundation of modern shipbuilding; that grew out of experimentation and innovation in steam and iron. The successful pioneering of the iron steamship transformed the scale and location of the industry, leading to the demise of the myriad small shipyards building wooden vessels, and the transformation of the traditional craft into a complex engineering assembly industry concentrated on the rivers of the North East coast, the Clyde, at Barrow, and on the Mersey. In the thirty years leading up to the First World War Britain's shipbuilders and marine engineers dominated world shipbuilding, their industry again transformed by the rapid adoption of steel in construction, and the innovations of quadruple-expansion engines and turbines to power their ships. To this was added the stimulus of naval demand for warships, and the emergence of great steel and armament combines to dominate the industry. The emergence of Britain as the leading financial power with a great empire and the world's largest and most modern merchant marine gave British shipyards a monopoly market they were quick to exploit. Before the First World War Britain's leadership in marine technology, and in ship design and construction, enabled its shipbuilders to crowd out foreign competition from the domestic market as they enjoyed scale economies not readily accessible to rival nations. At the beginning of the twentieth century British shipbuilding was the colossus of the world industry, its market ascendancy unrivalled by any other country. The British yards regularly launched over 60 per cent of world merchant tonnage, and supplied some 30 per cent of all tonnage for foreign registration. In contrast, no other nation built as much as a quarter of the tonnage launched by Britain's yards. While construction had fluctuated wildly in building cycles, the trend of output had been steadily upward, the industry growing ever larger year on year. All of this changed abruptly between the two world wars.

After the short post-war boom, the signing of the Washington Treaty in 1921 effectively liquidated the prosperous naval market for the private yards, enforcing the larger yards to compete in a cut-throat fashion in a merchant market where demand was weak and contracting. In contrast to the pre-war years, world trade barely grew at one per cent per year in the 1920s, and the wartime-enlarged merchant fleet fed over-capacity into the shipping market, forcing down freight rates and demand for new tonnage. World shipbuilding output was cut in half, averaging barely 2 million tons each year between 1924 and 1938. Britain's main source of orders, the domestic flag fleet, failed to grow while the world fleet expanded by half. Few foreign orders came to British yards. In these two difficult decades British shipbuilders were squeezed between the pressure of excess capacity and weak demand, a toxic combination leading to uneconomic competition and prices, yard closures and escalating unemployment and declining wages. In these depressing conditions Britain's market share declined from 60 to 42 per cent between 1920 and 1938. These difficult years were also ones which confronted the shipbuilders with new challenges and choices, as the motorship and the tanker emerged as new market areas. Foreign builders exploited these innovations more vigorously than did British yards, as Britain concentrated on reducing capacity more than investing in the new developments.

These two developments of weak demand and intense competition greatly weakened the competitive advantages which had taken British shipbuilding to world leadership before 1914. The international competitive environment moved against Britain with the growth in scale and capacity of shipbuilding in Europe and Japan. Moreover, the advantages Britain had derived from her role as the world's main carrier nation and financier weakened, as her merchant marine stagnated, trade volumes slumped, and as the USA displaced Britain as the world's creditor nation. As the demand from the domestic ship market languished, the dependence on the merchant marine for orders became a ceiling on the perspectives and operations of British shipbuilders, encouraging retrenchment and survival over risk taking and growth. By the end of the 1930s the international economic environment was less favourable to British builders, their leadership in technology was diminished, and their dominant market position was under threat.

The declaration of war on 3 September 1939 quickly transformed the condition of British shipbuilding. Wartime demands rapidly eliminated the long deficiency of demand, re-employed unused capacity, and full order books and profitable contracts replaced two decades of uneconomic work. The industry was launched into what became a twenty-year growth cycle, which for the most part was a sellers' market, initially unhindered by competition from the defeated Germany and Japan. Consequently

Britain's shipbuilders were presented with unprecedented opportunities to reconstruct their depleted resources.

In the absence of serious competitors British yards faced a tidal wave of orders from home and overseas, and between 1946 an 1948 launched over half the world's new tonnage, a feat regularly achieved before the First World War. This achievement was made in the context of a world shipbuilding market averaging around 3 million tons per year. This was a scale similar to that before the war, and one in which British builders were comfortable in responding to familiar levels of demand and production. In this sellers' market Britain's builders were able to overfill their order books and to allow them to lengthen in the knowledge that customers had no alternative to waiting patiently in the queue. However, between 1950 and 1958, world shipbuilding output trebled to over 9 million grt, and the world fleet expanded by 33 million grt. In this period world shipping and shipbuilding markets altered in scale in an unprecedented manner, and at a speed which left British shipbuilding standing still, as new shipbuilding nations, and the re-emerging German and Japanese industries, invested heavily in new facilities, capturing large shares of the growing market. West Germany and Japan re-established their shipbuilding with astonishing speed. West Germany launched only 154,000 grt in 1950, but 1.42 million grt in 1958; in 1948 Japan launched 148,000 grt, but in excess of 2 million grt a decade later. Both also added some 4 million tons to their flag fleets, all the work undertaken in their own yards, while the British flag fleet added barely 2.0 million tons in the same period. By 1953 West Germany built more tonnage for export than Britain, and in 1956 Japan displaced Britain as the first-ranking producer. Two years later West Germany pushed Britain down to third place. As a consequence Britain's market share plunged downward from half in 1948 to only 15 per cent in 1958. A century of world ascendancy had been lost abruptly, as alone among major shipbuilding nations Britain failed to expand its output in the post-war expansion of the world industry. While world output more than quadrupled from 2.1 million tons in 1946 to 9.3 million tons in 1958, British output held steady at 1.2–1.4 million tons per year.

When pressed to explain this failure to grow in response to the expansion of demand, Britain's builders consistently blamed post-war government restrictions, especially in the supply of steel, while also complaining of critical shortages of skilled labour. The level of steel supplied was consistent with an output of around 1.2 to 1.4 million tons, but with a nominal capacity of 1.75 million tons said to be available, British builders made no attempt to supplement steel supplies by importation. The steel supply clearly set a ceiling on UK output, but this stability of output seems also to be linked to the shipbuilding market expectations of both the government and the industry in the 1950s. Both were cautious and pessimistic, judging it desirable only to restore the merchant flag fleet to about 18.5 million tons. This again set a ceiling on the scale of orders to be expected which were to be sufficient to match an annual output of a little more than 1.0 million tons, this to be supplemented modestly by some export orders. Strongly influenced by the bitter experience of the 1920s and 1930s, the owners and managers of these decades were still mainly in control after 1945, and clearly favoured stability over growth, and capacity control over expansion. In this context, the loss of leadership to Germany and Japan did not seem immediately threatening. The order books were full and between 1954 and 1958 the industry achieved average annual launchings of 1.4 million tons, its best achievement since the five years leading up to the First World War. The industry seemed to be performing as well as it had ever done, and the shipbuilders seemed confident that they could cope with the challenging changes in markets, products and technology. What confronted them was the growing preference for tankers, the accelerating switch to the motorship, and the more extensive application of welding and prefabrication. Between 1948 and 1958, as these developments impacted on the world industry, Britain did not lag significantly behind competitors in the trend to the tanker and motorship, but unlike her rivals did not increase her scale of production in line with enlarging world demands, this stasis enforcing a loss of market share in both product markets.

The British pace and pattern in adopting welding and prefabrication was similarly less vigorous than in Sweden, Japan or Germany, and in other nations. In Britain, both the product preferences of domestic ship owners, and the stable-state philosophy of the shipbuilders, favoured a preference for familiar products, and dissuaded companies from disrupting production on the berths to enable new techniques and facilities to be introduced in a large scale or systematic way.

Although they opposed expansion of capacity, the shipbuilders did begin to invest in some modernisation. The level of investment between 1946 and 1950 was small, at about £5 million per year, but increased to £8 million from 1951 to 1956, and reached £14 million in 1957, and £18.5 million the following year. Even so, with some notable exceptions, this did not amount to a systematic investment programme for strategic modernisation. Most investment was to improve the capacity of cranes, the improvement and enlargement of berths and quays, and the introduction of welding and plate shops. These were essentially responses to cope with requirements arising from orders for particular types of vessels. In this sense the investment was order-book driven more than arising from a clear strategy. In the 1950s the industry was also experiencing the beginning of serious demarcation disputes arising from the attempts of employers to modernise, to introduce new techniques, and to negotiate new working practices. The benefits expected from the investments were slow to materialise and less than hoped for. A major outcome of this conjunction of circumstances was that British shipbuilding began to exhibit and develop delays in construction and delivery, and to work with a significantly slower building cycle than its competitors. This inevitably led to a widening gap in prices, British tenders in 1958 being frequently some 20–30 per cent above those of the main competitors of Sweden, Japan and Germany. The disparity in building times, delivery and price had become so serious by the second half of the 1950s that the industry admitted that it had acquired among foreign owners a reputation that it could not be relied upon to deliver ships on time, and that if domestic ship owners were enticed to leave the queue in British yards in favour of a foreign builder, it would be difficult for the industry to win them back.

When the twenty-year upward growth of world shipbuilding was halted with the onset of a recession beginning in 1958, Britain's shipbuilders suddenly found themselves translated from a sellers' to a buyers' market favouring fixed prices, one in which some old problems and many new challenges had to be faced. In the absence of expanding demand, excess capacity re-appeared and brought with it fierce competition and price cutting. This mainly confirmed British builders in their long-held opinion that boom was always followed by slump, and in this circumstance expanding capacity exacerbated the problem, and that it was folly to plan and invest for longer-term growth in shipbuilding. Even though world shipbuilding had enjoyed twenty years of expansion, British builders had not gone for growth as had those of Sweden, Germany and Japan. This was a policy decision and a strategy powerfully influenced by the experience of the 1930s. Consequently, as overseas builders invested heavily to meet expanding demand, Britain builders retrenched and kept their fixed capital low in relation to the value of work in progress. As competitors made longer-term judgements about changes in products and markets, Britain clung to a traditional short-term perspective of the nature of markets and demand, and relied principally on retaining long-standing builder–client relationships to deliver orders from British ship owners. Since the second half of the nineteenth century the underlying rationale shaping the investment decisions, product choices and market-sector preferences of the British shipbuilders, was the link of their capacity and expectations for orders to the needs of the British merchant fleet for replacement and new tonnage. This symbiotic relationship had powered the growth of the industry from the steam and steel era, and persisted into the age of the motorship and tanker. This inter-dependence had mainly been advantageous for Britain's shipbuilders. As long as world demand for new tonnage was substantially driven by the orders for new ships from British ship owners, this strategy secured a monopoly of the world's largest merchant ship market for British builders. In the century from the 1850s to the 1950s the equilibrium position of holding the growth and capacity of British shipbuilding in line with the growth and scale of the domestic fleet ensured world leadership for British shipbuilding. However, when the British flag fleet ceased to grow between 1945 and 1958, and as new shipbuilding capacity in competing nations came on stream in the 1950s, the equilibrium strategy that had long supported the ascendancy of British shipbuilding was converted into a dependency trap tying British shipbuilders to a stagnant sector of demand in an expanding world industry.

While the inter-dependency of British builders and ship owners was a two-way relationship, the growing price and delivery superiority of European and Japanese builders gave British ship owners a way out of the dependency on British shipyards, while simultaneously trapping the shipbuilders in the least profitable rump of the domestic market, while their uncompetitiveness gave them no easy means of capturing profitable orders in the world export market for new ships. The strategy of attempting modernisation and seeking to maintain stability in balance with the demands of the domestic fleet in a period of rapid investment and growth in the world industry pushed British shipbuilding into an equilibrium trap from which there was no obvious escape, and set the scene for the industry to suffer an unprecedented and precipitous loss of market share.

The period from 1958 to 1963 was the first significant break in the upward climb of world shipbuilding since the Second World War. The trade recession following hard upon the impact of the Suez crisis combined with excess shipping capacity to drive down freight rates. This recession held world shipbuilding in check for five years, with output averaging barely 8.5 million tons per year. Somewhat surprisingly in this static market, British shipbuilding regained second place in output behind Japan, its access to the still large market of the domestic fleet helping it to maintain an output of around 1.0 million tons. This residual advantage still kept the British order book a little ahead of the Japanese, though the dynamic was shifting rapidly in Japan's favour, their yards capturing the largest share of new orders in the weak recession market, while the British market share had contracted by 30 per cent by 1963.

The recession years of 1958–63 were a critical time for both the British and European industries. British shipbuilding was greatly weakened by intense Japanese and European competition for scarce orders which exposed Britain's problems of price competitiveness and its poorer access to credit support, and resurrected the spectre of surplus capacity. As it struggled to cope, the British industry was subjected to increasing public criticism of its lack of efficiency, its poor productivity, its adversarial labour relations, and the poor quality and performance of its management. As the shipbuilders analysed their situation they clung to their dependency on domestic ship owners for the majority of their orders, and concluded that it was the significant excess capacity in the world industry that was forcing down prices to uneconomic levels. Given the stagnation in the scale of the domestic flag fleet they also concluded that UK capacity was excessive in relation to the foreseeable overall demand from the British fleet. Indeed, they concluded that while the modernisation schemes had improved efficiency, they had come on stream as the recession deepened, and had instead contributed to their perceived problem of excess capacity.

As a consequence of this analysis, the shipbuilders sought assistance in retreating to their inter-war strategies of capacity reduction, price support and contract-allocation schemes. As in the 1930s they believed that the solution was to reduce capacity, and that such a reduction should mainly come from the countries which had increased their scale so vigorously in the 1950s. That was wishful thinking, but at home yard closures did cut back domestic capacity by 15–20 per cent, while overseas capacity continued to grow. In spite of these efforts, British shipbuilders remained trapped in their dependency on the domestic flag fleet, and as the crisis of orders deepened in 1963 their policy of capacity control and reduction was for the first time challenged by the Conservative government. It argued that seeking to reduce capacity to bring it into line with the immediate needs of UK ship owners was not the correct or effective approach to gaining orders. The government advocated that industry policy should focus instead on reducing its costs, for that was the key to improving competitiveness and winning more orders. The price issue reflected the impact of rising costs of materials, equipment and labour, and also arose from the lack of success by the industry in trying to negotiate new working practices with the unions. These efforts stalled in 1962 and exacerbated the growing problem of poor productivity and uncompetitive prices in comparison with its main competitors. Among these, Japan was perceived as the major threat, and British and European builders openly complained of the 'Japanese menace'. This was a shorthand for the belief that Japan deliberately increased its capacity, enjoyed the benefit of cheap labour and government support, and by these means forced uneconomic prices on other builders.

While the Japanese did begin to penetrate the British market, structural changes in the shipping market also weakened Britain's position through the dependence for orders from the domestic merchant marine. In the 1950s the ocean-liner market was beginning to contract in face of the growing popularity of long-distance jet travel. Equally threatening was the growing trend to ship owners ordering fewer but larger ships, this particularly reducing the volume of orders for cargo liner and tramp ships. As Britain's traditional market sectors weakened and contracted, the main growth sector emerged as demand for large-scale tankers, an area in which many British yards had little experience or expertise.

The crisis conditions of 1963, with order books rapidly drying up, presaged government intervention on an unprecedented scale in the run-up to the 1964 general election, which returned a Labour government under Harold Wilson. This also marked the beginning of the end of industry policy focused on the control and reduction of capacity designed to keep balance with domestic demand, and to preserve and protect the independence and survival of the shipbuilding companies. In its place there began to emerge an industry powerfully influenced by public-policy dictates and preference. In need of financial support the industry acquiesced in government-enforced amalgamations and structural changes following upon the Geddes Report and recommendations. Shipyard independence was replaced by horizontal amalgamations producing regional multi-yard groupings, these combining yards with varied and different cultures, products and performance. Alternative strategies of encouraging vertical integration, greenfield sites, or supporting individual companies to develop specialised niche-market products were rejected. The new groups were then encouraged to target their efforts on the growing market for larger-scale tankers and bulk carriers.

These government preferences began to be implemented from 1967, and the new groups began to function in a world market that was expanding rapidly, and entering upon a decade of explosive growth. Between 1964 and 1975 world annual launchings more than trebled to 35.8 million grt, and order books grew sixfold to 133 million grt. In contrast, in Britain the reorganised industry failed to capture a larger market share, and continued to launch around 1.0–1.2 million grt each year, its market share slipping from 10.0 per cent to 3.7 per cent. The dramatic changes enforced in company structures and groupings, in management reorganisation, and in work practices, produced major diseconomies and unexpectedly large costs. And as the groups were forced into taking orders at fixed prices to fill their order books, many then began to suffer significant financial losses. The costs were so large that they led to spectacular failures on the Upper Clyde, at Birkenhead, and across the Irish Sea at Belfast, these drawing in yet more and deeper government intervention. The groups had been caught by the speed of the changes in scale of tankers and bulk carriers which carried these orders beyond the capacity of the medium-scale facilities of the regrouped yards. In response, some like Scott Lithgow, Harland & Wolff, and to some extent Swan Hunter, moved to invest to enter the large ship market. What seemed to be positive policy choices were to be overtaken by the abrupt collapse of the tanker market in the wake of the oil price rises in 1973–74. The next public policy choice in support of the industry was to be nationalisation.

The bitter two-year-long opposition to nationalisation produced a period of uncertainty and a policy vacuum for British shipbuilding, this coinciding with the world industry slipping into crisis. Once achieved in 1977, the government delivered resources but no strategy for the new corporation, British Shipbuilders. In its ten-year existence BS was directed by six chief executives, and was responsible to no fewer than seven different ministers of state. Each chief executive significantly changed the organisational structure of BS, with all the corresponding costs, disruptions and diseconomies. The initial grouping was highly centralised, with poor and extended lines of communication with the management of its subsidiary companies. The pressure from government was to attract orders to sustain employment, while through pressure from the Ministry of Defence, preventing the corporation from attempting to rationalise the warship sector under its ownership. The low level of orders available in merchant shipbuilding also prompted BS to take the high-risk product strategy of entering the offshore market for oil rigs and support vessels. This resulted in disastrous losses, BS central management completely misunderstanding the complexity of the products and the impracticality of existing shipyard and management skills transferring to the new technologies. It was the costs of this failure that ensured that the Conservatives would privatise the profitable warship sector, and seek to cut back on the costs of sustaining the merchant yards.

Under the Labour government the nationalisation objective had been to support the industry to stabilise employment, and to await the expected cyclical recovery of demand. Though warned by Graham Day, there was no recognition that the oil-price rises and collapse of the tanker market, swiftly followed by the contraction of the dry cargo market, and the appearance of massive unused shipping capacity, signalled that shipbuilding and shipping had been plunged into a serious structural crisis of over-capacity and weak demand. When the Conservatives returned to power the public policy agenda retreated from sustaining employment to be replaced by an emphasis on returning warship building to private hands, and enforcing cost, capacity and employment rationalisation on the merchant yards. Without the cross-subsidisation from the warship yards, there was no prospect of BS operating the remaining merchant yards profitably. Indeed in the depressed market conditions, with cut-throat competition from state-supported industries in Japan and South Korea, the weakened merchant sector was unable to meet government expectations. Moreover, with the sale of the warship and mixed yards, privatisation had effectively destroyed critical mass in merchant shipbuilding, and with a decade of subsidy totalling £1.27 billion, the government washed its hands of the industry and disposed of it with extreme dispatch.

In announcing the sell-off of these yards, Kenneth Clarke had claimed that their only hope of survival lay in returning them to private ownership. However, the reality was that they had no hope of any long-term survival in the ferociously competitive conditions in world shipbuilding at that time. As small-scale enterprises in a market dominated by large corporations, with subsidies and aggressive construction policies supported by their governments, the privatised merchant yards quickly failed, or found more security in withdrawing from shipbuilding in favour of ship repair and conversion. The long run-down in employment, and the erosion of design and technical skills under nationalisation, also excluded them from attempting to compete in the growing market for leisure and cruise ships. Only Govan Shipbuilders, rescued by Kvaerner Industries, and subsequently sold to GEC and transferred into naval work, survived from the wreck of British Shipbuilders merchant division. Nationalisation, long desired by the unions as a guarantor of employment and for the survival of shipbuilding, had not been able to secure those aspirations in the cruel conditions in world shipbuilding in the late 1970s and into the 1980s. On the eve of nationalisation, the much-criticised shipbuilding industry still launched its customary 1.2 million gross tons each year. At the end of the decade of huge government support, British Shipbuilders was launching only around 230,000 grt, a mere 1.5 per cent of world production.

In the 1990s only the warship builders continued as representatives of Britain's once-great shipbuilding industry. Here the major market lay with the MoD, which favoured keeping as many yards as possible in play to ensure a competitive field of bidders for orders. In contrast, the warship builders looked to minimise and control competition. The main player in surface-ship construction was GEC which owned Yarrow, Govan and VSEL at Barrow. GEC's main objective was to become the prime contractor for all MoD business. Government and company objectives were completely opposed, and in pursuing its policy the MoD squandered resources in allocating orders to non-specialist yards such as Harland & Wolff and Swan Hunter. Since these yards had long been out of the naval market, and lacked the skills and resources to build technologically advanced warships, MoD's attempt to extend competition produced expensive cost over-runs and contract failures, and maintained excess capacity and inefficiency in the sector. The same desire encouraged MoD to draw the small specialist producer of mine-sweepers, Vosper-Thorneycroft, into competition with GEC, and later BAe, in the frigate-building programmes. The trajectory of the yards in the warship sector was substantially dictated by MoD allocations of orders. While MoD preferred to manufacture competition for its orders, the change in scale of building from the frigate to the destroyer programme, and even more in the Future Carrier Programme, eventually forced MoD to recognise that it needed to deal with a large-scale prime contractor. From this point on the objectives of MoD and the builders edged uneasily closer. BAe had clearly stated aims of competing as a prime contractor, but that outcome came only after MoD supported combines of firms in alliances to plan, design and contract for the two aircraft carriers. The path to agreement was rocky, with public and private policy conflicts between the government and BAe. These were eventually to be resolved, uneasily, when government essentially enforced a merger of BAe and Vosper Thorneycroft to create BVT Surface Ships to manage the carrier programme. This was a short-lived outcome, VT selling out to BAe within a year, BAESS then becoming the sole supplier of surface ships and submarines for the MoD.

This outcome is in essence a contractual partnership between MoD and BAESS, but such a relationship brings with it a legacy of abrasiveness through strains long embedded through engaging in the procurement process, and frequent disagreements over changes in specifications and over-runs in costs. This apparent symbiosis of MoD and BAESS is not in equilibrium. MoD is the sole market for British warships, and BAESS the sole provider. Yet BAE Surface Ships and BAE Submarine Solutions are only relatively small divisions in the global defence company that is BAE Systems. Government policy and power in this sector are constrained by a vulnerability to the ability of BAESS to close or dispose of yards if MoD fails to meet contractual commitments in the fifteen-year partnership agreement. The existing scale of surface-ship and submarine facilities is already close to falling below critical mass to deliver the ships in progress, and any further defence expenditure reductions could cause delays in construction, and gaps in building programmes, any of which could threaten employment and profitability in BAESS. This is a difficult balancing act for government, for turning to foreign builders for British warships is not a realistic alternative. Government intervention did not save the merchant shipbuilding industry, although that in the end was a conscious policy choice by the Thatcher government. In the current drive to reduce expenditure, defence expenditure is under threat. In these scenarios politics and economics are closely intertwined, but may be interpreted differently by BAESS and the government of the day. Issues of nationalism and independence may also complicate the scenarios by the end of 2014. Government policy choices, conscious or inadvertent, could threaten the continued existence of warship building, all that now remains of British shipbuilding.

# Measures of ships' tonnage

Over time there have been many different measures and ways of calculating a ship's tonnage. Mostly these express the volume of cargo-carrying capacity, rather than the weight of the vessel.

## Ship's Burthen

In medieval times it was common to express a ship's tonnage as, say, 100 tons (or 'tuns') burthen. A tun was a wine cask of 252 gallons weighing about 2,240 lbs – our imperial ton – each occupying about 100 cubic feet of ship's space. Hence a ship of 100 tons could carry 100 'tuns' of wine, each of 100 cubic feet in capacity. The simplest early formula to calculate the tonnage was a measure of *length × beam × depth*, divided by 100, the divisor being the unit of 100 cubic feet of capacity.

## Builder's Old Measure (BOM or bm)

From around the middle of the seventeenth century shipbuilders adopted a more detailed measure of calculating tonnage, this again based on length and maximum beam. From 1694 this was standardised as *tonnage = length × beam × depth*, divided by 94. From 1720 BOM was calculated by a more complex version. This 'measured' tonnage was from the Registration Act of 1786 required to be entered in the ship's registration documents, and hence also came to be called the ship's registered tonnage. BOM remained the usual measure of tonnage until replaced by new measures introduced in The Merchant Shipping Act of 1854. These were Gross Registered Tonnage and Net Registered Tonnage.

## Gross Registered Tonnage (GRT)

GRT is again a measure of volume, not weight. It measures the volume of enclosed space in a vessel, one gross registered ton being equivalent to 100 cubic feet of volume. GRT is a statutory measure employed in the registration of the vessel. Merchant shipbuilding output has commonly been expressed in terms of gross registered tonnage.

## Net Registered Tonnage (NRT)

NRT is calculated from GRT by deducting the space in a vessel taken up by machinery, stores, and fuel, and by the ship's company. NRT is again a measure of volume or capacity expressed in tons of 100 cubic feet. It is generally held to represent the fee-paying space available for cargo and passengers. It has also been used for the calculation of port dues, other charges, and for statistics of tonnage entering and clearing from UK ports.

## Deadweight Tonnage (DWT)

Unlike the former measures DWT is a true measure of weight, not of the ship, but of the maximum tonnage of cargo and fuel when the vessel is loaded down to its summer load line. It is widely employed in tonnage statistics relating to cargo vessels, especially tramps, tankers and container ships. It is not usually applied to passenger ships.

## Compensated Gross Registered Tonnage (C.GRT)

While it has long been usual to utilise GRT data as an indicator of the output of a shipyard, and of a shipbuilding industry, comparisons of performance utilising GRT can be misleading. It is widely recognised that it takes considerably longer to build, say, a 50,000 GRT container ship than a simpler 50,000 GRT bulk carrier. GRT makes no allowance for variations in work content in the tonnage produced. Consequently a new measure C.GRT has been introduced to take account of this. C.GRT is calculated by multiplying gross tonnage by agreed coefficients designed to measure the work involved in producing different types of ships. The coefficients are designed to reflect the 'standard man hours' required to produce different types of vessel. These coefficients were first introduced in 1978 jointly by the Association of West European Shipbuilders, and the Shipbuilders Association of Japan. It is now common practice to record national shipbuilding statistics in C.GRT, making possible a more reliable basis of comparison in performance.

## Displacement Tonnage

Displacement tonnage is utilised exclusively as a measure applied to naval vessels. Standard Displacement Tonnage is a measure of the weight of water displaced by a naval vessel when fully manned and equipped, including stores and ammunition, but excluding fuel and reserve feed water.

# Notes and references

## Chapter 1: Wood and sail, 1500–1815

1 William McNeill, *The Rise of the West. A History of the Human Community* (Chicago, 1963), pp. 565 et. seq.

2 Philip Banbury, *Shipbuilders of the Thames and Medway* (David & Charles, 1971), p. 25.

3 Sybil M. Jack, *Trade and Industry in Tudor and Stuart England*, Historical Problems. Studies and Documents, 27. G.R. Elton (ed.) (Allen & Unwin, 1977), p. 97.

4 Banbury, *Shipbuilders of the Thames*, p. 27.

5 Jack, *Trade and Industry*, p. 99. The main providers were Plymouth, Dartmouth, Bere Regis, Exeter, Saltash, Bradford, Bristol, Southampton, Exmouth, Poole, Ipswich, Brightlingsea, Yarmouth, Hull, Beverley, York.

6 Banbury, *Shipbuilding of the Thames*, p. 25.

7 Jack, *Trade and Industry*, p. 99.

8 Banbury, *Shipbuilders of the Thames*, pp. 28–31.

9 'Naval History in Three Periods', *Encyclopaedia Metropolitiana*, vol. VI, 1831.

10 Banbury, *Shipbuilding of the Thames*, p. 34.

11 Banbury, *Shipbuilding of the Thames*, p. 34.

12 Jack, *Trade and Industry*, p. 94, p. 96.

13 Jack, *Trade and Industry*, p. 94, p. 96.

14 J.F. Clarke, *Building Ships on the North East Coast, Part 1, 1640–1914* (Bewick Press, Whitley Bay, 1997), p. 1.

15 Ralph Davis, *The Rise of the English Shipping Industry in the 17th and 18th Centuries* (Newton Abbot, 1972), p. 15 and Appendix A.

16 L.A. Harper, *The English Navigation Laws* (Columbia Press, 1939), p. 326.

17 Richard W. Unger, *Dutch Shipbuilding before 1800. Ships and Guilds* (Amsterdam, 1978), p. 11.

18 J. Clapham, *A Concise History of Britain from Earliest Times to 1750* (CUP, 1951), p. 235.

19 Banbury, *Shipbuilders of the Thames*, pp. 38–9.

20 Ralph Davis, 'English Foreign Trade, 1660–1700', in W.E. Minchinton (ed.), *The Growth of English Overseas Trade in the Seventeenth and Eighteenth Centuries* (Methuen, 1969), p. 92.

21 Harper, *Navigation Laws*, p. 326.

22 *Encyclopaedia Metropolitiana*, vol. VII, 1831.

23 P. Deane and W.A. Cole, *British Economic Growth, 1688–1959* (CUP, 2nd edn, 1969), p. 48, Table 14.

24 Deane and Cole, *British Economic Growth*, p. 48, Table 14.

25  K. Neville Moss, 'A General Survey of the History of the Coal Mining Industry', *Historical Review of Coal Mining* (Mining Association of Great Britain, Fleetway Press, 1924), p. 10.

26  J.F. Clarke, *Building Ships*, p. 3.

27  Ralph Davis, *Rise of English Shipping*, p. 15, and L.A. Harper, N*avigation Laws*, p. 326.

28  Richard R. Brown, *Society and Economy in Modern Britain*, *1700–1850* (Routledge, 1991), p. 164.

29  J.F. Clarke, 'Shipbuilding in Britain about 1800', unpublished paper.

30  Banbury, *Shipbuilders of the Thames*, p. 41.

31  Roger Knight, 'Devil Bolts and Deception? Wartime Naval Shipbuilding in Private Shipyards 1739–1815', *Journal of Maritime Research* (April 2003), p. 6.

32  Banbury, *Shipbuilders of the Thames*, p. 41.

33  Knights, 'Devil Bolts and Deception?', pp. 7–8.

34  Joseph A. Goldenberg, 'An Analysis of Shipbuilding Sites in Lloyds Register of 1776', *The Mariners Mirror*, 59 (1973), No. 4, p. 424.

35  Goldenberg, 'Analysis of Shipbuilding Sites', pp. 424–35.

36  B.R. Mitchell and Phyllis Deane, *Historical Abstract of Statistics of the United Kingdom* (Cambridge, 1962), p. 217.

37  W.S. Cormack, 'An Economic History of Shipbuilding and Marine Engineering', unpublished Ph.D. thesis (University of Glasgow, 1930), vol. 2, Table 4C.

38  Mitchell and Deane, *Historical Abstract*, p. 217.

39  R. Porter, *The Progress of the Nation* (London, 1851), p. 396.

40  Clarke, 'Shipbuilding in Britain', pp. 9–10.

41  Clarke, 'Shipbuilding in Britain', pp. 9–10.

42  Clarke, 'Shipbuilding in Britain', p. 4.

43  Clarke, 'Shipbuilding in Britain', pp. 36–8.

44  Knight, 'Devil Bolts and Deception?', pp. 8–13.

45  Knight, 'Devil Bolts and Deception?', pp. 8–13.

46  Knight, 'Devil Bolts and Deception?', p. 11, for a list of merchant yards building naval ships, 1803–1815.

47  Knight, 'Devil Bolts and Deception?', p. 13, Table: Distribution of warship building by region, 1803–15.

48  Clarke, 'Shipbuilding in Britain', pp. 16–21.

49  Clarke, 'Shipbuilding in Britain', p. 16, for Table 'Shipyards over 50 in 1804'.

50  Clarke, *Building Ships*, p. 43, footnote 1.

51  Deane and Cole, *British Economic Growth*, p. 6, Table 2.

52  Deane and Cole, *British Economic Growth*, p. 156, Table 35, p. 161, Table 36.

53  Peter Mathias, *The First Industrial Nation: An Economic History of Britain*, *1700–1914* (2nd edn, 1983), p. 123.

54  Mathias, *The First Industrial Nation*, p. 102.

55  Mathias, *The First Industrial Nation*, p. 117.

56  Deane and Cole, *British Economic Growth*, p. 185, Table 54.

57  Deane and Cole, *British Economic Growth*, p. 234, Table 62.

58  Deane and Cole, *British Economic Growth*, p. 210, Table 51, p. 216, Table 54.

59  W.J. Bassett-Lowke and George Holland, *Ships and Men*, 2nd edn (Harrap, 1949), p. 124.

60  Banbury, *Shipbuilders of the Thames*, p. 56.

61  Anthony Burton, *The Rise and Fall of British Shipbuilding* (Constable, 1994), p. 49.

62  Banbury, *Shipbuilders of the Thames*, p. 58.

63  Burton, *Rise and Fall*, p. 45.

64  Burton, *Rise and Fall*, p. 49.

## Chapter 2: Two industries: from 1815 to the 1880s

1 Mitchell and Deane, *Historical Abstract*, pp. 217–18.
2 A.H. Imlah, *Economic Elements in the Pax Britannica* (Cambridge, 1958), pp. 96–7.
3 Imlah, *Economic Elements*, pp. 70–3.
4 J.R.T. Hughes and S. Reiter, 'The First 1945 British Steamships', *Journal of the American Statistical Association*, vol. 53, 1958, pp. 362–5.
5 J. Glover, 'The Decline of Shipbuilding on the Thames, "Statistics of Tonnage", and "Tonnage Statistics of the Decade, 1860–70"', *Journal of the Statistical Society*, vol. 32, 1869, pp. 26, 35, 45.
6 Hughes and Reiter, 'The First Steamships', passim.
7 The total internal volume of a ship was divided by 100 cubic feet (a measure of one ton) to give the gross tonnage of the vessel. The further deduction of the machinery and other unproductive space gave a measure of net tonnage. Bassett-Lowke and Holland, *Ships and Men*, p. 126.
8 Banbury, *Shipbuilders of the Thames*, p. 58.
9 Basil Lubbock, *The Blackwall Frigates* (Brown, Son & Ferguson; Glasgow, 1922), passim.
10 John G.B. Hutchins, 'History and Development of the Shipbuilding Industry in the United States', ch. II, p. 27, in F. G. Fasset (ed.), *The Shipbuilding Business in the United States*, vol. 1 (Society of Naval Architects and Marine Engineers, New York, 1948).
11 'Aberdeen Built Ships Project', Aberdeen Art Gallery and Museum website, www.aberdeenships.com
12 Burton, *Rise and Fall*, p. 48.
13 Michael Davies, *Belief in the Sea* (Lloyds of London Press, 1992), p. 60.
14 Bassett-Lowke and Holland, *Ships and Men*, p. 126.
15 *Historical Statistics of the United States; Colonial Times to 1957*, 2nd edn (US Department of Commerce, Bureau of Census, Washington, 1960), p. 448.
16 Hutchins, 'History and Development of Shipbuilding', p. 26.
17 John Scott Russell, *The Modern System of Naval Architecture* (London, 1865), passim.
18 Banbury, *Shipbuilders of the Thames*, p. 160.
19 Fred M. Walker, *Song of the Clyde: A History of Clyde Shipbuilding* (Patrick Stephens, Cambridge, 1984), p. 21.
20 Bassett-Lowke and Holland, *Ships and Men*, p. 167.
21 Walker, *Song of the Clyde*, p. 22.
22 James Williamson, *Clyde Passenger Steamers from 1812 to 1901* (Maclehose, Glasgow, 1904), pp. 348–77.
23 J.R. Raper and I. Buxton, 'Analysis Report of Register File of British Built Ships', *British Shipbuilding History Project* (University of Newcastle, 1992).
24 Porter, *Progress of the Nation*, p. 316.
25 C. Singer *et al.* (eds), *A History of Technology*, vol. 5 (Oxford, 1958), p. 153.
26 Bassett-Lowke and Holland, *Ships and Men*, p. 174.
27 Hutchins, 'History and Development of Shipbuilding', p. 27.
28 Bassett-Lowke and Holland, *Ships and Men*, p. 172.
29 Bassett-Lowke and Holland, *Ships and Men*, p. 175.
30 *Encyclopaedia Britannica*, 1886, vol. 22, p. 517.
31 Fred M. Walker, 'Early Iron Shipbuilding: a reappraisal of the Vulcan and other pioneer vessels', National Maritime Museum, November 1989, p. 3.
32 Walker, *Song of the Clyde*, p. 31.

33 Clarke, *Building Ships*, p. 62.

34 Walker, 'Early Iron Shipbuilding', p. 4.

35 A. Slaven, 'The Shipbuilding Industry', in Roy Church (ed.), *The Dynamics of Victorian Business* (London, 1980), p. 12.

36 A.J. Arnold, *Iron Shipbuilding on the Thames* (Ashgate Publishing, Aldershot, 2000), p. 11.

37 Arnold, *Iron Shipbuilding*, p. 12, and Banbury, *Shipbuilders of the Thames*, p. 60.

38 David Dougan, *The History of North East Shipbuilding* (Allen & Unwin, 1968), p. 38.

39 J. Grantham, *Iron as a Material for Shipbuilding* (London, 1842), p. 41.

40 Arnold, *Iron Shipbuilding*, p. 5.

41 *The Greenock Advertiser*, 1 April 1852.

42 J. Strang, 'Progress Extent and Value of Steamboat Building and Marine Engine Making on the Clyde', *Journal of the Statistical Society*, vol. xvi, 1852, p. 9, Table 4.

43 F. Neal, 'Liverpool Shipping in the Early Nineteenth Century', in J.R. Harris (ed.), *Essays in the Economic and Social History of the Port and its Hinterland* (Frank Cass, London, 1969), p. 146.

44 Arnold, *Iron Shipbuilding*, Appendix 3, pp. 168–86.

45 J. Strang, *Report on the Vital and Economic Statistics of Glasgow for 1858* (Glasgow, 1859), p. 25.

46 University of Glasgow Business Archive, *Alexander Stephen Papers*, UGD 4/1/1, 1859.

47 J.R. Ravenhill, 'Twenty Minutes with our Commercial Marine Steam Fleet in 1877', *Transactions of the Institute of Naval Architects*, vol. xvii, 1877, p. 283.

48 Bassett-Lowke and Holland, *Ships and Men*, pp. 181–2.

49 Ravenhill, 'Twenty Minutes', pp. 283–4.

50 *Encyclopaedia Britannica*, 1886, vol. 22, p. 519.

51 S. Ville, 'Shipbuilding in the North East of England in the Nineteenth Century', p. 21, in S. Ville (ed.), *Shipbuilding in the United Kingdom in the Nineteenth Century: A Regional Approach*, Research in Maritime History No. 4 (International Maritime History Association) St Johns, Newfoundland, 1993.

52 Banbury, *Shipbuilders of the Thames*, Part Four, Private Shipyards and Engine Builders; 1815 onwards, pp. 158–307.

53 Williamson, *Clyde Passenger Steamers*, pp. 348–69; Walker, *Song of the Clyde*, Appendix 3.

54 F. Neal, 'Shipbuilding in the North-west of England in the Nineteenth Century', in Ville, *Shipbuilding in the United Kingdom*, pp. 121–2.

55 S. Pollard, 'The Economic History of British Shipbuilding, 1870–1914', unpublished Ph.D. thesis, London 1951, p. 51.

56 *Stephen Papers*, University of Glasgow Business Archives, UGD 4/16/1, 14 January 1830.

57 Arnold, *Iron Shipbuilding*, p. 25.

58 Arnold, *Iron Shipbuilding*, p. 41.

59 Dougan, *History of North East Shipbuilding*, pp. 55–6.

60 Pollard, 'Economic History of British Shipbuilding', p. 55.

61 *Stephen Papers*, UGD 4/18/7, 1 September 1847, and UGD 4/11/1, 4 August 1858.

62 *Denny Papers*, UGD 3, Journal, 1 June 1859.

63 Arnold, *Iron Shipbuilding*, p. 61.

64 Arnold, *Iron Shipbuilding*, p. 62.

65 Arnold, *Iron Shipbuilding*, p. 74.

66 Clarke, *Building Ships*, p. 122.

67 Ian Johnston, *Ships for a Nation: John Brown & Company, Clydebank* (West Dunbartonshire Libraries and Museums, 2000), p. 42.

68 Johnston, *Ships for a Nation*, p. 56.

69 Pollard, 'Economic History of British Shipbuilding', p. 73.

70  M. Moss and J.R. Hume, *Shipbuilders to the World: 125 Years of Harland & Wolff, Belfast 1861–1986* (Blackstaff Press, Belfast, 1986), p. 37, Table 3.1.
71  Inspector of Factories Return on Factories and Workshops, Cmnd. 440, P.P. 1871, vol. lxii, pp. 23, 40, 102.
72  Slaven, 'The Shipbuilding Industry', p. 117, Table 5.1.
73  *Report of the Select Committee, 1833*, Evidence of Thomas Forrest, Henry Nelson and Edward Gibson, also, Pollard, 'Economic History of British Shipbuilding', p. 9.
74  K. Maywald, 'The Construction Costs and Value of the British Merchant Fleet 1850–1938', *The Scottish Journal of Political Economy*, vol. 3, 1956.
75  Slaven, 'The Shipbuilding Industry', p. 118.
76  Deane and Cole, *British Economic Growth*, p. 234, Table 62.
77  Arnold, *Iron Shipbuilding*, p. 59.
78  *Royal Commission on Trade Unions, 1867–68*, Ninth Report, PP 1867–68, vol. xxxix, Minutes of Evidence, p. 13, quoted in Arnold, *Iron Shipbuilding*, p. 107.
79  Pollard, 'Economic History of Shipbuilding', p. 208.
80  D.H. Aldcroft, 'The Mercantile Marine', in D.H. Aldcroft (ed.), *The Development of British Industry and Foreign Competition, 1875–1914*, University of Glasgow, Social and Economic Studies, 12 (Allen & Unwin, 1968), pp. 326–8.
81  Arnold, *Iron Shipbuilding*, Appendix I, pp. 156–7.
82  Clarke, *Building Ships*, pp. 224–8.

## Chapter 3: Leading the world: the 1880s to the First World War

1  A. Slaven, 'Modern British Shipbuilding, 1880–1990', in L.A. Ritchie (ed.), *The Shipbuilding Industry: A Guide to Historical Records* ( Manchester University Press, 1992), pp. 6–8.
2  Clarke, *Building Ships*, pp. 163–74, for a detailed discussion of the problems and timeline in adopting steel..
3  P.L. Payne, *Colvilles and the Scottish Steel Industry* (Clarendon, Oxford, 1979), p. 57, Table 4.3.
4  Dougan, *History of North East Shipbuilding*, p. 110, quoting Sir Stanley Goodall, 'Parsons Memorial Lecture', Royal Society of Arts, 26 March 1942.
5  Clarke, *Building Ships*, pp. 174–9.
6  D. Pollock, *The Shipbuilding Industry* (Methuen, London, 1905), ch. 4; Clarke, *Building Ships*, p. 208.
7  S. Pollard, 'The Decline of Shipbuilding on the Thames', *Economic History Review*, 2nd Series (1950–51), vol. 3, pp. 77–89.
8  Edward H. Lorenz, *Economic Decline in Britain. The Shipbuilding Industry, 1870–1970* (Oxford, 1991), p. 7.
9  Slaven, 'The Shipbuilding Industry', pp. 122–4.
10  S. Pollard and P.L. Robertson, *The British Shipbuilding Industry, 1870–1914* (Harvard University Press, 1979), p. 34.
11  H.W. Macrosty, *The Trust Movement in British Industry. A Study in Business Organisation* (London, 1907), p. 42.
12  *John Brown Papers*, University of Glasgow Business Archive, USC1/3/6.
13  M.S. Moss and J.R. Hume, *Beardmore: The History of a Scottish Industrial Giant* (Heineman, London, 1977), p. 82.
14  Macrosty, *The Trust Movement*, p. 45.
15  Edwin Green and Michael S. Moss, *A Business of National Importance: The Royal Mail Shipping Group, 1902–1937* (Methuen, 1982), p. 17.

16 Green and Moss, *A Business of National Importance*, p. 28.
17 Green and Moss, *A Business of National Importance*, p. 35.
18 Pollard and Robertson, *British Shipbuilding, 1870–1914*, p. 32.
19 Daniel Todd, *The World Shipbuilding Industry* (Croom Helm, London, 1985), p. 187, table 4.16.
20 A. Slaven, 'Scottish Shipbuilders and Marine Engineers; the Evidence of Business Biography, 1860–1960', in T.C. Smout (ed.), *Scotland and the Sea* (John Donald, Edinburgh, 1992), pp. 186–8.
21 Slaven, 'Scottish Shipbuilders', pp. 188–91.
22 Lorenz, *Economic Decline*, p. 55.
23 A.W. Kirkaldy, *British Shipping; Its History Organisation and Importance* (Kegan Paul, London, 1919), pp. 630–2, and Appendix XVI.
24 *Board of Trade*, 'Committee on Industry and Trade; A Survey of the Metal Industries' (1924), ch. 4. 'The Shipbuilding Industry', p. 273.
25 Pollard and Robertson, *British Shipbuilding, 1870–1914*, p. 31.
26 Hugh B. Peebles, *Warship Building on the Clyde* (John Donald, Edinburgh, 1987), p. 31.
27 Peebles, *Warship Building*, Appendix B, pp. 166–7.
28 Pollard and Robertson, *British Shipbuilding 1870–1914*, p. 219.
29 Peebles, *Warship Building*, p. 58.
30 Peebles, *Warship Building*, p. 81.
31 L. Jones, *Shipbuilding in Britain: Mainly between the Two World Wars* (Cardiff University Press, 1957), p. 8, Table 1.

## Chapter 4: War and depression: 1914–1939

1 Davies, *Belief in the Sea*, p. 96.
2 Davies, *Belief in the Sea*, p. 101.
3 Davies, *Belief in the Sea*, p. 96.
4 Davies, *Belief in the Sea*, p. 97.
5 Davies, *Belief in the Sea*, p. 100.
6 Davies, *Belief in the Sea*, p. 102.
7 Peebles, *Warship Building*, p. 169.
8 *Board of Trade*, 'Survey of the Metal Industries' (1928), p. 404.
9 Todd, *World Shipbuilding*, pp. 111–17.
10 *Board of Trade*, 'Survey of the Metal Industries', p. 404.
11 *Board of Trade*, 'Survey of the Metal Industries', p. 376, and Davies, *Belief in the Sea*, p. 103.
12 Jones, *Shipbuilding in Britain*, p. 27.
13 Davies, *Belief in the Sea*, pp. 106–7.
14 *Board of Trade*, 'Survey of the Metal Industries', pp. 387–8.
15 F. Capie and M. Collins, *The Inter-war British Economy: A Statistical Abstract* (Manchester University Press, 1983), p. 84.
16 F.C. Pyman, 'Shipbuilding Rationalisation', *Journal of Commerce and Shipping Telegraph* (1933), p. 8.
17 A. Slaven, 'A Shipyard in Depression: John Brown of Clydebank, 1919–38', *Business History* (vol. xix, 2, 1977), p. 197.
18 *Shipbuilding Employers Federation and Shipyard Trade Unions*, 'Report of the Joint Inquiry into Foreign Competition and Conditions in the Shipbuilding Industry' (1926), p. 14.
19 A. Slaven, 'British Shipbuilders; market trends and order book patterns between the wars', *The Journal of Transport History*, 3rd Series, vol. 3, 2 (1982), p. 39.

20  Peebles, *Warshipbuilding*, pp. 98–9.
21  S.G. Sturmey, *British Shipping and World Competition* (Athlone Press, London, 1962), chs IV–V, *passim*.
22  H.W. Nordvik, 'The Norwegian Shipbuilding Industry; The Transition from Wood to Steel, 1880–1939', in F.W. Walker and A. Slaven (eds), *European Shipbuilding; One Hundred Years of Change* (Maritime Publications International, London 1983), p. 198.
23  Sturmey, *British Shipping*, p. 75.
24  Slaven, 'British Shipbuilders; Market Trends', pp. 50–1.
25  Slaven, 'British Shipbuilders; Market Trends', pp. 52–3.
26  Slaven, 'A Shipyard in Depression', pp. 195–6.
27  *Board of Trade*, 'Survey of the Metal Industries', p. 371.
28  C.E. Fayle, *The War and the Shipping Industry* (Oxford University Press, 1927), pp. 207–8, pp. 336–40.
29  *The Glasgow Herald Trade Review* (1931), p. 41.
30  *The Glasgow Herald Trade Review* (1929), p. 43.
31  Davies, *Belief in the Sea*, p. 116.
32  Public Record Office (now The National Archives, *TNA*), 'Trade Facilities Acts', File T160, 550/F6930/1.
33  *TNA*, 'Trade Facilities Acts', File T160, 550/F6930/1.
34  *TNA*, 'Trade Facilities Acts', File T160, 550/F6930/1.
35  *TNA*, 'Trade Facilities Acts', File T160, 550/F6930/1. Letter, Niemeyer to Sainsbury, Trade Facilities Act Advisory Committee, 22 October, 1924.
36  *TNA*, 'Trade Facilities Acts', File T160, 550/F6930/1 (1924), Memorandum by the Minister of Labour 'Unemployment in Shipbuilding'.
37  *TNA*, 'Trade Facilities Acts', File T160, 550/F6930/3, 'Notes on a Deputation from Employers and Work People in the Shipbuilding Industry', 15 February 1927.
38  *TNA*, File T160, 550/F6930/3, 'Minutes of a Joint Deputation', 17 February 1927, p. 4.
39  Davies, *Belief in the Sea*, p. 111.
40  *TNA*, File T160, 550/F6930/3, 'Minutes of a Joint Deputation', p. 14.
41  *TNA*, File T160, 550/F6930/3, 'Minutes of a Joint Deputation', p. 19.
42  *TNA*, File T172, 1695, 'Deputation to the Chancellor of the Exchequer', 24 July 1930.
43  *TNA*, File T172, 1695, 'Deputation', 24 July 1930, pp. 4–5.
44  *TNA*, File T172, 1695, 'Deputation', 24 July 1930, p. 15, p. 25.
45  Davies, *Belief in the Sea*, p. 113.
46  *TNA*, 'Cabinet Files A, Parts 2 & 3', 8 December 1930.
47  *TNA*, 'Cabinet Files A, Parts 2 & 3', p. 3.
48  *TNA*, 'Cabinet Files A, Parts 2 & 3', p. 7.
49  Slaven, 'A Shipyard in Depression', p. 201.
50  *John Brown Papers*, Glasgow University Business Archive, UCS1/5/30, 'Letter, Sir Percy Bates to Thomas Bell', 1 December 1931.
51  *TNA*, File T160, 1313/F11798, 'Note to Sir Richard Hopkins', 15 February 1932.
52  *TNA*, File T160, 1313/F11798, 'Correspondence, Sir Richard Hopkins', 15 February 1932.
53  *TNA*, File T160, 1313/F11798/01, 'The Cunard Loan', 21 October 1930.
54  Davies, *Belief in the Sea*, p. 120.
55  Davies, *Belief in the Sea*, p. 120.
56  Davies, *Belief in the Sea*, p. 122.
57  Sturmey, *British Shipping*, p. 110.
58  *British Shipping (Assistance) Act*, 1935, 25 George V, c. 7.
59  Davies, *Belief in the Sea*, p. 123.

60  Davies, *Belief in the Sea*, p. 123.

61  Davies, *Belief in the Sea*, p. 124, and 'First Report of the Tramp Shipping Subsidy Committee', Cmnd, 5004 (1934–35).

62  *Board of Trade*, 'Survey of the Metal Industries', Appendix III, p. 404.

63  *National Maritime Museum* (NMM), 'Memorandum, Section 1, Warship Group', Sir Maurice Denny, Records of National Shipbuilders Security Ltd, SRNA, September 1940, p. 1.

64  NMM, 'Memorandum Section 1', para 3, 'Shipbuilding Conference Development', p. 1.

65  NMM, 'Memorandum', p. 2–3: Note of 10 February 1938.

66  *The Glasgow Herald Trade Review* (1930).

67  A. Slaven, 'Self-Liquidation: The National Shipbuilders Security Ltd and British Shipbuilding in the 1930s', in S. Palmer and G. Williams (eds), *Charted and Uncharted Waters* (Trustees of the National Maritime Museum, London 1981), p. 128.

68  *Bank of England*, SMT/2/280, Letter 11 March 1929.

69  *Bank of England*, SMT/2/280, File 142/4, 24 April 1929.

70  *Bank of England*, SMT/2/280, File 142/4, J. Frater Taylor to Montagu Norman, 20 June 1929.

71  *Bank of England*, SMT/2/280, File 142/4, Letter, J. Frater Taylor to Montagu Norman, 28 May 1929.

72  *Bank of England*, SMT/2/280, File 142/4, Note of Meeting Norman and Frater-Taylor, 29 October 1929.

73  NMM, 'National Shipbuilders Security Ltd', Articles of Association and Deeds of Covenant, 27 February 1930.

74  NMM, National Shipbuilders Security Ltd (NSS), Minutes, 10 April 1930.

75  *Bank of England*, SMT/2/280, File 142/4, Memorandum, H.C. Bischoff to C. Bruce Gardner, 30 May 1930.

76  *Bank of England*, SMT/2/280, File 142/4, Memorandum, 30 May 1930; Note appended by E.D.H. Skinner.

77  NMM, 'Prospectus, National Shipbuilders Security Ltd, 1930.

78  NMM, 'Prospectus, National Shipbuilders Security Ltd, 1930.

79  *Bank of England*, SMT/2/280, File 142/4, 'Servicing the Loan', 10 November 1930.

80  *Bank of England*, SMT/2/280, File 142/4, 'Servicing the Loan', 10 November 1930.

81  NMM, NSS Minutes, 31 July 1930.

82  NMM, NSS Balance Sheets, 1930–39; Annual Returns to the Registrar of Companies.

83  NMM, NSS Minutes, 16 December 1932.

84  NMM, NSS Fourth General Meeting, Minutes, 24 May 1933.

85  NMM, NSS Minutes, 26 January 1933.

86  NMM, NSS Minutes, 23 February 1933, Meeting of Warship and Liner Builders.

87  NMM, NSS Minutes, 27 April 1933.

88  *Bank of England*, SMT/3/282, Personal Letter, Montagu Norman to Sir Andrew Duncan, 18 July 1932.

89  *Bank of England*, SMT/3/282, Letter, Norman to Duncan, 9 June 1933.

90  NMM, NSS Minutes, 23 July 1934.

91  NMM, NSS Minutes, 23 July 1934.

92  NMM, NSS Minutes, 6 November 1935.

93  NMM, NSS Minutes, 27 March 1935.

94  NMM, 'A Review of the Operations of National Shipbuilders Security Ltd: The Position and Outlook at March 1937', NSS Papers, para 9; An Abbreviated version, February 1938, circulated confidentially to members of NSS Ltd, and The Shipbuilding Conference.

95  'A Review of the Operations of National Shipbuilders Security Ltd: The Position and Outlook

at March 1937', NSS Papers, para. 9; An Abbreviated version, February 1938, circulated confidentially to members of NSS Ltd, and The Shipbuilding Conference.

96  NMM, NSS Minutes, 21 October 1932.

97  NMM, NSS Minutes, 12 April 1934.

98  NMM, NSS Minutes, 1 December 1934.

99  *John Brown Papers*, University of Glasgow Business Archive, UCS1/9/74, 'Notes on the Segregation Scheme', December 1937.

100  *John Brown Papers*, UCS1/9/79, Memorandum, Shipbuilding Conference, p. 3, December 1938.

101  Davies, *Belief in the Sea*, pp. 133–4.

## Chapter 5: War and recovery: 1939–1958

1  TNA, MT73/13, 'Note on Control of Merchant Shipbuilding during the War', October 1945.

2  Davies, *Belief in the Sea*, p. 147.

3  TNA, MT73/13, 'Note on Control', para. 12.

4  Davies, *Belief in the Sea*, p. 149, footnote 78.

5  TNA, MT73/13, 'Note on Control', para. 21.

6  NMM, *Shipbuilding Conference*, 'Statistical Summary', June 1945.

7  I.L. Buxton, *British Warship Building and Repair during World War 2* (Centre for Business History in Scotland, Research Papers No. 2, 1998), p. 14.

8  Davies, *Belief in the Sea*, p. 151.

9  NMM, National Shipbuilders Security Ltd; 'yards formerly closed by NSS and now used for shipbuilding', 7 May 1945.

10  Buxton, *British Warship Building*, p. 15.

11  *Ministry of Labour Gazette*, June 1945.

12  NMM, *Shipbuilding Conference*, Statistical Summary, June 1945.

13  *Fairfield Papers*, University of Glasgow Business Archive, 'Profit and Loss Accounts', UCS2/1–6, 1930–36.

14  *John Brown Papers*, University of Glasgow Business Archive, UCS1/21/17, Board Papers; Letter Piggot to Crease on Admiralty Cost Investigation, UCS1/21/26.

15  *John Brown Papers*, University of Glasgow Business Archive, UCS1/5/45, 'Report to the Board', 7 October 1941.

16  *John Brown Papers*, University of Glasgow Business Archive, UCS1/8/22 and UCS1/21/26–27.

17  NMM, NSS Minutes, 1 July 1938 and 13 October 1938.

18  NMM, NSS Minutes, 23 January 1941.

19  NMM, NSS Minutes, 26 April 1941.

20  NMM, *Shipbuilding Conference*, 'Memorandum on the Shipbuilding Corporation Ltd', June 1943.

21  NMM, *Shipbuilding Conference*, 'Memorandum', June 1943.

22  NMM, 'History of the Shipbuilding Corporation', SRNA Circular File 3.

23  NMM, 'Shipbuilding Memorandum', SRNA, Draft TAW/JB, Table P, 4 March 1949.

24  Davies, *Belief in the Sea*, pp. 152–3.

25  Davies, *Belief in the Sea*, p. 156.

26  Davies, *Belief in the Sea*, p. 153.

27  Slaven, 'British Shipbuilders: Market Trends', p. 38, Table 1.

28  J. Foreman-Peck, *A History of the World Economy* (Wheatsheaf Books, Brighton, 1986), p. 271.

29 Foreman-Peck, *World Economy*, p. 273.

30 Foreman-Peck, *World Economy*, p. 280.

31 Peter J. Hillditch, *Management Strategy in the British Shipbuilding Industry, 1945–1986*, Unpublished Ph.D. thesis, University of Kent, 1986.

32 *Lloyds List and Shipping Gazette*, 22 January 1958.

33 *Report of the Shipbuilding Inquiry Committee, 1965–66*, Cmnd. 2937, p. 183 (Geddes Cttee).

34 Davies, *Belief in the Sea*, p. 159.

35 TNA, SC76, MT73, 'Final Report of the Shipbuilding Committee', p. 146.

36 TNA, 'Draft Memorandum on the Control of Merchant Shipbuilding during the War and up to the Present Time', MT73/6, 7 January 1948.

37 TNA, File BT199/5, 'Steel Allocations to the Merchant Shipbuilding and Repairing Industry', SAC 128 (1949).

38 TNA, File MT73/6, 'Shipbuilding Advisory Committee: Steel Allocations to the Shipbuilding Industry', Note by the Chairman submitted for the information of the First Lord [of the Admiralty] and the Minister of Transport, SAC 133 (1949).

39 TNA, File BT 199, 'Memorandum by the Admiralty and Ministry of Transport on the Future Labour Force required in the Shipbuilding Industry', SAC III, Section III, p. 3 (1949).

40 NMM, *The Shipbuilding Conference*, 'Report of the Executive Board', No. 1/53, Thursday 12 February 1953, Section V, p. 8.

41 NMM, *The Shipbuilding Conference*, 'Report of the Executive Board', No. 1/53, Thursday 12 February 1953, Section V, p. 8.

42 TNA, 'Final Report of the Shipbuilding Committee', MT 73/2 (1946).

43 TNA, File BT 199, 'Memorandum by the Admiralty and Ministry of Transport', SAC III, and SAC II7.

44 *The Glasgow Herald Trade Review*, January 1949.

45 NMM, *Shipbuilding Conference*, Executive Board Report, 1/53, 12 February 1953.

46 A. Slaven, 'From Rationalisation to Nationalisation; the capacity problem and strategies for survival in British Shipbuilding, 1920–1976', in Wilfried Feldenkirchen *et al.*, *Hans Pohl, Liber Amicorum, Wirtschaft, Gesellschaft, Unternekemen* (Stuttgart, 1995), Section V, pp. 1128–55.

47 NMM, SRNA, *Merchant Shipbuilding in Great Britain and Ireland*, vol. iv, 1946–50; summary of the value of output, 1946–50, p. 521.

48 Moss and Hume, *Shipbuilders to the World*, p. 360.

49 Hillditch, *Management Strategy*, ch. 3, p. 13.

50 Hillditch, *Management Strategy*, ch. 3, p. 18.

51 NMM, SRNA, *Shipbuilding Conference*, Executive Board Reports, No. 1/53, p. 5, Thursday 12 February 1953.

52 Todd, *World Shipbuilding*, p. 170.

53 *Department of Scientific and Industrial Research*, 'Report on the Research and Development Requirements of the Shipbuilding Industry' (1960), p. 4.

54 J.R. Parkinson, *The Economics of Shipbuilding in the United Kingdom* (Cambridge, 1960), p. 88.

55 NMM, SRNA, *Merchant Shipbuilding in Great Britain and Northern Ireland*, vol. v, 1951–55, pp. 303–4.

56 *The Glasgow Herald Trade Review*, January 1950.

57 NMM, SRNA, *Merchant Shipbuilding*, vol. v, 1951–55, Summary of the value of output 1951–55, showing principal types of ships, p. 437, p. 441.

58 Davies, *Belief in the Sea*, p. 58.

59 *Report of the Committee of Inquiry into Shipping*, 1970, Cmnd. 4337, para. 64 (Rochdale Report).

60 Davies, *Belief in the Sea*, p. 164.

61 Davies, *Belief in the Sea*, p. 164 and Rochdale Report, Cmnd. 4337, paras 499 and 573.

62  J. Ramsay Gebbie, 'Shipbuilding: Five Years of Achievement', *Lloyds List Annual Review*, 1950.

63  TNA, MT73/6, Shipbuilding Advisory Committee, December 1948.

64  NMM, SRNA, 'Minutes of an Informal Meeting of Shipbuilders from North West European Countries', Thursday 21 June 1951, Agenda point 5; statement by Sir Amos Ayre, pp. 6–7.

65  *The Times*, London, 4 December 1953.

66  Parkinson, *Economics of Shipbuilding*, pp. 208–9.

67  A.H. Whyte, *The Glasgow Herald Trade Review*, January 1951.

68  *Lloyds List and Shipping Gazette*, 'Disappointing year for UK yards', 22 January 1958.

69  *Lloyds List and Shipping Gazette*, 'The Shipyard Outlook', 23 July 1958.

70  T. Chida and P.N. Davies, *The Japanese Shipping and Shipbuilding Industries: A History of Their Modern Growth* (Athlone Press, London 1990), p. 114.

71  E.H. Lorenz, *Economic Decline*, p. 81.

72  *Fairplay*, 10 January 1957.

73  *The Financial Times*, London, 'A Sharp Upturn', 24 July 1957. *F.T. Historical Archive, 1888–2006* (Gale Cengage Learning).

74  G. Cameron, 'Post-war strikes in the North-East shipbuilding and shiprepairing industry, 1946–1961', *British Journal of the Industrial Relations*, vol. 2 (1964), p. 22.

75  NMM, *Shipbuilding Conference*, 'Memorandum. The Present Position of the British Shipbuilding Industry', Executive Board Report No. 1/53, 23 February 1953.

76  *The Times*, 4 December 1953.

77  *The Times*, 2 October 1957.

78  NMM, *Shipbuilding Conference*, 'Meeting of the Shipbuilding Conference and Shipbuilding Employers Federation with Confederation of Shipbuilding and Engineering Unions', 14 January 1959.

79  *The Economist*, 'Export Credits for Exports', 5 December 1953.

80  Hillditch, *Management Strategy*, ch. 3, p. 3.

81  H. Gerrish Smith and L.C. Brown, 'Shipyard Statistics', in Fassett (ed.), *The Shipbuilding Business*, vol. 1, pp. 99–103.

82  K. Olsson, 'Tankers and Technical Development in the Swedish Shipbuilding Industry', in J. Kuuse and A. Slaven (eds), *Scottish and Scandinavian Shipbuilding: Development Problems in Historical Perspective* (University of Goteborg, 1980), p. 69.

83  Hillditch, *Management Strategy*, ch. 3, p. 3.

84  D. McKeown, 'Welding, the Quiet Revolution', in F.M. Walker and A. Slaven (eds), *European Shipbuilding: One Hundred Years of Change* (Maritime Publications International, London, 1983), p. 103.

85  Hillditch, *Management Strategy*, ch. 3, p. 10.

86  R.T. Harrison, *Industrial Organisation and Changing Technology in UK Shipbuilding* (Gower Publishing, Avebury, 1990), p. 105; see also J. McGoldrick, 'Industrial Relations and The Division of Labour in the Shipbuilding Industry since the War', *British Journal of Industrial Relations*, vol. 21, pp. 197–220.

87  Lorenz, *Economic Decline*, p. 106.

88  J.M. Goldrick, 'Crisis and the Division of Labour; Clydeside Shipbuilding in the Inter-war Period', in T. Dickson (ed.), *Capital and Class in Scotland* (Edinburgh, 1982), pp. 78–9.

89  Lorenz, *Economic Decline*, p. 112.

90  Slaven, 'British Shipbuilders: Market Trends', p. 44.

91  Slaven, 'British Shipbuilders: Market Trends', p. 41.

92  *Lloyds Register of Shipping*. Annual Summaries, 1946–58.

93  Parkinson, *Economics of Shipbuilding*, p. 31.

94 *The Glasgow Herald Trade Review*, January 1958; also, Hillditch, *Management Strategy*, ch. 3, p. 27.

## Chapter 6: Deterioration: 1958–1963

1 *American Bureau of Shipping*, 'Bulletin', 1958.

2 *British Shipping Statistics*, 1976–77, Table 6.1 (Chamber of Shipping, London, 1977).

3 *British Shipping Statistics*, 1976–77, p. 146.

4 *British Shipping Statistics*, 1976–77, p. 73, Table 3C.

5 *Shipbuilding Inquiry Committee, 1965–66: Report* (London, 1966), Cmnd. 2937, p. 172 (The Geddes Committee).

6 NMM, 'Shipyards closed down etc. since 1945', NSS Files. SRNA Papers.

7 TNA, *Shipbuilding Advisory Committee*, File BT 199/1, Minutes of the 49th meeting, 26 September 1957.

8 NMM, *Shipbuilding Conference*, 'Meeting of Executive Board, 11 February 1959, 'State of the Industry'; Result of a Special Enquiry to Member Firms on the Firmness of the Order Book. SRNA File S42/6/1.

9 NMM, *Shipbuilding Conference*, 'Agenda for Policy Committee, Wednesday 12 November 1958'. SRNA File 5028.

10 NMM, *Shipbuilding Conference*, 'Agenda for Policy Committee, Wednesday 12 November 1958'. SRNA File 5028.

11 NMM, *Shipbuilding Conference*, 'Meeting of Policy Committee, 12 November 1958; Paper B, 'The Shipbuilding Industry Between 1920 and 1958'. SRNA File 5028.

12 NMM, *Shipbuilding Conference*, Meeting of Executive Board, 11 February 1959, 'State of the Industry'. SRNA File S42/6/1.

13 NMM, *Shipbuilding Conference*, Meeting of Executive Board, 11 February 1959, 'State of the Industry'. SRNA File S42/6/1.

14 NMM, *Shipbuilding Conference*, Meeting of Executive Board, 11 February 1959, 'State of the Industry'. SRNA File S42/6/1.

15 NMM, *Shipbuilding Conference*, Meeting Executive Board, 13 April 1961.

16 NMM, *Shipbuilding Conference*, Meeting Executive Board, 13 April 1961.

17 NMM, *Shipbuilding Conference*, Meeting of Executive Board, 8 February 1961. SRNA File S42/6/1.

18 NMM, *Shipbuilding Conference*, Meeting of Executive Board, 11 July 1962, item 11. SRNA File S42/6/1.

19 NMM, *Shipbuilding Conference*, Meeting of Executive Board, 11 July . 1962; 'Memo; Reduction of Shipyard Capacity'. SRNA File S42/6/1.

20 NMM, *Shipbuilding Conference*, Meeting of Executive Board, 11 July. 1962; 'Memo; Reduction of Shipyard Capacity'. SRNA File S42/6/1.

21 NMM, *Shipbuilding Conference*, 'Notes on a Meeting with Geoffrey Parker, Under Secretary Board of Trade, 9 October 1962. SRNA File S42/6/1.

22 NMM, *Shipbuilding Conference*, 'Scheme for Reduction of Shipyard Capacity', 9 January 1963. SRNA File S42/3/1.

23 NMM, *Shipbuilding Conference*, 'Note on Meeting with Minster of Transport, Ernest Marples, 21 July 1964, para. 1. SRNA File S42/7.

24 NMM, *Shipbuilding Conference*, 'Meeting with Minister of Transport, Ernest Marples', 9 January 1964. SRNA File S42/7.

25 NMM, *Shipbuilding Conference*, 'Informal meeting between the Shipbuilders Employers

Federation, The Shipbuilding Conference, and the Confederation of Shipbuilding and Engineering Unions', 14 January 1959; Statement by the SEF President, Mr R.W. Johnson.

26 NMM, *Shipbuilding Conference*; Statement by R.W. Johnson, p. 6, 14 January 1959.

27 NMM, *Shipbuilders Employers Federation*, 'Obstacles to Maximum Output', File 4611², 1961.

28 NMM, *Shipbuilding Conference*, 'Informal Meeting of SC, SEF and CSEU, 1 March 1961, Note, p. 6. SRNA File 5028.

29 NMM, *Shipbuilding Conference*, Ministry of Labour; Minutes of a joint meeting of representatives of SEF, SC, and CSEU', para. 2, 25 May 1962. SRNA File 5117.

30 NMM, *Shipbuilding Employers Federation*, 'Scheme for the Reorganisation of Labour and Conditions of Employment in United Kingdom Shipyards', October 1962. SRNA File 5117 a⁴.

31 J. M. Goldrick, 'Trade Unions and Industrial Relations in the British Shipbuilding Industry', in F.M. Walker and A. Slaven (eds), *European Shipbuilding; One Hundred Years of Change* (Maritime Publications International Limited, London, 1953), p. 182.

32 NMM, SEF Circulars, 189/62 and 199/62.

33 NMM, SEF Circular 105/63, 11 July 1963, 'Scheme for the Reorganisation of Labour'. SRNA File 5117 a⁵.

34 NMM, 'Industrial Relations and Competitive Position of the Industry': Working Party meetings, 14 November 1963. SRNA File 5117 a⁶.

35 NMM, SRNA File 5117 a⁶, p. 7.

36 NMM, SRNA File 5117 a⁶, 'Letter, D.B. Kimber, Fairfield Shipbuilding and Engineering Co. Ltd, to N.A. Sloan, Shipbuilding Employers Federation, 3 February 1964.

37 The Financial Times, London, 27 September 1958, *F.T. Historical Archive 1888–2006* (Gale Cengage Learning).

38 *British Shipping Statistics*, 1967, Table 4, p. 84.

39 NMM, *Shipbuilding Conference*, 'Informal Meeting Between the SC, SEF, and CSEU, 14 January 1959: Statement by Mr J. A. Milne, President SEF. SRNA File 5028.

40 NMM, *Shipbuilding Conference*, 'Preliminary Factual Report to the Minister of Transport on Shipbuilding Prices' (Peat, Marwick and Mitchell Report): A Joint Report by the Shipbuilding Conference, The Shipbuilders Employers Federation, Messrs. Peat Marwick and Mitchell, accountants, and Officials of the Ministry of Transport, 1963, Section IV and paras 30–38, Appendix A.

41 NMM, *Shipbuilding Conference*, Peat Marwick and Mitchell Report, Appendix IV and 'Report on Japan', 1 November 1963, pp. 7–8. SRNA File J1/2.

42 NMM, *Shipbuilding Conference*, Paper 'Can Japanese Shipbuilders get out of the present situation of "Prosperity without Profit?"', SRNA File J1/2.

43 NMM, *Shipbuilding Conference*, Paper 'Can Japanese Shipbuilders get out of the present situation of "Prosperity without Profit?"', SRNA File J1/2.

44 NMM, *Shipbuilding Conference*, Paper, 'Shipping and Shipbuilding in the Federal Republic of Germany: Report on a West European Study Visit, 1964', p. 4. SRNA File G23/1.

45 *The Times*, 2 October 1957.

46 NMM, *Shipbuilding Conference*, 'Peat Marwick and Mitchell Report, Section V, paras. 30–38, Appendix A.

47 K.J.W. Alexander and C.L. Jenkins, *Fairfields: A Study in Institutional Change* (London, 1970), p. 38.

48 NMM, *Shipbuilding Conference*, 'Memorandum Export Credits Guarantee Department', Paper D41/58, 27 November 1958, SRNA File E 42/A.

49 NMM, *Shipbuilding Conference*, 'Sources of Finance Available to Foreign Shipbuilders', Report, 7 April 1960. SRNA File E 42/4.

50 NMM, *Shipbuilding Conference*, 'Memorandum on Credit Facilities: Part II, Credit Insurance', Meeting with ECGD, 7 January 1960. SRNA File E 42/4.

51 NMM, *Shipbuilding Conference*: Credit Terms, April 1960: SRNA File E 42/4.

52 NMM, *Shipbuilding Conference*. 'Report on Findings of the Patton Committee into the problems relating to Productivity and Operational Research in Shipbuilding', 1962: Summary of Report, Section 3, SRNA File R 17/2.

53 NMM, *Shipbuilding Conference*, 'Patton Report: Confidential Supplement, Section 5, Scandinavia (1962). SRNA File R17/2.

54 NMM, *Shipbuilding Conference*, 'Summary of Patton Report', Section 6. SRNA File R17/2.

55 NMM, *Shipbuilding Conference*, 'Interim Report of the Policy Committee', 11 February 1959. SRNA File S42/6/1.

56 NMM, *Shipbuilding Conference*, 'Report of the Policy Committee', 13 April 1961. SRNA File S42/6/1.

57 NMM, *Shipbuilding Conference*, 'The Export Organisation', September 1962. SRNA File E40/3.

58 NMM, *Shipbuilding Conference*, 'Note of Meeting with the Minister of Transport, the Rt. Hon. Ernest Marples, 9 January 1964. SRNA File S42/7.

## Chapter 7: Intervention: 1964–1977

1 *Business Monitor*, MR 15, 1981, p. 42.

2 *National Maritime Museum*, here after *NMM*, SRNA, File 5028. *Shipbuilding Conference*. Meeting with the Minister of Transport, Rt. Hon. Ernest Marples, 21 July 1964.

3 NMM, SRNA File S42/9. *Shipbuilding Conference*, 'Memorandum to Governments on the West European Shipbuilding Industry', 12 November 1964.

4 NMM, SRNA File S42/9. *Shipbuilding Conference*, 'Memorandum to Governments on the West European Shipbuilding Industry', 12 November 1964.

5 T. Chida and P.N. Davies, *The Japanese Shipping and Shipbuilding Industries; A History of their Modern Growth* (Athlone Press, London, 1990), p. 89.

6 NMM, SRNA File E 40/3. *Shipbuilding Conference*, Meeting with Mr Roy Mason, Minister of State at the Board of Trade, 23 December 1964. NMM, SRNA File E 40/3. Confidential Memorandum, 'Government's Proposed Independent Committee of Inquiry into the Shipbuilding Industry', 31 December 1964.

7 NMM, SRNA File 5117 a[6]. *Shipbuilding Conference*, 'Memorandum. Meeting with Conservative MPs on 4 November 1965, House of Commons'.

8 *Shipbuilding Inquiry Committee, 1965–1966, Report*, London, HMSO, March 1966, Cmnd. 2937, p. 3 (Geddes Report).

9 Hillditch, *Management Strategy*, ch. 7, pp. 7–40, p. 45.

10 NMM, SRNA File F19. *Shipbuilding Conference*, 'Letter from Sinclair Scott, President, Shipbuilding Conference, and George Hilton, President, Shipbuilders Employers Federation, to the Rt. Hon. Harold Wilson, The Prime Minister', 9 December 1965.

11 NMM, SRNA File F 19. *Shipbuilding Conference*, 'Further Notes on Developments in Regard to Governments Participation in Management of Fairfield's, 20 December 1965.

12 NMM, SRNA File 19. *Shipbuilding Conference*, Statement by the First Secretary of State, Mr George Brown MP, House of Commons, Wednesday 22 December 1965 (Copy From Hansard).

13 *Shipbuilding Inquiry Committee*, 1966, p. 8.

14 *Shipbuilding Inquiry Committee*, 1966, p. 81.

15  *Shipbuilding Inquiry Committee*, 1966, p. 81.

16  *Shipbuilding Inquiry Committee*, 1966, p. 153.

17  *Shipbuilding Inquiry Committee*, 1966, p. 145 and pp. 154–5.

18  *John Brown Papers*, University of Glasgow Business Archive, UCS1/5/101, 'Shipbuilding Conference response to the Shipbuilding Inquiry Committee'.

19  *John Brown Papers*, UCS 1/5/101, p. 4 para 22.

20  B. Hogwood, *Government and Shipbuilding: The Politics of Industrial Change* (Farnborough, 1979), p. 82.

21  Davies, *Belief in the Sea*, p. 218 and footnote 123.

22  Hogwood, *Government and Shipbuilding*, pp. 85–6.

23  A. Slaven, 'Marketing Opportunities and Marketing practices; The Eclipse of British Shipbuilding 1957–76' in L.R.F. Fischer (ed.), *Essays in Maritime Business History*. Research in Maritime History No. 2 International Maritime History Association (1992), pp. 125–51.

24  Booz-Allen and Hamilton, *British Shipbuilding 1972*, A Report to the Department of Trade and Industry, London (HMSO, 1973), p. 102, Summary of UK Industry Delivery Record, 1967–71.

25  Davies, *Belief in the Sea*, pp. 214–15.

26  Davies, *Belief in the Sea*, p. 216.

27  B.R. Mitchell and P. Deane, *Abstract of British Historical Statistics* (Cambridge, 1962), p. 175, Table 35.

28  Michael Moss and John R. Hume, *Shipbuilders to the World; 125 years of Harland & Wolff, Belfast, 1861–1986* (Blackstaff Press, Belfast, 1986), p. 404.

29  Moss and Hume, *Shipbuilders to the World*, pp. 409–10.

30  Moss and Hume, *Shipbuilders to the World*, pp. 415–18.

31  Moss and Hume, *Shipbuilders to the World*, p. 421.

32  Moss and Hume, *Shipbuilders to the World*, p. 425.

33  Moss and Hume, *Shipbuilders to the World*, p. 427.

34  Moss and Hume, *Shipbuilders to the World*, p. 431.

35  Moss and Hume, *Shipbuilders to the World*, p. 442.

36  Moss and Hume, *Shipbuilders to the World*, p. 435.

37  NMM, SRNA File S42/11 and File 7/317/A, Professor David Flint, *Confidential Report. Upper Clyde Shipbuilders Limited (In Liquidation)*, Companies Act 1948 Section 332 (1), November 1973, p. 5.

38  Hillditch, *Management Strategy*, ch. 7, p. 6, quoting HC544, 1970–71, p. 2.

39  Hillditch, *Management Strategy*, ch. 7, p. 60.

40  Flint Report, p. 10.

41  Flint Report, p. 11.

42  Flint Report, p. 11, para. 4.4.

43  Flint Report, p. 11, para. 4.7.

44  Flint Report, p. 13.

45  Flint Report, p. 14.

46  Flint Report, p. 15.

47  Flint Report, p. 18.

48  Flint Report, p. 19.

49  NMM, SRNA File S42/11, Letter: 'Official Liquidator to the Secretary of State for Industry', 4 October 1974.

50  Booz-Allen and Hamilton, *British Shipbuilding 1972*, Exhibit 29, p. 89.

51  Hillditch, *Management Strategy*, ch. 7, pp. 64–5, and Johnman and Murphy, *British Shipbuilding*, p. 187.

52   NMM, SRNA Document S42/13. *Shipbuilding Conference*, 'Executive Council Meeting of 20 January 1972', Appendix A.
53   Booz-Allen and Hamilton, *British Shipbuilding 1972*, pp. 4–14.
54   NMM, SRNA Document S42/13/3. *Shipbuilding Conference*, 'Government Policy and the Industry', 1973. Comment on Report to the Department of Trade and Industry by Booz-Allen and Hamilton.
55   Hillditch, *Management Strategy*, ch. 10, p. 41.
56   Hillditch, *Management Strategy*, ch. 10, p. 45.
57   Hillditch, *Management Strategy*, ch. 10, p. 45.
58   Hillditch, *Management Strategy*, ch. 9, p. 24.
59   Booz-Allen and Hamilton, *British Shipbuilding 1972*, p. 176, Cmnd. 71.
60   Hillditch, *Management Strategy*, ch. 9, p. 31.
61   Hillditch, *Management Strategy*, ch. 9, p. 30.
62   Hillditch, *Management Strategy*, ch. 10, p. 19.
63   Hillditch, *Management Strategy*, ch. 10, pp. 10–13.
64   Davies, *Belief in the Sea*, pp. 242–3.
65   Lewis Johnman and Hugh Murphy, *Scott Lithgow: Déjà-vu all over again!: The Rise and Fall of a Shipbuilding Company*, Research in Maritime History No. 30 (International Maritime Economic History Association, Newfoundland 2005), p. 241.
66   Johnman and Murphy, *Déjà-vu*, p. 246.
67   Johnman and Murphy, *Déjà-vu*, p. 248.
68   Johnman and Murphy, *Déjà-vu*, p. 232.
69   Johnman and Murphy, *Déjà-vu*, p. 248.
70   Davies, *Belief in the Sea*, pp. 240–1.
71   Moss and Hume, *Shipbuilders to the World*, p. 458.
72   Davies, *Belief in the Sea*, p. 241.
73   *British Shipping Statistics*, General Council of British Shipping (1975), Table 3.1, p. 61.
74   NMM, SRNA File S/42/9/3. 'Record of Meeting with the Rt. Hon. Anthony Wedgwood Beam, Secretary of State for Industry', 22 April 1974.
75   NMM, SRNA File S/42/9/3. 'Notes of a Meeting with Mr. Varley', November 1976.
76   NMM, SRNA File S/42/9/3. 'Notes of a Meeting with Mr. Varley', November 1976.
77   NMM, SRNA File S/42/1. 'A Possible Policy for a Conservative Government: The Present Situation', May 1975.
78   NMM, SRNA File S/42/1, May 1975.
79   Slaven, 'Marketing Opportunities', passim.
80   NMM, SRNA File S/42/1. 'A Possible Policy', May 1975, passim.
81   NMM, SRNA File S/42/1. 'A Possible Policy', May 1975, passim.
82   NMM, SRNA File S/42/1. 'A Possible Policy', May 1975, passim.
83   NMM, SRNA File S/42/1. 'A Possible Policy', May 1975, passim.
84   NMM, SRNA File S/42/1. 'A Possible Policy', May 1975, passim.
85   NMM, SRNA File S/42/1. 'A Possible Policy', May 1975, passim.
86   NMM, SRNA File S/42/9/3. 'Report of the Working Party on Shipbuilding Comprising Representatives of the Confederation of Shipbuilding and Engineering Unions, Members of the Organising Committee for British Shipbuilders, and Officials' (1976).
87   NMM, SRNA File S42/9/3, 'Report of the Working Party', p. 2.
88   NMM, SRNA File S42/9/3, 'Report of the Working Party', p. 5.
89   NMM, SRNA File S42/9/3, 'Report of the Working Party', p. 6.
90   NMM, SRNA File S42/9/3, 'Report of the Working Party', p. 10.

# Chapter 8: End game: 1978–2010

1 'Nationalisation of the Shipbuilding and Ship Repair and Marine Engineering Industries', Joint Report of the Labour Party, TUC and CSEU, British Labour Party Research Department Memorandum and Information Papers (Labour History, Series One, Paper No. 800, July 1973).

2 *The Aircraft and Shipbuilding Industries Bill*, HC Deb. 30 April 1975, vol. 891 cc 477–8.

3 *The Economist*, 9 November 1974, p. 6.

4 *The Economist*, 'Shipyards in the Storm', 15 February 1975, p. 8.

5 *Aircraft and Shipbuilding Industries Act*, 1977.

6 Interview, *J. Graham Day*, 27 August 1991.

7 Interview, *J. Graham Day*, 27 August 1991.

8 Michael Casey, *A History of British Shipbuilders, 1977–1980*, unpublished MSS (1980), p. 1.

9 Casey, *History of British Shipbuilders*, p. 4, 'Employment by Sector and Region on Vesting Day'.

10 V. Marchant, 'The Nationalisation of an Industry: the Case of British Shipbuilders', unpublished paper.

11 Casey, *History of British Shipbuilders*, ch. 1, Appendix A; Insolvency of Subsidiary Companies'.

12 British Shipbuilders (BS) *Board Papers*, Minutes of 4th meeting, 24 November 1977.

13 BS, *Executive Committee of the Board*, Minutes of 14 September 1979.

14 BS, *Board Papers*, Minutes of 8th meeting, 23 June 1978.

15 BS, *Board Papers*, Minutes of 7th meeting, 17 April 1978.

16 BS, *Board Papers*, Minutes of 6th meeting, 23 February 1978.

17 BS *Corporate Plan 1978–83*, ch. 17, p. 7.

18 BS *Corporate Plan 1978–83*, ch. 17, p. 7.

19 BS *Corporate Plan 1978–83*, ch. 17, p. 7.

20 BS, *Corporate Plan 1978–83*, ch. 17, p. 11.

21 BS, *Board Papers*, Sixth Special Meeting of the Board, Minute 5.2, 21 December 1978.

22 Casey, *History of British Shipbuilders*, ch. 6, 'Restructuring of Merchant Shipbuilding and General Restructuring Picture'.

23 BS, *Board Papers*, Minutes of 15th meeting, 26 July 1979.

24 BS, *Board Papers*, Minutes of the Ninth Special Meeting of the Board, 28 August 1979.

25 Casey, *History of British Shipbuilders*, ch. 4, 'Merchant Marketing'.

26 BS, *Annual Report and Accounts*, 1980–81 p. 11.

27 The companies were Wallsend Slipway, Wallsend Dry Dock, Green Silley Weir, Silley Cox, London Graving Dock, and Thames Ship Repairers.

28 BS, *Board Papers*, Minutes of the 12th meeting, 25 January 1979.

29 BS, *Board Papers*, Minutes of the Fifth Special Meeting of the Board, 11 December 1978.

30 BS, *Board Papers*, Minutes of the Executive Committee meeting, 28 September 1979.

31 BS, *Board Papers*, Minutes of the Twelfth Special Meeting of the Board, 10 December 1979.

32 BS, *Board Papers*, Minutes of the 12th Meeting, 25 January 1979.

33 *The Financial Times*, 'British Shipbuilders wins £80m oil rig order', Friday 13 November 1981, p. 8. *FT Historical Archive, 1888–2006* (Gale Cengage Learning).

34 BS, *Board Papers*, Minutes of Executive Committee, 21 March 1980.

35 Johnman and Murphy, *Déjà-vu*, p. 292.

36 Johnman and Murphy, *Déjà-vu*, p. 296, quoting the *Greenock Telegraph*, 28 July 1983.

37 Interview with *K.P. Griffin*, 22 March 1992.

38  Interview with *Maurice Phelps*, 8 October 1991.

39  Interview with *Robert Atkinson*, 28 August 1991.

40  Interview with *Robert Atkinson*, 28 August 1991.

41  House of Commons, *Parliamentary Debates*, sixth series, vol. 46, c 130.

42  Interview with *J. Graham Day*, 27 August 1991.

43  Interview, *K.D. Griffin*, 22 March 1992.

44  Interview, *K.D. Griffin*, 22 March 1992.

45  Interview, *G.H. Fuller*, 3 June 1991.

46  Interview, *Maurice Phelps*, 8 October 1991.

47  *The Financial Times*, 'British Shipbuilders to axe 3000 Scott Lithgow jobs', Wednesday, 18 January 1984, p. 1. *FT Historical Archive, 1888–2006* (Gale Cengage Learning).

48  Davies, *Belief in the Sea*, p. 306, quoting Parliamentary Debates, 6th Series, c 1093.

49  Interview, *J. Graham Day*, 27 August 1991.

50  BS, *Annual Report and Accounts, 1985–86*, p. 9.

51  B. Baxter, 'The Nationalised Shipbuilding Industry, in the United Kingdom: The First Decade, 1977–87', Andrew Laing Memorial Lecture, 1987. Presented to The North East Coast Institution of Engineers and Shipbuilders (Newcastle 1987).

52  Baxter, 'Laing Memorial Lecture', Table 1.

53  Baxter, 'Laing Memorial Lecture', Table 1.

54  Interview, *Geoff Fuller*, 3 June 1991.

55  Interview, *J. Graham Day*, 27 August 1991.

56  *The Financial Times*, 15 May 1986. *FT Historical Archive, 1888–2006* (Gale Cengage Learning).

57  *The Financial Times*, 16 March 1987. *FT Historical Archive, 1888–2006* (Gale Cengage Learning).

58  BS, *Annual Reports and Accounts*, 1986–88.

59  Davies, *Belief in the Sea*, p. 311.

60  Davies, *Belief in the Sea*, p. 311, quoting Parliamentary Debates, sixth series, vol. 131, c. 554.

61  Davies, *Belief in the Sea*, p. 311, quoting Parliamentary Debates, sixth series, vol. 131, c. 1106.

62  Johnman and Murphy, *British Shipbuilding*, p. 234.

63  Johnman and Murphy, *British Shipbuilding*, p. 234.

64  George H. Parker, *At the Sharp End: A Shipbuilding Autobiography* (Brown, Son & Ferguson, Glasgow, 1992), pp. 167–71.

65  Davies, *Belief in the Sea*, p. 313, quoting Parliamentary Debates, sixth series, vol. 139, c 286 and c 300.

66  Moss and Hume, *Shipbuilders to the World*, p. 486, Table 14.2.

67  Moss and Hume, *Shipbuilders to the World*, ship delivery dates abstracted from ship list, p. 561.

68  Moss and Hume, *Shipbuilders to the World*, p. 478.

69  *The Financial Times*, 'Harland & Wolff wins £30m defence contract', Saturday 3 March 1984. *FT Historical Archive, 1888–2006* (Gale Cengage Learning).

70  *The Financial Times*, 'Harland & Wolff launches naval ship', Thursday 26 March 1987, p. 6. *FT Historical Archive, 1888–2006* (Gale Cengage Learning).

71  Moss and Hume, *Shipbuilders to the World*, p. 486, Table 14.2, and Trade and Industry Committee, 'The Privatisation of Harland & Wolff', HC 131 p. x. Also, Johnman and Murphy, *British Shipbuilding*, p. 238

72  *The Financial Times*, 'Belfast shipyard fears future will slip away', Friday 21 October 1988, p. 9. *FT Historical Archive* (Gale Cengage Learning).

73  *The Financial Times*, 'Buy-out plan for Harland & Wolff accepted', Thursday 23 March 1989, p. 1. *FT Historical Archive* (Gale and Cengage Learning).

74  *The Financial Times*, 'Harland & Wolff delays buy-out announcement', Wednesday 6 September 1989, p. 9. *FT Historical Archive* (Gale Cengage Learning).

75  *The Financial Times*, 'Buy-out plan for Harland & Wolff accepted', Thursday 23 March 1989, p. 1. *FT Historical Archive* (Gale Cengage Learning).

76  Johnman and Murphy, *British Shipbuilding*, p. 239.

77  BBC News (Scotland), 'Ayrshire Shipyard closing', Friday 18 August 2000.

78  *Associated British Ports*, 'ABP News', 30 June 2002.

79  *The Scotsman*, Edinburgh, 'Ferguson Shipbuilders wins £3.2m refit contract', 10 February 2010.

80  Johnman and Murphy, *British Shipbuilders*, pp. 233–4.

81  *The Financial Times*, 'Govan wins £200m shipbuilding order', Thursday 19 December 1991, p. 22. *FT Historical Archive* (Gale Cengage Learning).

82  *Management Today*, 1 May 1992.

83  *The Financial Times*, 6 July 1999. *FT Historical Archive* (Gale Cengage Learning).

84  *The Financial Times*, 11 October 1999. *FT Historical Archive* (Gale Cengage Learning).

85  *The Financial Times*, 'Shy Shipowner sails to the rescue', Thursday 23 March 1989, p. 12. *FT Historical Archive* (Gale Cengage Learning).

86  *The Financial Times*, 'Harland & Wolff tops £11m', Wednesday 20 March 1989, p. 39. *FT Historical Archive* (Gale Cengage Learning).

87  *The Financial Times*, 'Harland & Wolff wins £223m bulk carrier order', Wednesday 28 August 1991, p. 1. *FT Historical Archive* (Gale Cengage Learning).

88  *The Financial Times*, 'Harland & Wolff losses treble', Saturday 8 April 1995, p. 10. *FT Historical Archive* (Gale Cengage Learning).

89  *The Financial Times*, 'Flexibility holds key to future of shipyard', Friday 21 March 1997, p. 9. *FT Historical Archive* (Gale Cengage Learning).

90  *The Financial Times*, 'Harland & Wolff "threatened" by dispute', Thursday 21 October 1999, and 'Harland & Wolff to cut workforce by half', Friday 22 September 2000. *FT Historical Archive* (Gale Cengage Learning).

91  *The Financial Times*, 'Jobs threat as Harland & Wolff fails to win Queen Mary II contract', Friday 10 March 2000, p. 1. *FT Historical Archive* (Gale Cengage Learning).

92  *The Financial Times*, 'Receivers appointed at Hall Russell Shipyard', Thursday 10 November 1988, p. 12. *FT Historical Archive* (Gale Cengage Learning).

93  *The Financial Times*, 'Appledore buys Hall Russell Shipyard', Tuesday 21 February 1989, p. 10. *FT Historical Archive* (Gale Cengage Learning).

94  *The Financial Times*, 'Swan Hunter to shed 1,400 workers', Saturday 29 August, 1992, p. 5. *FT Historical Archive* (Gale Cengage Learning).

95  *The Financial Times*, 'Receivers called in at Swan Hunter', Friday 14 May 1993. *FT Historical Archive* (Gale Cengage Learning).

96  *The Financial Times*, 'Swan Hunter loses by £50m order from Oman to French shipyard', Thursday 2 September 1993. *FT Historical Archive* (Gale Cengage Learning).

97  *The Financial Times*, 'Swan Hunter set to close as Rosyth gains £40m order', Wednesday 20 July 1994, p. 1. *FT Historical Archive* (Gale Cengage Learning).

98  *The Financial Times*, 'Canadians torpedo VSEL bid to fill submarine orderbook', Friday 28 April 1989, p. 14. *FT Historical Archive* (Gale Cengage Learning).

99  *The Financial Times*, 'VSEL submarine yard plans further job cuts', Saturday 17 November 1990, p. 6. *FT Historical Archive* (Gale Cengage Learning)

100  *The Financial Times*, 'Shipyard closure costs 900 jobs', Thursday 3 December 1992, p. 22. *FT Historical Archive* (Gale Cengage Learning).

101  *The Financial Times*, 'BAe and Sema link to bid for defence contracts', Friday 2 August 1991, p. 16. *FT Historical Archive* (Gale Cengage Learning).

102   *The Financial Times*, 'Submarines in BAe's sights', Thursday 13 October 1994, Lex Column. *FT Historical Archive* (Gale Cengage Learning).

103   *The Financial Times*, 'GEC offers £532m for VSEL', Saturday 29 October 1994, p. 1. *FT Historical Archive* (Gale Cengage Learning).

104   *The Financial Times*, 'VSEL put into deep freeze', Thursday 8 December 1994, p. 27. *FT Historical Archive* (Gale Cengage Learning).

105   *The Financial Times*, 'Shift in balance of power over VSEL', Wednesday 24 May 1995, p. 22. *FT Historical Archive* (Gale Cengage Learning).

106   *The Financial Times*, 'BAe pulls out of £835m bid battle for VSEL', Thursday 22 June 1995, p. 1. *FT Historical Archive* (Gale Cengage Learning).

107   *The Financial Times*, 'GEC-Marconi secures £2Bn submarine deal', Friday 14 March 1997, and Wednesday 26 March 1997. *FT Historical Archive* (Gale Cengage Learning).

108   *The Financial Times*, 'BAe and DASA discuss proposals for merger', 24 July 1998. *FT Historical Archive* (Gale Cengage Learning).

109   *The Financial Times*, 'BAe pays £77m for stake in naval systems specialist', Friday 11 September 1998, p. 22. *FT Historical Archive* (Gale Cengage Learning).

110   *The Financial Times*, 'BAe wins Marconi with £7.8 bn bid', Tuesday 19 January 1999, p. 1. *FT Historical Archive* (Gale Cengage Learning).

111   *The Daily Telegraph*, 14 July 2006.

112   *The Financial Times*, 'Vosper plans £10m injection for shipyard', Wednesday 17 November 1999, p. 31. *FT Historical Archive* (Gale Cengage Learning).

113   *The Glasgow Herald*, 24 November 1999.

114   *The Financial Times*, 'Warship makers at odds over destroyer production', Monday 11 December 2000, p. 3. *FT Historical Archive* (Gale Cengage Learning).

115   *The Financial Times*, 'Vosper wins bigger share of BAE contract', Wednesday 11 July 2001, p. 2. *FT Historical Archive* (Gale Cengage Learning).

116   *Strategic Defence Review*, 8 July 1998, Cm. 3999, HOC Session 1997–98.

117   Claire Taylor and Tom Walderman, *British Defence Policy since 1997*, House of Commons Library Research Paper 08/57, 27 June 2008, p. 16.

118   Taylor and Walderman, RP 08/57, p. 38.

119   *Defence Industry News*; 25 July 2007.

120   *Navy Matters*, 'Future Aircraft Carrier, Part 9.

121   *Defence Industry Daily*, 20 October 2009.

122   *The Guardian*, 23 March 2010.

123   *The Times*, 31 December 2006.

124   *The Financial Times*, 'BAe examines sale of warship building division', Monday 26 April 2004, p. 21. *FT Historical Archive* (Gale Cengage Learning).

125   *Public Accounts Committee*, HC 372, 'Ministry of Defence: Type 45 Destroyers; 2009.

126   *The Scotsman*, 28 October 2010.

127   *The Financial Times*, 'BAE Systems navigates treacherous waters', Wednesday 22 January 2003, p. 24. *FT Historical Archive* (Gale Cengage Learning).

128   *House of Commons Defence Committee*, 'Defence Equipment 2010', Sixth Report of Session 2009–2010, 23 February 2010. HC 99.

129   *North West Evening Mail*, 6 March 2010.

130   *Defence News*, 'Lots of Losers in UK Defence Review', 19 October 2010.

131   *Royal United Services Institute (RUSI)*, Future Defence Review, Working Paper No. 5, M. Chalmers, 'Capability Cost Trends; Implications for the Defence Review', January 2010.

# Select bibliography

## Chapter 1: Wood and sail, 1500–1815

The literature on the early history of shipbuilding makes it clear that the earliest concentrations of activity were on the river Thames and along the rivers and coasts of the north-east of England. The most detailed account of developments on the Thames is by Philip Banbury, *Shipbuilding on the Thames and Medway* (David & Charles, 1971); parts 1–4 trace the growth of the industry from Tudor times to the Napoleonic Wars, and cover the emergence of the Royal Dockyards and the appearance of the private shipyards in the seventeenth and eighteenth centuries. Developments in the North East are comprehensively set out in J.F. Clarke, *Building Ships on the North East Coast, Part 1, 1640–1914* (Bewick Press, Whitley Bay, 1997). Chapters 1–3 focus on the developments from the seventeenth century to 1815. A supplementary account is by David Dougan, *The History of North East Shipbuilding* (Allen & Unwin, 1968). The more general development and evolution of the wooden ship and the skills of the shipwright are set out by Anthony Burton, *The Rise and Fall of British Shipbuilding* (Constable, 1994), ch. 2 . An account of the early legislation designed to support the growth of English trade and shipping is detailed in Michael Davies, *Belief in the Sea* ( Lloyds of London Press, 1992), ch. 1. Early Scottish shipbuilding is less well researched. T.C. Smout, *Scottish Trade on the Eve of the Union, 1660–1707* (Edinburgh, 1963), provides insight for early Scottish trade and shipping. Brief comment on early developments on the river Clyde are included in John Shields, *Clyde Built: A History of Shipbuilding on the River Clyde* (William McClellan, Glasgow, 1947).

## Chapter 2: Two industries: from 1815 to the 1880s

The interplay of the advance and refinement of building ships in wood and sail, and the parallel beginnings of the early steamship are succinctly set out in Anthony Burton, *The Rise and Fall of British Shipbuilding*, ch. 2 Advances in design in the Blackwall Frigates and in the clipper ships are reviewed in Basil Lubbock, *The Blackwall Frigates* (Brown, Son & Ferguson, Glasgow, 1922), and by the same author and publisher in a series of books, *The China Clippers* (1914), *The Colonial Clippers* (1914), *The Nitrate Clippers* (1932), and *The Opium Clippers* (1933). A detailed account of the technological innovations in the steam engine and its application to ships can be consulted in C. Singer *et al.* (eds), *A History of Technology, vol. 5* (Oxford, 1958). A brief account of the complexity of the technical changes involved in the introduction of steam power and metal hulls in shipbuilding is set out by Richard T. Harrison, *Industrial Organisation and Changing Technology in UK Shipbuilding* (Gower Publishing, Aldershot, 1990), ch. 3. The national context in which these events took place, especially the expansion of the coal, metal, engineering and shipbuilding industries is well covered in Roy Church (ed.), *The Dynamics of Victorian Business: Problems and Perspectives to the 1870s* (Allen & Unwin, 1980).

The growth of the iron and steam shipbuilding industry had a profound influence on the location of the shipbuilding districts, and initiated the long decline of the industry on the Thames. How different districts responded is well explained in Simon Ville (ed.), *Shipbuilding in the United Kingdom in the Nineteenth Century: A Regional Approach* (Research in Maritime History, no. 4, St Johns, Newfoundland, 1993). The decline of traditional shipbuilding on the Thames is reviewed by Philip Banbury, *Shipbuilding on the Thames and Medway* (1971), ch. 6, while the parallel expansion of iron shipbuilding there is examined in detail in A.J. Arnold, *Iron Shipbuilding on the Thames, 1832–1915* (Ashgate Publishing, Aldershot, 2000). A detailed study of these changes as they affected shipbuilding in the North East is provided by J.F. Clarke, *Building Ships on the North East Coast*, Part 1, *c.1640–1914* ( 1997), chs 3–8. Shipbuilding developments on the Clyde receive a detailed examination in Fred M. Walker, *Song of the Clyde: A History of Clyde Shipbuilding* (Patrick Stephens, Cambridge, 1984). The consequences of these developments for marine legislation and for British shipping are clearly summarised in Michael Davies, *Belief in the Sea* (1992), ch. 3.

## Chapter 3: Leading the world: the 1880s to the First World War

The world  supremacy of British shipbuilding before 1914 is reviewed in detail in S.Pollard and P.L. Robertson, *The British Shipbuilding Industry, 1870–1914* (Harvard University Press, 1979), while the consequences for British shipping are explored in Michael Davies, *Belief in the Sea* (1992), ch. 4. An older but still valuable account of the evolution of the ship from wood to steel, together with a the development of the marine engine, may be found in Adam W. Kirkaldy, *British Shipping*, *Its History*, *Organisation and Importance* (Kegan Paul, 1919, 2nd edn); the appendices include details of the tonnage produced in each yard for 1911–12, together with the capitalisation and earnings of the major companies. Another contemporary account, David Pollock, *The Shipbuilding Industry* (Methuen 1905), provides information on the changes in the type of ships being produced, and comparative data on district and national merchant tonnage produced.

The growth of the main shipbuilding districts has been the subject of a number of studies. The contribution of the North East is reviewed in David Dougan, *The History of North East Shipbuilding*, (1968); chapter 4 outlines the major trends in this period, including the major companies and warship as well as merchant production. J.F. Clarke, *Building Ships on the North East Coast*, *Part 1* (1997), outlines developments on each of the main rivers, Tyne, Wear and Tees, and discusses the changeover from iron to steel hulls, and the importance of warship production before 1914. Additional information on the development of the main companies on the Wear is included in J.W. Smith and T.S. Holden, *Where Ships are Born: Sunderland, 1346–1946* (Thomas Reed, Sunderland, 1953). For the Clyde, Fred M. Walker, *Song of the Clyde*, reviews the development and importance of the individual yards. A fine photographic record of these developments is presented in John Hume and Michael Moss, *Clyde Shipbuilding from Old Photographs* (B.T. Batsford, 1975). The dominance of the Clyde in warship production is explored in detail in Hugh B. Peebles, *Warship Building on the Clyde* (John Donald, Edinburgh, 1987). Information on individual regions, the north-east of England, south-east England, south-west England, north-west England, Scotland, and Ireland, is in Simon Ville (ed.), *Shipbuilding in the Nineteenth Century: A Regional Approach* (St Johns, Newfoundland, 1993). More detail on Harland & Wolff is in Michael Moss and John R. Hume, *Shipbuilders to the World* (1986), and the fate of the Thames yards is detailed in A.J. Arnold, *Iron Shipbuilding on the Thames, 1832–1915* (2000); chs 6–8 and the appendices provide great detail on the yards and their output.

## Chapter 4: War and depression: 1914–1939

A succinct account of the general condition of the British economy between the two world wars is given by M.W. Kirby, *The Decline of British Economic Power Since 1870* (Allen & Unwin, 1981), chs 2–3, while an excellent account of the fortunes of shipbuilding is in L. Jones, *Shipbuilding in Britain, Mainly Between the Wars* (Cardiff, 1957). A more modern account is given by Lewis Johnman and Hugh Murphy, *British Shipbuilding and the State since 1918* (2002), chs 1–2, while Anthony Burton, *The Rise and Fall of British Shipbuilding* (1994), focuses in ch. 8 on the inter-war depression in the industry. Conditions in the industry in the North East are set out in detail in J.F. Clarke, *Building Ships on the North East Coast, Part 2, c.1914–1980* (1997), chs 21–22, while a more general overview is given in David Dougan, *The History of North East Shipbuilding* (1968), ch. 5–6; the appendices contain detailed data on ship launches, employment, and profit and loss, for the main builders.

The dislocation of industry in Scotland between the wars is outlined in Anthony Slaven, *The Development of the West of Scotland, 1750–1960* (Routledge & Kegan Paul, 1975), ch. 8, and in R.H. Campbell, *The Rise and Fall of Scottish Industry, 1707–1939* (John Donald, Edinburgh, 1980), ch. 6. The consequences for naval orders are explored in detail by Hugh B. Peebles, *Warship Building on the Clyde* (1987), chs 7–10. Across the Irish Sea, the inter-war problems of Harland & Wolff are explained in Michael Moss and John R.Hume, *Shipbuilders to the World* (1986), chs 8–10. Some information on the history of the yards in Belfast, Barrow, and on Merseyside, is included in Norman L. Middlemiss, *British Shipbuilding Yards, Volume 3* (Shield Publications, Newcastle-Upon-Tyne, 1995). The significance of State policy for shipping and shipbuilding from 1913 to 1939 is examined by Michael Davies, *Belief in the Sea* (1992), chs 5–6.

## Chapter 5: War and recovery, 1939–1958

A good analysis of the industry in this period is given in J.R. Parkinson, *The Economics of Shipbuilding in the United Kingdom* (Cambridge, 1960), and Michael Davies, *Belief in the Sea* (1992), also provides a neat overview in ch. 8. A more recent detailed analysis is developed by Lewis Johnman and Hugh Murphy in *British Shipbuilding and the State Since 1918* (2002), chs 3–4. The consequences for naval orders are explored in detail in Ian Buxton, *Warship Building and Repair during the Second World War* ( Research papers in the History of British Shipbuilding, no. 2, Centre for Business History in Scotland, Glasgow, 1998). The experience of the industry in the north-east of England is outlined in David Dougan, *The History of North East Shipbuilding* (1968), ch. 8, and in more detail by J.F. Clarke, *Building Ships on the North East Coast, Part 2* (1997), chs 24–25. Developments in Scotland are covered by A. Slaven, *Growth and Stagnation in Scottish/British Shipbuilding, 1913–1977*, in J. Kuuse and A. Slaven (eds), *Scottish and Scandinavian Shipbuilding: Development Problems in Historical Perspective* (University of Goteborg, 1980). The experience of the Vickers yard at Barrow is outlined in Leslie M. Shore, *Vickers' Master Shipbuilder, Sir Leonard Redshaw* (Black Dwarf Publications, 2011), chs 3–5, and developments at Harland & Wolff are assessed by Michael Moss and John R.Hume, *Shipbuilders to the World* (1986), ch. 12.

## Chapter 6: Deterioration: 1958–1963

This pivotal period for British shipbuilding is examined closely by Lewis Johnman and Hugh Murphy in *British Shipbuilding and the State Since 1918* (2002), ch. 5, and in J. Kusse and A. Slaven (eds), *Scottish and Scandinavian Shipbuilding: Development Problems in Historical Perspective* (Goteborg, 1980).The nature and condition of the industry is also clearly set out in the *Shipbuilding*

*Inquiry Committee, 1965–1966 Report* (Cmnd. 2937, London, HMSO, 1966). A key issue of the period, that of productivity in the industry, is closely explored in James Patton, *Productivity and Research in Shipbuilding* (Gresham Press, London, 1962). A discussion setting the problems of the industry in a longer perspective is provided by Edward H. Lorenz, *Economic Decline in Britain: The Shipbuilding Industry, 1890–1970* (Oxford, 1991), chs 4–5. The situation in the North East industry is reviewed in David Dougan, *The History of North East Shipbuilding* (1968), ch. 7, and in detail by J.F. Clarke, *Building Ships on the North East Coast, Part 2* (1997), ch. 25. At Barrow the beginnings of nuclear submarine construction is outlined by Leslie M. Shore, *Vickers' Master Shipbuilder* (2011), ch. 6, while across the Irish Sea, developments at Harland & Wolff are assessed by Michael Moss and John R. Hume, *Shipbuilders to the World* (1986), ch. 12.

## Chapter 7: Intervention: 1964–1977

The condition of British shipbuilding is clearly spelt out in two official reports. The first is the *Shipbuilding Inquiry Committee, 1966* (HMSO, London, 1966). The second is Booz-Allen and Hamilton, *British Shipbuilding, 1972, A Report to the Department of Trade and Industry* (HMSO, 1973). This growing involvement of the government with the industry is explored in B. Hogwood, *Government and Shipbuilding: The Politics of Industrial Change* (Farnborough, Saxon House, 1979). A different perspective on this relationship is argued by Bo Strath, *The Politics of Deindustrialisation: The Contraction of the West European Shipbuilding Industry* (Croom Helm, London, 1987), ch. 5. The decline of the industry is also examined by Edward H.Lorenz, *Economic Decline in Britain: The Shipbuilding Industry, 1890–1970* (Oxford, 1991), chs 4–6. Another explanation is offered by Karel Williams, John Williams and Dennis Thomas in *Why are the British Bad at Manufacturing?* (Routledge & Kegan Paul, 1983), 'case study no. 2: shipbuilding'. The deepening intervention in the affairs of the industry is also examined in detail in Lewis Johnman and Hugh Murphy, *The State and British Shipbuilding Since 1918* (2002), chs 6-7. The decline of the industry in Scotland is the subject of a case study in T.L. Johnston, N.K. Buxton and D. Mair, *Structure and Growth of the Scottish Economy* (Collins, 1971), ch. 5, 'case study no. 3: shipbuilding'. The decline of the industry in Scotland is also set in the context of the general contraction of the heavy industries, by Peter L. Payne, *The Decline of Scottish Heavy Industries, 1945–1983*, in Richard Saville (ed.), *The Economic Development of Modern Scotland, 1950–1980* (John Donald, Edinburgh, 1985). An extended version of this analysis is in Peter L. Payne, *Growth and Contraction: Scottish Industry, c.1866–1990*, Studies in Scottish Economic and Social History No 2 (Economic and Social History Society of Scotland, 1992).

The 1965 crisis at the Fairfield yard is explored in Sydney Paulden and Bill Hawkins, *Whatever Happened at Fairfields?* (Gower Press, 1989), and in K.W. Alexander and C.L. Jenkins, *Fairfield's, A Study in Institutional Change* ( 1970). The growing problems on the Lower Clyde are examined in Lewis Johnman and Hugh Murphy, *Scott Lithgow: Déjà vu all Over Again! The Rise and Fall of a Shipbuilding Company* (Research in Maritime History No. 30, St John's, Newfoundland, 2005), while the demise of the Clydebank yard is studied by Ian Johnston, *Ships for a Nation, 1847–1971: John Brown & Company Clydebank* (West Dunbartonshire Libraries and Museums, 2000).

Developments in the North East are explored by J.F. Clarke, *Building Ships on the North East Coast, Part 2* (1997), ch. 27, and the Belfast situation is detailed in Michael Moss and John R. Hume, *Shipbuilders to the World* (1986), chs 13–14. Developments at Barrow are outlined in Leslie M. Shore, *Vickers' Master Shipbuilder* (2011), chs 10–11.

293

## Chapter 8: End Game: 1978–2010

The path to nationalisation and the subsequent privatisation and demise of merchant shipbuilding is succinctly explained in Michael Davies, *Belief in the Sea* (1992), chs 11–12. This saga is also explored by Lewis Johnman and Hugh Murphy, *British Shipbuilding and the State Since 1918* (2002), chs 7–8 and Epilogue. The same authors examine the fate of the Scott Lithgow group in *Scott Lithgow: Déjà Vu all Over Again* (2005), chs 7–9. These events are also recounted in George H. Parker, *Astern Business: 75 years of UK Shipbuilding* (World Shipbuilding Society, Kendal, 1996), chs 5–8, and similarly in Anthony Burton, *The Rise and Fall of British Shipbuilding* (1994), ch. 11. The effort to keep Harland & Wolff as a going concern is assessed to 1985 in Michael Moss and John R. Hume, *Shipbuilders to the World* (1986), chs 14–15. On naval shipbuilding the eventual rationalisation of the companies can be seen in the context of the *Strategic Defence Review* (Cm 3999), July 1998, and Claire Taylor and Tom Walderman, *British Defence Policy Since 1997* (House of Commons Library Research Paper 08/57, June 2008). Implications for the future of warship building are explored in M.Chalmers, *Capability Cost Trends: Implications for the Defence Review* (Royal United Services Institute, Future Defence Review, Working Paper No. 5).

# Index